THE WAY IT REALLY WAS

at Gettysburg ("On they came . . . Our men were shot with
rebel muskets at their breasts . . . Good God! The line at the
stone wall gives way!") . . . *in besieged Vicksburg* ("We are
entirely cut off from the world . . . I think all the dogs and
cats must be killed or starved. We don't see any more pitiful
animals prowling around") . . . *under fire at Antietam* ("The
truth is, when bullets are whacking against tree trunks and solid
shot are cracking skulls like eggshells, the consuming passion
in the breast of the average man is to get out of the way" . . .
in Sherman's path ("Poor, bleeding, suffering South Carolina!")
. . . *with Captain Abner Doubleday at Fort Sumter* ("It was
determined not to return their fire until after breakfast. I
remained in bed") . . . *with General Lee at Appomattox* ("There
is nothing left me but to go and see General Grant, and I had
rather die a thousand times") . . . *and in all the other places
in the country and in the hearts and minds that the Civil War
was fought. . . .*

VOICES OF THE
CIVIL WAR

RICHARD WHEELER is a former Marine and a full-time author.
He has specialized in Civil War history, with eight of his thirteen
books dealing with that momentous conflict.

Lincoln reading the Emancipation Proclamation to his cabinet.

VOICES
OF THE
CIVIL
WAR

RICHARD WHEELER

A MERIDIAN BOOK

MERIDIAN
Published by the Penguin Group
Penguin Books USA Inc., 375 Hudson Street,
New York, New York 10014, U.S.A.
Penguin Books Ltd, 27 Wrights Lane,
London W8 5TZ, England
Penguin Books Australia Ltd, Ringwood,
Victoria, Australia
Penguin Books Canada Ltd, 2801 John Street,
Markham, Ontario, Canada L3R 1B4
Penguin Books (N.Z.) Ltd, 182-190 Wairau Road,
Auckland 10, New Zealand

Penguin Books Ltd, Registered Offices:
Harmondsworth, Middlesex, England

Published by Meridian, an imprint of New American Library, a division of Penguin Books USA
Inc. This is an authorized reprint of a hardcover edition published by Thomas Y. Crowell
Company.

First Meridian Printing, October, 1990
10   9   8   7   6   5   4   3

REGISTERED TRADEMARK—MARCA REGISTRADA

Library of Congress Number: 98-13289

PRINTED IN THE UNITED STATES OF AMERICA
Original hardcover book designed by S. S. Drate

To Hugh Rawson
with gratitude

BOOKS BY RICHARD WHEELER

Voices of the Civil War
Voices of 1776
In Pirate Waters
The Bloody Battle for Suribachi

FOREWORD

During the last two or three decades, America has absorbed a great many books on the Civil War: scholarly books, once-over-lightlies, exciting books, dull books—and, when you stop to consider it, probably too many books. The story of that war is a tale that has been told. What do we gain by having it told once more?

That depends, of course, on who is doing the telling. Here was the greatest, most terrible, and the most profoundly significant, single experience in our national existence, and it merits all of the study it gets; and now and then it occurs to a student that the telling may be best accomplished by the people who were actually in it, whether soldiers, politicians, or innocent stay-at-homes. One man who feels this way about it is Richard Wheeler, and his *Voices of the Civil War* presents his selection of remarks by those who were among those present. His selection is good and the remarks are worth listening to. Through them the reader gets a fresh understanding of the generation that went into that war—the astounding innocence with which the war was begun, the deep knowledge with which it was ended.

Probably no one will ever again begin a war with the lightness of heart that was on display in 1861. In upstate New York, as the first troops march off to war, a massed crowd sings fervently, "It is sweet, it is sweet for one's country to die!" And in Virginia, at the same time, a correspondent wrote to a northern friend: "You cannot meet with one man in a thousand who is not influenced with a passion for war." North and South alike, the troops reflected that spirit, acquiring a soldier's bitter wisdom by degrees as they moved from the parade ground to battle's reality. General McDowell, the unlucky professional who commanded the Union's unready troops at Bull Run, summed up his men's lack of preparation with the words: "They were not used to denying themselves much; they were not used to journeys on foot." Henry M. Stanley, who later became famous for African explorations, remembered a young Confederate soldier who pinned a handful of violets to his hat just before the fearful battle of Shiloh with the hopeful comment that if he wore those flowers maybe the Yanks would not shoot him "because violets are a sign of peace." (It would be interesting to know whether this lad survived his grubby handful of flowers.)

In some cases, to be sure, these unsophisticated people adjusted themselves to reality better than their generals did. Big talk seems to have served commanding generals much as this quaint faith in violets served the young soldier, which is to say that it nerved them for an experience that was altogether too big for them. Both McClellan and Hooker bragged too confidently, too far in advance, of the great things they were going to do; leading Lincoln, some time later, to the wry comment: "The hen is the wisest of all the animal creation because she never cackles until the egg is laid."

By and large, the things that strike home now are not so much the pronouncements of the famous as the stray glimpses we get of the ordinary citizen in the act of bearing up under the weight of war. There was a Southern officer at Second Bull Run, telling how his outfit, ordered to hold a bit of ground until evening no matter what the cost, hung on and did what it was supposed to do—"But the sun went down so slowly." There was a Confederate foraging party in Maryland, filling its canteens with fresh well water; pouring that out to fill them with cold milk from a farmer's spring house; pouring the milk out to fill them with fresh cider, and discarding that a few minutes later for refills from a keg of apple brandy. A Northern officer after Fredericksburg, reflecting on the impossibility of making those who were not there understand what battle was like, mused sadly that a future generation, "when the dimness of time shall have enhanced the romance, will dearly love to hear the tale of the great rebellion." Well, maybe we are the future generation he was talking about, at that.

If it seems too romantic we might reflect what General Sherman had to say when the mayor of Atlanta begged him not to exile its citizens and burn its buildings:

"You cannot qualify war in harsher terms than I will. War is cruelty, and you cannot refine it. . . . You might as well appeal against the thunderstorm as against these terrible hardships of war."

And a veteran from Maine, writing in 1882, considered that some day there would be no veterans present at the annual Memorial Day observances, and reflected that the men who had fought would rest easily if, a century later, their countrymen understood what the war had cost and what it meant for the future of the nation.

Again, we are the countrymen he was talking about.

—Bruce Catton

PREFACE

Voices of the Civil War is intended to be a kind of companion book to the author's previous work, *Voices of 1776*, an eyewitness account of the American Revolution. The Civil War lends itself especially well to this treatment, since so many participants left behind rich accounts of their experiences. No apology will be made for adding yet another volume to the great profusion of books dealing with this period. Not only does the topic seem inexhaustible; the demand seems insatiable.

But perhaps a point has been reached where a new book on the topic should make at least one claim to uniqueness. *Voices of the Civil War* is not simply a loose compilation of eyewitness material in which errors and false impressions have been allowed to stand as "part of the times." The quotes have been selected, researched, and linked together in such a way as to present a continuous narrative that makes every effort to be historically veracious.

The book, however, is not an historical study. It does not go deeply into causes and effects. Even strategic and tactical military detail has been kept at a minimum. This information can be found, repletely covered, in many other places. The present book's purpose is to portray the war's leading military events as participants saw them; and, hopefully, to give the reader an idea of what it must have been like to be there when these events occurred.

Since the work is intended primarily for the general reader rather than the scholar, the sources of the individual quotes are not given; the author was unwilling to clutter the narrative with numbers. Most of the quotes, however, can be traced through the bibliography. In transposition, some alterations have been made in paragraphing, punctuation, and, occasionally, in spelling. Any other tampering that has been done—for the sake of clarity and conciseness, and also to rid certain passages of faulty information—is indicated by brackets and ellipses.

The book's illustrations, except for a few of the maps, are from the war years and the period immediately after, and they range from realistic on-the-spot sketches to engravings of romanticized studio paintings. Among the better-known artists represented are Edwin Forbes, Alfred R. Waud, Frank Beard, Alonzo Chappel, Benson J. Lossing, and Allen C. Redwood.

CONTENTS

ILLUSTRATIONS

MAPS

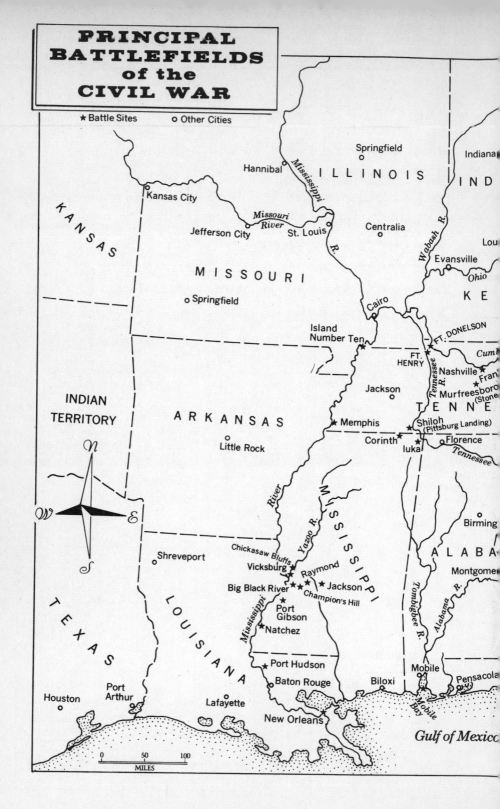

PRINCIPAL
BATTLEFIELDS
of the
CIVIL WAR

★ Battle Sites   ○ Other Cities

KANSAS

MISSOURI

INDIAN
TERRITORY

ARKANSAS

TEXAS

LOUISIANA

ILLINOIS

IND

INDIANA

Springfield

Hannibal

Kansas City

Missouri River

Jefferson City   St. Louis

Centralia

Evansville

KE

Ohio

Springfield

Cairo

Island
Number Ten

FT. DONELSON

FT.
HENRY

Cum

Nashville

Fran

Jackson

Murfreesboro
(Stone

TENNE

Memphis

Shiloh
(Pittsburg Landing)

Little Rock

Corinth   Iuka   Florence

Tennessee

River

Yazoo R.

MISSISSIPPI

Birming

ALABA

Chickasaw Bluffs

Shreveport

Vicksburg   Raymond

Big Black River   ★★★ ★ Jackson
Champion's Hill

Montgome

Port
Gibson

Natchez

Mississippi

Tombigbee R.

Alabama R.

Port Hudson

Houston

Port
Arthur

Lafayette

Baton Rouge

Biloxi

New Orleans

Mobile
Bay

Mobile

Pensacola

Gulf of Mexico

0   50   100
MILES

N
W   E
S

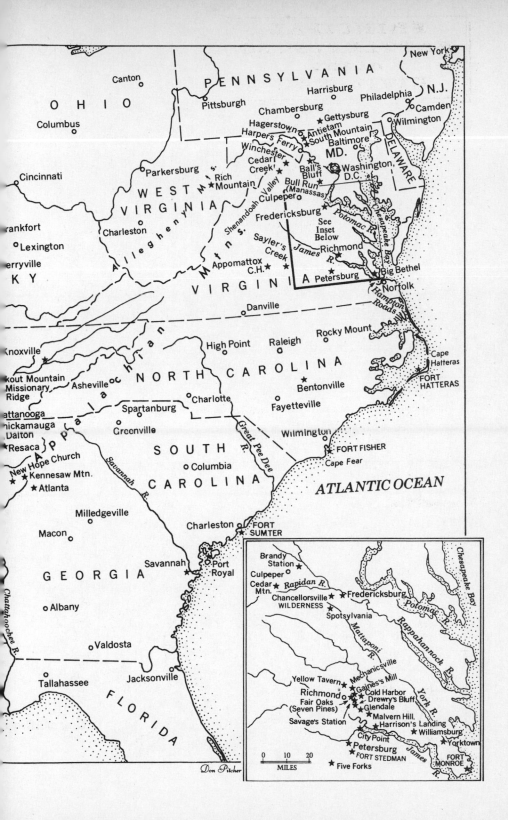

New York

P E N N S Y L V A N I A

O H I O

Canton

Harrisburg

Pittsburgh

Chambersburg

Philadelphia

N. J.

Camden

Columbus

Hagerstown

Gettysburg

Antietam

Wilmington

Harpers Ferry

South Mountain

Baltimore

Winchester

Cedar

Creek

MD.

Parkersburg

Rich

Mountain

Ball's

Bluff

Washington

D.C.

DELAWARE

Cincinnati

W E S T

Shenandoah Valley

Culpeper

Bull Run

(Manassas)

Chesapeake Bay

V I R G I N I A

Fredericksburg

Potomac R.

rankfort

Charleston

Alleghenynia

Mtns.

See

Inset

Below

Lexington

Sayler's

Creek

James

Richmond

R.

erryville

Appomattox

C.H.

Big Bethel

K Y

V I R G I N I A

Petersburg

Norfolk

Hampton

Roads

Danville

Rocky Mount

Knoxville

High Point

Raleigh

Cape

Hatteras

kout Mountain

N O R T H   C A R O L I N A

FORT

Missionary

Ridge

Asheville

Bentonville

HATTERAS

attanooga

Appalachian

Charlotte

hickamauga

Spartanburg

Fayetteville

Dalton

Greenville

Wilmington

Resaca

S O U T H

Great Pee Dee R.

FORT FISHER

New Hope Church

Columbia

Cape Fear

Kennesaw Mtn.

C A R O L I N A

A T L A N T I C   O C E A N

Atlanta

Savannah R.

Milledgeville

Charleston

FORT

SUMTER

Macon

G E O R G I A

Savannah

Port

Royal

Chattahoochee R.

Albany

Valdosta

Tallahassee

Jacksonville

F L O R I D A

Don Pitcher

Brandy

Station

Chesapeake Bay

Culpeper

Cedar

Mtn.

Rapidan R.

Fredericksburg

Chancellorsville

WILDERNESS

Potomac R.

Spotsylvania

Rappahannock R.

Mattaponi R.

Yellow Tavern

Gaines's Mill

Mechanicsville

Richmond

Cold Harbor

Fair Oaks

(Seven Pines)

Drewry's Bluff

Glendale

York R.

Savage's Station

Malvern Hill

Harrison's Landing

Williamsburg

City Point

Petersburg

James R.

Yorktown

FORT STEDMAN

FORT

MONROE

0   10   20

MILES

Five Forks

INTRODUCTION

By the year 1860, which saw Abraham Lincoln elected President of the United States, the North and the South had been at odds for half a century. The two sections had developed along different lines. The North was a populous, bustling, commercial place, its economy geared to industrial growth. In the less populous South, where aristocratic values had a strong influence, the pace was slower and prosperity was centered in large-scale agriculture, with cotton the leading crop, the system dependent upon the labor of slaves.

The North—except for some of its shipowners, who played a prominent part in bringing the Negroes from Africa—had never found slavery to be very profitable. A great many of the farms were small enough to be run by their owners, and large urban populations were available for industrial labor. Consequently, it wasn't hard for Northerners to view slavery with disapproval.

With the opening of the great territories to the west, which led to the formation of new states, slavery became a burning issue. The South, in order to ensure the growth of its economy and its influence (with the added consideration that some of its older cotton lands were played out), strove to extend the practice, while the North wanted it restricted in favor of its own economic system. Slave labor was seen as a threat to this system.

Statesmen such as Henry Clay of Kentucky realized that the only way to ward off explosive trouble was to try to keep the power of the free states and the slave states on a parity, and a vital piece of legislation enacted from this standpoint was the Missouri Compromise (1820). Other momentous laws growing out of the rivalry were the Compromise of 1850 and the Kansas-Nebraska Act (1854).

Tied in with the sectional strife was the issue of states' rights. Since the nation was formed, various political figures, North and South, had regarded the powers of the Federal government as being limited to those explicitly mentioned in the Constitution, and the powers of the individual states as embracing all of those not explicitly denied them. In line with this doctrine, the Southern states argued that Congress had no right to regulate slavery, nor to pass any other law that infringed upon their sovereignty.

In 1832, a tariff that seemed to benefit the North at the expense of the South prompted South Carolina to declare the legislation null and void within her borders and also to threaten to secede from the Union. Getting no substantial support from the other Southern states, she mitigated her stand after a show of force by President Andrew Jackson, who insisted: "Our Federal Union—it must be preserved!" The tariff was reenacted on a compromise basis.

Complicating the slavery problem were the North's abolitionists, among whom were such effective spokesmen as William Lloyd Garrison, publisher of *The Liberator,* and Harriet Beecher Stowe, author of *Uncle Tom's Cabin.* This group demanded a quick end to slavery, yet advanced no acceptable ideas as to how this could be done without ruining the South's economy and precipitating a general turmoil. Even Lincoln, in a speech delivered in 1854, said that he could not blame the South "for not doing what I should not know how to do myself." Lincoln was not an abolitionist, advocating instead that slavery be allowed no further advances.

In the latter 1850s the dispute grew louder and more furious. The North clamored against the Supreme Court's Dred Scott Decision, which stated not only that a slave, being property, had no constitutional rights as a citizen, but also that it was unconstitutional for Congress to legislate the exclusion of slavery from new territories. The South, though encouraged by the Dred Scott Decision, was appalled when John Brown, a fanatical abolitionist, made an attempt to steal Federal weapons from the arsenal at Harpers Ferry, Virginia (later West Virginia), for the purpose of arming a Negro uprising.

In both North and South, all the while, there were those who averred that the best way to settle the dispute was to dissolve the Union.

By 1859, there were eighteen free states and only fifteen slave states, and the South was at a disadvantage in both houses of Congress. The climax came the following year when the Republican party, which represented Northern interests, won with Lincoln. The South now considered herself to be politically overwhelmed, and many people could see no other course but withdrawal from the Union. South Carolina led the way, declaring for secession on December 20, 1860.

The organization of the Confederate States of America, with Jefferson Davis as president and Alexander Stephens as vice-president, was launched in February, 1861. At this time the Confederacy was made up of six states: South Carolina, Mississippi, Florida, Alabama, Georgia, and Louisiana. Texas made it seven on March 2.

Even before their official organization, the seceded states had begun seizing Federal property—mostly that of a military nature—within their borders. Backed by Washington, the garrison at Fort Sumter, in the harbor of Charleston, South Carolina, refused to move out. In early spring, 1861, the new Confederate government decided to force the issue. This seemed the best way to draw the wavering states away from Washington and consolidate Southern power.

The half-century dispute between the two sections of the country had now departed the realm of words and entered the realm of war.

1

CRISIS AT
FORT SUMTER

I T WAS *the afternoon of April 11, 1861, and Major Robert Anderson, commander of the Union troops at Fort Sumter, found himself in a crucial spot. A deputation of Confederates had come to demand that he and his men evacuate the fort without further delay. Sumter had not yet been fired upon, but it was heavily besieged and its food stores and other supplies were running out. Until recently, the Confederates had allowed Anderson to obtain some of his supplies from Charleston, but now this traffic was banned. (The ban, however, hadn't prevented two of the more friendly Confederate officers from presenting Anderson's officers with a generous supply of wine and cigars.)*

Located near the center of the entrance to Charleston Harbor, Fort Sumter was a five-sided brick structure that rose directly from the water, its foundations resting upon a shoal. Built to accommodate a garrison of 650 men, it was presently occupied by about 125, some 40 of whom were noncombatant workmen. On points of land across the encircling waters were lesser fortifications, some old and some new, all in the hands of Confederate troops numbering in the thousands, their commander being Brigadier General Pierre G. T. Beauregard.

Some twenty years earlier, Beauregard, a Louisianan, had studied artillery under Anderson at West Point. Anderson himself, inciden-

5

Fort Sumter before the bombardment.

tally, was a Southerner, coming from Kentucky. Both men had gone on to serve the national flag in the Mexican War, and both had been wounded. Unlike Beauregard, Anderson had chosen to remain with the Union. Now Beauregard had Anderson ringed with cannons and mortars, the deployment doubtless influenced by Anderson's own teachings.

Beauregard, through the aides he had sent to the fort on this day in April, offered his old instructor the best of terms: The Federals would be allowed to leave with the honors of war, to include their giving a formal salute to their flag before departing. They would be guaranteed safe conduct north.

Major Anderson was expecting Washington to make an attempt to resupply him from the sea, so he did not submit. However, he doubted that the operation would be successful, and as he accompanied the Confederates to their boat in the late afternoon, he said, "Gentlemen, if you do not batter the fort to pieces about us, we shall be starved out in a few days."

About twelve-thirty that same night, a reverberating signal shot announced that the Confederate boat was returning. The fort was in deep darkness, being equipped with only a few improvised oil lamps. Many of the Federals tumbled from their cots "to see what was the matter." Major Anderson soon learned that the Confederates wanted

*to resume negotiations, and he took them to the guardroom, where
one of the lamps glimmered.*

*This time the major said he would evacuate the fort in three days,
provided he wasn't resupplied or sent contrary orders by then. But
the Confederates had orders from Beauregard to deny Anderson the
opportunity to await a possible change in his situation. At 3:20 A.M.
they composed and penned a brief note which they presented as their
reply. Anderson held the paper up to the dim light, and read:*

By authority of Brigadier General Beauregard, commanding the
Provisional Forces of the Confederate States, we have the honor to
notify you that he will open the fire of his batteries on Fort Sumter in
one hour from this time.

*According to the note's penman, Stephen D. Lee, Anderson "was
much affected."*

He seemed to realize the full import of the consequences and the
great responsibility of his position. Escorting us to the boat at the
wharf, he cordially pressed our hands in farewell, remarking, "If we
never meet in this world again, God grant that we may meet in the
next."

*Some of Anderson's men had remained up after being awakened by
the signal gun. Others were asleep during the critical moments of the
parley. The latter included even the fort's second-in-command, Captain Abner Doubleday (later to be credited, though not with historic
certainty, with creating the modern version of baseball):*

. . . I was [now] awakened by someone groping about my room in
the dark and calling out my name. It proved to be Anderson, who
came to announce to me that he had just received a dispatch from
Beauregard . . . to the effect that he should open fire upon us in an
hour. Finding it was determined not to return the fire until after
breakfast, I remained in bed. As we had no lights, we could in fact do
nothing [worthwhile] before that time. . . .

*Doubleday's kind of calmness was hardly the rule on either side of the
dispute at this moment. Even many of the civilians in Charleston,
which lay three miles across the bay from Sumter, were alert and anxious. Mary Boykin Chesnut, the wife of one of Beauregard's aides and
a guest in a mansion overlooking the harbor, wrote in her diary:*

I do not pretend to go to sleep. How can I? If Anderson does not

A Confederate mortar battery.

accept terms at four, the orders are he shall be fired upon. I count four [as] St. Michael's bells chime out, and I begin to hope.

Even as the bells chimed, fresh campfires were springing up on the several points of land that held the Confederate guns and mortars. Up to this time, some of the Federals peering from Sumter's ramparts had believed that Beauregard might be bluffing. Now all such speculation ended. In the words of the garrison's surgeon, Dr. S. Wylie Crawford:

The night was calm and clear, and the sea was still. . . . [A]t 4:30 A.M. the silence was broken by the discharge of a mortar from a battery near Fort Johnson. . . .

Adds Union artillerist James Chester:

The eyes of the watchers easily detected and followed the burning fuse which marked the course of the shell as it mounted among the stars and then descended with ever-increasing velocity. . . .

A "capital shot," the shell burst directly over the fort. Writes Stephen Lee, of Beauregard's staff:

The firing of the mortar [the signal for the start of a general bombardment] woke the echoes from every nook and corner of the harbor, and in this the dead hour of night before dawn, that shot was a sound of alarm that brought every soldier in the harbor to his feet, and every man, woman, and child in the city of Charleston from their beds.

Mary Boykin Chesnut fell at once to her knees:
. . . I prayed as I never prayed before. There was a sound of stir all over the house, pattering of feet in the corridors. All seemed hurrying one way. I put on my double gown and a shawl and went too. It was to the housetop. The shells were bursting. . . . The regular roar of the cannon—there it was. . . . The women were wild there on the housetop. Prayers came from the women, and imprecations from the men. And then a shell would light up the scene. . . . We watched up there, and everybody wondered that Fort Sumter did not fire a shot.

Says the garrison's James Chester:
. . . shot and shell went screaming over Sumter as if an army of devils were swooping around it. As a rule the guns were aimed too high, but all the mortar practice was good. In a few minutes the novelty [of the situation] disappeared in a realizing sense of danger, and the watchers retired to the bomb-proofs, where they discussed probabilities until reveille. . . . No serious damage was being done to the fort.

The imperturbable Abner Doubleday takes up:
When it was broad daylight, I went down to breakfast. I found the officers already assembled at one of the long tables in the mess hall. Our party were calm, and even somewhat merry.

We had retained one colored man to wait on us. He was a spruce-looking mulatto from Charleston, very active and efficient on ordinary occasions, but now completely demoralized by the thunder of the guns and crashing of the shot around us. He leaned back against the wall . . . his eyes closed, and his whole expression one of perfect despair.

Our meal was not very sumptuous. It consisted of pork and water. But Doctor Crawford triumphantly brought forth a little farina, which he had found in a corner of the hospital.

When this frugal repast was over, my company was told off in three details for firing purposes, to be relieved afterward by [Captain Truman] Seymour's company. As I was the ranking officer, I took the first detachment and marched them to the casemates [the series of brick gun rooms] which looked out upon the powerful iron-clad battery of Cummings Point.

In aiming the first gun fired against the rebellion I had no feeling of self-reproach, for I fully believed that the contest was inevitable and was not of our seeking. . . .

Our firing now became regular and was answered from the rebel guns which encircled us on four sides of the pentagon upon which the fort was built. The other side faced the open sea. Showers of balls . . . and shells . . . poured into the fort in one incessant stream, causing great flakes of masonry to fall in all directions. When the immense mortar shells, after sailing high in the air, came down in a vertical direction and buried themselves in the parade ground, their explosion shook the fort like an earthquake.

General Beauregard watched the performance of his crews with satisfaction: ". . . the fire of my batteries was kept up most spiritedly, the guns and mortars being worked in the coolest manner. . . ."

"At the end of the first four hours," relates Union artillerist James Chester,

Doubleday's men were relieved from the guns and had an opportunity to look about [the harbor]. Not a man was visible near any of the batteries, but a large party, apparently non-combatants, had collected on the beach of Sullivan's Island, well out of the line of fire. . . . Doubleday's men were not in the best of temper. They were irritated at the thought that they had been unable to inflict any serious damage on their adversary, and although they had suffered no damage in return they were dissatisfied.

The crowd of unsympathetic spectators was more than they could bear, and two veteran sergeants determined to stir them up a little. For this purpose they directed two 42-pounders [i.e., two guns made for 42-pound solid projectiles] on the crowd; and, when no officer was near [to deter them], fired. The first shot struck about fifty yards short, and, bounding over the heads of the astonished spectators, went crashing through the Moultrie House. The second followed an almost identical course, doing no damage except to the Moultrie House, and the spectators scampered off in a rather undignified manner.

Scattered everywhere about the harbor were other spectators, some on housetops, some on the wharves and beaches, and some in hover-

ing boats. Mary Boykin Chesnut divided her time between her house-top observation point and her bedroom: "Boom, boom, goes the cannon all the time. The nervous strain is awful. . . ."

The men in the fort, says James Chester, soon noted that the expected relief vessels from the North were beginning to arrive in the waters outside the harbor bar: ". . . orders were given to dip the flag to them. This was done, and the salute was returned. . . ."

The expedition was ill-prepared for an emergency of so grave a nature, and its commander felt that an attempt to reach the fort would result in too great a sacrifice of lives; so nothing was done. The ships rode at anchor, their crews merely swelling the ranks of the spectators.

Again in Abner Doubleday's words:

The firing continued all day without any special incident of importance, and without our making much impression on the enemy's works. They had a great advantage over us, as their fire was concentrated on the fort, which was in the center of the circle, while ours was diffused over the circumference. Their missiles were exceedingly destructive to the upper exposed portion of the work, but no essential injury was done to the lower casemates which sheltered us.

Several times the wooden barracks within the fort's walls were set afire by specially heated projectiles ("red-hot shot"), but the flames were soon extinguished.

James Chester says that Sumter was sufficiently supplied with shot, shell, and powder, but that it was short of friction primers and, in particular, of cartridge bags—bags for holding the individual powder charges:

The scarcity of cartridge bags drove us to some strange makeshifts. . . . [S]everal tailors were kept busy making cartridge bags out of soldiers' flannel shirts; and we fired away several dozen pairs of woolen socks belonging to Major Anderson.

With the coming of dusk, the Federals ceased firing and closed their embrasures. Beauregard's batteries continued to fire at ten- or fifteen-minute intervals. The night was stormy, the wind and waves high. The men in the fort were apprehensive that the Confederates would attempt an assault in spite of the weather, but nothing happened.

At last, writes Chester,

. . . reveille sounded, and the men oiled their appetites with the fat pork at the usual hour by way of breakfast. The second day's bombardment began at the same hour as did the first; that is, on the Sumter side. The enemy's mortars had kept up a very slow fire all night, which gradually warmed up after daylight as their batteries seemed to awaken. . . . Fire broke out once or twice in the officers' quarters, and was extinguished.

Over in Charleston, Mary Boykin Chesnut did not go down to break-fast. Early in the day, she wrote in her diary:

Anderson has not yet silenced any of our guns. . . . But the sound of those guns makes regular meals impossible. . . . Tea trays pervade the corridors, going everywhere. Some of the anxious hearts lie on their beds and moan in solitary misery. Mrs. [Louis T.] Wigfall and I solace ourselves with tea in my room. . . .

Not by one word or look can we detect any change in the de-meanor of these Negro servants. Lawrence sits at our door, sleepy and respectful, and profoundly indifferent. So are they all, but they carry it too far. You could not tell that they even heard the awful roar go-ing on in the bay. . . . People talk before them as if they were chairs and tables. They make no sign. Are they stolidly stupid? Or wiser than we are; silent and strong, biding their time?

While Mrs. Chesnut and Mrs. Wigfall sipped their morning tea and worried about a slave insurrection, Beauregard's batteries succeeded in starting new and more serious fires in the fort's barracks. When the columns of smoke were seen, says Beauregard,

. . . the fire of our batteries was increased as a matter of course, for the purpose of bringing the enemy to terms as speedily as possible, inasmuch as his flag was still floating defiantly above him. Fort Sumter continued to fire from time to time. . . . Our brave troops, carried away by their naturally generous impulses, mounted the different batteries, and at every discharge from the fort cheered the garrison for its pluck and gallantry, and hooted the fleet lying inactive just out-side the bar.

By this time the fires in the fort's barracks were burning out of con-trol, and the magazine, or ammunition repository, was threatened. Men rushed in and began rolling out barrels of powder to be taken to the casemates where the gun crews were stationed. A good many bar-rels were thus transferred; but soon the heavy copper door had to be swung shut and insulated with a pile of earth.

The conflagration, according to Abner Doubleday, was now one of "terrible and disastrous" proportions:

One fifth of the fort was on fire, and the wind drove the smoke in dense masses into the angle where we had all taken refuge. It seemed impossible to escape suffocation. Some lay down close to the ground with handkerchiefs over their mouths, and others posted themselves near the embrasures [in the casemates] where the smoke was somewhat lessened by the draught of air. . . . Had not a slight change of wind taken place, the result might have been fatal to most of us.

Our firing having ceased and the enemy being very jubilant, I thought it would be as well to show them that we were not all dead yet, and ordered the gunners to fire a few rounds more. . . .

The scene at this time was really terrific. The roaring and crackling of the flames, the dense masses of whirling smoke, the bursting of the enemy's shells and our own [stored shells] which were exploding in the burning rooms, the crashing of the shot, and the sound of masonry falling in every direction, made the fort a pandemonium.

Adds John Gray Foster, another of the garrison's officers:

The clouds of smoke and cinders which were sent into the casemates by the wind . . . made it dangerous to retain the powder which had been saved from the magazine. The commanding officer accordingly gave orders to have all but five barrels thrown out of the embrasures into the water, which was done.

A bobbing accumulation of these barrels was hit by a Confederate shell, and the gun whose muzzle loomed at the nearest embrasure was blown out of position.

In the early afternoon the flagstaff, which rose from the ground inside the fort, was snapped off; but, says James Chester, "the old flag was rescued and nailed to a new staff . . . [and] was carried to the ramparts. . . ."

In spite of the screen of smoke, the Confederates had been quick to note the flag's disappearance. Some wondered if it had been lowered by the garrison. Before the banner reappeared on the ramparts, Colonel Louis T. Wigfall (until lately a United States senator from Texas) headed for the fort.

Returning to Doubleday's account:

About 2 P.M. Senator Wigfall, in company with W. Gourdin Young, of Charleston, unexpectedly made his appearance at one of the embrasures, having crossed over from Morris Island in a small boat rowed by Negroes. . . . An artilleryman serving his gun was very much astonished to see a man's face at the entrance and asked him what he was doing there. Wigfall replied that he wished to see Major Anderson.

Since he was starkly exposed to the shot and shell still coming from the Confederate batteries, the senator added, "For God's sake, let me in!" A hand was extended to help him through the embrasure into the casemate. Notwithstanding the fort's condition, one of the Federal officers was quick to show Wigfall the flag on the ramparts. Wigfall responded with, "Let us quit this!"

Doubleday goes on:

Wigfall, in Beauregard's name, offered Anderson his own terms, which were the evacuation of the fort, with permission to salute our flag and to march out with the honors of war, with our arms and private baggage. . . .

Anderson ordered the fort's flag lowered and a bed sheet raised in its place, and the shooting stopped. The fort's barracks still burned, the air remaining acrid with smoke and sparks.

As it turned out, the impetuous Wigfall had no authority from Beauregard to negotiate with Anderson; but an authorized deputy soon arrived, and by evening the terms as offered by Wigfall were official. The Federals agreed to evacuate the fort the next day.

Among the Confederates present at the surrender that evening was Stephen Lee:

Major Anderson, his officers, and men were blackened by smoke and cinders, and showed signs of fatigue and exhaustion. . . . It was soon discovered, by conversation, that it was a bloodless battle. Not a man had been killed or seriously wounded on either side during the entire bombardment of nearly forty hours [actually, thirty-four]. Congratulations were exchanged on so happy a result.

The lack of casualties on the Federal side (except for a few men with nicks, burns, and bruises) was all the more remarkable in light of the fact that the Confederates had fired more than three thousand rounds of shot and shell.

According to an unnamed Federal officer, the Confederate ranks included men who had qualms about their part in the affair:

Many of the South Carolina officers who came into the fort . . .

Interior view of Fort Sumter after the bombardment.

who were formerly in our service, seemed to feel very badly at firing upon their old comrades and flag.

In Charleston, the surrender had been anticipated since the conflagration started. Said an evening dispatch from the city:
The bells have been chiming all day, guns firing, ladies waving handkerchiefs, people cheering, and citizens making themselves generally demonstrative. It is regarded as the greatest day in the history of South Carolina.

Mary Boykin Chesnut told her diary:
I did not know that one could live such days of excitement. . . . As far as I can make out, the fort surrendered to Wigfall. But it is all confusion. . . . Fire engines have been sent for, to put out the fire. Everybody tells you half of something, and then rushes off to tell something else, or to hear the last news.

Charleston celebrated the victory far into the night. The weary Federals, writes Doubleday, got some rest:
The next morning, Sunday the 14th, we were up early, packing

our baggage in readiness to go on board the transport [sent to the fort by the Confederates]. The time having arrived, I made preparations, by order of Major Anderson, to fire a national salute to the flag.

Though intended to be one of a hundred guns, or discharges, the salute was limited to fifty because of an accident. Doubleday explains:
    . . . owing to the recent conflagration, there were fire and sparks all around the cannon. . . . It happened that some flakes of fire had entered the muzzle of one of the guns after it was sponged. Of course, when the gunner attempted to ram the cartridge down it exploded prematurely, killing Private Daniel Hough instantly, and setting fire to a pile of cartridges underneath, which also exploded . . . wounding five men.

The injuries of one of these men were mortal. Thus it was that the war's first deaths were accidental.
    The new garrison sent by Beauregard marched into the fort as the salute ended, and a Confederate chaplain assisted at Daniel Hough's burial, made on the rubble-strewn parade ground. The Confederate soldiers joined the Federals in uncovering their heads during the ceremonies.
    Doubleday says that Major Anderson now ordered him to march the Federals to the wharf:
    I told him I should prefer to leave the fort with the flag flying [at the head of the column] and the drums beating "Yankee Doodle," and he authorized me to do so. As soon as our tattered flag came down [from above the fort, where it had flown for the salute] and the silken banner made by the ladies of Charleston was run up, tremendous shouts of applause were heard from the vast multitude of spectators; and all the vessels and steamers [scattered about the harbor] with one accord made for the fort.

After a delay caused by tidal conditions, the vessel boarded by the Federals crossed the bar to the Union fleet. The men were transferred to the steamship Baltic, *which soon weighed anchor to take them north. Writes Dr. Crawford:*
    Many an eye turned toward the disappearing fort, and as it sunk at last upon the horizon, the smoke-cloud still hung heavily over its parapet.

2

THE RUSH TO ARMS

D URING THE *bombardment of Fort Sumter, streams of telegraph dispatches kept the people of North and South alike informed of all that happened. In the North, perhaps no one took a keener interest in the situation than Mary Ashton Livermore, a public-spirited woman who was soon to join the United States Sanitary Commission, a volunteer organization dedicated to looking after the health and welfare of Union soldiers and their families. On April 11, 1861, just before the Sumter crisis exploded, Mrs. Livermore completed a train trip across the Northeast:*

The opening of the War of the Rebellion found me in Boston, my native city. My own home had been in Chicago for years, but my aged father was thought to be dying, and the stern speech of the telegram had summoned me to his bedside. It was a time of extreme and unconcealed anxiety. The daily papers teemed with the dreary records of secession. . . . Everyone was asking his neighbor, "What will be the end?"

. . . The day after my arrival, came the news that Fort Sumter was attacked, which increased the feverish anxiety. . . . When . . . the telegraph, which . . . registered for the astounded nation the hourly progress of the bombardment, announced the lowering of the Stars and Stripes and the surrender of the beleaguered garrison, the news fell on the land like a thunderbolt. . . .

The next day, April 14, was Sunday. The pulpits thundered with denunciations of the rebellion. . . . Some of the ministers counselled war. . . . Better that the land should be drenched with fraternal blood than that any further concessions should be made to the slaveocracy. . . . The same vigorous speech was heard on the streets, through which surged hosts of excited men. . . .

Monday dawned, April 15. Who that saw that day will ever forget it! For now . . . there rang out the voice of Abraham Lincoln calling for seventy-five thousand volunteers for three months. They were for the protection of Washington and the property of the government. . . . This proclamation was like the first peal of a surcharged thunder-cloud, clearing the murky air. The . . . whole North arose as one man. . . .

Everywhere the drum and fife thrilled the air with their stirring call. Recruiting offices were opened in every city, town, and village. . . . Hastily formed companies marched to camps of rendezvous, the sunlight flashing from gun-barrel and bayonet, and the streets echoing the measured tread of soldiers. Flags . . . blossomed everywhere. . . .

To my father, this uprising of the country was the very elixir of life. The blood came again to his cheek, and vigor to his system. And when, on the morning of Tuesday, volunteers began to arrive in Boston . . . he insisted on being lifted into a carriage and on going to witness their arrival and reception.

As they marched from the railroad stations, they were escorted by crowds cheering vociferously. Merchants and clerks rushed out from stores, bareheaded, saluting them as they passed. Windows were flung up; and women leaned out into the rain, waving flags and handkerchiefs. Horse-cars and omnibuses halted for the passage of the soldiers, and cheer upon cheer leaped forth from [their] thronged doors and windows. . . . As the men filed into Faneuil Hall, in solid columns, the enthusiasm knew no bounds. . . .

I had never seen anything like this before. I had never dreamed that New England . . . could be fired with so warlike a spirit. . . .

By six o'clock on the afternoon of Tuesday, April 16, three regiments were ready to start for Washington, and new companies were being raised in all parts of the state. On the afternoon of the next day, the Sixth Massachusetts, a full regiment one thousand strong, started from Boston by rail. . . . An immense concourse of people gathered in the neighborhood of the Boston and Albany railroad station to witness their departure. . . . The long train backed down where the

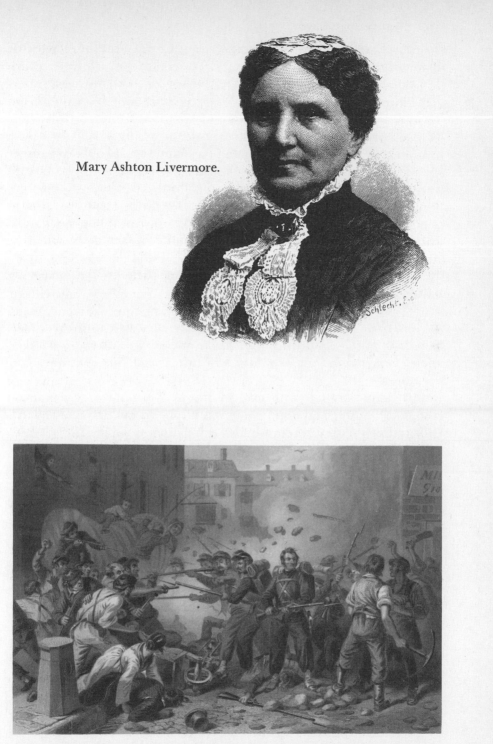

Mary Ashton Livermore.

Massachusetts troops fighting their way through Baltimore.

soldiers were scattered among mothers, wives, sweethearts, and friends uttering last words of farewell.

"Fall into line!" was the unfamiliar order that rang out. . . . The blue-coated soldiers released themselves tenderly from the clinging arms of affection . . . and were marched into the cars. The two locomotives, drawing the long train slowly out of the station, whistled a shrill good-bye—every engine in the neighborhood shrieked back an answering farewell—[and] from the crowded streets, the densely packed station, the roofs of houses, the thronged windows, and the solid mass of human beings lining both sides of the track . . . there rang out a roar of good wishes and parting words, accompanied with tears and sobs and the waving of hats and handkerchiefs—and the Sixth Massachusetts was on its way to Washington. Ah, how little they, or we, foresaw the reception awaiting them in the streets of Baltimore!

By this time Mrs. Livermore's father was so much improved that there was no longer any need for her to remain in Boston, and a day or two later she began her return trip to Chicago. She continues her narrative:

All along the route were excited groups of people, eager for news from Washington, and everywhere was displayed the national flag. At Albany [New York], where we halted for dinner, we learned [about] the reception given the Massachusetts Sixth in their passage through Baltimore the day before. A vast and angry crowd [of secessionists] had opposed their progress; showers of stones and other missiles were hurled at them from the streets and housetops; the soldiers had defended themselves and fired into the mob; and the dead, dying, and wounded lay in the streets. . . . The war had indeed begun. . . .

I was detained . . . over Sunday in Auburn, N.Y. The war spirit was rampant there, as everywhere. A newly recruited company of volunteers were to leave on Monday morning for New York, and they were honored with a public leave-taking in one of the churches that evening. The spacious church was crowded to suffocation—[with] as large an audience waiting outside. . . . The pulpit was decked with the national colors. Bunting festooned the walls and the sides of the gallery. The great audience rose, clapping and applauding, as the soldiers filed into the pews reserved for them. . . .

The sermon . . . was a radical discourse, and recognized slavery as the underlying cause of the outbreak, which, it predicted, would result in the freedom of the Southern serfs. The choir sang patriotic odes, the audience joining with one voice in the exultant refrain, "It is sweet, it is sweet, for one's country to die!" The great congregation [out-of-doors] caught it, thrilling the evening air with the spirit of the hour, "It is sweet, it is sweet, for one's country to die!"

. . . In Chicago, there was more stir and excitement than I had seen elsewhere. The war spirit, war news, and war preparations engrossed everybody. The day presented scenes of din and bustle, and the night was scarcely [more] tranquil. The streets were thronged with eager men and women rushing here and there as incidents called them.

As it was throughout the North, so it was in the South. Lincoln's proclamation precipitated secession proceedings on the part of four more states: Virginia, Arkansas, North Carolina, and Tennessee. This resulted in bringing the Confederacy's total to eleven states, the limit of its strength.

John Minor Botts, an influential Virginian who was devoted to the Federal Union, deplored Lincoln's act in a letter to Washington written on April 19:

. . . I cannot begin to give you a just conception of the excitement created, not only here but throughout the whole Southern country, by the proclamation. . . . [T]he Union party and the Union feeling has been almost entirely swept out of existence. You cannot meet with one man in a thousand who is not influenced with a passion for war. . . .

Jefferson Davis reacted to Lincoln's move by inviting Southern ship-owners to help "resist aggression" by operating as privateers (licensed pirates) against the North's seaborne commerce. Lincoln, in turn, ordered a blockade of Southern ports. At the same time, however, the Federal navy yard at Norfolk, Virginia, had to be abandoned to the Confederates, an attempt to destroy it being only partly successful. Also abandoned was the Federal arsenal at Harpers Ferry. These were encouraging gains for the Confederacy.

Many of the aroused Southerners had begun to think in terms of attacking the Northern capital. According to the Richmond, Virginia, Examiner *of April 23:*

From the mountain-tops and valleys to the shores of the sea, there is one wild shout of fierce resolve to capture Washington City. . . . That filthy cage of unclean birds must and will assuredly be purified by fire. . . . It is not to be endured that this flight of abolition harpies shall come down from the black North for their roosts in the heart of the South, to defile and brutalize the land. . . .

The fanatical yell for the immediate subjugation of the whole South is going up hourly from the united voices of all the North; and, for the purpose of making their work sure, they have determined to hold Washington City as the point whence to carry on their brutal warfare. Our people can take it—they *will* take it. . . .

Though hardly ready for such an effort, the South was rapidly grow-ing stronger. Preparations were everywhere evident. The picture on the Gulf Coast is given by Confederate naval officer Raphael Semmes:

I found Mobile, like the rest of the Confederacy, in a great state of excitement. It was boiling over with enthusiasm. The young mer-chants had dropped their day-books and ledgers, and were forming and drilling companies by night and day, while the older ones were discussing the question of the Confederate Treasury, to see how it could be supported. . . .

I arrived in New Orleans on Monday, the 22d of April. . . . War now occupied the thoughts of the multitude, and the sound of the drum and the tramp of armed men were heard in the streets. The balconies were crowded with lovely women in gay attire to witness the military processions, and the Confederate flag in miniature was pinned on every bosom.

Mrs. Mary A. Ward, a citizen of Rome, Georgia, tells how the first troops (apparently all aristocrats) left that community:

The young men carried dress suits with them, and any quantity of fine linen. . . . Every soldier, nearly, had a servant with him, and a whole lot of spoons and forks, so as to live comfortably and elegantly in camp, and finally to make a splurge in Washington when they should arrive there, which they expected would be very soon indeed.

That is really the way they went off; and their sweethearts gave them embroidered slippers and pin-cushions and needle-books, and all sorts of such little et ceteras. . . .

These men were on their way to Virginia, where the Confederacy's main army was gathering. Virginia herself, of course, was raising many troops for this army. Among them was a company of cavalry originating in Bedford County and led by Captain William R. Terry. It included a Private John Goode, who later set down the story of the unit's departure from home:

Never can I forget . . . that beautiful May morning. The birds were sweetly singing in the trees, the flowers were beautifully blooming, and all nature seemed to be rejoicing. In the presence of a large concourse of sympathizing people . . . Reverend John E. Wharton invoked the Divine blessing upon Captain Terry and his men as they went forth with all the buoyancy of young manhood, and all the enthusiasm of the volunteer soldier. They left many sorrowing and aching hearts behind them. They were followed by the prayers and benedictions of the pure, the virtuous, the patriotic, and the good. . . .

After remaining a few weeks in a camp of instruction at Lynchburg, Captain Terry marched with his [mounted] company to the neighborhood of Manassas Junction to join the Confederate forces. On our march we camped one night in a vacant lot adjoining a female seminary at Gordonsville. When we went to the pump the next morning to wash our faces, the young girls belonging to the seminary brought out their nice clean towels and offered them to us.

After we had mounted to resume our march, and were drawn up in line in front of the long portico where the young girls stood to witness our departure, Captain Terry cried out, "Attention! Private Goode will advance two paces to the front and return thanks for our hospitable treatment."

If I had heard a thunderclap from a cloudless sky, I could not have been more astonished; but believing that the first duty of a soldier is to obey orders, I spurred my horse, advanced two paces in front of the line, doffed my military cap, and proceeded to harangue the young ladies in an impromptu address in which I said a great many foolish things. Among other things, I told them that when the war was over we would return . . . and, like the troubadours of old, would sing under their windows the songs of love.

War preparations, both North and South, were made in a kind of holiday atmosphere, with both sides highly confident and neither having any real idea of what lay ahead—the usual manner in which belligerents undertake hostilities. Explains Northern historian Joel Tyler Headley, who recorded the story of the war even while it was happening:

Civil war was an evil we had never contemplated. Besides, we had been taught so long to regard it as a political bugbear, a mere party menace, that we looked upon it with little or no alarm. More than this, the North had been told so long by unscrupulous politicians that the South dare not fight, that at the first call to arms the slaves would rush into insurrection—that it really believed at the first show of determination the South would decline the contest.

The people at the South had been beguiled in the same manner by their leaders. They had been assured over and over again that the money-loving North would never go to war with [a] source of their wealth—a "race of shop keepers" would never fight for a sentiment; and if they attempted it, would be crushed at the first onset by the chivalrous, warlike South. Thus the two sections were hurried, through ignorance and blind presumption, towards all the untold horrors of civil war.

Though the North was greatly superior to the South in population and material resources, the war's outcome was by no means a foregone conclusion. The South had many competent leaders and thousands of outdoorsmen adept with horses and firearms. Moreover, the Confederate armies would do most of their fighting on their own ground, aided by friendly civilians. The North, on the other hand, would have to stretch its supply lines over vast areas of hostile territory. Also advantageous to the South was that the North had a strong "peace party." A stiff resistance might well increase the pressure on Washington to end the war on Southern terms. Finally, since cotton was economically important in Europe, the South could look that way for aid in the form of arms and other supplies. She could even harbor a substantial hope for open intervention in her favor.

3

FIRST BULL RUN

THE WAR'S FIRST THREE MONTHS *saw only minor fighting. On June 10, 1861, the Confederates beat back a Federal attack at Big Bethel, on the Virginia coast northwest of Hampton. Additional clashes occurred in the border state of Missouri and in western Virginia (soon to become the border state of West Virginia). The victor at the Battle of Rich Mountain, western Virginia (July 11), was a young Union general named George Brinton McClellan, who managed to win newspaper acclaim that gave him a reputation greater than he merited.*

Events were now moving toward the war's first great battle. At Alexandria, Virginia, on the Potomac River below Washington, a Federal army under General Irvin McDowell was ready to heed the North's cry, "On to Richmond!" Responsible for blocking the Federal approach to the Confederate capital was Pierre Beauregard, the hero of Fort Sumter, who had deployed his army along Bull Run, a stream near Manassas, about twenty-five miles southwest of Washington. McDowell and Beauregard had been classmates at West Point.

Roughly fifty miles northwest of the Alexandria–Manassas arena, at the northern end of Virginia's Shenandoah Valley, two more forces faced each other, the Federals under General Robert Patterson and the Confederates under General Joseph E. Johnston. Patterson had orders from Washington to keep Johnston occupied, and by no means to let him slip to Manassas to reinforce Beauregard.

S. Emma E. Edmonds.

Confederate troops on the way to Manassas.

The Federal march from the Alexandria vicinity through Con-
federate territory to Bull Run was begun on July 16. The columns
included foot soldiers, artillery and cavalry units, white-topped sup-
ply wagons, and dark-hued ambulances. Many of the men were three-
month volunteers assembled immediately after the war's beginning
at Fort Sumter, and their day of discharge was already close at hand.

The roads were hot and dusty, but according to a Federal nurse
named S. Emma E. Edmonds:

In gay spirits the army moved forward, the air resounding with
the music of the regimental bands and patriotic songs of the soldiers.
No gloomy forebodings seemed to damp the spirits of the men for a
moment. . . . "On to Richmond!" was echoed and re-echoed. . . .

Accompanying the army—on foot, on horseback, and in a variety of
horse-drawn vehicles—were crowds of civilians. As explained in an
account of the battle written by John G. Nicolay, private secretary to
President Lincoln:

The business of war was such a novelty that McDowell's army accumulated an extraordinary number of camp-followers and non-
combatants. The vigilant newspapers of the chief cities sent a cloud
of correspondents to chronicle the incidents of the march and conflict.
The volunteer regiments carried with them . . . companionships
unknown to regular armies. . . . [S]enators and representatives . . .
in several instances joined in what many rashly assumed would be a
mere triumphal parade.

Confederate historian Edward A. Pollard, who spent the war years as
editor of the Richmond Examiner, *writes that the procession in-*
cluded a throng of "gay women and strumpets"; that the senators and
representatives had prepared "carriage loads of champagne for festal
celebration of the victory that was to be won"; and that many people
were carrying tickets that had been printed "for a grand ball in Rich-
mond."

Gatherings of apprehensive Virginia inhabitants, both whites and
Negroes, watched the progress of the army and its followers through
the farmlands and villages.

General McDowell says of the troops:

They stopped every moment to pick blackberries or get water;
they would not keep in the ranks, order as much as you pleased.
When they came where water was fresh, they would pour the old
water out of their canteens and fill them with fresh water. They were

not used to denying themselves much; they were not used to journeys on foot.

Confidence in a quick victory was sustained by the way the Confederate outposts retreated before the advance, doing little more than leave some trees felled across the road. The rate of march was less than ten miles a day. On July 17, according to Nurse Edmonds:

The main column reached Fairfax toward evening and encamped. . . . Notwithstanding the heat and fatigue of the day's march, the troops were in high spirits. . . . Some built fires while others went in search of, and appropriated, every available article which might in any way add to the comfort of hungry and fatigued men. The whole neighborhood was ransacked for milk, butter, eggs, poultry, etc. . . . There might have been heard some stray shots fired in the direction of a field where a drove of cattle were quietly grazing; and soon after the odor of fresh steak was issuing from every part of the camp. I wish to state, however, that all raids made upon hen-coops, etc., were contrary to the orders of the general in command. . . .

But the depredations included even some sportive barn-burning and some vandalizing and burning of homes from which the occupants had fled. One group of soldiers delighted the military multitude by walking the streets of Fairfax dressed in pilfered female clothing. This wasn't funny, however, to Union journalist George Wilkes. He was especially offended when "a fellow passed by with a pair of ladies' ruffled drawers hauled up over his pantaloons."

Next morning the drummers beat an early reveille, and the army marched to Centreville, only a few miles from Bull Run. Here General McDowell called a halt. One of his divisions, however, commanded by General Daniel Tyler, continued forward to make a reconnaissance of the Confederate lines, which extended along the Run for about eight miles. Tyler sent Colonel Israel B. Richardson's brigade to the section of the Run that held the two fords known as Mitchell's and Blackburn's. This was the ground occupied by General Beauregard's center. In coordination with a demonstration in front of Mitchell's, a probe in force was made at Blackburn's. Covered by a cannonade, the infantry closed in.

As recorded by Charles Carleton Coffin, correspondent for the Boston *Journal:*

Suddenly there comes a volley from beneath the green foliage along the winding stream, and the air is thick with leaden rain. A

James Longstreet.

white cloud rises above the trees, and a wild yell—not a cheer, not a hurrah, but more like the war whoop of the painted warrior of the Western plains—is heard above the din of battle. It was [General James] Longstreet's brigade, delivering its first volley and sending out its first battle-cry. . . .

Richardson's men hurrah in return. The firing is quick and sharp. Longstreet's men are thrown into confusion, and he sends to [Colonel Jubal A.] Early for assistance. General Tyler [Richardson's superior] is beneath the peach trees near a small house overlooking the field. He walks nervously, and finally orders the troops to withdraw.

The withdrawal order, actually, was issued after Richardson's men had begun to fall back. They were pursued by cannon fire. Confederate General Beauregard writes that many "were plainly seen to break and scatter . . . as our parting shells were thrown among them."

One of the Union officers on the field at this time was a forty-one-year-old colonel named William Tecumseh Sherman: ". . . for the first time in my life I saw cannon-balls strike men and crash through the trees and saplings above and around us. . . ."

The Union cannon fire had been equally fierce. Says Beauregard:

A comical effect . . . was the destruction of the dinner of myself and staff by a Federal shell that fell into the fire-place of my head-quarters. . . .

The unexpected fury of this skirmish divested some of the Federal participants of their military ardor, and they began to clamor for their discharge, which was about due.

McDowell's army now delayed for two days at Centreville to do additional reconnoitering and to await the arrival of supplies from the rear. This time was well used by Joe Johnston, Confederate commander in the Shenandoah Valley. He managed to elude the Federals under Robert Patterson and move about two-thirds of his troops, part of the way by rail, to the Bull Run lines. Since he outranked Beauregard, Johnston assumed top command. Confederate strength was now about 30,000 men, while McDowell had about 35,000.

The Federals began their advance from Centreville westward to Bull Run in the hours preceding the dawn of Sunday, July 21. Writes Nurse Edmonds:

. . . column after column wound its way over the green hills and through the hazy valleys, with the soft moonlight falling on the long lines of shining steel. Not a drum or bugle was heard during the march, and the deep silence was only broken by the rumbling of artillery, the muffled tread of infantry, or the low hum of thousands of subdued voices.

At the same time, a small fragment of the army was marching in the opposite direction—back toward Washington. The three-month volunteers who had proved gun-shy at Blackburn's Ford—a Pennsylvania infantry regiment and a New York artillery battery—had secured their discharge, spurning patriotic appeals from both General McDowell and the Secretary of War, who was then making a visit of encouragement to the army.

The columns marching westward to the attack followed the Warrenton Turnpike. Says James Tinkham, a volunteer from Massachusetts:

Near Cub Run we saw carriages and barouches which contained civilians who had driven out from Washington to witness the operations. A Connecticut boy said, "There's our Senator!" and some of our men recognized . . . other members of Congress. . . . We thought it wasn't a bad idea to have the great men from Washington come out to see us thrash the Rebs.

According to Edmund Clarence Stedman, of the New York World:

The spirit of the soldiery was magnificent. . . . There was glowing rivalry between the men of different states. "Old Massachusetts will not be ashamed of us tonight." "Wait till the Ohio boys get at them." "We'll fight for New York today," and a hundred similar utterances were shouted from the different ranks.

The Warrenton Turnpike led toward the Stone Bridge over Bull Run, where lay the extreme left, or northern flank, of the Confederate lines. One of the men stationed at the Stone Bridge, where Colonel Nathan G. Evans commanded, was Virginia's Private John Goode:

Before sunrise . . . great clouds of dust might be seen . . . plainly indicating that the enemy were advancing; and soon the roar of heavy artillery was heard; shot and shell came screaming like lost spirits through the air; and the advancing hosts were momentarily expected to appear.

But this firing, from Tyler's division, was only part of a demonstration intended to deceive the Confederates. Additional units under Colonel D. S. Miles were making a feint before the center of the entrenchments, several miles down the Run. The idea was to make Johnston and Beauregard believe that the main attack was coming directly in their front, while, in reality, McDowell was sending two divisions on a wide semicircle to his right (to the north), with the intention of striking the Confederates on their left flank. Johnston and Beauregard, coincidentally, had been readying an attack of their own, but McDowell's early-morning advance frustrated their plans.

The two Union divisions, commanded by Colonels Samuel P. Heintzelman and David Hunter, were in a position to push southward across Bull Run at Sudley Springs, less than two miles from the Confederate left, about 9:30 A.M. But now they took a break to drink, to fill their canteens, and to rest from the march. One of the correspondents present was Charles Coffin, of the Boston Journal:

Looking south . . . you see clouds of dust floating over the forest trees. The Rebels have discovered the movement and are marching in hot haste [from several points along the Bull Run line] to resist the impending attack. . . . Rebel officers ride furiously and shout their orders. The artillerymen lash their horses to a run. The infantry are also upon the run, sweating and panting in the hot sunshine.

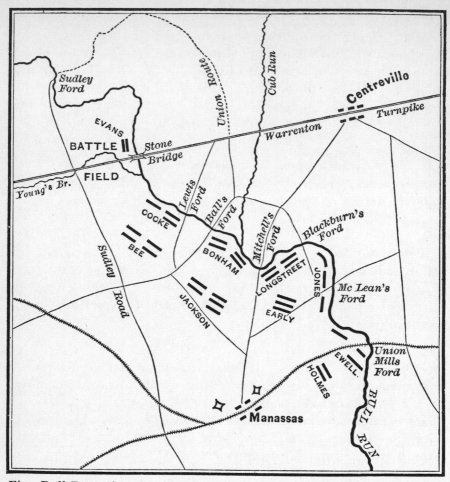

First Bull Run. Situation just prior to the battle. Map shows the Confederate positions along Bull Run and the route of the Union flanking march from the Warrenton Turnpike.

First to reach a ridge overlooking the Union approach route was Colonel Evans with the greater part of his force from the Stone Bridge, chiefly South Carolinians and Louisianans. Two 6-pound cannon were positioned, and the infantry concealed themselves in scattered patches of brush.

Newsman Coffin goes on:

The Union troops at Sudley Springs move across the stream. [Colonel Ambrose E.] Burnside's brigade is in advance. The Second Rhode Island infantry is thrown out, deployed as skirmishers. The men are five paces apart. They move slowly, cautiously, and nervously

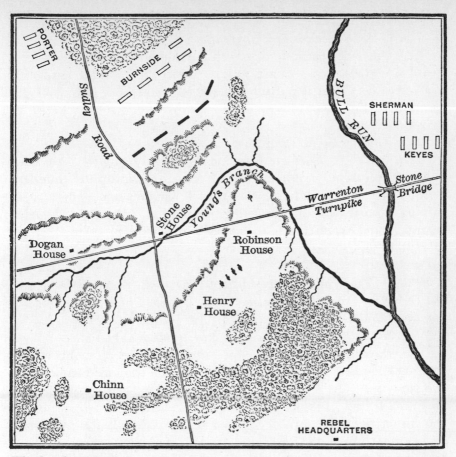

The battle of Bull Run begins. Confederate units who have hurried from their original positions are shown (as black rectangles) facing the Union flank attack.

through the fields and thickets. Suddenly, from bushes, trees, and fences there is a rattle of musketry. . . . Evans's skirmishers are firing. There are jets of flame and smoke, and a strange humming in the air. There is another rattle, a roll, a volley. The cannon join.

Union Colonel Burnside was shortly reinforced by Colonel Andrew Porter's brigade. Joining the Union artillery batteries already on the field were those under Captains Charles Griffin and James B. Ricketts, a dozen guns in all, which were to play a notable part in the battle. On the Confederate side, Evans was reinforced by two of the brigades that Joe Johnston had brought from the Shenandoah Valley, those under South Carolina's General Barnard E. Bee and Georgia's Colonel Francis S. Bartow.

Writes the Union's Nurse Edmonds:

Now the battle began to rage with terrible fury. Nothing could be heard save the thunder of artillery . . . and the continuous roar of musketry. Oh, what a scene for the bright sun of a holy Sabbath morning to shine upon!

Again in Charles Coffin's words:

Men fall. . . . They are bleeding, torn, and mangled. . . . The trees are splintered, crushed, and broken, as if smitten by thunderbolts. Twigs and leaves fall to the ground. There is smoke, dust, wild talking, shouting; hissings, howlings, explosions. It is a new, strange, unanticipated experience to the soldiers of both armies, far different from what they thought it would be.

This stage of the battle as viewed from a distance, from a hill between the Cub Run bridge and Centreville, is described by a correspondent for the London Times, *William Howard Russell, who was to be dubbed "Bull Run Russell" as a result of his vivid depictions:*

. . . the sounds which came upon the breeze and the sights which met our eyes were in terrible variance with the tranquil character of the landscape. The woods far and near echoed to the roar of cannon; and thin, frayed lines of blue smoke marked the spots whence came the muttering sound of rolling musketry. . . . Clouds of dust shifted and moved through the forest, and . . . I could see the gleam of arms and the twinkling of bayonets.

On the hill beside me there was a crowd of civilians on horseback and in all sorts of vehicles, with a few of the fairer, if not gentler, sex. . . . The spectators were all excited, and a lady with an opera glass who was near me was quite beside herself when an unusually heavy discharge roused the current of her blood: "That is splendid! Oh, my! Is not that first-rate? I guess we will be in Richmond this time tomorrow."

Though soon heavily outnumbered, the green Confederate troops, with General Bee in charge, managed to stand fast for about an hour. It was later to be said by professionals in the Southern army that Bee's men were whipped but were too new at combat to know it.

Finally, with the pressure on their front still growing as additional Federal units came forward, the Confederates began to fall back, leaving behind their dead and incapacitated and a number who had been taken prisoner. Now the battered troops began to receive trouble

William T. Sherman.

from the flank. General Tyler, who had been making a feint on the other side of the Stone Bridge, ordered the brigades of Colonels William T. Sherman and Erasmus D. Keyes across Bull Run to join the attack, he himself accompanying Keyes.

    Cheering and flourishing their battle flags, the Federals in both quarters surged forward. Says James Tinkham, of Massachusetts:

We . . . fired a volley, and saw the Rebels running. . . . Then we were ordered to lie down and load. We aimed at the puffs of smoke we saw rising in front and on the left of us. The men were all a good deal excited. Our rear rank had singed the hair of the front rank, who were more afraid of them than of the Rebels.

The next thing I remember was the order to advance, which we did under a scattering fire. . . . The boys were saying constantly, in great glee: "We've whipped them." "We'll hang Jeff Davis to a sour apple tree." "They are running." "The war is over."

Adds Lieutenant William Thompson Lusk, of a New York regiment in Sherman's brigade:

From many a point not long since covered by secession forces, the American banner now floated. What wonder we felt our hearts swelling with pride, and saw, hardly noticing, horse and rider lying stiff, cold, and bloody together! What, though we stepped unthinking over the pale body of many a brave fellow still grasping convulsively his gun, with the shadows of Death closing around him! We were following the foe . . . and were dreaming only of victory.

William Howard Russell, of the London Times, *tells how the news reached his observation point east of the Cub Run bridge:*

. . . a man dressed in the uniform of an officer, whom I had seen riding violently across the plain in an open space below, galloped along the front [of the spectators], waving his cap and shouting at the top of his voice. He was brought up, by the press of people round his horse, close to where I stood.

"We've whipped them on all points," he cried. ". . . They are retreating as fast as they can, and we are after them."

Such cheers as rent the welkin! The congressmen shook hands with each other and cried out: "Bully for us! Bravo! Didn't I tell you so?"

Writes J. C. Nott, a Confederate doctor who was treating the wounded as they came to the rear:

At this stage of the game the enemy was telegraphing to Washington that the battle had been won, and secession was about to be crushed. My heart failed me as I saw load after load of our poor wounded and dying soldiers brought and strewed on the ground along the ravine where I was at work. Dr. Fanthray, who belonged to

General Johnston's staff, and myself were just getting fully to work when an old surgeon, whom I do not know, came to us . . . and ordered us to fall back to another point with the wounded, as . . . the battle would soon be upon us.

General Bee's troops had retreated over a stream called Young's Branch and were being pushed up sloping ground leading to a plateau that held two houses, one owned by a free Negro, James Robinson, and the other by Mrs. Judith Henry, an aged and invalided widow.

A fresh unit from the Confederate rear now crossed the plateau and joined the men on the slope. This was "Hampton's Legion," six hundred men equipped and led by the rich South Carolina planter Wade Hampton.

Approaching the plateau from the rear at this time, intending to make a stand there against the Federal assault, was General Thomas J. Jackson's brigade, which had marched from a position near the center of the original Bull Run lines. (Jackson, like Bee and Bartow, was a recent arrival from the Shenandoah Valley.) Relates D. B. Conrad, who served on one of Jackson's regimental staffs:

Reaching the top [of the slope], a wide clearing was discovered . . . and far away over the hill in front [i.e., in the valley dropping from the farther rim of the plateau] was the smoke of musketry . . . and on the hills beyond could be seen clearly Griffin's and Ricketts' batteries. In their front, to their rear, and supported on each side, were long lines of blue. To our right, about one hundred yards off, was . . . the . . . Henry house.

Stationed near the Henry house since the fight had begun was a Confederate artillery battery commanded by Captain John D. Imboden. Now, says Imboden, the battery came under heavy fire from Griffin and Ricketts, and was forced to retire:

More than half of our horses had been killed. . . . Those that we had were quickly divided among the guns and caissons [i.e., ammunition wagons], and we limbered up and fled. Then it was that the Henry house was riddled . . . for our line of retreat was so chosen that . . . the house would conceal us from Griffin's battery, and, in a measure, shelter us from the dreaded fire of the infantry when they should reach the crest we had just abandoned. Several of Griffin's shot passed through the house, scattering shingles, boards, and splinters all around us.

Unfortunately, the Widow Henry was in the house. Laments an unnamed correspondent for the Richmond Enquirer:

This estimable lady, who had spent here a long life . . . was now bed-ridden. There she lay amid the horrid din, and no less than three of the missiles of death that scoured through her chamber inflicted their wounds upon her. It seems a strange dispensation of Providence that one whose life had been so gentle and secluded should have found her end amid such a storm of human passions. . . .

The rolling infantry battle was now nearing the edge of the plateau. According to Southerner D. B. Conrad, of Jackson's brigade:

. . . we could hear the sound and see the white smoke. At this time there rode up fast toward us from the front a horse and rider, gradually rising to our view. . . . He was an officer, all alone, and as he came closer, erect and full of fire, his jet-black eyes and long hair and . . . uniform of a general officer made him the cynosure of all. In a strong, decided tone he inquired of the nearest aide what troops we were. . . . The strange officer then advanced [to Jackson]. . . .

The "strange officer" was the top commander at the front, General Bee. In the words of Henry Kyd Douglas, another of Jackson's men:

The struggle for the plateau at Bull Run.

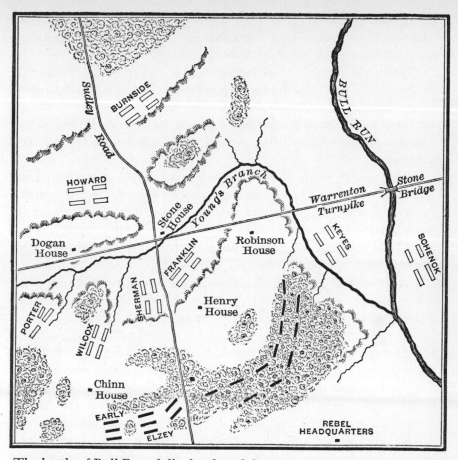

The battle of Bull Run, fully developed, becomes a contest for the plateau holding the Henry and Robinson houses. Confederate lines at bottom of map. Federal units are shown as white rectangles.

General Bee . . . reported that the enemy were beating him back.

"Very well, General; it can't be helped," replied Jackson.

"But how do you expect to stop them?"

"We'll give them the bayonet!" was the answer. . . .

General Bee wheeled his horse and galloped back to his command. . . . In the storm which followed . . . he was soon on foot, his horse shot from under him. With the fury of despair he strode among his men and tried to rally and to hold them . . . and finally, in a voice which rivalled the roar of battle, he cried out, "Oh, men, there are Jackson and his Virginians standing behind you like a stone wall!"

. . . It was Bee who gave [Jackson] the name of "Stonewall," but it was his own Virginians who made that name immortal.

Soon to be fatally wounded, the brave and forceful Bee had earned a fame destined to "follow that of Jackson as a shadow."

The battle was now developing into a contest for possession of the plateau, with Confederate reinforcements arriving and forming around Jackson. Others, however, were still on the march from the far end of the original Bull Run lines; and General E. Kirby Smith's brigade, the last of the troops from the Shenandoah Valley, had not been heard from.

Confederate morale was stimulated when "at about 12 meridian" Generals Johnston and Beauregard were seen approaching at a gallop. They had come from their headquarters near Mitchell's Ford. Writes Beauregard:

As soon as General Johnston and myself reached the field, we were occupied with the reorganization of the heroic troops. . . . It was now that General Johnston impressively and gallantly charged to the front with the colors of the 4th Alabama regiment by his side, all the field officers of the regiment having been previously disabled.

At this stage of the battle, a Union observer, Edwin S. Barrett, was sitting among the topmost branches of a high persimmon tree:

. . . I had an unobstructed view of the whole line, and I could see into the enemy's intrenchments, where the men looked like so many bees in a hive; and I could plainly see their officers riding about, and their different columns moving hither and thither. Their batteries on the right and left were masked with trees so completely that I could not distinguish them except by the flash from their guns. . . .

The valley . . . in front of the enemy's works was filled with our infantry, extending to some patches of woods on our right. Our batteries were placed on various eminences on the flank and rear, shifting their positions from time to time. The fire from our lines in this valley was terrific, and as they kept slowly advancing, firing, retreating to load, and then advancing again, it was a sight which no words could describe.

Adds Northern newsman Charles Coffin:

There is not much order. Regiments are scattered. The lines are not even. . . . There are a great many stragglers on both sides; more, probably, from the Rebel ranks than from McDowell's army, for thus far the battle has gone against them. . . . The artillery crashes louder than before. There is a continuous rattle of musketry.

. . . There are desperate hand-to-hand encounters. . . . Hundreds fall, and other hundreds leave the ranks.

Again in the words of Unionist Edwin Barrett, the man in the persimmon tree:

. . . a continuous stream of wounded were being carried past me to the rear. The soldiers would cross their muskets, place their wounded companions across, and slowly carry them past; another soldier would have a wounded man with his arm around his neck, slowly walking back; and then two men would be bearing a mortally wounded comrade in their arms, who was in convulsions and writhing in his last agonies. These were to me the most affecting scenes I witnessed. . . .

There was now a lull in the battle, though sporadic cannon and musket fire were still heard. Before two o'clock, under a blazing sun, the pace picked up again, beginning with a mistake on the part of the Union command. The artillery batteries of Ricketts and Griffin were drawn from their support positions in the rear and ordered to take up exposed positions inside the edge of the plateau. With only green infantry available as protection for the guns, this was a dangerous move.

    According to newsman Coffin:

Ricketts does not like the order, but he is a soldier in the regular army and believes in obeying commands. The battery . . . ascends the hill towards the Henry house and opens fire at close range. . . . Griffin comes, with his horses upon the gallop . . . and takes position to the left of Ricketts.

Several Confederate batteries under Jackson's command, only about three hundred yards away, replied almost at once; and a terrific contest ensued. Southern battery commander John Imboden suddenly found his duties expanded:

Jackson ordered me to [ride] from battery to battery and see that the guns were properly aimed and the fuses cut the right length. This was the work of but a few minutes. On returning to the left of the line of guns, I stopped to ask General Jackson's permission to rejoin my battery. [Jackson was astride his horse.] The fight was just then hot enough to make him feel well. His eyes fairly blazed.

He had a way of throwing up his left hand with the open palm toward the person he was addressing. And as he told me to go, he made this gesture. The air was full of flying missiles, and . . . he jerked down his hand, and I saw that blood was streaming from it.

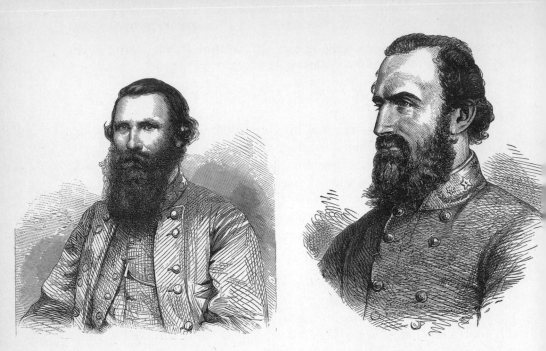

Jeb Stuart.   Stonewall Jackson.

I exclaimed, "General, you are wounded!"

He replied, as he drew a handkerchief from his breastpocket and began to bind it up, "Only a scratch—a mere scratch," and galloped away along his line.

Writes Jackson himself:

Although under a heavy fire for several continuous hours, I received only one wound, the breaking of the longest finger of my left hand. . . . My horse was wounded, but not killed.

The artillery duel raged for about twenty minutes. Then a regiment of Confederate infantry, covered by woods, circled to the attack. When the men made their appearance in the open, they were believed to be Union troops and were not fired upon. They moved closer and took deliberate aim.

Then [says an unidentified member of Griffin's battery] came a tremendous explosion of musketry, and all was confusion. Wounded men . . . were clinging to caissons, to which were attached frightened and wounded horses. . . . I saw three horses galloping off, dragging a fourth, which was dead. The dead cannoneers lay with the rammers . . . sponges and lanyards still in their hands. The battery was annihilated by those volleys in a moment. Those who could get away didn't wait. We had no supports near enough to protect us properly. . . .

Ricketts' battery was also hit, with Ricketts himself falling badly wounded. The ineffectual support units, which included New York's colorful Fire Zouaves (a regiment dressed in fezzes, waist-length jackets, red bloomers, and gaiters, in the fashion of the French soldiers of North Africa), were assaulted by both infantry and cavalry. Leading the saber-swinging horsemen was a young colonel from Virginia with the impressive name of James Ewell Brown Stuart. All of the support units fled in disorder, though enough shots were fired by the Zouaves to empty a few of "Jeb" Stuart's saddles.

Union commander McDowell reacted to this reverse by renewing his forward pressure. The lines moved determinedly, with Colonel Sherman's men showing exemplary spirit. Acting with great personal effectiveness was Colonel Samuel Heintzelman. The Confederates noted that he was "a gray-haired man, sitting sideways on horseback," and they admired his "coolness and gallantry" as he "directed the movements of each regiment as it came up the hill."

The attack recovered the lost guns and gained control of a good part of the plateau. Confederate hopes hit a new low.

But [says a writer for the Richmond *Dispatch*] there was at hand the fearless general whose reputation as a commander was staked on this battle. . . . Gen. Beauregard rode up and down our lines, between the enemy and his own men, regardless of the heavy fire, cheering and encouraging our troops.

Beauregard was on his second horse, his first having been killed under him. General Johnston, at Beauregard's urging, had gone to the rear to send up reinforcements as they arrived. This left Beauregard in command at the front. He relates:

Now . . . I gave the order for the right of my line, except my reserves, to advance to recover the plateau. It was done with uncommon resolution and vigor; and at the same time Jackson's brigade pierced the enemy's centre with the determination of veterans and the spirit of men who fight for a sacred cause; but it suffered seriously.

With equal spirit the other parts of the line made the onset, and the Federal lines were broken and swept back at all points from the open ground of the plateau. Rallying soon, however . . . the Feder-

alists returned, and by weight of numbers pressed our lines back, recovered their ground and guns, and renewed the offensive.

General McDowell was now exultant:
    . . . it was supposed by us all that the repulse was final, for [the
enemy] was driven entirely from the hill, and so far beyond it as not
to be in sight; and all were certain the day was ours.

But Beauregard wasn't through:
    . . . between half past two and three o'clock . . . I . . . ordered
forward . . . the whole line . . . which, at this crisis of the battle, I
felt called upon to lead in person. . . . The whole open ground was
again swept clear of the enemy, and the plateau around the Henry and
Robinson houses remained finally in our possession, with the greater
part of the Ricketts and Griffin batteries and a flag of the 1st Michigan
regiment, captured by . . . Jackson's brigade.

*This hot work, however, had left the Confederate ranks badly frag-
mented. Though a like condition existed among the Federals, their
numbers were still strong and their position on the field tactically
promising.*
    But [explains General McDowell] we had been fighting since half
past ten o'clock in the morning, and it was after three o'clock in the
afternoon. The men had been up since two o'clock in the morning,
and had made what, to those unused to such things, seemed a long
march before coming into action . . . and though they had three
days' provisions served out to them the day before, many, no doubt
. . . either threw them away on the march or during the battle, and
were, therefore, without food. They had done much severe fighting.

Says Southerner D. B. Conrad, of Jackson's brigade:
    . . . the fate of the field hung in the balance. . . . Both sides
were exhausted and ready to say, "Enough!" The critical moment
which comes in all actions had arrived. . . .

*Then telegraph signals from Beauregard's observers in high places
warned him to "look out for the enemy's advance on the left."*
    *As recorded by Confederate historian Edward Pollard, who fol-
lowed the progress of the battle as editor of the Richmond* Examiner:
    At the distance of more than a mile, a column of men was ap-
proaching. At their head was a flag which could not be distinguished.

. . . Gen. Beauregard was unable to determine whether it was the Federal flag or the Confederate flag. . . .

"At this moment," said Gen. Beauregard, in speaking afterwards of the occurrence, "I must confess my heart failed me. I came reluctantly to the conclusion that, after all our efforts, we should at last be compelled to leave to the enemy the hard-fought and bloody field. I again took the glass to examine the flag of the approaching column . . . but I could not tell to which army the waving banner belonged. . . . The only person with me was the gallant . . . Colonel Evans. . . . I told him that I feared the approaching force was in reality Patterson's division [from the Shenandoah Valley]. . . ."

. . . Both officers fixed one final, intense gaze upon the advancing flag. A happy gust of wind shook out its folds, and Gen. Beauregard recognized the Stars and Bars of the Confederate banner!

Beauregard's battle-begrimed face lighted up, and cheer after cheer was raised along the Confederate lines.

"Slowly they came onto the field," relates Southerner D. B. Conrad,

not from want of spirit, but tired out by double-quicking in the heat and dust. As they passed through and by our squads . . . the enemy were pointed out to them, and . . . from out their dusty and parched throats came the . . . "rebel yell."

. . . These new troops were Kirby Smith's delayed men [from the Shenandoah Valley]. The train had that morning broken down, but on arriving at the station . . . and hearing the sound of the fighting, he had . . . arrived on the field at the supreme moment.

Also arriving at this time was Confederate Colonel Jubal Early, who had brought his brigade from its position on the right wing of the original Bull Run lines. The reinforcements had an extraordinary effect on the battle. Says Union General McDowell:

They threw themselves in the woods on our right, and towards the rear of our right, and opened a fire of musketry on our men, which caused them to break and retire down the hillside. This soon degenerated into disorder for which there was no remedy. Every effort was made to rally them . . . but in vain.

Adds Colonel Andrew Porter, of McDowell's second division:

Soon the slopes . . . were swarming with our retreating and disorganized forces, while riderless horses and artillery teams ran furiously through the flying crowd. All further efforts were futile. The words, gestures, and threats of our officers were thrown away upon men who had lost all presence of mind, and only longed for absence of body.

The turn of events was viewed by Union writer Edwin Barrett (no longer in his persimmon tree) with "utter astonishment." He was swept along with the retreat, but soon stopped on a hill to look back:

I did not leave the hill until the enemy's infantry came out from their intrenchments and slowly moved forward, their guns glistening in the sun; but they showed no disposition to charge. . . . Had they precipitated their columns upon our panic-stricken army, the slaughter would have been dreadful, for so thorough was the panic that no power on earth could have stopped the retreat and made our men turn and fight.

Actually, not all of the men had lost their heads. Present were experienced units of the regular army, as well as volunteer units who had occupied reserve positions, who maintained their order. Some of the regulars, in fact, took up stations to help cover the retreat. But thousands of men were indeed panic-stricken. According to an unnamed correspondent for the New York Tribune:

All sense of manhood seemed to be forgotten. . . . Even the sentiment of shame had gone. . . . Every impediment to flight was cast aside. Rifles, bayonets, pistols, haversacks, cartridge-boxes, canteens, blankets, belts, and overcoats lined the road.

The "road" was the Warrenton Turnpike, which became the main route of retreat, the troops heading back toward Cub Run and Centreville.

The Confederates, their own ranks disorganized and in a state of confusion, made only a limited pursuit. A few parties of cavalry, including Jeb Stuart's command, swirled among the flying men and took numerous prisoners. An artillery battery belonging to the Seventh Virginia Regiment galloped after and did some damage. With this battery was Edmund Ruffin, an elderly Yankee-hater with "flowing white locks," who had fired one of the first shots at Fort Sumter; and he added to his record. In the words of Union Colonel Ambrose Burnside:

Upon the bridge crossing Cub Run a shot took effect upon the horses of a team that was crossing. The wagon was overturned directly in the centre of the bridge, and the passage was completely obstructed. The enemy continued to play his artillery upon the carriages, ambulances, and artillery wagons that filled the road, and these were reduced to ruin. . . . The infantry, as the files reached the bridge, were furiously pelted with a shower of grape and other shot, and several persons were here killed or dangerously wounded.

At this point the panic reached its peak. Fortunately for the Federals, the bridge could be bypassed. Cub Run was narrow and shallow. The desperate men and surviving vehicles splashed across and raced after the masses that had crossed the bridge before it was obstructed.

Edmund Clarence Stedman of the New York World, *traveling with the fugitives, soon saw two congressmen standing fast and calling for an end to the rout, one of them flourishing a bayoneted musket:*

Both these Congressmen bravely stood their ground till the last moment. . . . But what a scene! . . . For three miles, hosts of Federal troops . . . were fleeing along the road, but mostly through the lots on either side. Army wagons, sutlers' teams [sutlers being retail merchants who followed the army with wagonloads of goods], and private carriages choked the passage, tumbling against each other amid clouds of dust and sickening sights and sounds. Hacks containing unlucky spectators of the late affray were smashed like glass, and the occupants were lost sight of in the debris.

Horses . . . many of them in death agony [from battlefield wounds], galloped at random forward. . . . Those on foot who could catch them rode them bareback, as much to save themselves from being run over as to make quicker time. Wounded men lying along the banks . . . appealed with raised hands to those who rode horses . . . but few regarded such petitions.

Then the artillery, such as was saved, came thundering along, smashing and overpowering everything. . . .

Who ever saw such a flight? . . . It did not slack in the least until Centreville was reached.

Meanwhile:

The loyal people in Washington [writes presidential secretary John Nicolay] were rejoicing over a victory, steadily reported during the greater part of the day, when suddenly, at about five o'clock, came the startling telegram: "General McDowell's army in full retreat through Centreville. The day is lost. . . ."

. . . By midnight, officers and civilians who were lucky enough to have retained horses began to arrive, and the apparent proportions of the defeat to increase. It was a gloomy night, but yet gloomier days followed. Next day, Monday, the rain commenced falling. . . . Through this rain the disbanded soldiers began to pour into Washington City, fagged out, hungry, and dejected, and having literally nowhere to turn their feet or lay their head.

History owes a page of honorable mention to the Federal capital . . . on this occasion. The rich and poor, the high and low of her loyal people . . . opened their doors and dealt out food and refreshments to the footsore, haggard, and half-starved men . . . so unexpectedly reduced to tramps and fugitives.

Nearly 3,000 casualties (killed, wounded, captured, and missing) had been inflicted on the Union army, at a cost of about 2,000 to the Confederates. As the news of the great disaster swept the North, the people were at first incredulous, then filled with mortification and disappointment. In the South, of course, the joy was boundless. Says editor and historian Edward Pollard:

The victory . . . was taken by the Southern public as the end of the war, or, at least, as its decisive event. . . . President Davis . . . assured his intimate friends that the recognition of the Confederate States by the European powers was now certain. The newspapers declared that the question of manhood between North and South was settled forever; and the phrase of "one Southerner [is] equal to five Yankees" was adopted in all speeches about the war—although the origin . . . of the precise proportion was never clearly stated. . . .

It is remarkable that the statesmen of Richmond did not observe the singular temper of the authorities at Washington. . . . On the very day that Washington was crowded with fugitives from the routed army . . . the House of Representatives [Congress being in special session] passed unanimously the following resolution:

"*Resolved,* That the maintenance of the Constitution, the preservation of the Union, and the enforcement of the laws, are sacred trusts which must be executed; that no disaster shall discourage us from the most ample performance of this high duty; and that we pledge to the country and the world the employment of every resource, national and individual, for the suppression, overthrow, and punishment of rebels in arms."

4

McCLELLAN
TAKES COMMAND

SOON AFTER MAKING *his first call for volunteers on April 15, 1861, President Lincoln had foreseen the necessity of raising a more substantial army, based on longer enlistments, and had issued a proclamation launching such an effort. Thus the Union's strength was not substantially hurt by the Bull Run debacle and the disbandment of the three-month volunteers. Writes Lincoln's secretary John Nicolay:*

The three-year quota [of volunteers] and the increase of the regular army . . . had so far progressed that garrisons and camps suffered no serious diminution. Congress . . . now legalized their enlistment. . . . It authorized an army of five hundred thousand men. . . .

Pending the change and transformation of the volunteer forces from the three months to the three years service, military operations necessarily came to a general cessation. Washington City . . . and the fortified strip of territory held by the Union armies on the Virginia side of the Potomac . . . [was] a great military camp.

Though General McDowell was in many ways a capable commander, the failure at Bull Run caused Washington to replace him at once. In the words of Charles Coffin, of the Boston Journal:

. . . General McClellan, who had won the battle of Rich Mountain, in West Virginia [strictly speaking, in "western Virginia," since West Virginia was still in process of forming as a new state], was

49

George B. McClellan.

selected. That battle was a small affair, but it had compelled the Confederates to abandon that section of country, and General McClellan was already regarded as a great commander. He was called to Washington and commissioned by President Lincoln.

The thirty-four-year-old general assumed command of all the troops in the Washington area only six days after Bull Run. He was later to write:

All was chaos, and the streets, hotels, and bar-rooms were filled with drunken officers and men absent from their regiments without leave. . . .

The first and most pressing demand upon me was the immediate safety of the capital and the government. This was provided for by at once exacting the most rigid discipline and order. . . .

I lost no time in acquiring an accurate knowledge of the ground in all directions, and by frequent visits to the troops made them personally acquainted with me, while I learned all about them, their condition, and their needs, and thus soon succeeded in inspiring full confidence and a good morale in place of the lamentable state of affairs which existed on my arrival.

Thus I passed long days in the saddle and my nights in the office—a very fatiguing life, but one which made my power felt everywhere and by everyone.

According to Charles Coffin, McClellan soon included the press in his sphere of influence:

"General McClellan would like to meet the correspondents [on assignment] in Washington. Please be at Willard's Hotel this evening at eight o'clock." Such was the invitation which the newspaper correspondents received on the morning of August 1, 1861.

They assembled at the hotel, stepped into omnibuses [drawn by horses], were taken to General McClellan's headquarters, and introduced to him.

"I have one request to make—that you will be careful not to write anything from which the enemy will learn what is going on," he said.

His words were few, but pleasant. The next day, all the country was reading about the interview; how General McClellan looked and acted. One correspondent said that he resembled Napoleon Bonaparte, and the people began to speak of him as "Little Napoleon" [or, more generally, as "the Young Napoleon"], and to have great expectations of victory with such an officer as commander-in-chief.

Street scene in Washington.

After paying a visit to the Senate, McClellan wrote his wife:

When I . . . found those old men flocking around me; when I afterwards stood in the library, looking over the Capitol of our great nation, and saw the crowd gathering around to stare at me, I began to feel how great the task committed to me. . . . Who would have thought, when we were married [in May, 1860], that I should so soon be called upon to save my country?

Soon he was adding: "Things are improving daily. I received three new regiments today."

The troops, says newsman Coffin, were coming from all parts of the North:

People left their occupations—the farmer his plough, the mechanic his hammer, the joiner his plane, the salesman his yardstick, scholars their books. Men worth a million dollars enlisted as privates. . . . In every village drums were beating, soldiers marching.

The Confederacy, too, waking to the fact that the war wasn't over, was recruiting new regiments, though at a lesser pace than the North.

On both sides, the ladies were eager to do their part. Says Mary Ashton Livermore, of Chicago:

The transition of the country from peace to the tumult and waste of war was appalling and swift—but the regeneration of its women kept pace with it. They lopped off superfluities, retrenched in expenditures, became deaf to the calls of pleasure, and heeded not the mandates of fashion. . . . The fetters of caste and conventionalism dropped at their feet, and they sat together, patrician and plebeian, Protestant and Catholic, and scraped lint [made linen softer by scraping it], and rolled bandages, or made garments for the poorly clad soldiery.

According to a Confederate periodical, Southern Field and Fireside:

Instead of finding our women at the piano or on the fashionable promenade, we find them busy at their looms, busy at their wheels, busy making soldiers' uniforms, busy making bandages, busy in hospitals, busy girding up their sons, their husbands, and their fathers for the battlefield.

In fighting spirit, North and South were doubtless about equal. But by this time the North had begun to flex its superior economic muscles. Again in Coffin's words:

[The soldiers] must be fed and clothed; they must have guns, cartridge-boxes, knapsacks, tents, and wagons. For the closing of the Southern seaports, ships must be built. Never before was there such a commotion in the Northern States. Labor . . . suddenly became a giant, and was getting ready to put forth its strength. . . .

It takes much money to carry on a great war. . . .

"Which will win, the North or the South?" was the question a banker in London asked of Baron Rothschild, who had a great deal of money. . . .

"The North."

"Why?"

"Because it has the longest purse."

. . . Baron Rothschild knew that the Southern people had no [major] manufactories . . . that their property was in land and slaves. He knew that they had only cotton and tobacco to sell; that with all the seaports blockaded they would have no market. . . .

But thanks to England, Coffin goes on to say, the South's hope was at first high:

Very soon after the surrender of Fort Sumter . . . the British Government recognized the Confederates as belligerents—or as a people exercising war powers—which the people of the United States regarded as a very unfriendly act. But the great manufacturers of England who wanted cotton, the merchants who wanted to sell goods [to the South], saw that if the Southern ports were blockaded all trade with the Southern States would cease. They were greatly offended, also, because Congress, in order to get money to carry on the war, put a high tax on all goods manufactured in other countries and brought to the United States for sale.

So it came about that the manufacturers, merchants, and traders of Great Britain sympathized with the Southern people. They subscribed money to buy cannon, muskets, powder, and shells, which they gave to the Confederates. They built fast-sailing ships, and loaded them with all kinds of goods to run the blockade . . . carrying cotton back to England.

As for General McClellan, he proved to be a superb organizer. He had an extraordinary way with troops. His men dubbed him "Little Mac" and raised a zealous cheer when he appeared among them on his black charger. As he acknowledged their homage with a bow, a smile, and a twirl of his cap, they cheered still louder.

"I can see every eye glisten," he told his wife.

As the training continued, the men often rent the air with a new military song that included the lines, "McClellan's our leader, he's gallant and strong; for God and our country we're marching along!"

By the end of August, McClellan's army had grown to 75,000 men, and Washington was strongly fortified. But McClellan was worried. Thanks to a poor intelligence system and to his proneness to regard the enemy as being all-powerful, he believed that Confederate General Joe Johnston and his second-in-command, Pierre Beauregard, headquartered at Manassas, had more than 100,000 men. In reality they had about 40,000. They were strong only in audacity.

Newsman Coffin relates that General Johnston

. . . pushed his troops almost up to General McClellan's lines, taking possession of Munson's Hill, which is only five miles from the Long Bridge [over the Potomac] at Washington. . . . From the hill they could see the spires of the city. . . . No doubt they longed to have it in their possession; but there were thousands of men in arms and hundreds of cannon and a wide river between them and the city.

One . . . morning I rode to Bailey's Cross-roads, which is about a mile from Munson's Hill. Looking across a cornfield, I could see the Rebels behind their breastworks. Their battle-flags were waving gayly. Their bayonets gleamed in the sunshine. A group of officers had gathered on the summit of the hill. With my field-glass, I could see what they were doing. They examined maps, looked towards Washington, and pointed out the position of the Union fortifications. There were ladies present, who looked earnestly towards the city and chatted merrily with the officers. . . .

The summer passed away and the golden months of autumn came round. The troops were organized into brigades and divisions. They were drilled daily. . . . At sunset each regiment had a dress parade. . . .

In the evening there were no military duties to be performed, and the soldiers told stories around the campfires, or sang songs, or had a dance, for in each company there was usually one who could play the violin. . . . Some sat in their tents and read the newspapers or whatever they could find to interest them, with a bayonet stuck in the ground for a candlestick. There were some who, at home, had attended the Sabbath school. . . . The Bible was precious to them. . . . Sometimes they had a prayer-meeting. . . .

But at the tap of the drum at nine o'clock the laughter, the songs, the dances, the stories, the readings, and the prayer-meetings, all were brought to a close; the lights were put out, and silence reigned throughout the camp, broken only by the step of the watchful sentinel. . . .

There were grand reviews of troops during the fall. . . . Each regiment tried to outdo all others in its appearance and its marching. They moved by companies past the President, bands playing national airs, the drums beating, and the flags waving. There were several hundred pieces of artillery and several thousand cavalrymen. The ground shook beneath the steady marching of the great mass of men and the tread of thousands of hoofs. It was the finest military display ever seen in America.

Many Northerners felt it was time this grand army began to shake the ground around Richmond; but McClellan wasn't ready. After all, his spies had told him that Johnston and Beauregard had an even greater army. He needed more troops, more equipment, more time to organize and train. Suggestions from government officials that he plan a campaign made him angry.

"I am becoming daily more disgusted with this administration," he wrote his wife.

A little later, he added:

When I returned yesterday after a long ride, I was obliged to attend a meeting of the cabinet at eight P.M., and was bored and annoyed. There are some of the greatest geese in the cabinet I have ever seen—enough to tax the patience of Job. . . .

Lincoln, though, with his many pertinent and amusing anecdotes, was "a rare bird" who could be viewed with toleration. "The President is honest and means well."

But McClellan grew impatient with Lincoln's frequent visits to his headquarters, sometimes keeping him waiting while he transacted business with others, and sometimes finding ways to dodge him. This discourtesy did not escape the notice of the press. Said Lincoln: "I will hold McClellan's horse if he will only bring us success."

Sporadic gunfire was heard along the Potomac as McClellan's men skirmished with Confederate pickets, or outguards. On October 21 there was a graver clash, disastrous to the Federal participants, at Ball's Bluff, near Leesburg. Lincoln received the news by telegraph at McClellan's headquarters. Included in the message was that Colonel Edward D. Baker, a member of the Senate and one of Lincoln's oldest and closest friends, had been killed.

Charles Coffin, who was present when the news arrived, says that Lincoln left the building unattended, with his head bowed and with tears running down his cheeks:

His hands were clasped upon his heart; he walked with a shuffling, tottering gait, reeling as if beneath a staggering blow. He did not fall, but passed down the street, carrying not only the burden of the nation but a load of private grief which, with the swiftness of the lightning's flash, had been hurled upon him.

Lincoln's concerns were not confined to the East. During the past three months, added clashes had occurred in the border states of West Virginia and Missouri. At the same time, both sides had begun seizing strategic spots in Kentucky, another border state.

The Union's navy was growing apace. This was disturbing news to the South, whose naval capabilities were modest. John Beauchamp Jones, a clerk in the Richmond war offices, penned in his diary:

The most gigantic naval preparations have been made by the enemy. . . . They are building great numbers of gunboats, some of them iron-clad, both for the coast and for the Western rivers. If they get possession of the Mississippi River, it will be a sad day for the Confederacy.

New strength was already being added to Lincoln's blockade of the South's seaports. The navy, with the army's help, was beginning to seize and occupy strategic coastal points. As early as August, Fort Hatteras, North Carolina, was taken; and the capture of the forts at Port Royal, South Carolina, was achieved in November.

Also occurring in November was the "Trent Affair," which nearly brought about the entry of England into the war. Two commissioners appointed by the Confederacy to represent their interests in England and France, having slipped through the blockade, were taken from the British mail steamer Trent *on the high seas by a Union sloop of war. At first the North rejoiced over the capture, but England reacted so strongly to this violation of her neutrality that the two men had to be released to continue their journey. The South, however, was not happy over the affair's outcome.*

The concession [says Confederate historian Edward Pollard] . . . was a blow to the hopes of the Southern people. The . . . spectacle of their enemy's humiliation . . . was but little compensation for their disappointment of a European complication in the war.

A visitor to the Washington camps in late autumn was Julia Ward Howe of Boston, a poet and a staunch abolitionist. To her, the Union army's mission was nothing less than a holy one. She was thrilled by the sight of the nightly campfires, and her ear was caught by the stirring tune, originally a revival hymn, to which the soldiers sang, "John Brown's body lies a mouldering in the grave. . . ." Urged by a friend to provide the tune with a better set of words, she wrote a poem that began, "Mine eyes have seen the glory of the coming of the Lord. . . ." The mighty "Battle Hymn of the Republic" was soon being sung not only by the troops in the camps but by Northern civilians everywhere.

Both McClellan's and Johnston's armies now turned to making themselves as comfortable as possible for the winter. Writes A. F. Hill, a Union enlisted man:

. . . to dwell in tents . . . during the frosts and snows . . . was no very delightful prospect. . . . Having obtained permission . . . we . . . set about erecting rustic habitations, arranging them in the usual form of an encampment. The huts we built were eight by ten feet in dimensions. We built them of small logs, to the height of four or five feet, and pitched our tents upon the top of the walls, for coverings. A fireplace and chimney adorned a corner of each building, imparting a cheerful, domestic appearance.

John B. Gordon.

Those men who were obliged to remain in tents equipped them with stoves. The thin walls were banked with earth and evergreen boughs. Snug evergreen stables were made for the horses.

"Once fairly settled and established in our winter quarters," says Hill, "we began to resort to all manner of games, mental and gymnastic, for amusement."

Johnston's army lived in similar makeshift camps. Georgia's John B. Gordon, then a major, was later to write:

My men were winter-quartered in the dense pine thickets on the rough hills that border the Occoquan [about twenty miles southwest of Washington].

Christmas came, and was to be made as joyous as our surroundings would permit by a genuine Southern eggnog with our friends. The country was scoured far and near for eggs, which were exceedingly scarce. Of sugar we still had at that time a reasonable supply; but our small store of eggs and other ingredients could not be increased in all the country round about.

Mrs. Gordon superintended the preparation of this favorite Christmas beverage, and at last the delicious potion was ready. All stood anxiously waiting with camp cups in hand.

The servant started toward the company with full and foaming bowl, holding it out before him with almost painful care. He had taken but a few steps when he struck his toe against the uneven floor of the rude quarters and stumbled. The scattered fragments of crockery and the aroma of the wasted nectar marked the melancholy wreck of our Christmas cheer.

The winter was a severe one, and the men suffered greatly—not only for want of sufficient preparation, but because those from farther south were unaccustomed to so cold a climate. There was much sickness in camp. It was amazing to see the large number of country boys who had never had the measles. Indeed, it seemed to me that they ran through the whole catalogue of complaints to which boyhood and even babyhood are subjected. They had everything almost except teething, nettle-rash, and whooping-cough. I rather think some of them were afflicted with this latter disease.

According to Union historian Joel Tyler Headley:

The new year [1862] opened with comparative quiet around Washington, and indeed all along the great line of defense that crossed half the continent. Even at Richmond, the rebel capital, more than usual gaiety prevailed. . . .

Charles Coffin says that Washington's newspaper correspondents were obliged to repeat the dispatch "All quiet along the Potomac" so often that it became a byword:

New troops were constantly arriving, and by midwinter the army around Washington numbered nearly two hundred thousand. The inaction of General McClellan was producing discontent throughout the country. . . . The "peace party," which was opposed to the war, applauded his inaction, and the natural result was that those who were earnest for its prosecution began to think that his heart was not in it.

Even Lincoln, who had done everything he could to support McClellan, began to have doubts about his intentions and abilities. To make matters worse, the conduct of the Union generals in the lines to the west seemed equally unpromising. Lincoln himself knew little about military science. In frustration, he began to study books on the topic.

Then, in February, thanks to an obscure brigadier general named Ulysses S. Grant, the Western picture changed dramatically. With the help of Flag Officer Andrew H. Foote and a fleet of gunboats,

Grant took two Confederate forts near the northern border of Tennessee—Fort Henry on the Tennessee River and Fort Donelson on the Cumberland. Fort Henry was taken by gunboat action alone, but sharp land fighting developed before Donelson. In the end, when the garrison commander, General Simon B. Buckner, sent a note to Grant in which he agreed to discuss terms, Grant wrote back:

No terms except an unconditional and immediate surrender can be accepted. I propose to move immediately upon your works.

This decisiveness was praised in Northern newspapers, and the people rejoiced at the victory. Apprehension pervaded the South. Writes Richmond's Edward Pollard:

The fall of Fort Donelson was the heaviest blow that had yet fallen on the Confederacy. It opened the whole of West Tennessee to Federal occupation. . . .

Lincoln immediately nominated "Unconditional Surrender" Grant for promotion to major general. Here was a leader worth watching. Instead of asking for more troops, more equipment, and more time for preparation, he made full use of the resources at hand and got results.

Supporters of the Union found it both appropriate and auspicious that in addition to a "Father" Abraham they now had a "U. S." Grant.

As for Lincoln, even as his hope for the war effort rose, he was subjected to profound private sorrow. His two youngest sons, Willie and Tad, had been ill for about two weeks, and on February 20, four days after the Donelson victory, Willie died. Lincoln was so stricken that those close to him worried about his ability to carry on, but by February 24 the New York Evening Post *was reporting:*

Mr. Lincoln . . . is again at his ordinary duties, spending, not infrequently, eighteen out of the twenty-four hours upon the affairs of the nation.

The North's strategy for victory was by this time firmly established. Her aims were to keep the disputed border states of West Virginia, Kentucky, and Missouri in the Union, to capture Richmond, to perfect her blockade of Southern seaports, to gain control of the Mississippi River (which would cut the South in half), and to isolate and defeat the Confederate armies, east and west.

5

THE *MONITOR*
AND THE *MERRIMAC*

ARLY MARCH, *1862, saw the war on the water take a turn that
had no historical precedent. The scene was Hampton Roads,
the channel through which Virginia's James, Nansemond, and Elizabeth rivers flow into the mouth of Chesapeake Bay. On the northern
shore of the channel were Fort Monroe and Newport News, manned
by Union forces; the shores to the south held Norfolk and the Gos-
port Navy Yard, occupied by the Confederates. The waters of the
Roads were controlled by a Union blockading fleet, a situation particularly vexatious to the Confederates, since Richmond was located up
the James. Even before First Bull Run they undertook a project calculated to meet the problem. According to Southerner Edward
Pollard:*

In the early summer of 1861 the Navy Department at Richmond
. . . designed an iron-clad war vessel. . . . A plan originated with
Lieut. [John M.] Brooke [and naval constructor John L. Porter] to
convert the hull of the frigate *Merrimac* [actually, *Merrimack*, but
rarely so designated], which vessel had been scuttled and sunk by the
Federals on their abandonment of Norfolk at the opening of the war,
into a shot-proof steam battery. . . . The plates to protect her sides
were prepared at the Tredegar Iron Works at Richmond. . . .

61

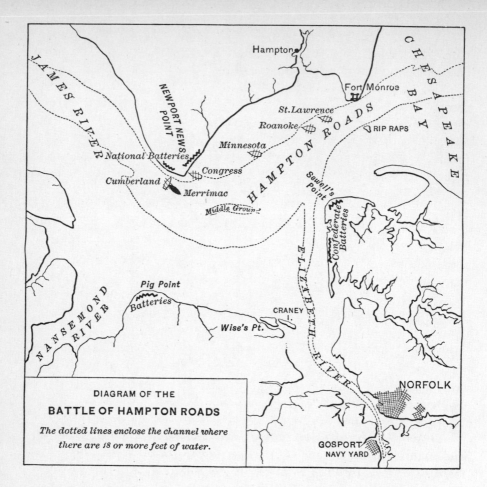

DIAGRAM OF THE
BATTLE OF HAMPTON ROADS
*The dotted lines enclose the channel where
there are 18 or more feet of water.*

Though steam was replacing sail, most of the warships of the day were wholly wooden. Only lately had experiments with iron sheathing been achieving prominence.

The Confederates tried to keep secret that they were converting the salvaged *Merrimac* into an ironclad—one stronger than any yet afloat—but the news soon reached Washington.

In the words of Gideon Welles, Lincoln's Secretary of the Navy:

We, of course, felt great solicitude in regard to this proceeding of the rebels. . . . When the contract for the *Monitor* [a specially designed ironclad to be built in New York City] was made in October, with a primary condition that she should be ready for sea in one hundred days, the Navy Department intended that the battery should, immediately after reaching Hampton Roads, proceed up Elizabeth River to the Navy Yard at Norfolk, place herself opposite the dry-dock, and with her heavy guns destroy both the dock and the *Merri-*

mac. This was our secret. . . . But the hundred days expired, weeks passed on, and the *Monitor* was not ready.

Late in February [1862] a Negro woman who resided in Norfolk came to the Navy Department and desired a private interview with me. She and others had closely watched the work upon the *Merrimac,* and she, by their request, had come to report that the ship was nearly finished, had come out of the dock, and was about receiving her armament. The woman had passed through the lines, at great risk to herself, to bring me the information; and, in confirmation of her statement, she took from the bosom of her dress a letter from a Union man [i.e., a Union sympathizer], a mechanic in the Navy Yard, giving briefly the facts as stated by her. This news, of course, put an end to the [plan] . . . of destroying the *Merrimac* in the dry-dock; but made us not less anxious for the speedy completion of the battery.

John Ericsson, a Swedish immigrant with an international reputation as an engineer, was the Monitor's *designer. He made her somewhat raftlike in appearance. On deck, she was 172 feet long and 41 feet wide, and she drew about 10 feet of water. Her machinery and her accommodations for equipage and her fifty-eight-man crew were below the waterline.*

Says an unnamed Northern newspaperman:

Externally, she presents to the fire of the enemy's guns a hull rising but about eighteen inches above the water, and a sort of Martello tower [a gun turret] twenty feet in diameter and ten feet high. . . . The hull is sharp at both ends. . . . No railing or bulwark of any kind appears above the deck. . . . [The] turret is a revolving, bombproof fort, and mounts two 11-inch guns. It is protected by eight thicknesses of inch-iron. . . . A spur-wheel . . . moved by a double-cylinder engine, turns the turret, guns and all. . . .

The turret, of course, was in the deck's center. Short twin smokestacks rose from the afterdeck, but, being retractable, offered no target during combat. Well forward of the turret, up near the prow, was a pilothouse. Rising 4 feet above the deck, it was made of heavy iron logs, bolted together, and had only a narrow slit for visibility.

The Merrimac, or Virginia, as she had been renamed by the Confederates, was about 90 feet longer than the Monitor and had room in her hull, which drew 22 feet of water, for about 320 men in addition to her machinery and stores. In appearance above the water she resembled a huge turtle "with a large round chimney about the middle of its back." This ironclad shield was pierced by ten gun ports, the largest guns being designed for 9-inch shells. Her prow, a cast-iron projection weighing 1,500 pounds, was intended for use as a ram.

Writes a Southern correspondent:

Commodore [Franklin] Buchanan commands her, and the second in command is Catesby Jones—both men of the highest order of courage. Buchanan has confidence in her, and says he is going to glory or a grave in her. Jones is less confident, but says she is as good a place to die in as a man could have.

As summed up by Southern editor Edward Pollard:

The other vessels of the Confederate squadron in the [Norfolk area] . . . were the *Patrick Henry*, six guns; the *Jamestown*, two guns; the *Raleigh*, the *Beaufort*, and the *Teazer*, each of one gun. . . .

[A] considerable naval force of the enemy had been collected in Hampton Roads, off Fortress Monroe . . . the *Cumberland*, of 24 guns; the *Congress*, 50 guns; the *St. Lawrence*, 50 guns; the steam-frigates *Minnesota* and *Roanoke*, 40 guns. . . .

With the force of twenty[-one] guns, Capt. Buchanan proposed to engage this formidable fleet, besides the enemy's [shore] batteries at Newport News and several small steamers armed with heavy rifled guns. Everything had to be trusted to the experiment of the *Virginia*.

Working in the ironclad's favor, of course, was that the vessels she was going against were wooden ones.

The Monitor *won the race to completion—by two days. Unfortunately, she was three hundred miles from Hampton Roads. Her second-in-command, Lieutenant S. Dana Greene, was later to write:*

We left New York in tow of the tug-boat *Seth Low* at 11 A.M. of Thursday, the 6th of March. On the following day a moderate breeze was encountered, and it was at once evident that the *Monitor* was unfit as a sea-going craft. . . . The berth-deck hatch leaked in spite of all we could do, and the water [also] came down under the turret like a waterfall. It . . . came through the narrow eye-holes in the pilot-house with such force as to knock the helmsman completely round from the wheel.

The waves also broke over the blower-pipes, and the water came down through them in such quantities that the belts of the blower-engines slipped, and the engines consequently stopped. . . . [T]he fires [coal being the fuel] could not get air for combustion. [First Assistant Engineer Isaac] Newton and [Chief Engineer Alban C.]

Stimers, followed by the engineer's force, gallantly rushed into the engine-room and fire-room to remedy the evil, but they were unable to check the inflowing water, and were nearly suffocated with escaping [coal] gas. They were dragged out. . . .

The water continued to pour through the hawse-hole, and over and down the smoke-stacks and blower-pipes in such quantities that there was imminent danger that the ship would founder. . . . Fortunately, toward evening the wind and the sea subsided. . . . But at midnight . . . rough water was again encountered, and our troubles were renewed. . . . [T]he safety of the ship depended entirely on the strength of the hawser which connected her with the tug-boat. . . . [D]uring the greater part of the night we were constantly engaged in fighting the leaks, until we reached smooth water again just before daylight.

It was now Saturday, March 8. Down at Norfolk, the early-morning hours found the Merrimac *preparing to steam forth to battle. She was crowded with workmen up to the hour of sailing. The Union fleet was about ten miles distant, the position of the various vessels known to the Confederates. Explains John Taylor Wood, who served as one of the* Merrimac's *lieutenants:*

At anchor . . . off Fort Monroe were the frigates *Minnesota, Roanoke,* and *St. Lawrence,* and several gun-boats. . . . Off Newport News, seven miles [along the shore to the southwest], which was strongly fortified and held by a large Federal garrison, were anchored the frigate *Congress* . . . and the sloop *Cumberland.* . . .

The two vessels off Newport News were chosen for the Merrimac's *first attentions. It was a bright, calm day, and the unsuspecting vessels were "swinging lazily by their anchors." Laundered clothes were strung about in the rigging to dry.*

About quarter past eleven, the Merrimac *cast loose from her moorings at the navy yard and, in the company of two small wooden steamers, started down the Elizabeth River. Troops and civilians lining the shore cheered lustily, many of the men also waving their hats.*

Over at Newport News, the Union tugboat Zouave *had completed her morning duties and was tied up at the wharf. Relates her master, Henry Reaney:*

A little after dinner, about 12:30, the quartermaster on watch called my attention to black smoke in the Elizabeth River, close to Craney Island. We let go from the wharf and ran alongside the *Cum-*

berland. The officer of the deck ordered us to . . . find out what was coming down from Norfolk. It did not take us long to find out, for we had not gone over two miles when we saw what to all appearances looked like the roof of a very big barn belching forth smoke as from a chimney on fire. We were all divided in opinion as to what was coming. The boatswain's mate was the first to make out the Confederate flag, and then we all guessed it was the *Merrimac* come at last.

Back on the anchored Cumberland, *the pilot A. B. Smith, studied the approaching vessel with his glass:*

As she came ploughing through the water . . . she looked like a huge half-submerged crocodile. Her sides seemed of solid iron, except where the guns pointed from the narrow ports. . . . At her prow I could see the iron ram projecting straight forward, somewhat above the water's edge. . . .

By this time, large numbers of soldiers, sailors, and civilians were hurrying to the shores between Newport News and Fort Monroe. On the Confederate shores, the crowds were increasing.

The tugboat Zouave, *the Union vessel nearest the* Merrimac, *began the action. In Henry Reaney's words:*

When we were satisfied it was the enemy, we went to quarters and fired our 30-pounder Parrott, which was not answered. We fired again, taking deliberate aim, and were rather surprised that it was unnoticed. We fired, I think, about six shots when our recall signal was hoisted on the *Cumberland.* By this time the [shore] batteries at Newport News had commenced firing; the *Congress* had gone to quarters and opened fire; when we got close to the *Cumberland* she also began firing.

The *Merrimac* kept on until abreast of the *Congress,* when she opened fire, pouring a broadside in passing, and came right on for the *Cumberland,* which vessel was using her guns as fast as they could be fired.

Writes A. B. Smith, the Cumberland's *pilot:*

Still she came on, the balls bouncing upon her mailed sides like India-rubber, apparently making not the least impression, except to cut off her flag-staff and thus bring down the Confederate colors. . . . We had probably fired six or eight broadsides when a shot was received from one of her guns which killed five of our marines.

It was impossible for our vessel to get out of her way, and the *Merrimac* soon crushed her iron horn, or ram, into the *Cumberland* . . . knocking a hole in the side . . . and driving the vessel back upon her anchors with great force. The water came rushing into the hold.

Southerner John Taylor Wood says that the blow was "hardly perceptible" on board the Merrimac:

Backing clear of her, we went . . . up the river . . . and turned slowly. . . . As we swung, the *Congress* came in range . . . and we got in three raking shells. She had slipped her anchor . . . and tried to escape, but grounded. Turning, we headed for her and took a position within two hundred yards, where every shot told. In the meantime the *Cumberland* continued the fight, though our ram had opened her side wide enough to drive in a horse and cart.

The Cumberland's *A. B. Smith describes the vessel's plight:*

The water was all the while rushing in the hole. . . . In the meantime [the *Merrimac*'s] broadsides swept our men away, killed and maimed, and also set our vessel on fire in the forward part. The fire was extinguished. . . .

The fight lasted about three-fourths of an hour, the *Cumberland* firing rapidly, and all the time the water pouring in the hold, and by and by [into] the ports, as her bow kept sinking deeper and deeper.

Near the middle of the fight . . . one of the crew of the *Merrimac* came out of a port to the outside of her iron-plated roof, and a ball from one of our guns instantly cut him in two. That was the last and only rebel that ventured within sight, the rest remaining in their safe, iron-walled enclosure. We fired constantly, and the *Merrimac* [only] occasionally, but every shot told upon our wooden vessel and brave crew.

As learned by a correspondent of the Baltimore American, *a Union newspaper:*

They worked desperately and unremittingly, and amid the din and horror of the conflict gave cheers for their flag and the Union, which were joined in by the wounded. The decks were slippery with blood, and arms and legs and chunks of flesh were strewed about.

The *Merrimac* laid off at easy point-blank range, discharging her broadsides alternately at the *Cumberland* and the *Congress*.

The water by this time had reached the after-magazine of the

Cumberland. . . . Several men in the after shell-room lingered there too long . . . and were drowned.

The water . . . reached the . . . main gun-deck, and it was felt hopeless and useless to continue the fight longer. The word was given for each man to save himself; but after this order, gun No. Seven was fired when the adjoining gun, No. Six, was actually under water. This last shot was fired by an active little fellow named Matthew Tenney, whose courage had been conspicuous throughout the action. As his port was left open by the recoil of the gun, he jumped to scramble out, but the water rushed in with so much force that he was washed back and drowned.

When the order was given . . . to look out for their safety in the best way possible, numbers scampered through the portholes, whilst others reached the spar-deck by the companionways. Some were incapable to get out by either of these means and were [trapped in] the rapidly sinking ship.

A. B. Smith says that the Cumberland *went down with "the Stars and Stripes still waving."*

That flag was finally submerged, but after the hull grounded on the sands, fifty-four feet below the surface of the water, our pennant was still flying from the top-mast above the waves. None of our men were captured, but many were drowned. . . . Very few of our men swam ashore, most of those who were rescued from the water being saved by small boats.

The Merrimac, *in company with the one-gun steamers* Raleigh *and* Beaufort, *now turned her full attention to the grounded* Congress. *Franklin Buchanan, the* Merrimac's *commander, wasn't deterred by the fact that his brother, Paymaster McKean Buchanan, was serving on the Union vessel.*

The vessel's second-in-command, Lieutenant Austin Pendergrast, was later to write:

. . . the *Merrimac* . . . raked us fore and aft with shells, while one of the smaller steamers kept up a fire on our starboard quarter. In the meantime, the *Patrick Henry* and the [*Jamestown*], rebel steamers, appeared from up the James River, firing with precision and doing us great damage. Our two stern-guns were our only means of defence. These were soon disabled. . . . The men were knocked away from them with great rapidity and slaughter by the terrible fire of the enemy.

Among the ship's officers slain was the commander, Lieutenant Joseph B. Smith. He was succeeded by Lieutenant Pendergrast:

Seeing that our men were being killed without the prospect of any relief from the *Minnesota,* which vessel had run [aground] in attempting to get up to us from Hampton Roads, [and] not being able to get a single gun to bear upon the enemy, and the ship being on fire in several places . . . we deemed it proper to haul down our colors. . . .

Says John Taylor Wood, of the Merrimac:

As soon as the *Congress* surrendered, Commander Buchanan ordered the gun-boats *Beaufort* . . . and *Raleigh* . . . to steam alongside. . . . Lieutenant Pendergrast . . . surrendered to Lieutenant [W. H.] Parker, of the *Beaufort.*

According to a Confederate report in the Norfolk Day-Book:

The scene around the *Congress* is represented as heartsickening. The officers of the *Beaufort* . . . who boarded her for the purpose of removing the wounded . . . represented the deck of the vessel as being literally covered with the dead and dying. One of them assured us that as he went from fore to aft his shoes were well-nigh buried in blood and brains. Arms, legs, and heads were found scattered in every direction, while here and there, in the agonies of death, would be found poor deluded wretches with their breasts torn completely out.

The Merrimac's *John Taylor Wood goes on to explain:*

All this time the [Union] shore batteries and small-arm men were keeping up an incessant fire on our vessels. Two of the officers of the *Raleigh* . . . were killed while assisting the Union wounded out of the *Congress.* A number of the [Union vessel's] men were killed by the same fire.

One of the Northern soldiers on shore asked the commanding general, Joseph Mansfield, "Since the ship has surrendered, has not the enemy the right to take possession of her?" The general snapped, "I know the damned ship has surrendered, but we haven't!"

John Taylor Wood continues:

Finally it became so hot that the gun-boats were obliged to haul off with only thirty prisoners, leaving Lieutenant Pendergrast and most of his crew on board, and they all afterward escaped to the shore by swimming or in small boats. While this was going on, the white flag was flying at her mainmasthead.

Among the survivors was Paymaster McKean Buchanan, brother of the Confederate commodore, who had been so busy at a volunteer combat post that he was unable to save a large sum of payroll money locked in the ship's safe.

Again in Wood's words:

Not being able to take possession of his prize, the commodore ordered hot shot to be used, and in a short time she was in flames fore and aft. While directing this [from an exposed position on the *Merrimac*'s deck], both himself and his flag-lieutenant . . . were severely wounded [by small-arms fire from shore]. The command then devolved upon Lieut. Catesby Jones.

About five o'clock in the afternoon the Merrimac, Jamestown, *and* Patrick Henry *turned their attention to the Union's steam frigate* Minnesota, *which had run aground while approaching the scene from Fort Monroe. Writes the* Minnesota's *commander, G. J. Van Brunt:*

Very fortunately, the iron battery drew too much water to come within a mile of us. She took a position on my starboard bow, but did not fire with accuracy, and only one shot passed through the ship's bow. The other two steamers took their position on my port bow and stern, and their fire did [the] most damage in killing and wounding men. . . .

Aided by tugboats, the Union frigates Roanoke *and* St. Lawrence *were now making their way from Fort Monroe toward the battle scene. Their route brought them within distant range of heavy batteries at Sewell's Point, on the Confederate shore, and a duel resulted.*

The overall picture at this time is given by Confederate observer General R. E. Colston, who says it was "one of unsurpassed magnificence."

The bright afternoon sun shone upon the glancing waters. The fortifications of Newport News were seen swarming with soldiers . . . and the flames were . . . bursting from the abandoned *Congress*. The stranded *Minnesota* seemed a huge monster at bay, surrounded by the *Merrimac* and the gun-boats. The entire horizon was lighted up by the continual flashes of the artillery of these combatants, the broadsides of the *Roanoke* and *St. Lawrence*, and the [fire from] the Sewell's Point batteries. Clouds of white smoke rose in spiral columns to the skies, illumined by the evening sunlight, while land and water seemed to tremble under the thunders of the cannonade.

The *Minnesota* was now in a desperate situation. It is true that, being aground, she could not sink; but, looking through the glass, I could see a hole in her side, made by [one of] the *Merrimac's* rifle shells. She had lost a number of men, and had once been set on fire. Her destruction or surrender seemed inevitable, since all efforts to get her afloat had failed.

But just then the *Merrimac* turned away from her toward the *Roanoke* and the *St. Lawrence.* These vessels had suffered but little from the distant fire of the Sewell's Point batteries, but both had run aground and had not been floated off again without great difficulty, for it was very hazardous for vessels of deep draught to manoeuvre over these comparatively shallow waters.

When the *Merrimac* approached, they delivered broadsides and were then towed back with promptness. The *Merrimac* pursued them but a short distance—for by this time darkness was falling upon the scene of action, the tide was ebbing, and there was great risk of running aground. . . . [She] then steamed toward Norfolk. . . .

The vessel was taken only as far as Sewell's Point, where she was anchored for the night, her crew not resting until preparations had been made to renew the fight in the morning.

Laments the Baltimore American's *correspondent:*

The day . . . closed most dismally for our side, and with the most gloomy apprehensions of what would occur the next day. The *Minnesota* was at the mercy of the *Merrimac,* and there appeared no reason why the iron monster might not clear the Roads of our fleet, destroy all the stores and warehouses on the beach, drive our troops into the Fortress, and command Hampton Roads against any number of wooden vessels the Government might send there. Saturday was a terribly dismal night at Fortress Monroe.

For the Confederates, the night was one of exultation. Their experimental ironclad had proved a great success. Writes Richmond's editor and historian, Edward Pollard:

She had already in a single half-day achieved one of the most remarkable triumphs ever made on the water. She had destroyed two powerful vessels carrying three times her number of men and full six times her weight of armament. . . . The *Cumberland* went into action with 376 men. When the survivors were mustered there were only 255. . . . The crew of the *Congress* were 434 officers and men; of these, 298 got to shore. . . .

Many of the survivors of both ships had suffered wounds. Confederate losses were about twenty in killed and wounded. As for the condition of the Merrimac:

The armor [says John Taylor Wood] was hardly damaged, though at one time our ship was the focus on which were directed at least one hundred heavy guns afloat and ashore. But nothing outside escaped. Two guns were disabled by having their muzzles shot off. The ram was left in the side of the *Cumberland.* One anchor, the smokestack, and the steam-pipes were shot away. Railings, stanchions, boat-davits —everything was swept clean. The flag-staff was repeatedly knocked over, and finally a boarding-pike was used.

Though battered, the vessel had lost but little of her original strength. She was still quite ready for anything the Union chose to pit against her.

And where was the Monitor *while the* Merrimac *had been having her way that afternoon? Not far off. She entered the mouth of Chesapeake Bay about 4:00 P.M., at which time her crew could hear "the distant booming of heavy guns." While she was still ten miles from Fort Monroe, says second-in-command S. Dana Greene, she met the Union fleet's pilot boat and was told the fate of the* Cumberland *and* Congress:

We could not credit it at first, but as we approached Hampton Roads we could see the fine old *Congress* burning brightly; and we knew it must be true. Sad indeed did we feel to think those two fine old vessels had gone to their last homes with so many of their brave crews. . . .

At 9 P.M. we anchored near the frigate *Roanoke,* the flagship [of the Union fleet] . . . and received orders to proceed to Newport News and protect the *Minnesota*—then aground—from the *Merrimac.* We got under way and arrived at the *Minnesota* at 11 P.M. I went on board in our cutter. . . . I . . . told [Captain Van Brunt] we should do all in our power to protect him from the *Merrimac.* He thanked me kindly and wished us success.

Just as I arrived back to the *Monitor* the *Congress* blew up, and certainly a grander sight was never seen; but it went straight to the marrow of our bones.

The night "dragged slowly on" aboard the Monitor, *which stayed near the* Minnesota, *alert for any emergency. Three miles away, the crew of the* Merrimac *slept at their guns, "dreaming of other victories in the morning."*

By this time, news of the Merrimac's *great triumph was spreading north and south from Hampton Roads. Washington learned the details by telegram early the following morning, Sunday, March 9. Lincoln hastened to call a cabinet meeting at the White House. Secretary of the Navy Gideon Welles writes that he arrived to find Secretary of State William H. Seward, Secretary of the Treasury Salmon P. Chase, and Secretary of War Edwin M. Stanton already there, consulting with the President in much alarm:*

Each inquired what had been, and what could be done, to meet and check this formidable monster, which in a single brief visit had made such devastation, and would . . . repeat her destructive visit with still greater havoc, probably, while we were in council. . . .

I had expected that our new iron-clad battery . . . would have reached the Roads on Saturday, and my main reliance was upon her. We had, however, no information as yet of her arrival. . . .

Mr. Stanton, impulsive and always a sensationalist . . . walked the room in great agitation. . . .

"The *Merrimac*," said Stanton . . . "will change the whole character of the war; she will destroy, seriatim, every naval vessel; she will lay all the cities on the seaboard under contribution. . . . Port Royal [South Carolina] must be abandoned. I will notify the governors and municipal authorities in the North to take instant measures to protect their harbors."

. . . He had no doubt, he said, that the monster was at this moment on her way to Washington; and, looking out of the window, which commanded a view of the Potomac for many miles, [he said it was] "not unlikely we shall have a shell or cannon-ball from one of her guns in the White House before we leave this room."

Most of Stanton's complaints were directed to me. . . . I had little to impart, except my faith in the untried *Monitor* experiment. . . .

"What," asked Stanton, "is the size and strength of this *Monitor*? How many guns does she carry?"

When I replied two, but of large calibre, he turned away with a look of mingled amazement, contempt, and distress that was painfully ludicrous. . . .

Turning to Stanton, [Seward] said we had, perhaps, given away too much to our apprehensions. He saw no alternative but to wait and hear what our new battery might accomplish. Stanton left abruptly after Seward's remark. The President ordered his carriage and went to the Navy Yard to see what might be the views of the naval officers.

Returning to my house . . . I stopped at St. John's Church and called out Commodore [Joseph] Smith, to whom I communicated the tidings we had received, and that the *Congress,* commanded by his son . . . had been sunk.

"The *Congress* sunk!" he exclaimed, at the same time buttoning up his coat and looking me calmly and steadily in the face; "then Joe is dead."

I told him . . . the officers and crew doubtless escaped, for the shore was not distant.

"You don't know Joe . . . as well as I do. He would not survive his ship."

The commodore, of course, was right; Joe was dead—though it hadn't been a matter of choice, the Confederates having hit him with their gunfire.

Even while the two men spoke, the waters of Hampton Roads were resounding with the noises of another battle. It had begun early that morning. Says the Merrimac's *John Taylor Wood:*

. . . at daybreak we discovered, lying between us and the *Minnesota,* a strange-looking craft, which we knew at once to be Ericsson's *Monitor,* which had long been expected in Hampton Roads. . . . She appeared but a pigmy compared with the lofty frigate which she guarded.

One Confederate spectator, getting his first glimpse of the Monitor *as she was touched by the sun's earliest rays, exclaimed, "A tin can on a shingle!"*

Writes S. Dana Greene, the Monitor's *second-in-command:*

At about half-past 7 o'clock the enemy's vessels [the *Merrimac* and two wooden steamers] got under way and steered in the direction of the *Minnesota.* At the same time the *Monitor* got under way, and her officers and crew took their stations for battle.

The moment was one of unique historical significance. In the words of Naval Medical Director Charles Martin, who watched from the Union shore:

. . . David goes out to meet Goliath, and every man who can walk to the beach sits down there, spectators of the first iron-clad battle in the world.

The Monitor's *Greene was aware at this time that he had a friend on the* Merrimac. *Lieutenant Walter R. Butt had been his roommate at Annapolis. "Little did we think at the Academy," says Greene, "we should ever be firing 150-pound shot at each other, but so goes the world."*

Greene explains that the Monitor's *commanding officer, Lieutenant John L. Worden, was stationed in the pilothouse at the vessel's bow:*

. . . by his side were [Samuel] Howard, the pilot, and Peter Williams, quartermaster, who steered the vessel throughout the engagement. My place was in the turret, to work and fight the guns. With me were [Acting Master Louis N.] Stodder and [Chief Engineer Alban] Stimers and sixteen brawny men, eight to each gun. . . .

The physical condition of the officers and men of the two ships at this time was in striking contrast. The *Merrimac* had passed the night quietly near Sewell's Point, her people enjoying rest and sleep. . . . The *Monitor* had barely escaped shipwreck twice within the last thirty-six hours, and since Friday morning, forty-eight hours before, few if any of those on board had closed their eyes in sleep or had anything to eat but hard bread, as cooking was impossible. She was surrounded by wrecks and disaster, and her efficiency in action had yet to be proved.

Worden lost no time in bringing it to test. . . . [H]e steered direct for the enemy's vessels, in order to meet and engage them as far as possible from the *Minnesota*. As he approached, the wooden vessels quickly turned and left. Our captain . . . made straight for the *Merrimac,* which had already commenced firing; and when he came within short range . . . he gave the order, "Commence firing!"

I . . . ran out [a] gun, and, taking deliberate aim, pulled the lockstring. The *Merrimac* was quick to reply, returning a rattling broadside . . . and the battle fairly began. The turret and other parts of [our] ship were heavily struck, but the shots did not penetrate. The tower . . . continued to revolve. A look of confidence passed over the men's faces. . . .

The power of the fire coming from the Monitor's *"tin can" surprised the* Merrimac's *crew. "Damn it," said one, "the thing is full of guns!"*

The *Monitor* and the *Merrimac*.

Naval Medical Director Charles Martin gives this description of the opening of the fight as seen from the Union shore:

The day is calm, the smoke hangs thick on the water, the low vessels are hidden by the smoke. They are so sure of their invulnerability, they fight at arm's length. They fight so near the shore, the flash of their guns is seen, and the noise is heard of the heavy shot pounding the armor.

Deeply thrilling to the Union spectators was the realization that the little Monitor *was holding her own against the South's "monster." The shoreline rang with cheers. "Men were frantic with joy." Though the Confederate spectators did their share of cheering as the* Merrimac's *powerful broadsides were loosed, the mood was less exuberant than that of the day before.*

Watching from the deck of the grounded Union vessel Minnesota, *along with the hundreds that made up her crew, was Captain Van Brunt, who regarded the turn of events with "astonishment":*

Gun after gun was fired by the *Monitor,* which was returned with whole broadsides from the rebels, with no more effect, apparently, than so many pebble-stones thrown by a child. . . . [W]hen they struck the bomb-proof tower, the shot glanced off . . . clearly establishing the fact that wooden vessels cannot contend successfully with iron-clad ones, for never before was anything like it dreamed of by the greatest enthusiast in maritime warfare.

The battle developed into one of maneuvering and firing, with neither vessel gaining the advantage. The Monitor *was far the more agile of the two, the* Merrimac *being handicapped not only by her size and draft, but by defects in her machinery, which was old and had been ravaged by fire and water at the time of her abandonment by the Union. John Taylor Wood calls her "as unwieldy as Noah's ark."*

Relates the Monitor's *S. Dana Greene:*

The fight continued . . . as fast as the guns could be served, and at very short range. . . . Worden skillfully manoeuvred his quick-turning vessel, trying to find some vulnerable point in his adversary. Once he made a dash at her stern, hoping to disable her screw, which he thinks he missed by not more than two feet.

Our shots ripped [into] the iron of the *Merrimac,* while the reverberation of her shots against the tower caused anything but a pleasant sensation. While Stodder, who was stationed at the machine which controlled the revolving motion of the turret, was incautiously leaning against the side of the tower, a large shot struck in the vicinity and disabled him. He left the turret and went below, and Stimers, who had assisted him, continued to do the work.

The drawbacks to the position of the pilot-house were soon realized. We could not fire ahead nor within several points of the bow, since the blast from our own guns would have injured the people in the pilot-house, only a few yards off. . . . As the engagement continued, the working of the turret was not altogether satisfactory. It was difficult to start it revolving, or, when once started, to stop it, on account of the imperfections of the novel machinery, which was now undergoing its first trial.

Switching to the Merrimac *and John Taylor Wood:*

More than two hours had passed, and we had made no impression on the enemy so far as we could discover, while our wounds were slight. Several times the *Monitor* ceased firing, and we were in hopes she was disabled, but the revolution again of her turret and the heavy blows of her 11-inch shot on our sides soon undeceived us.

. . . observing a division [of gunners] standing at ease, Lieutenant [Catesby] Jones inquired, "Why are you not firing, Mr. Eggleston?"

"Why, our powder is very precious . . . and after two hours' incessant firing I find that I can do her about as much damage by snapping my thumb at her every two minutes and a half."

Writes Captain Van Brunt, of the grounded Minnesota:

The *Merrimac,* finding that she could make nothing of the *Monitor,* turned her attention . . . to me. . . . I opened upon her with all my broadside-guns and ten-inch pivot—a broadside which would have blown out of water any timber-built ship in the world. She returned my fire with her rifled bowgun, with a shell which passed through the chief-engineer's state-room, through the engineers' mess-room amidships, and burst in the boatswain's room, tearing four rooms all into one, in its passage exploding two charges of powder, which set the ship on fire, but it was promptly extinguished. . . . Her second went through the boiler of the tugboat *Dragon,* exploding it. . . .

I had concentrated upon her an incessant fire . . . and . . . at least fifty solid shot struck her . . . without producing any apparent effect. By the time she had fired her third shell, the little *Monitor* had come down upon her, placing herself between us, and compelled her to change her position, in doing which she grounded, and again I poured into her all the guns which could be brought to bear upon her. As soon as she got off, she stood down the bay, the little battery chasing her with all speed. . . .

It was now the Merrimac's *intention, says John Taylor Wood, to make an attempt either to ram the* Monitor *or board her:*

For nearly an hour we manoeuvred for a position. . . . At last an opportunity offered [to ram her]. . . . But before the ship gathered headway the *Monitor* turned, and our disabled ram only gave a glancing blow, effecting nothing.

Again she came up on our quarter, her bow against our side, and at this distance fired twice. Both shots struck about half-way up the shield . . . and the impact forced the side in bodily two or three inches. All the crews of the after guns were knocked over by the concussion, and bled from the nose or ears. Another shot at the same place would have penetrated.

While alongside, [our] boarders were called away; but she dropped astern before they could get on board.

The battle continued at close quarters. S. Dana Greene of the Monitor *takes up the narrative:*

Soon after noon, a shell from the enemy's gun, the muzzle not ten yards distant, struck the forward side of the pilot-house directly in the sight-hole, or slit, and exploded, cracking the second iron log and partly lifting the top, leaving an opening. Worden was standing immediately behind this spot, and received in his face the force of the blow, which partly stunned him, and, filling his eyes with powder, utterly blinded him. . . .

The flood of light rushing through the top of the pilot-house . . . caused Worden, blind as he was, to believe that the pilot-house was seriously injured, if not destroyed. He therefore gave orders to . . . "sheer off." Thus the *Monitor* retired temporarily from the action. . . . At the same time, Worden sent for me; and leaving Stimers the only officer in the turret, I went forward at once, and found him standing at the foot of the ladder leading to the pilot-house.

He was a ghastly sight, with his eyes closed and the blood apparently rushing from every pore in the upper part of his face. He . . . directed me to take command. I assisted in leading him to a sofa in his cabin. . . . When I reached my station in the pilot-house, I found that . . . the steering gear was still intact. . . . In the confusion of the moment . . . the *Monitor* had been moving without direction [in water too shallow to permit the *Merrimac* to follow]. . . .

During this time the *Merrimac* . . . had started in the direction of the Elizabeth River; and on . . . turning the [*Monitor's*] head in the direction of the *Merrimac,* I saw that she was already in retreat. A few shots were fired at the retiring vessel, and she continued on to Norfolk. . . . The fight was over.

The Merrimac *hadn't left the field in haste, but had waited for some time for the* Monitor's *return to deep water and a resumption of the fight. However, the Southern vessel was leaking as a result of her attempt to ram the* Monitor, *was in need of many other repairs, and was carrying a crew now worn out from two days of work with their heavy guns, much of the time in a haze of acrid powder smoke. Moreover, the tide was ebbing and the cumbrous vessel was in danger of running aground and not getting off.*

The Merrimac's *John Taylor Wood offers this objective summation:*

Although there is no doubt that the *Monitor* first retired . . . the battle was a drawn one, so far as the two vessels engaged were concerned. But in its general results the advantage was with the *Monitor*.

. . . [She] saved the *Minnesota* and the remainder of the fleet at Fort Monroe.

After assuring herself that the Merrimac *wasn't coming back, the* Monitor, *her armor bearing many marks from the enemy's shells, returned to the side of the grounded* Minnesota. *As the little ironclad's crew climbed from her dark confines to her sunny deck, with the men of the turret "perfectly black with smoke and powder," the* Minnesota's *crew cheered themselves hoarse. Captain Van Brunt had made every preparation to destroy his vessel if the* Monitor *was bested.*

The joy at the battle's outcome, of course, extended to the crowds of spectators between Newport News and Fort Monroe. And soon the word was crackling over the telegraph wires to all parts of the North.

The South found its satisfaction in the results of the first day's fighting. John Taylor Wood went to Richmond with the flag of the Congress, *secured at the time she surrendered, for an audience with President Davis:*

I told at length what had occurred. . . . Mr. Davis made many inquiries. . . . During the evening the flag of the *Congress* . . . was brought in, and to our surprise, in unfolding it we found it in some places saturated with blood. On this discovery it was quickly rolled up and sent to the Navy Department. . . .

John Worden, disabled commander of the Monitor, *the man who had saved the North's control of Hampton Roads and had mitigated her fear of the* Merrimac, *was taken to Washington. President Lincoln, quick to pay him a visit, found him lying on a couch, his eyes bandaged and his face discolored. As Lincoln took his hand, Worden said, "Mr. President, you do me great honor by this visit."*

Tears swelling in his eyes, Lincoln replied warmly, "Sir, I am the one who is honored by this interview."

Happily, Worden's condition wasn't as bad as it seemed; his blindness was only temporary.

The two-day affair at Hampton Roads attracted worldwide attention and was destined for inclusion among the great naval battles of history. It dramatized the superiority of ironclad warships over wooden ones. The example had a particular impact on England and France, pioneers in experimentation with ironclads. Observed the London Times:

Whereas we had available for immediate purposes one hundred

and forty-nine first-class warships, we have now two . . . the *Warrior* and her sister *Ironside*. There is not now a ship in the English Navy, apart from these two [ironclads] that it would not be madness to trust to an engagement with that little *Monitor*.

6

SHILOH

THE MONTH *of the great naval battle—March, 1862—saw two significant developments on land. George Brinton McClellan, the Young Napoleon, finally opened his campaign against Richmond, and the Federals in the West, now in control of the border states of Kentucky and Missouri, began to invade the South. The Western events were first to climax.*

After General Grant's capture of Forts Henry and Donelson in northwestern Tennessee in February, Union forces had been sent to reduce the Confederate works at New Madrid, Missouri, and Island Number Ten, under jurisdiction of Kentucky, points on the Mississippi River lying about ten miles apart. They had to be taken in order to open the lower Mississippi to the Union's river fleet.

Not waiting for the completion of this effort, a strong Union army had pushed down through western Tennessee. At the beginning of April, about 42,000 men under Grant were stationed at Pittsburg Landing and nearby Crump's Landing, on the west bank of the Tennessee River, only a few miles from the northern border of Mississippi. Another Federal army, led by Major General Don Carlos Buell, was marching to join Grant from Columbia, Tennessee, eighty-five miles to the northeast.

The retreating Confederates had regrouped at Corinth, Missis-

Ulysses S. Grant.

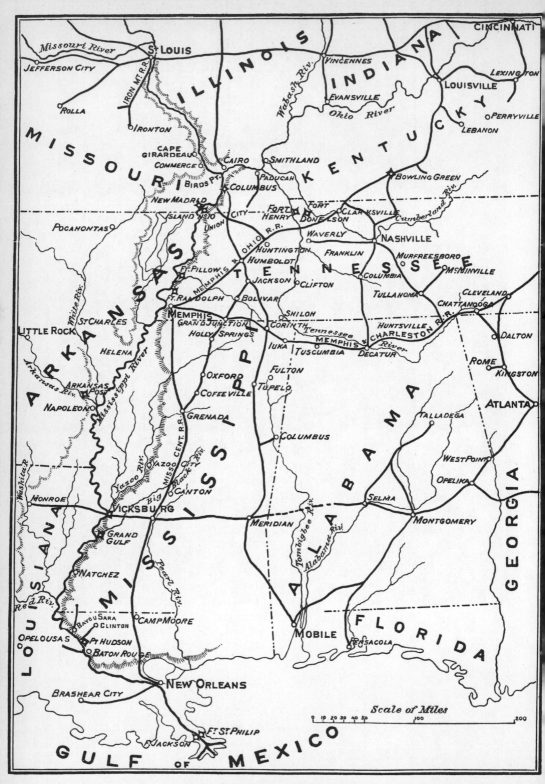

Field of operations in the West.

sippi, about twenty miles southwest of Grant's position. Their strength approximated that of Grant's army, without Buell. The Confederate commander was General Albert Sidney Johnston (not to be confused with Joseph E. Johnston, then commanding in the East). Second-in-command in the West was a newcomer: Pierre Beauregard. President Davis had sent him to help run things in this critical theater because of his effective work at Fort Sumter and Bull Run. He was presently in the grip of a bronchial infection that made it hard for him to carry on.

Johnston and Beauregard decided that their best chance against the Union forces in Tennessee lay in attacking Grant before Buell arrived to reinforce him. With Grant defeated, attention could be turned to Buell. The plan had more in its favor than the Confederates realized. Grant, underestimating their resolve, felt there was little danger of his being attacked at Pittsburg Landing while awaiting Buell. He believed that the Confederates, after their recent setbacks, would choose to remain at Corinth and brace for the next Federal advance. Grant's men had no entrenchments. (This early in the war, the soldiers of both sides tended to be careless about their security.) The Federals occupied tent camps scattered over a great area of woods and fields in the vicinity of Shiloh Church, a log structure two and a half miles inland from the river.

The Confederate columns—made up of foot soldiers, horsemen, artillery batteries, supply wagons, and ambulances—began their advance toward Grant's encampment on April 3, at which time Johnston issued a general order that included these lines:

Soldiers of the Army of the Mississippi: I have put you in motion to offer battle to the invaders of your country. . . . You can but march to a decisive victory over . . . mercenaries sent to subjugate and despoil you of your liberties, property, and honor. Remember the precious stake involved; remember the dependence of your mothers, your wives, your sisters, and your children on the result; remember the fair, broad, abounding lands, the happy homes that will be desolated by your defeat. The eyes and hopes of eight million people rest upon you.

Writes General Beauregard:

It was expected we should be able to reach the enemy's lines in time to attack them early on the fifth instant. The men, however, for the most part, were unused to marching. The roads, narrow and traversing a densely wooded country, became almost impassable after a severe rainstorm on the night of the fourth, which drenched the troops in bivouac. Hence, our forces did not reach . . . the immediate vicinity of the enemy until late Saturday afternoon [April 5]. It was then decided that the attack should be made on the next morning, at the earliest hour practicable. . . .

Amazingly enough, the Union troops had no indication that a great army was only about two miles away. Their pickets were posted too close to camp, and no cavalry patrols were out. A few of the Union officers, however, were uneasy as the men settled down to their usual night's rest. Colonel Wills de Hass, who occupied a tent at the edge of the camp nearest the Confederate bivouac, was later to write:

. . . the whole camp was asleep. How unconscious of danger lay the army of the Union that night! . . . [The men's] visions were of home and the loved ones who looked so fondly for their return. . . . At midnight, stepping from my tent . . . I listened. . . . But all was still save the measured tread of the sentinel and the gentle whispers of the genial night breeze. No sound came from the distant wood. . . . [Q]uietness reigned . . . throughout the rebel camps.

Among the Confederate soldiers was young Henry Morton Stanley, later an internationally known journalist, adventurer, and explorer, whose exploits in Africa included tracking down Dr. David Livingstone. Stanley relates:

At four o'clock in the morning, we rose from our damp bivouac, and, after a hasty refreshment, were formed into line. We stood in rank for half an hour or so, while the military dispositions were being completed along the three-mile front. . . . Day broke with every promise of a fine day.

Next to me . . . was a boy of seventeen. Henry Parker. . . . [W]hile we stood at ease, he drew my attention to some violets at his feet and said, "It would be a good idea to put a few into my cap. Perhaps the Yanks won't shoot me if they see me wearing such flowers, for they are a sign of peace."

"Capital," said I. "I will do the same."

We . . . arranged the violets in our caps. The men in the ranks laughed at our proceedings. . . .

As the order to begin the advance was passed up and down the lines, General Johnston asked General Beauregard, "Can it be possible they are not aware of our presence?" Beauregard answered, "It can scarcely

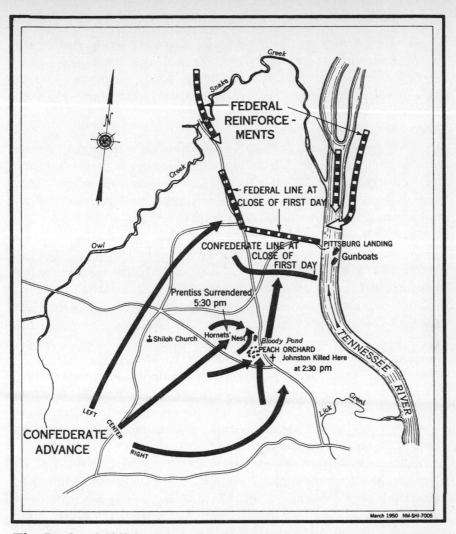

The Battle of Shiloh. When the battle began, the Union front faced toward the southwest at Shiloh Church, the lines stretching between Owl and Lick Creeks. This map shows the direction of the Confederate attack and the positions of the two armies at the end of first day. On the second day the Federals, having been strongly reinforced during the night, counterattacked and drove the Confederates from the field.

be possible." Beauregard had developed misgivings about making the attack, since they were a day late. He pictured the Federals now strongly entrenched, with cannons and muskets at the ready.

The reality, of course, was much different in the Northern camp. Corporal Charles Wright tells how the men of an Ohio company greeted the dawn:

We came out of our tents about the time the sun began to show itself in the east. It was Sunday morning, the air soft and balmy, and everyone remarked, "What a beautiful morning this is." . . . [A] smile was on each face, pleasant salutations passed between officers and privates, and I heard such remarks as these:

"Say, Bob, how would you like to be back in old Ohio today?"

"O, pshaw! Keep still! Don't tempt a fellow to desert!"

"Say, John, how would it suit to be back in Highland County this morning, fixin' to go to meetin' with that little girl of yours?"

And so in pleasant jest and repartee a short time was passed. Then came our breakfast of coffee, beans, meat and crackers. . . .

The Union divisions encamped closest to the advancing Confederates were those under Brigadier Generals Benjamin M. Prentiss and William Tecumseh Sherman (the latter promoted from colonel after Bull Run). A great many of the troops, says one of Sherman's officers, were "fresh from the recruiting camps, and wholly unpracticed, even in the simplest company manoeuvres."

A brigade commander serving under Prentiss, Colonel Everett Peabody, had sent out a patrol early that morning, and contact had been made with the enemy, but the warning was insufficient. The Confederates managed to spring what Beauregard calls "one of the most surprising surprises ever achieved."

Among Sherman's troops was a boy named Jesse Bowman Young, who later recorded:

The robins had been chirping in the woods since dawn, and the trees were full of music, when suddenly a sound not so melodious broke in on the ears of the soldiers, an occasional shot from the picket line a mile beyond the camp. . . . [A]s the firing continued . . . wild birds in great numbers, rabbits in commotion, and numerous squirrels came flocking toward the Union lines as though they were being driven from the woods. . . .

It was now almost six o'clock, and the neighboring infantry regiments showed tokens of alarm, and some of them began to form line of battle. By the time that hour actually came the firing had become quite heavy, a cannon shot now and then being heard in the midst of the musketry.

An officer said, ". . . The rebels must be attacking our outposts."

The words were scarcely spoken when a straggling squad of men came running by in great excitement, their officers in vain trying to keep them in order. They shouted the news that the Confederates were making an attack on the picket line with a heavy force. . . .

By this time the bugles had sounded, "Fall in—mount!" and the cavalry was soon in line. The long roll was beaten among the infantry regiments in every direction. The men were just at breakfast, and many of them had to spring into the ranks in a hurry, without waiting to drink their coffee or eat their hardtack.

Following pellmell after the first squad of retreating men came the whole regiment of infantry to which they belonged, and one or two wounded soldiers, all very much frightened, and running in dismay.

In a short time the Confederates were in sight, and young Jesse, suddenly under fire, took to his heels to escape injury or capture. Achieving momentary safety in a section of the line that was standing fast under Sherman's personal leadership, the boy found himself thinking: "I reckon this is going to be a great battle, such as I have been anxious to see for a long time. I think I have seen enough of it. I wish I was safely out of it and at home."

The attack soon began to develop along the whole Union front, which extended in a three-mile semicircle between two creeks that flowed toward the river, Owl Creek on the right and Lick Creek on the left. Colonel Wills de Hass writes that the encircling woods, so quiet the night before, now resounded with "the deep roar of heavy cannon and the sharp rattle of musketry."

The lines closed steadily on us, the enemy moving forward at all points. . . . Onward came the surging masses, backward fell our lines; then rallying would, by a terrific fire, check the shouting legions in gray! Checked again and again, they still pressed forward.

Often heard amid the general din was "the ear-piercing and peculiar Rebel yell." Jesse Young explains that

. . . there was a good deal of a panic at the beginning of the battle. The roads were filled with all manner of fugitives. . . . Army wagons, some empty and others full of rations and camp stores and baggage, were being driven toward the landing [on the Tennessee River], and other wagons with ammunition were trying to get to the front. . . . Sutlers' wagons were jammed into the midst of the throng of pale and frightened men, some of whom were only half dressed. . . .

Colored servants . . . were scampering out of the reach of the rebel bullets. Here and there a soldier had seized a mule or a horse and . . . had mounted the animal and was trying to force his way to the river. Officers were in vain attempting to quiet the alarm and organize the wild, surging, frantic mob that was pressing toward the place where the transports were tied up. Word was sent quickly down to the landing to have the steamers anchor in the middle of the stream and to let no one come on board.

The disorder wasn't wholly one-sided. General Beauregard laments that some of the Confederates "abandoned their colors . . . to pillage the captured encampments," and that others, coming under Union cannon and musket fire, "retired shamefully from the field." Many of the Confederates, like many of the Federals, were seeing their first combat.

The principal commanders under Johnston and Beauregard were Generals William J. Hardee, Braxton Bragg, Leonidas Polk, and John C. Breckinridge. Grant's top generals, in addition to Sherman and Prentiss, were Stephen A. Hurlbut, John A. McClernand, W. H. L. Wallace, and Lewis Wallace. The last-named (later to become famous as the author of Ben-Hur) *was stationed with about 7,000 men at Crump's Landing, about five miles northward along the river.*

Grant wasn't on the field when the battle opened. He had his headquarters at the Cherry Mansion in Savannah, about ten miles northward along the river, on the opposite shore. His reason for this was that General Buell's army, marching to reinforce him from Columbia, was coming by way of Savannah.

Grant had a painfully swollen ankle, acquired two days earlier as the result of a horseback accident, but he did not allow the injury to interfere with his response to the emergency:

While I was at breakfast . . . heavy firing was heard in the direction of Pittsburg Landing, and I . . . [sent] a hurried note to Buell informing him of the reason why I could not meet him at Savannah. On the way up the river I directed the dispatch-boat to run in close to Crump's Landing so that I could communicate with General Lew Wallace. I found him waiting on a boat apparently expecting to see me, and I directed him to get his troops in line ready to execute any orders he might receive. He replied that his troops were already under arms and prepared to move.

Grant arrived on the battlefield to find the Federals under heavy pressure all along their front. But, says Jesse Young, "He was cool and self-possessed in the midst of all the excitement, and seemed to mind the confusion no more than the scenes of a review."

In the words of Junius Henri Browne, special war correspondent of the New York Tribune:

Hotter and hotter grew the contest. . . . The light of the sun was obscured by the clouds of sulphurous smoke, and the ground became moist and slippery with human gore. . . . Men glared at each other as at wild beasts; and when a shell burst with fatal effect among a crowd of the advancing foe, and arms, legs, and heads were torn off, a grim smile of pleasure lighted up the smoke-begrimed faces of the transformed beings who witnessed the catastrophe. . . .

Men with knitted brows and flushed cheeks fought madly over ridges, along ravines, and up steep ascents, with blood and perspiration streaming down their faces. . . . Everywhere was mad excitement; everywhere was horror. Commanders galloped wildly to the front of their regiments and cheered them on . . . urging their spirited steeds wherever the troops were falling back, careless of their own life, as if they had a million souls to spare. . . .

There was no pause in the battle. The roar of the strife was ever heard. The artillery bellowed and thundered, and the dreadful echoes went sweeping down the river, and the paths were filled with the dying and the dead. The sound was deafening, the tumult indescribable. No life was worth a farthing. . . . Yonder a fresh regiment rushed bravely forward, and ere they had gone twenty yards a charge of grape sent the foremost men bleeding to the earth. . . . Death was in the air, and bloomed like a poison-plant on every foot of soil.

By this time the surgeons on both sides had set up field hospitals and were busy with the wounded. Amputation was commonly resorted to, with the discarded arms and legs beginning to form "gory, ghastly heaps."

General Beauregard says that the Confederate attack moved for-

ward "like an Alpine avalanche," and General Grant admits that "the National troops were compelled several times to take positions to the rear nearer Pittsburg Landing [on the river]."

Grant continues:

It was a case of Southern dash against Northern pluck and endurance. . . . I was continuously engaged in passing from one part of the field to another, giving directions to division commanders. In thus moving along the line, however, I never deemed it important to stay long with Sherman. . . . [He] inspired a confidence in officers and men that enabled them to render services on that bloody battlefield worthy of the best of veterans. . . .

A casualty to Sherman that would have taken him from the field that day would have been a sad one for the troops engaged at Shiloh. And how near we came to this! . . . Sherman was shot twice, once in the hand, once in the shoulder, the ball cutting his coat and making a slight wound, and a third ball passed through his hat. In addition to this, he had several horses shot during the day.

The nature of this battle was such that cavalry could not be used in front. I therefore formed ours into line in rear, to stop stragglers. . . . When there would be enough of them to make a show, and after they had recovered from their fright, they would be sent to reinforce some part of the line. . . .

On one occasion . . . I rode back as far as the river and met General Buell, who had just arrived. . . . [A]t that time there probably were as many as four or five thousand stragglers lying under cover of the river bluff, panic-stricken, most of whom would have been shot where they lay, without resistance, before they would have taken muskets and marched to the front to protect themselves.

This meeting between General Buell and myself was on the dispatch-boat used to run between the landing and Savannah. It was brief, and related specially to his getting his troops over the river. As we left the boat together, Buell's attention was attracted by the men lying under cover of the river bank. I saw him berating them and trying to shame them into joining their regiments.

Similar efforts were made by other commanders. Writes Douglas Putnam, Jr., one of Grant's aides:

I remember well seeing a mounted officer, carrying a United States flag, riding back and forth on top of the bank, pleading and entreating in this wise:

"Men, for God's sake, for your country's sake, for your own sake, come up here, form a line, and make one more stand."

The appeal fell on listless ears. No one seemed to respond, and the only reply I heard was someone saying, "That man talks well, don't he?"

Not all of the skulkers were at the river. Some crouched in ravines, others behind rocks or trees. Corporal Charles Wright, of Ohio, says that a member of his company named John Blake, who was on the sicklist that day, met with a strange sight while making his way from the battle zone to a safer place in the rear:

On coming to a large hollow log . . . he looked in . . . and beheld the insignia denoting a certain officer or rank in the United States Army. The patriot whose rank was thus shown had crawled the farthest into the log, and, crouched up to him as closely as possible, were two blue-coats who as yet bore no distinguishing marks, but who, no doubt, when they enlisted promised to follow where he led!

The number of Confederate stragglers, too, became "dangerously large," and cavalry units were assigned the task of rounding up as many as they could and sending them to the front.

For green troops in particular, the scenes at the front were appalling. Writes an unnamed Union captain:

I saw an intelligent-looking man with his whole diaphragm torn off. He was holding up nearly all of his viscera with both hands and arms. His face expressed a longing for assistance and an apprehension of fatality.

The same narrator adds:

After our regiment had been nearly annihilated, and [we] were compelled to retreat under a galling fire, a boy was supporting his dying brother on one arm . . . trying to drag him from the field and the advancing foe. He looked at me imploringly and said, "Captain, help him—won't you? Do, captain; he'll live."

I said, "He's shot through the head, don't you see? and can't live. He's dying now."

"O, no he ain't, captain. Don't leave me."

I was forced to reply, "The rebels won't hurt him. Lay him down and come, or both you and I will be lost."

The rush of bullets and the yells of the approaching demons hurried me away—leaving the young soldier over his dying brother.

*Among the spots on the battlefield where the attacking forces encoun-
tered strong opposition was a peach orchard on the Union left. The
trees were in full bloom, and the bullets, cannon fire, and reverbera-
tions of the fight caused the petals to fall like snow.*

It was near the peach orchard that the Confederates suffered one
of their worst blows. About two o'clock in the afternoon, an aide to
Albert Sidney Johnston noted with alarm that the general had begun
to turn pale and was swaying in the saddle. "General," cried the aide,
"are you wounded?" Johnston answered, "Yes, and I fear seriously."
It was learned that a rifle ball had severed a leg artery and that his
boot was filling with blood. He needed immediate first aid, but his
surgeon, by his orders, was some distance away, caring for a gathering
of wounded men, some of whom were Federals.

Writes General Beauregard:

Our commander-in-chief . . . died on the field at half-past two
P.M., after having shown the highest qualities of the commander and
a personal intrepidity that inspired all around him and gave resistless
impulsion to his columns at critical moments.

The chief command then devolved upon me, though at the time I
was greatly prostrated and suffering from the prolonged sickness with
which I had been afflicted. . . . The responsibility was one which, in
my physical condition, I would have gladly avoided, though cast upon
me when our forces were successfully pushing the enemy back upon
the Tennessee River. . . .

*At this time the Union center, having reformed after falling back
under the early attacks, was still standing fast. It was made up of elements of the divisions under Prentiss, Hurlbut, and W. H. L. Wallace.*

Explains Beauregard:

. . . in a strong, sheltered position, well backed by artillery and
held with great resolution, they repulsed a series of uncombined assaults. . . . Here General Bragg was directing operations in person. . . .

Relates Bragg's chief engineer, Colonel S. H. Lockett:

I witnessed the various bloody and unsuccessful attacks on the
"Hornet's Nest." During one of the dreadful repulses of our forces,
General Bragg directed me to ride forward to the central regiment of
a brigade of troops that was recoiling across an open field, [and] to
take its colors and carry them forward. "The flag must not go back
again," he said.

. . . I dashed through the line of battle, seized the colors from the [retreating] color-bearer, and said to him, "General Bragg says these colors must not go to the rear." While I was talking to him, the color-sergeant was shot down.

A moment or two afterward I was almost alone on horseback in the open field between the two lines of battle. An officer [Colonel H. W. Allen, later to become governor of Louisiana] came up to me with a bullet-hole in each cheek, the blood streaming from his mouth, and asked, "What are you doing with my colors, sir?"

"I am obeying General Bragg's orders, sir, to hold them where they are," was my reply.

"Let me have them," he said. "If any man but my color-bearer carries these colors, I am the man. Tell General Bragg I will see that these colors are in the right place. But he must attack this position in flank. We can never carry it alone from the front."

The position was now subjected to a heavy cannonade, and a combination attack followed. While pressure was maintained in front, other units swung to the right and left. The outcome is described by Union General Prentiss, who had succeeded in maintaining good communications with Hurlbut and W. H. L. Wallace, the other two division commanders involved:

When the gallant Hurlbut was forced to retire, General Wallace and myself consulted, and agreed to hold our positions at all hazards . . . we having been now informed . . . that all others had fallen back to the vicinity of the river. A few minutes [later] . . . Wallace received the wound of which he shortly afterwards died. Upon [his] fall . . . his division, excepting [four regiments] . . . retired from the field.

Perceiving that I was about to be surrounded . . . I determined to assail the enemy. . . . [But] I found him advancing in mass, completely encircling my command, and nothing was left but to . . . retard his progress so long as might be possible. This I did until 5:30 P.M., when, finding that further resistance must result in the slaughter of every man in the command, I had to yield the fight. The enemy succeeded in capturing myself and 2,200 rank and file, many of them being wounded.

Confederate Colonel S. H. Lockett says of the capture:

. . . [It] was a dear triumph to us—dear for the many soldiers we had lost in the first fruitless attacks, but still dearer on account of the valuable time it cost us [with the day fast waning]. The time consumed in gathering Prentiss's command together, in taking their arms, in marching them to the rear, was inestimably valuable. Not only that; the news of the capture spread, and grew as it spread. Many soldiers and officers believed we had captured the bulk of the Federal army, and hundreds left their positions and came to see the "captured Yanks."

Since the start of the battle at dawn, Grant's lines had been driven back nearly two miles. His left flank lay at Pittsburg Landing, his right about two miles inland. According to Whitelaw Reid, correspondent of the Cincinnati Gazette, *writing on the battlefield:*

We have lost nearly all our camps and camp equipage. We have lost nearly half our field artillery. We have lost a division general and two or three regiments of our soldiers as prisoners. We have lost . . . dreadfully . . . in killed and wounded. The hospitals are full to overflowing. . . . And our men are discouraged by prolonged defeat. Nothing but the most energetic exertion on the part of the officers prevents them from becoming demoralized.

Fortunately for the Federals, the Confederate effort was about spent for the day. Aided by a line of artillery set up near the river, and by the heavy weapons of the wooden gunboats Tyler *and* Lexington, *Grant's troops were able to withstand the final attacks.*

Since early afternoon, Grant had been looking anxiously for his expected reinforcements. The orders he had sent to General Lew Wallace at Crump's Landing had been misunderstood, and Wallace had marched his division on a circuitous route and was only now nearing the field. General Buell's troops from Columbia, now gathered at Savannah more than 20,000 strong, were beginning to cross the river on steam transports.

The first indication that many of the Federals on the battlefield had that reinforcements were crossing came in the nature of three great cheers from the skulkers under the river bank. For them to be cheering struck the more courageous observers as highly incongruous.

One of the tired and disheartened Union men positioned near the landing during the last exchanges of fire was Private Leander Stillwell, of Illinois:

As we were lying there I heard the strains of martial music and saw a body of men marching . . . up the road. I slipped out of ranks and walked out to the side of the road to see what troops they were.

Shiloh: the final clash of the first day.

Their band was playing "Dixie's Land." . . . The men were marching at a quick step. . . . I saw that they had not been in a fight, for there was no powder smoke on their faces.

"What regiment is this?" I asked of a young sergeant marching on the flank.

Back came the answer in a quick, cheery tone, "The 36th Indiana, the advance guard of Buell's army."

. . . I gave one big, gasping swallow, and . . . the blood thumped in the veins of my throat and my heart fairly pounded against my little infantry jacket in the joyous rapture of this glorious intelligence.

The Confederates had no certain knowledge at this time that Grant was being reinforced.

Beauregard takes up the narrative:

We had now had more than eleven hours of continuous fighting. . . . [T]he Confederate troops were not in a condition to carry such a position as that which confronted them at that late hour. . . . In fact, the troops had got out of the hands either of corps, divisional, or brigade commanders, and for the most part . . . at the front, were out of ammunition. . . . Comprehending the situation as it was, at six P.M. I dispatched . . . orders to cease hostilities, withdraw the troops from under fire of the Federal gunboats, and to sleep on their arms. . . . My headquarters for the night were established at the Shiloh Meeting House in the tent that General Sherman had occupied.

Returning to the Union lines and to Colonel Wills de Hass:

The Sabbath closed upon a scene which had no parallel on the Western Continent. . . . Night fell upon, and spread its funereal pall over, a field of blood where death held unrestrained carnival! Soon after dark the rain descended in torrents, and all through the dreary hours of that dismal night it rained unceasingly. The groans of the dying, and the solemn thunder of the gunboats [as they threw their heavy missiles toward the Confederate lines] came swelling at intervals high above the peltings of the pitiless storm.

In one way, the rain was a blessing. It extinguished brushfires that had started during the day and threatened the wounded who hadn't been carried from the field. Lightning flashed, and nature's thunder was added to that of the guns. With many of their tents in Confederate hands, large numbers of Federal troops lay unprotected on the ground. One of the lucky ones who found a tent was Jesse Young, the boy with Sherman's division. He writes of himself in the third person:

As the boy peered out of the tent through the woods, he saw them alternately lighted up with the glare of the lightning and then darkened with the gloom of the tempest. In a moment the darkness would be illuminated once more by the firing off of the cannon on the hill in front, and through the forest he could dimly discern the details of men who were searching with hurrying feet for the wounded and bearing them to hospitals in the rear. Mixed with other horrid sounds that smote his ears, he would catch every now and then an occasional cry of a maimed and mangled soldier crawling over the ground in quest of aid or lying helpless and bleeding on the wet earth. . . .

Even General Grant, though severely troubled by the injury he had suffered in the horseback accident two days before the battle, was exposed to the elements:

I made my headquarters under a tree a few hundred yards back from the river bank. My ankle was so much swollen . . . and the bruise was so painful that I could get no rest. The drenching rain would have precluded the possibility of sleep without this additional cause. Some time after midnight, growing restive under the storm and the continuous pain, I moved back to the log-house under the bank. This had been taken as a hospital, and all night wounded men were being brought in, their wounds dressed, a leg or an arm amputated, as the case might require, and everything being done to save life or alleviate suffering. The sight was . . . unendurable . . . and I returned to my tree in the rain.

Among the Confederates, the general mood that night was one of exhilaration—this in spite of their heavy losses, the relentless rain, and the Federal shellfire. As recorded by Southern historian Edward Pollard:
    . . . with the exception of a few thousand disciplined troops . . . the whole army degenerated into bands of roving plunderers, intoxicated with victory, and scattered in a shameful hunt for the rich spoils of the battle-field. All during the night thousands were out in quest of plunder. Hundreds were intoxicated with wines and liquors found; and . . . scenes of disorder and shouts of revelry arose around the large fires which had been kindled, and mingled with the groans of the wounded. . . .

Relates Unionist Charles Wright, the corporal from Ohio:
    Cold, hungry, and chilled through, we impatiently awaited the coming of another day. . . . [A]s soon as daylight made its appearance [the rain having stopped] we were on our feet and ready for the second act in the bloody drama. It had been our custom on being aroused in the morning to stir around and get breakfast, but the first order on the morning of the seventh of April was "Fall in, men! Dress on the colors!"
    . . . I could hear men remarking, "I wish they would give us time to make coffee!" We had not had any of that delicious and strengthening beverage since yesterday morning, and were growing faint for want of it.
    Finding that the forward movement without breakfast would soon take place, some of the 81st [Ohio Volunteer Infantry] began to wonder if their guns would go off, as they had lain on the ground all night in the rain. Bang! Bang! began to be heard along the line.
    Orders were issued immediately to "Stop firing, and draw your loads!" But some of the boys did not have the necessary implement to draw the load [i.e., remove it], and an irregular firing commenced, sounding much like a skirmish. I heard a plucky blue-coat in Com-

pany C remark, "I wonder if they think that we're going to march out there to be shot at, when maybe our guns won't go off and we can't shoot back!" Bang! went his Enfield. . . .

Here we stand in battle-array, in the early dawn . . . awaiting the order to move forward and renew the strife. . . . Buell's forces [and those under Lew Wallace] had arrived during the night and . . . were in the positions assigned them. When we lay down in line on the evening before, the enemy's flags fluttered within gunshot of us, but during the night they had fallen back, selected and occupied a strong position.

All is ready, and "Forward, march!" is the command. I glance to the left and catch glimpses of long lines of blue moving grandly against the enemies of my country; and waving proudly above the serried ranks was the dear old flag, doubly dear since the scenes of yesterday.

Many of the waiting Confederates had countered the chill dampness of the dawn with steaming cups of good Union coffee, those men who had spent much of the night in drunken revelry finding the liquid a particular blessing. Henry Morton Stanley felt refreshed "after a hearty replenishment of my vitals with biscuit and molasses." He was apprehensive, however, knowing that if the Federals had been reinforced during the night, "we had a bad day's work before us."

In General Beauregard's words:

About six o'clock . . . a hot fire of musketry and artillery—opened from the enemy's quarter on our advanced line—assured me of the junction of his forces; and soon the battle raged with a fury which satisfied me I was attacked by a largely superior force. But from the onset our troops, notwithstanding their fatigue and losses from the battle of the day before, exhibited the most cheering veteran-like steadiness. . . . Again and again our troops were brought to the charge . . . invariably to drive back their foe. But . . . opposed to an enemy constantly reinforced, our ranks were perceptibly thinned under the unceasing, withering fire. . . .

The gains made by the Confederate charges were only temporary. "This day," says General Grant, "everything was favorable to the Union side. . . . The enemy was driven back . . . as we had been the day before. . . ."

The ratio of confusion had also changed. Today it was the Confederates who were the more afflicted. One brigade commander,

Preston Pond, Jr., claims that he spent most of his time marching his men around the field:

I was ordered by General [Daniel] Ruggles to form on the extreme left and rest my left on Owl Creek. While proceeding to execute this order, I was ordered to move by the rear of the main line to support the extreme right of General Hardee's line. Having taken my position . . . I was . . . ordered by General Beauregard to advance and occupy the crest of a ridge in the edge of an old field. My line was just formed in this position when General Polk ordered me forward to support his line. While moving to the support of General Polk, an order reached me from General Beauregard to report to him with my command at his headquarters.

The new Federal spirit infected even the skulkers at the river, thousands of whom "seemed to be imbued with genuine manhood, and . . . returned to the front to render good service."

Corporal Wright of Ohio, one of the first to advance in the morning, tells how his unit, failing initially to hold its ground, pressed forward again:

We crossed a ravine where the dead of both armies lay thick. . . . We moved slowly and cautiously, knowing the enemy were close at hand, but whom the density of the undergrowth through which we were passing prevented us from seeing. . . . We emerge from the bushes, and there, directly in our front, not far away, are the rebels. They were moving. Both lines seemed to halt at the same instant, and the fire bursts from both lines simultaneously. . . .

While loading and firing as fast as possible, I happened to glance to the rear, and from that direction came a black man with gun in hand. . . . He came up on my left, gazed for a moment along the line of our blazing Enfield rifles, then shouted, "Give 'em hell, boys!" and running forward to an oak tree . . . he began to load and fire with an amazing rapidity. . . . He seemed to thoroughly enjoy the fight. . . .

Writes the unidentified Union captain already quoted in connection with the previous day's carnage:

. . . our regiment strode on . . . over wounded, dying, and dead. . . . I had an opportunity to notice incidents about the field. The regiment halted amidst a gory, ghastly scene. I heard a voice calling, "Ho, friend! Ho! For God's sake, come here." I went to a gory pile of dead human forms in every kind of stiff contortion. I saw one arm raised, beckoning me. I found there a rebel, covered with clotted blood, pillowing his head on the dead body of a comrade. Both were red from head to foot. The dead man's brains had gushed out in a reddish and grayish mass over his face. The live one had lain across him all that horrible long night in the storm.

The first thing he said to me was, "Give me some water. Send me a surgeon, won't you? O, God! What made you come down here to fight us? We never would have come up there."

. . . I filled his canteen nearly, reserving some for myself. . . . I told him we had no surgeon in our regiment . . . that other regiments were coming, and to call on them for a surgeon. . . . "Forward!" shouted the colonel, and . . . I left him. . . .

I ate my dinner . . . within six paces of a rebel in four pieces. Both legs were blown off. His pelvis was the third piece, and his head and chest were the fourth. . . . I saw five dead rebels in a row, with their heads knocked off by a round shot. Myself and other amateur anatomists, when the regiment was resting temporarily on arms, would . . . examine the internal structure of man. We would examine brains, heart, stomach, layers of muscles, structure of bones, etc., for there was every form of mutilation. At home I used to wince at the sight of a wound or of a corpse; but here, in one day, I learned to be among the scenes I am describing without emotion. . . .

Another Federal soldier who later penned a vivid account of the things he saw was sixteen-year-old John A. Cockerill. A regimental musician who had become detached from his unit, he followed in the wake of the attack as a spectator. Among the first things to catch his notice was "a motley crowd of Confederate prisoners" marching to the rear under guard. Another observer, he says, asked what company the prisoners belonged to:

A proud young chap in gray threw his head back and replied, "Company Q, of the Southern Invincibles—and be damned to you!" That was the spirit of that day and hour. . . .

The underbrush had literally been mowed off by the bullets, and great trees had been shattered by the terrible artillery fire. . . . All the bodies had been stripped of their valuables, and scarcely a pair of boots or shoes could be found upon the feet of the dead. In most instances, pockets had been cut open, and one of the pathetic sights that I remember was a poor Confederate lying on his back, while by his side was a heap of ginger cakes and sausage which had tumbled out of

the trousers pocket cut by some infamous thief. The unfortunate man
. . . had been killed before he had an opportunity to enjoy his
bountiful store. . . .

Further on, I passed . . . the corpse of a beautiful boy in gray
who lay with his blond curls scattered about his face and his hands
folded peacefully across his breast. He was clad in a bright and neat
uniform, well garnished with gold, which seemed to tell the story of
a loving mother and sisters who had sent their household pet to the
field of war. His neat little hat lying beside him bore the number of a
Georgia regiment. . . . He was about my age. . . . At the sight of
that poor boy's corpse, I burst into a regular boo-hoo, and started on.

Here beside a great oak tree I counted the corpses of fifteen men.
. . . The blue and the gray were mingled together. . . . It was no
uncommon thing to see the bodies of Federal and Confederate lying
side by side as though they had bled to death while trying to aid each
other. . . .

Here and there in the field, standing in the mud, were . . . poor
wounded horses, their heads drooping, their eyes glassy and gummy,
waiting for the slow coming of death, or for some friendly hand to
end their misery. . . .

As I pushed onward to the front, I passed the ambulances and the
wagons bringing back the wounded, and talked with the poor, bleeding fellows who were hobbling toward the river along the awful roads
or through the dismal chaparral.

*The number of dead produced by the battle astonished even General
Grant:*

I saw an open field . . . over which the Confederates had made
repeated charges the day before, so covered with dead that it would
have been possible to walk across . . . in any direction, stepping on
dead bodies without a foot touching the ground.

Grant relates a personal story:

. . . I had been moving from right to left and back, to see for
myself the progress made. In the early part of the afternoon, while
riding with Colonel James B. McPherson and Major J. P. Hawkins,
then my chief commissary, we got beyond the left of our troops. We
were moving along the northern edge of a clearing. . . .

. . . suddenly a battery [supported] with musketry opened upon
us from the edge of the woods on the other side of the clearing. The

shells and balls whistled about our ears very fast for about a minute. I do not think it took us longer than that to get out of range and out of sight. In the sudden start we made, Major Hawkins lost his hat. He did not stop to pick it up.

When we arrived at a perfectly safe position, we halted to take an account of damages. McPherson's horse was panting as if ready to drop. On examination it was found that a ball had struck him forward of the flank, just back of the saddle, and had gone entirely through. In a few minutes the poor beast dropped dead. He had given no sign of injury until we came to a stop.

A ball had struck the metal scabbard of my sword, just below the hilt, and broken it nearly off. . . . There were three of us: one had lost a horse . . . one a hat, and one a sword-scabbard. All were thankful that it was no worse.

Writes Union General Lew Wallace, whose division fought on the right:

. . . step by step, from tree to tree, position to position, the rebel lines went back . . . infantry, horses, and artillery—all went back. The firing was grand and terrific. . . . To and fro, now in my front, then in Sherman's, rode Gen. Beauregard, inciting his troops and fighting for his fading prestige of invincibility.

The desperation of the struggle may be easily imagined. While this was in progress, far along the lines to the left the contest was raging with equal obstinacy. As indicated by the sounds, however, the enemy seemed retiring everywhere. Cheer after cheer rang through the woods, and each man felt the day was ours.

The officers of General Beauregard's staff were now gravely concerned. Says Adjutant General Thomas Jordan:

. . . our losses were swelling perilously, and the straggling was growing more difficult to restrain. A little after two o'clock, Governor [Isham G.] Harris of Tennessee . . . taking me aside, asked . . . whether there was not danger in tarrying so long in the field as to be unable to withdraw in good order. . . . Having an opportunity a moment later to speak to General Beauregard in private, I brought the subject before him. . . .

"General, do you not think our troops are very much in the condition of a lump of sugar thoroughly soaked with water, but yet preserving its original shape though ready to dissolve? Would it not be judicious to get away with what we have?"

Beauregard had already made up his mind to disengage "from so unequal a conflict."

Officers of my staff were immediately despatched with the necessary orders to make the best disposition for a deliberate, orderly withdrawal from the field, and to collect and post a reserve to meet the enemy, should he attempt to push after us.

The withdrawal began, with the Federals making no earnest move to disrupt it. The Confederate reserve was posted on a ridge overlooking the ground around Shiloh Church, where the battle had begun the day before. Beauregard continues:

. . . from this position our artillery played upon the woods beyond for a while, but upon no visible enemy and without reply. Soon satisfied that no serious pursuit would be attempted, this last line was withdrawn. . . . A second position was taken up about a mile in the rear, where the approach of the enemy was waited for nearly an hour, but no effort to follow was made, and only a small detachment of horsemen could be seen at a distance . . . warily observing our movements.

There seemed to be a consensus among both officers and men on the Union side that they had endured more than enough savage fighting, and that their objectives had been accomplished. Writes Whitelaw Reid, of the Cincinnati Gazette:

The camps were regained. The rebels were repulsed. Their attack had failed. We stood where we began. . . . And so ended the battle. . . .

With pride in their success, and with a profound sense of relief, the Union survivors set about reestablishing themselves in their camps. A private from Ohio, R. H. Griner, expressed what was probably the basic feeling of the great majority, when, pausing in the midst of appeasing his hunger with a ration of pigs' feet and crackers, he heaved a deep sigh and said, "Well, I'm here yet!"

By this time the Confederates had formed into columns and were on the march back to Corinth, Mississippi. Wounded men were everywhere in evidence. Lieutenant William G. Stevenson was later to write:

. . . I saw more of human agony and woe than I trust I will ever again be called on to witness. The retreating host wound along a narrow and almost impassable road. . . . Here was a long line of wagons loaded with wounded, piled in like bags of grain, groaning and cursing; while the mules plunged on in mud and water. . . . Next came a straggling regiment of infantry, pressing on past the train of wagons; then a stretcher borne upon the shoulders of four men, carrying a wounded officer; then soldiers staggering along, with an arm broken and hanging down, or other fearful wounds. . . .

And to add to the horrors of the scene, the elements of heaven marshalled their forces. . . . A cold, drizzling rain commenced about nightfall, and soon came harder and faster, then turned to pitiless, blinding hail. . . . I passed long wagon trains filled with wounded and dying soldiers, without even a blanket to shield them. . . . Some three hundred men died during that awful retreat. . . .

In and around the Union encampment, of course, were many assemblages of wounded belonging to both sides. Large hospital camps were set up. As recorded by an officer named M. F. Force:

When news of the two days' fighting was received at the North, the people of the Ohio Valley and St. Louis were stirred to active sympathy. Steamboats bearing physicians, nurses, sisters of charity, and freighted with hospital supplies were at once despatched and soon crowded the shore of Pittsburg Landing. There was need for all the aid that was brought. Besides the thousands of wounded, were other thousands of sick.

Adds Jesse Young, the boy with Sherman's troops:

It was wonderful the attraction and reverence and admiration that the sight of a woman created in that wilderness. . . . The soldiers, hungry to see a woman's face and form, stood about the hospitals and transports, waiting by scores until one of the female nurses appeared. Then they would crowd up with grateful and respectful attentions and beg permission simply to shake hands.

Shiloh's final casualty figures staggered both the Union and the Confederacy. In killed, wounded, captured, and missing, the Federals lost over 13,000 men, while the Confederates lost about 10,700. Receipt of the tragic news was everywhere coupled with an awakening to the fact that the war was not to be settled quickly, as had been hoped for on both sides, but was very likely to be long and bloody.

In General Grant's words:

Up to the battle of Shiloh I, as well as thousands of other citizens, believed that the rebellion against the Government would collapse suddenly and soon if a decisive victory could be gained over any of its armies. Donelson and Henry were such victories. . . . But when [shortly afterward] Confederate armies were collected which not only attempted to hold a line farther south . . . but assumed the offensive and made such a gallant effort to regain what had been lost, then, indeed, I gave up all idea of saving the Union except by complete conquest.

7

McCLELLAN
APPROACHES RICHMOND

W HEN GENERAL MC CLELLAN, *after spending nearly eight months organizing and training his Army of the Potomac, finally yielded to the demands of the public and the government that he begin a move against Richmond, he insisted upon a plan that President Lincoln did not like. Instead of proceeding directly southward by land, as Lincoln wished, the Young Napoleon aimed to float his troops down the Potomac into the Chesapeake, make a landing on the Virginia coast, and march upon the city from the east.*

McClellan maintained that Virginia's coastal terrain was better suited to the march of a large army than that of the direct route, and that this way of approaching, since it would shorten the march, would enable him to make a quick strike at the Confederacy's heart. A march southward from Washington, he said, would probably require him to fight several battles along the way. (The Confederates, however, were no longer positioned close to Washington, having fallen back toward their own capital.)

The final version of McClellan's plan called for him to float his forces to Union-held Fort Monroe, at the tip of the Virginia Peninsula, the neck of land between the York and James rivers. A march up the Peninsula to Richmond, he felt, could be made in "complete security," since his flanks would be protected by the York and James.

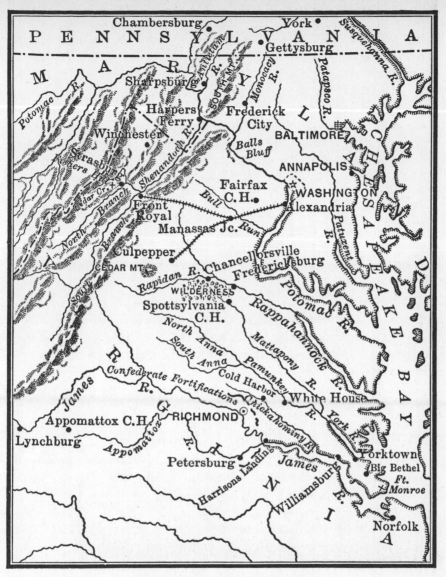

Field of operations in Virginia.

He expected these waterways to be seized on his behalf by the Union navy.

Though Lincoln consented to McClellan's plan, he feared that it might have the effect of leaving Washington unprotected, susceptible to an advance not only from the direction of Richmond, but also from the Shenandoah Valley, roughly fifty miles west of Washington. (Among the Confederates in the Valley at this time, incidentally, was the little-known but resourceful Stonewall Jackson.)

In mid-March, 1862, McClellan's army began assembling on the banks of the Potomac between Washington and Alexandria for an amphibious operation which "had scarcely any parallel in history." Some 400 makeshift transports of all types and sizes, from canal boats to three-decked steamers, had been gleaned from the waterways of the Northeast. Requiring more space than the troops themselves was their equipage, which included more than 1,200 wagons and ambulances, about 300 pieces of artillery, many tons of ammunition, 15,000 horses, mules, and beeves, mountains of crated rations, and numberless bales of forage.

The Reverend A. M. Stewart, chaplain of a Pennsylvania regiment, says that on the day he and his unit arrived at Alexandria at least a hundred vessels were lying within sight. They were being loaded with equipage and with "regiments, brigades, whole divisions of the great army."

At the passing of some general (or other exciting event) ten thousand voices would well up in shouts together, while numerous bands of martial music made river, hills, and adjacent cities vocal. The multitudes had come from their camps of long confinement and were wild with excitement.

. . . On Thursday morning [March 27] the vast armament began to move down the river. . . . We presently glided past Mount Vernon, the nation's shrine; and the . . . tomb of Washington showed itself from among the overhanging trees. . . . Could the Father of His Country have looked out from his tomb on the passing pageant . . . his exclamation would, no doubt, have been, "What! And where are you going?"

Few of the troops could have answered such a query, for Little Mac's plans had not been circulated. Writes Warren Lee Goss, a soldier from Massachusetts:

The general opinion among us was that at last we were on our way to make an end of the Confederacy. We gathered in little knots on the deck, here and there a party playing penny ante; others slept or dozed; but the majority smoked and discussed the probabilities of our destination. . . . That we were sailing down the Potomac was apparent. The next day we arrived . . . at Fortress Monroe, huge and frowning.

Adds French-born P. Regis de Trobriand, a Union officer from New York:

P. Regis de Trobriand.

The Reverend A. M. Stewart.

There, as at Alexandria, the river was covered with vessels. But one alone drew all eyes and absorbed all attention. . . . [T]he little *Monitor,* at anchor but always under steam, still watched, night and day, for a possible sortie of the *Merrimac.* . . .

Chaplain Stewart found himself impressed by the sight of "the troops busy landing, forming into long lines, and marching away . . . across the sandy beach and out towards the dark woods of the Peninsula." Camps were set up a mile or two inland. They stretched across the Peninsula from Newport News to Hampton. A few days later, the chaplain wrote:

The whole region seems literally filled with soldiery. One of the finest armies ever marshalled on the globe now wakes up these long stagnant fields and woods. Gen. McClellan is here, and commands in person.

Relates enlisted man Warren Goss:

One morning [April 4] we broke camp and went marching up the Peninsula. The roads were very poor, and muddy with recent rains, and were crowded with the indescribable material of the vast army which was slowly creeping through the mud over the flat, wooded country.

The few Confederate soldiers sighted during the day fell back before the advance. Regis de Trobriand writes that his regiment encountered only "some troops of hogs, half wild and complete rebels, who furnished a welcome addition to the soldiers' supper." He says of the next day:

The small number of houses . . . which were on the line of our march were all abandoned. Their occupants had left on our approach. . . . [N]ear a deserted hut we met four children crouched at the side of the road. . . . Their mother was dead, and their father had abandoned them. They wept while asking for something to eat. The soldiers immediately gave them enough provisions to last them several days. . . . But what became of these children? One does not like to think about such things. This is the horrible side of war.

According to Goss, the foot troops were now beginning to feel the weight of their knapsacks:

Castaway overcoats, blankets, parade-coats, and shoes were scattered along the route in reckless profusion. . . . The colored people along our route occupied themselves in picking up this scattered property. They had on their faces a distrustful look, as if uncertain of the tenure of their harvest.

That day the Federal columns were brought to a standstill before a line of Confederate entrenchments that extended across the Peninsula at Yorktown. The works held less than 15,000 men, but they looked very strong to McClellan, and he chose to encamp before them rather than attack. Lincoln quickly urged by letter: "I think it is the precise time for you to strike a blow." But the cautious McClellan "sat quietly down to a siege." Thousands of Union men were set to digging entrenchments and preparing emplacements for siege guns.

This gave the Confederates time to bring in reinforcements. The area where they had chosen to make their first stand was an historic one. Eighty years earlier, events at Yorktown had played a leading part in settling the American Revolution. Now the Reverend Nicholas A. Davis, chaplain of a Texas regiment, was moved to write:

How many pleasing recollections crowd upon the mind of each soldier as he walks over these grounds, or, sitting thoughtfully by his fagots, recalls the history of the past and compares it with the scenes of the present. The patriots of the Revolution were struggling for liberty, and so are we.

The hallowed soil was at this time miserably muddy as the result of repeated rainstorms, but the besieged men had to huddle close to it, for McClellan's army boasted many sharpshooters. On the other hand, explains the Union's Warren Goss:

The firing from the enemy's lines was of little consequence, not amounting to over ten or twelve [artillery] shots each day, a number of these being directed at the huge balloon which went up daily . . . from near General Fitz John Porter's headquarters.

Some of this observation work was done by General Porter himself, and Northern newspapers were soon saying of one of his ascents:

. . . when about one hundred feet above the ground, the rope anchoring the balloon broke, and the general sailed off . . . toward Richmond at a greater speed than the Army of the Potomac is moving. He . . . had sufficient calmness to pull the valve rope, and gradually descended, reaching the ground in safety [and received by friendly hands] about three miles from camp.

These were anxious days in Richmond, which lay about sixty miles northwest of Yorktown. Citizen John Minor Botts, then in jail as a result of his Union sympathies, tells of conditions in mid-April:

I . . . expected "Little Mac" in Richmond before the end of the week . . . as the authorities were then prepared for an evacuation rather than meet his greatly superior force, which they were by no means prepared to encounter—McClellan's force at that time being certainly not less than from eighty to a hundred thousand, and Johnston's not exceeding forty-five thousand. . . .

When finding "Little Mac" would listen neither to the persuasion nor . . . orders of his superiors . . . their alarm abated, and . . . they passed the first conscript act, under which the young conscripts poured into Virginia from all parts of the Confederacy. . . .

According to Constance Cary Harrison, another Richmond resident:

The gathering of many troops around the town filled the streets with a continually moving panorama of war, and we spent our time in greeting, cheering, choking with sudden emotion, and quivering in anticipation of what was yet to follow. . . .

. . . President Davis was a familiar and picturesque figure on the streets, walking through the Capitol square from his residence to the executive office in the morning, not to return until late in the afternoon, or riding just before nightfall to visit one or another of the encampments near the city.

Also in Richmond at this time was General Robert E. Lee, recently appointed the President's chief military adviser. Joe Johnston continued to command in the field.

In early May, a month after he had opened his siege, McClellan prepared to hit the Yorktown lines with an all-out bombardment and follow with an assault. But he was anticipated. Knowing that they had delayed the Federal advance as long as they could without suffering heavily, the Confederates began retiring up the Peninsula. The lines were taken without a fight. McClellan was highly pleased with his work, and he telegraphed Washington:

The success is brilliant, and you may rest assured that its effects will be of the greatest importance. There shall be no delay in following up the rebels.

The roads were still bad from too much rain, and one Confederate officer later claimed that the retreat was made "neither by land nor water, but by a half-and-half mixture of both."

On May 5, the day after the occupation of the Yorktown works, advance units of McClellan's army fought a daylong battle with the Confederate rear guard, entrenched at Williamsburg. McClellan himself, delayed by administrative matters at Yorktown, did not reach the field till near the day's end, when the fight was dwindling to an indecisive close. Says McClellan in a letter to his wife:

I found everybody discouraged . . . our troops in wrong positions . . . no system, no co-operation, no orders given, roads blocked up. As soon as I came upon the field the men cheered like fiends, and I saw at once that I could save the day. I immediately reinforced [General Winfield S.] Hancock and arranged to support [General Joseph] Hooker, advanced the whole line . . . filled up the gaps, and got everything in hand for whatever might occur. The result was that the enemy saw that he was gone if he remained in his position, and scampered during the night.

McClellan convinced himself that his army had given the foe "a tremendous thrashing," and he informed Washington: "The victory is complete." Actually, the Federals had suffered the greater losses (about 2,200, compared to about 1,700); and the Confederates viewed the affair as only a delaying action intended to ensure the safe retreat

Robert E. Lee.

*of their baggage. Many soon came to believe that the stand had gained
them something further. Writes Adjutant Robert Stiles, of the Richmond Howitzers:*

Williamsburg . . . let General McClellan see that it would not
be well for him to seriously interfere with . . . our "change of base,"
or "retreat," if one prefers that term. . . . [A]fter Williamsburg our
army was allowed to pursue its march very leisurely up the Peninsula. . . .

*In fairness to McClellan, it must be explained that he had begun the
campaign with a set of concerns he hadn't anticipated when he
planned it. In the first place, two-thirds of General Irvin McDowell's
corps had been withheld from his army; Lincoln felt that McClellan
had not allotted an adequate force to the defense of Washington.
Though McClellan brought this on himself by not consulting carefully with Lincoln about Washington's security, the deduction from
his forces threw him off balance; he considered his strength to be
seriously diminished. To make matters worse, he was getting inaccu-
rate information from his intelligence service, headed by Allan Pinkerton, a private detective before the war. Pinkerton's men persisted
in seeing double when it came to Confederates under arms, and Mc-
Clellan, who at this point had far the stronger force, came to believe
that he had the weaker!*

*A concern more solidly based was that the naval vessels at Fort
Monroe hadn't been able to give him the vigorous flank support (on
the York and James rivers) that he had expected. Actually, the campaign plan hatched in Washington hadn't been explicit regarding the
navy's cooperation, and the captains at Fort Monroe considered it
their primary concern to keep the* Merrimac *from interfering with
McClellan's advance. This problem was removed after McClellan
occupied Yorktown and Williamsburg, which forced the Confederates
to abandon Norfolk, home of the formidable ironclad. Despairing of
getting the deep-drafted vessel up the James to Richmond, her crew
ran her ashore near Craney Island, across Hampton Roads from the
scene of her triumph of March 8, and set her afire. About 4:30 A.M. on
May 11, according to a Union report from Fort Monroe:*

. . . an explosion took place which made the earth and water
tremble for miles around. In the midst of the bright flame which
shot up . . . the timbers and iron of the monster steamer could be
seen flying through the air. No doubt was entertained that the . . .
Merrimac had ceased to exist.

Writes the Monitor's *second-in-command, S. Dana Greene:*

With the evacuation of Norfolk and the destruction of the *Merrimac,* the *Monitor* moved up the James River with the squadron under the command of Commander John Rodgers, in connection with McClellan's advance upon Richmond by the Peninsula.

The Merrimac's *crew were still in the picture. John Taylor Wood says that they marched to Suffolk, Virginia, and boarded a train for Richmond:*

It only remains now to speak of our last meeting with the *Monitor.* Arriving at Richmond, we heard that the enemy's fleet was ascending James River, and the result was great alarm; for, relying upon the *Virginia* [the *Merrimac*], not a gun had been mounted to protect the city from a water attack. We were hurried to Drewry's Bluff, the first high ground below the city, seven miles distant. Here, for two days, exposed to constant rain, in bottomless mud, and without shelter, on scant provisions, we worked unceasingly, mounting guns and obstructing the river. In this we were aided by the crews of small vessels which had escaped up the river before Norfolk was abandoned. . . .

. . . on the 15th of May the iron-clad *Galena* [the Union navy's newest experiment in revolutional warships] . . . followed by the *Monitor* and three others, hove in sight. We opened fire as soon as they came within range, directing most of it on the *Galena.* . . . Coming up within six hundred yards . . . she anchored, and . . . presented her broadside. . . . The *Monitor,* and others anchored just below, answered our fire deliberately; but owing to the great elevation of [our] battery, their fire was in a great measure ineffectual, though two guns were dismounted and several men were killed and wounded. While this was going on, our sharp-shooters were at work on both banks. . . .

Finding they could make no impression on our works, the *Galena,* after an action of four hours, returned down the river with her consorts. . . . Had Commander Rodgers been supported by a few brigades . . . Richmond would have been evacuated. The *Virginia's* crew alone barred his way to Richmond. . . .*

---

* The *Monitor* survived the *Merrimac* by only seven and a half months. She foundered in heavy seas off Cape Hatteras, North Carolina, on December 30, 1862, taking down with her sixteen of her crew, the rest being rescued by the vessel that had her in tow.

This is the way it was on the James. On the York, across the Peninsula to the northeast, there was also activity. Though the greater part of McClellan's army advanced toward Richmond by land, several divisions went part of the way by water, the transports being protected by naval gunboats. These divisions were soon followed by fleets of supply vessels that entered the mouth of the Pamunkey and continued to White House, some twenty miles east of Richmond. Here was established a combination supply depot and base of operations.

By May 20, McClellan's troops were beginning to form along a fifteen-mile front reaching around Richmond's northeast side. The Chickahominy River lay along this line, and McClellan divided the army, placing three of his corps along the north bank and two along the south. It was necessary for him to keep troops north of the river in order to maintain contact with his supplies at White House, and also because he was looking northward for Irvin McDowell's corps (reinforced, since the campaign began, to nearly 40,000 men), which Lincoln, after several appeals, had agreed to send to his support.

Unhappily for McClellan, McDowell's corps failed to arrive. Stonewall Jackson, operating in the Shenandoah Valley, saw to that. With inferior numbers, he conducted a whirlwind campaign (one to be studied ever after by serious military men the world over) that kept the area's several Union commands badly off balance, caused alarm for the safety of Washington, and prompted Lincoln to retain McDowell to deal with the crisis.

McClellan and his men were now within sight of Richmond's church spires. The situation from the Confederate point of view is described by Edward Pollard, at the time editor of the Richmond Examiner:

The investment of the line of the Chickahominy brought the two armies face to face . . . and opened one of the grandest scenes of the war. . . .

For nearly a year an immense labour had been expended upon the fortifications of Richmond. Earthworks . . . swept all the roads, crowned every hillock; and mounds of red earth could be seen in striking contrast with the rich green of the landscape. . . .

Beyond, through the open and cultivated country . . . stretched the camp of the enemy. . . . [T]he numerous tents . . . the vast trains of wagons, the powerful park of artillery, together with the fleet of steamers and transports [far away to the rear, on the Pamunkey] presented a striking contrast to the usually quiet country. . . .

There were alarm and excitement in the mixed and restless population of Richmond; and the popular feeling found but little assurance in the visible tremour of the authorities. The Confederate Congress had adjourned in such haste as to show that the members were anxious to provide for their own personal safety. President Davis sent his family to North Carolina. . . . At the railroad depots were piles of baggage awaiting transportation, and the trains were crowded with women and children going to distant points in the country. . . .

But the panic . . . was soon subdued on reflection, and shamed by the counsels of the brave and intelligent. The newspapers rebuked it in severe terms. . . .

The tardy battle for Richmond yet lingered. Public confidence and public courage rose each day of the delay.

McClellan had now been on the Peninsula for nearly two months. On May 25, Lincoln informed him: "I think the time is near when you must either attack Richmond or give up the job and come to the defense of Washington." The capital wasn't really in danger, but Stonewall Jackson kept the North thinking it might be. An attack on Richmond would end the threat.

But McClellan was beginning to have nagging doubts about his ability to capture the Confederate capital. He had decided, as he had at Yorktown, that no attack was possible unless preceded by extensive artillery fire. He considered himself to be in a precarious spot. A very real problem was that the weather continued wet, which not only kept the mud deep but swelled the rivers and creeks. McClellan's biggest concern, however, was his army's size. The "scoundrels" and "hounds" in Washington kept demanding quick action but failed to send him reinforcements in the numbers he told them he needed.

(Far behind were the days when the white-haired solons paid McClellan homage as the Union's Great Hope. Now some of them—particularly the more radical Republicans, who were impatient to see the South crushed—were calling him a traitor. McClellan, it must be noted, was a Democrat serving a Republican administration.)

Actually, a point had been reached where a larger army would have been a distinct asset to McClellan. He had given the enemy time to increase his fighting strength to about 80,000 men, while his own army numbered about 100,000. His edge was none too great for a general who planned to attack a heavily fortified position. McClellan, unfortunately, wasn't aware that he had any edge at all. The Pinkertons—and his own imagination—had him believing that he was outnumbered nearly 2 to 1.

McClellan's one great solace in this time of anxiety was that he continued to hold the confidence and affection of his army, the army he himself had created and brought to an excellent state of organization. The chief reasons for his popularity were that he showed an abiding interest in the men's welfare and never missed an opportunity to praise them. It did no harm that he also had an engaging way about him and made a dashing picture on horseback. His visits of encouragement to the various units were much looked for, and the men considered it a privilege to get the chance to cheer him.

Some of the regimental chaplains, however, suddenly found cause to question Little Mac's rectitude. Wrote the Reverend A. M. Stewart on May 26:

There is at present the most serious apprehension that the Grand Army of the Potomac is on the eve of a terrible and disgraceful defeat, not from the rebels but from *rum*. An order has been . . . carried into execution to issue each morning to every officer and soldier of the army half a gill [one-eighth of a pint] of whiskey. Gen. McClellan is said to be the author of this monstrous wrong, both to soldier and country. . . . All this . . . under profession of kindness to the soldier, a medicine . . . to prevent him from getting sick! . . . One day the barrel of poison failed to reach our regiment; the next, two half gills were issued; the result, *drunkenness*. . . . Never did I feel so tempted and pressed to relinquish the chaplain service and yield all to the control of Satan.

These were days of few duties for many of the troops, and, says enlisted man Warren Goss:

Considerable foraging was done, on the sly, about the neighboring plantations. . . . There was much tobacco raised in this section of country, and we found the barns filled with the best quality of tobacco in leaf. This we appropriated. . . . As all trades were represented in our ranks, that of cigar-maker was included, and the army rioted in cigars without enriching the sutlers.

The weather continued rainy, the Chickahominy stayed high, and there was widespread swampiness. In the Confederate lines, Colonel John B. Gordon was amused to note, the excess of water was often treated as a great joke:

. . . the Southern troops, as they returned from outpost duty, kept the camp in roars of laughter with soldier yarns about their experiences at night at the front: how one man . . . lay down on a log to catch a brief nap, and dreaming that he was at home in his little bed, turned himself over and fell off the log into the water at its side; how another, whose imagination had been impressed by his [swampy] surroundings, made the outpost hideous with his frog-like croaking or snoring. . . .

I recall one private who had a genius for drawing. . . . He would represent this or that comrade with a frog-like face and the body and legs of a frog, standing in the deep water, with knapsack high up on his back, his gun in one hand and a johnny-cake in the other—the title below it being Bill or Bob or Jake "on picket in the Chickahominy."

At the end of May, while McClellan still hesitated, Confederate General Joe Johnston decided to take the initiative, a move anxiously awaited by the people of Richmond, who, according to Constance Cary Harrison, "had begun to feel like the prisoner of the Inquisition in Poe's story, cast into a dungeon of slowly contracting walls." Johnston determined to throw a great part of his army against McClellan's left wing: the two corps (commanded by Generals Erasmus Keyes and Samuel Heintzelman) on the side of the Chickahominy closest to the city.

F. Colburn Adams, an officer with a New York cavalry unit stationed on the side of the river farthest from Richmond, says that Johnston's attack was preceded by one on the part of nature:

The morning of the 30th came in hot and sultry . . . and about noon heavy storm clouds rolled up in threatening masses and filled the heavens with darkness. Then a fierce wind howled through the forest and over the camps, spreading alarm everywhere. A fearful storm soon broke upon us in all its fury. Vivid flashes of lightning . . . coursed along our batteries from one end of the line to the other. . . . Now the lightning has killed two men in a shelter tent; now a battery has been struck and a gun carriage shattered. . . . Then the thunder crashed and rolled fiercely, the animals started and pricked up their ears at each flash of lightning, and the roar and violence of the storm increased. . . .

When night set in, the rain fell like a deluge, and continued, accompanied by this violent thunder and lightning, until nearly morning. Trees were uprooted, tents blown down, the bridges over the Chickahominy nearly swept away, and the very earth flooded.

Never did the prospect look so gloomy for an army. . . . The enemy could not fail to see his opportunity and take advantage of it. If he could crush our left wing while there was no hope of getting reinforcements over [the river], his victory would give new confidence to his troops, and be an advantage from which we should not soon recover.

Saturday morning, the 31st, was dull and wet. The storm had ceased; but the roads were flooded, the woods were weeping, and a pale gray mist hung over . . . the long belt of forest on the opposite side of the river. . . . The dark turbulent waters of the Chickahominy were rushing and surging through the meadow, filled with wreckwood from the bridges. All eyes were turned instinctively to the other side of the stream, to those woods and fields where our almost isolated left wing stood. . . .

At 10 o'clock the mysterious movement of a column of the enemy . . . was reported. At fifteen minutes to one o'clock our whole camp was startled by the sudden, crashing sound of infantry, and the deep roar of cannon. It seemed as if twenty thousand infantry had discharged simultaneously . . . in such rapid succession that it were impossible to count the volleys. . . . Then we heard the long roll beating on the opposite hills.

"As I thought," said General [William B.] Franklin, who had been nearly washed out of his tent during the night, and stood . . . in front of the door; "they have attacked us in our weakest point."

In another minute all was bustle and motion at General McClellan's headquarters [in the same area as Franklin's]. Staff officers and orderlies went and came at a rapid speed. . . . Bugles sounded along the line, cavalry began saddling up, artillerymen harnessed their batteries, infantry prepared to move, and all with a spirit and quickness that proved how anxious they were to proceed [across the river, if the surviving bridges permitted] to the relief of their comrades, now engaged in the terrible struggle.

This was the Battle of Fair Oaks—or Seven Pines, as the Confederates called it. The two points were about a mile apart, and the fight embraced both. The Southern attack was made by divisions under Generals G. W. Smith, James Longstreet, D. H. Hill, and Benjamin Huger. Though hampered by the watery terrain and by poor coordination, the attack advanced strongly. As described by the Prince de Joinville, a Frenchman serving as a volunteer aide to McClellan:

The pickets and sentries are violently driven in; the woods which surround Fair Oaks and Seven Pines are filled with clouds of the enemy's sharpshooters. The troops rush to arms and fight in desperation; but their adversaries' forces constantly increase, and . . . losses

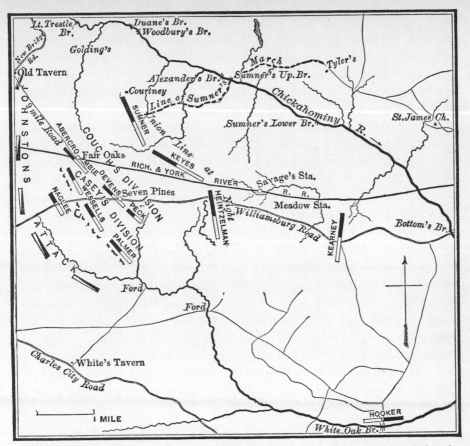

Battle of Fair Oaks, or Seven Pines. Johnston is attacking from left of map. Union troops are shown in their original position at Fair Oaks and Seven Pines, and also in their second position, closer to the Chickahominy. Broken line at top-center indicates Sumner's route across the river to reinforce the Union right.

do not stop them. The redoubt of the Seven Pines is surrounded, and its defenders die bravely. . . .

. . . Heintzelman rushes to the rescue with his two divisions. . . . [General Philip] Kearny arrives in good time. . . . [General Hiram G.] Berry's brigade, of this division, composed of Michigan regiments and an Irish battalion, advances firm as a wall into the midst of the disordered mass . . . and does more by its example than the most powerful reinforcements.

The action was nowhere hotter than in the section of the line occupied by Confederate Colonel John B. Gordon and his regiment.

Gordon says that he soon lost the three officers serving nearest him:

. . . I was left alone on horseback, with my men dropping rapidly around me. My soldiers declared that they distinctly heard the command from the Union lines, "Shoot that man on horseback." In both armies it was thought that the surest way to demoralize troops was to shoot down the officers. . . . Still I . . . marvellously escaped, with only my clothing pierced. As I rode up and down my line, encouraging the men forward, I passed my young brother, only nineteen years old but captain of one of the companies. He was lying with a number of dead companions near him. He had been shot through the lungs and was bleeding profusely. I did not stop. I could not stop; nor would he permit me to stop. There was no time for that—no time for anything except to move on and fire on. . . .

McClellan's men were slowly being pressed back into and through the Chickahominy swamp . . . but at almost every step they were pouring terrific volleys into my lines. . . . My field officers and adjutant were all dead. Every horse ridden into the fight, my own among them, was dead. Fully one half of my line officers and half my men were dead or wounded. A furious fire still poured from the front. . . . In water from knee- to hip-deep, the men were fighting and falling, while a detail propped up the wounded against stumps or trees to prevent their drowning.

On the Union side, the Pennsylvania regiment to which Chaplain Stewart belonged was having an altogether different experience with the water:

No enemy appeared in our front, for the reason, as we learned, of an intervening swamp. There we stood, for three hours, listening to that awful rage and din of battle, all the while vexed that we could not see the scene of strife, by reason of an intervening wood. At times the earth almost seemed to be tearing open, as ten thousand small arms, with scores of cannon, crashed together and mingled their roar with whizzing bullets, bursting shells, and the shouts and cheers of advancing or retiring columns. Whenever aught especially exciting happened, our whole regiment would send up three grand cheers.

These men finally received orders to march around to the right of the swamp, and they were shortly part of "a scene of horrid carnage."

Up to this point, writes the Union's Prince de Joinville:

About a mile of ground has been lost . . . but now . . . a sort of line of battle is formed across the woods . . . and there the repeated assaults of the enemy's masses are resisted. The left cannot be turned [by the enemy because of] . . . the White Oak Swamp, an impassable morass; but the right may be surrounded. At this very moment, in fact, [late in the afternoon] a strong column of Confederates has been directed against that side. . . .

But precisely at this moment . . . new actors appear on the scene. [Corps commander Edwin V.] Sumner, who has succeeded in passing the Chickahominy with [General John] Sedgwick's division, over the bridge constructed by his troops [before the flood, and designed with just enough strength to withstand it], and who, like a brave soldier, has marched straight through the woods to the sound of the cannon, arrives suddenly on the left flank of the [enemy] column. . . .

He plants in the clearing a battery which he has succeeded in bringing with him. . . . The simple and rapid discharging of these pieces makes terrible havoc in the opposing ranks. In vain Johnston sends against this battery his best troops. . . . Nothing can shake the Federals, who, at nightfall, valiantly led by Gen. Sumner in person, throw themselves upon the enemy at the point of the bayonet. . . .

In Confederate General Johnston's words:
It was . . . evident . . . from the obstinacy of our adversaries . . . that the battle would not be decided that day. I said so to the staff-officers near me, and told them that each regiment must sleep where it might be standing when the firing ceased for the night, to be ready to renew it at dawn next morning.

About half-past 7 o'clock I received a musket-shot in the shoulder, and was unhorsed soon after by a heavy fragment of shell which struck my breast. I was borne from the field. . . . The firing ceased before I had been carried a mile from it. The conflict . . . was terminated by darkness only.

Casualties were heavy on both sides. The South's John B. Gordon says of his regiment:
Nearly two-thirds . . . were killed or wounded. My young brother . . . who had been shot through the lungs, was carried back with the wounded. [The boy would make a good recovery—only to die of a similar wound later in the war.]

Writes F. Colburn Adams, of New York:
No pen can describe the agonies of that battlefield during this

Union wounded gathered in rows after the Battle of Fair Oaks. Signal
station in treetop.

fearful night. . . . [T]he dead of both armies, sometimes mingled
promiscuously, are scattered over the wet ground for a distance of
four miles. The groans and cries of the wounded and dying are heard
in every clump of trees. . . . Nourishment is not to be had. Medical
attendance is not a tithe of what it should be. . . .

According to Union narrator the Prince de Joinville:
   At the earliest dawn of day the combat was resumed with great
fury. . . . They fought with fierce determination on both sides. . . .
Toward midday the fire gradually diminished, then ceased. The enemy retreated, but the Federals were not in a position to pursue
them. . . . The conflict was a bloody one, for the North had lost
5,000 men, the South at least 8,000 [actually, about 6,000]; but the
results were as barren on one side as on the other.

*In Richmond, says Constance Cary Harrison, the battle's aftermath
was attended with great commotion:*
   . . . the whole town was on the street. Ambulances, litters, carts,
every vehicle that the city could produce, went and came with a
ghastly burden. Those who could walk limped painfully home, in
some cases so black with gunpowder they passed unrecognized.
Women with pallid faces flitted bareheaded through the streets

searching for their dead or wounded. The churches were thrown open
. . . for . . . prayer. The lecture-rooms of various places of worship
were crowded with ladies volunteering to sew, as fast as fingers could
fly, the rough beds [i.e., pads] called for by the surgeons. Men too old
or infirm to fight went on horseback or afoot to meet the returning
ambulances, and in some cases served as escort to their own dying
sons. By afternoon of the day following the battle, the streets were one
vast hospital. . . .

Day by day we were called to our windows by the wailing dirge of
a military band preceding a soldier's funeral. One could not number
those sad pageants: the coffin crowned with cap and sword and gloves,
the riderless horse following with empty boots fixed in the stirrups of
an army saddle; such soldiers as could be spared from the front
marching after with arms reversed and crape-enfolded banners; the
passers-by standing with bare, bent heads. Funerals less honored out-
wardly were [also] continually occurring.

*General McClellan emerged from the Battle of Fair Oaks feeling
deeply distressed over the "mangled corpses and poor suffering
wounded," but he was reanimated with optimism about his chances
for success. He wrote the Secretary of War:*

I only wait for the river to fall, to cross with the rest of the force
and make a general attack. Should I find them holding firm in a very
strong position, I may wait for what troops I can bring up from Fortress Monroe. But the morale of my troops is now such that I can venture much. I do not fear for odds against me.

He told his troops that the "final and decisive battle" was at hand:

Soldiers, I will be with you in this battle and share its dangers
with you. Our confidence in each other is now founded upon the past.
Let us strike the blow which is to restore peace and union to this dis-
tracted land.

*But even though reinforcements in substantial numbers shortly be-
gan arriving (some from Fort Monroe, others from points north), the
bold stroke wasn't ventured. The weather continued rainy, keeping
the river high and the earth muddy. Moreover, McClellan's bent for
caution reasserted itself. His army was much too important to the
Union cause to be exposed to "the slightest risk of disaster."*

*In mid-June the Confederates made another move—not a major
one but one that received major publicity. Dashing cavalryman Jeb*

Stuart, upon orders from General Robert E. Lee (who had assumed command of the Confederate forces in the field when Johnston was wounded), made a combination raid and reconnaissance around Mc-Clellan's right flank, then decided, on his own initiative, to continue the ride all the way around the Union army.

Writes Union trooper F. Colburn Adams:

Let us see what we did to intercept or cut off this bold raider. . . . Stuart had a father-in-law in our army . . . and what could be better than to send him in pursuit of his rebel son. If they came to sabres, and one got killed—why, it would all be in the family. . . . [General] Philip St. George Cooke . . . proceeded, with a force . . . of cavalry and a battery of artillery, in pursuit of his rebel son. . . . Whether this was a serious effort to overtake the bold raider or not I am unable to determine. . . . [T]he gallant father seems to have had some grave apprehensions of being captured and entertained by his rebel son, for he [soon] gave up the pursuit . . . and came back safe to us to report.

Other pursuers were equally ineffectual. Stuart's ride, according to one of his troopers, W. T. Robins, was completed at a cost of one man killed and a few wounded:

The [Confederacy] rang out with praises of the men who had raided entirely around General McClellan's powerful army, bringing prisoners and plunder from under his very nose. The Southern papers were filled with accounts of the expedition, none accurate, and most of them marvelous.

Union trooper Adams says that two or three days after the great ride . . . a smart little newsboy [from the Confederate camp] . . . came into our lines with a bundle of Richmond *Dispatches* containing an elaborate and well-written account of the deeds of valor performed by Stuart and his troopers. The boy had evidently been sent over by Confederate officers anxious that we should see their heroism in print. The boy sold his papers readily . . . but was much distressed when told that we should want him to stay and spend some time with us. . . . [O]ver the campfire that night . . . the little newsboy sang us songs and entertained us with stories concerning Richmond until nearly midnight.

The success of Jeb Stuart's ride not only embarrassed McClellan but also set him worrying about the possibility of his being cut off from

White House, on the Pamunkey, his supply depot and base of opera-
tions. Stuart had passed, raiding as he went, between White House
and the army.

Sickness was now rife in the Union ranks. The men had been
camped for a month in swampy terrain, much of it malarial. Pure
water was scarce. Since the Battle of Fair Oaks a terrible stench hung
over parts of the field, emphasizing another health hazard. Hundreds
of dead horses, only partly covered with earth, lay rotting. The same
was true of numbers of dead men. A letter written by Pennsylvania's
Chaplain Stewart says that "many a black, decaying hand and foot, or
even head, makes a ghastly projection."

The chaplain explains in the same letter that the attempt to com-
bat the swamp's evils with a daily ration of whiskey for each man had
been discontinued:

Let us bless the Lord together. . . . What new light has beamed
into the noddles of sage medical advisers and headquarter influences
can . . . only be guessed at. . . . Should no additional blindness induce the powers that be to renew the whiskey ration, we will . . .
have an absence of drunkenness among our rank and file. Get it here
they cannot.

The rains stopped at last, and McClellan concluded his preparations
to attack Richmond. "I will yet succeed," he wrote his wife, "not-
withstanding all they do, and leave undone, in Washington to pre-
vent it."

Only one of McClellan's corps, commanded by Fitz John Porter,
was now north of the Chickahominy, its mission to cover the supplies
at White House and to link up with Irvin McDowell's corps, still ex-
pected to make its appearance from the north.

As for the remarkable Stonewall Jackson, whose exploits in the
Shenandoah Valley had been detaining McDowell: Upon orders from
General Lee, he was presently in the process of bringing his army
secretly from the Valley to Richmond to help against McClellan.
Washington would not get certain information of this move until it
was too late to send McDowell to McClellan's support.

On June 23, McClellan wrote his wife that he believed himself
"ready for any eventuality," and that he expected to make a decisive
move on the twenty-fifth.

Says a Union enlisted man, John W. Urban:

Two armies—the largest ever marshalled on the Western continent—now stood confronting each other in such close proximity that

the advance pickets of the contending forces could converse together, and all felt that a mighty struggle was close at hand. And yet an amazing amount of good feeling, and even jollity, cropped out between these opposed pickets at times. A brisk trade in newspapers was kept up almost continually. The exchange of coffee for tobacco was a very usual thing.

Among the facetious things of these perilous posts was the conference between the Reb who called out, "Hello, Yank! What regiment do you belong to?"

"To the Ninety-ninth Rhode Island," was the ready reply.

". . . Good heavens!" cried the astonished questioner. "How many regiments must New York have if Rhode Island has ninety-nine?"

If McClellan heard this story, he probably wasn't amused, for he continued to believe that the Confederates had many more regiments than he.

The showdown between the two armies, coming after three months of preliminaries, wasn't to occur as McClellan had pictured it —that is, as one great battle. It was to be made up of a series of battles lasting for seven days.

8

THE SEVEN DAYS

THE SEVEN DAYS' *battles began on June 25, 1862, with a sharp but limited action in which McClellan advanced his lines a little closer to Richmond. This was intended to set the stage for a general advance the next day. But the move had come too late. General Lee, with Stonewall Jackson nearing the field from the northwest, was ready to take the offensive. Lee's numbers, with Jackson included, were now in the vicinity of 90,000 men, a strength finally beginning to make at least a respectable approach to that of McClellan.*

Confirmation of Jackson's proximity, which he already suspected, reached McClellan even as the action of the twenty-fifth was ending. In a bitter and despairing mood, he promptly informed Washington that reports indicated he was about to be assailed by 200,000 Confederates.

I regret my great inferiority in numbers, but feel that I am in no way responsible for it, as I have not failed to represent repeatedly the necessity of reinforcements. . . . I will do all that a general can do with the splendid army I have the honor to command, and, if it is destroyed by overwhelming numbers, can at least die with it and share its fate. But if the result of the action, which will probably occur tomorrow or within a short time, is a disaster, the responsibility cannot be thrown on my shoulders; it must rest where it belongs.

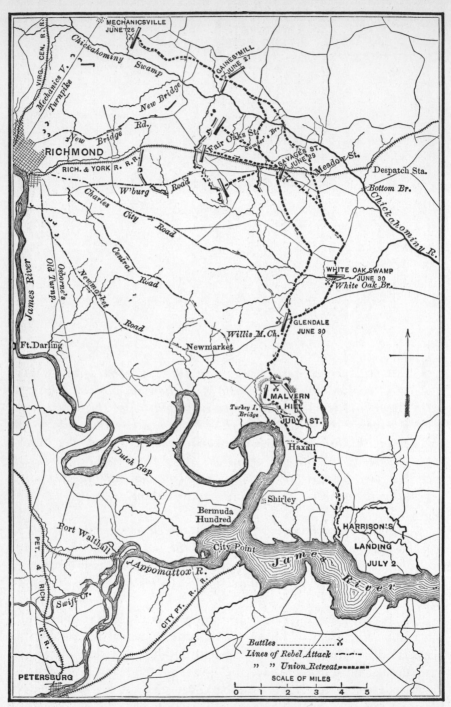

Battles .... ✕
Lines of Rebel Attack ·––·––·––·
  „   „   Union Retreat ▬▬▬▬▬▬

SCALE OF MILES

0   1   2   3   4   5

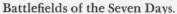
Battlefields of the Seven Days.

A. P. Hill.

But it wasn't McClellan's main body that Lee planned to attack. These lines, just east of Richmond, were very strong. Lee decided to steal northward from the Richmond defenses, cross the Chickahominy near Mechanicsville, and press down the north bank for an attack on the isolated corps under Fitz John Porter. Stonewall Jackson was expected to arrive from the northwest at the same time to hit Porter on the flank. Lee reasoned that this way of attacking McClellan would prompt him to do an about-face from Richmond in order to concentrate on saving his supplies at White House.

The plan was a daring one, for it would leave an inferior force in the Richmond defenses. This deficiency was to be overcome by the use of theatricals, their director being General John B. ("Prince John") Magruder. Early on the morning of June 26, with Lee's attack force—the divisions of Generals Longstreet, D. H. Hill, and A. P. Hill —already assembled at the river crossings, the men in the defenses began to maneuver and make a lot of noise, pretending to be a great army preparing for desperate combat. All day the show would continue, accompanied by periods of cannon fire and some busy minor attacks; and it would serve its purpose well, convincing McClellan that the defenses had been left strongly manned.

But McClellan had not been caught unaware by Lee's move toward Fitz John Porter's corps. A reception for such a move had been prepared. Porter relates:

The morning . . . dawned clear and bright, giving promise that the day would be a brilliant one. The formation of the ground south of the Chickahominy . . . largely concealed from view the forces gathered to execute an evidently well-planned and well-prepared attack upon my command. For some hours, on our side of the river, all was quiet, except at Mechanicsville and at the two bridge-crossings. At these points our small outposts were conspicuously displayed for the purpose of creating an impression of numbers and of an intention to maintain an obstinate resistance. We aimed to invite a heavy attack [on the outposts], and then, by [their] rapid withdrawal [down the river bank to join the main force in a strongly entrenched position], to incite such confidence in the enemy as to induce incautious pursuit.

In the northern and western horizon vast clouds of dust arose, indicating the movements of Jackson's advancing forces. They were far distant, and we had reason to believe that the obstacles to their rapid advance, placed in their way by detachments sent for that purpose, would prevent them from making an attack that day.

Jackson's failure to reach the field caused the Confederates to hesitate until well into the afternoon. Fitz John Porter continues:

About 2 o'clock . . . the boom of a single cannon in the direction of Mechanicsville resounded through our camps. This was the signal which had been agreed upon, to announce the fact that the enemy were crossing the Chickahominy. The curtain rose; the stage was prepared for the first scene of the tragedy. . . . About 3 o'clock the enemy . . . in large bodies commenced rapidly to cross the Chickahominy. . . .

The attack on the outpost line at Mechanicsville, as observed from the hills of Richmond, is described by citizen Edward Pollard:

As the Confederates advanced . . . artillery on both sides opened with a terrific roar. . . . The flash of guns and long lines of musket fire could be seen in bright relief against the blue and cloudless sky.

A party of civilians that included President Davis and his Secretary of War appeared on the battlefield at this time, much to the displeasure of General Lee, who was worried about their safety. He told them sternly that they did not belong there. They dropped back a short way and took cover, not for safety's sake but to escape the eye of Lee, "who at that moment was more to be dreaded than the enemy's guns."

According to Edward Pollard, the Confederates soon began rushing upon the Federal line "through infernal showers of grape."

A few moments more and the Federal guns were silent; a loud noise of many voices was heard; and then a long, wild, piercing yell, and the place was ours.

The Federals of the outposts withdrew down the river to Fitz John Porter's main entrenchments, and the Confederates prepared to follow.

Writes Union trooper F. Colburn Adams:

The enemy's line presents an imposing appearance . . . stretching back for a distance of two miles. His banners are flaunting, his drums beating; his arms flash and gleam in the sun's rays, and his cavalry and artillery add their force to the grand display.

Adams goes on to say that the Confederate advance, covered by artillery fire, was made "with a bold and defiant air."

In the Union entrenchments, which lay just behind Beaver Dam Creek (a tributary of the Chickahominy), the foremost lines were manned by General George A. McCall's division, with the brigade of General John F. Reynolds on the right, and that of General Truman Seymour on the left. Relates Union soldier John W. Urban:

As the enemy's troops came within range of McCall's artillery, the batteries . . . opened on them with the most terrific effect; but the enemy . . . pressed forward to the assault with the most desperate courage. . . .

. . . a part of the ground was low and swampy, making it almost impossible for troops to cross. Into this a part of the rebel column charged, and a scene of the most indescribable confusion, horror, and tumult ensued. Hundreds of the men and horses sank into the mire and were shot down by the deadly rifles of the first brigade [that of Reynolds]. . . .

Gen. Lee, finding he could not storm [the right of] the position . . . sent a strong column . . . for the purpose of turning the left. . . . [T]he enemy met the same repulse they had received on our right.

Fitz John Porter takes up:

Late in the afternoon . . . they renewed the attack with spirit and energy, some reaching the borders of the stream, but only to be repulsed with terrible slaughter, which warned them not to attempt a renewal of the fight. . . . [W]hen night came on, they all fell back beyond the range of our guns.

Lingering smoke deepened the field's shadows, and the sounds of battle were replaced by "the moans of the dying and the shrieks of the wounded."

General McClellan, who had spent the afternoon with Fitz John Porter and his corps, lost no time telegraphing Washington: "Victory today complete and against great odds. I almost begin to think we are invincible." In this mood, McClellan considered planning a new offensive. But his concern about Lee's "overwhelming numbers" quickly regained the upper hand. He saw proof of Lee's strength in that he had divided his forces. Lee would not have made an attack north of the river, McClellan reasoned, without leaving a large army in the Richmond defenses. McClellan was particularly worried about Stonewall Jackson, who had reached a point near Fitz John Porter's right flank. A sweep around this flank would place the Confederates between McClellan and White House, cutting the army's supply line.

McClellan's answer to this threat was to order the evacuation of White House and the establishment of a new base at Harrison's Landing, which lay southward across the Peninsula, on the James River. Actually, as a precaution, he had begun preparing for such a move more than a week earlier, at which time he had sent a flotilla of supply-laden vessels down the York and up the James. Of the rest of the supplies, some would have to be destroyed, others would follow the first flotilla, and still others would be transported by land—the operation to include a great drive of beef cattle. In conjunction with these measures, the entire army was to make its way across the Peninsula to the same place. Years later, McClellan was to explain (professing a confidence he did not really feel at the time):

To that end, from the evening of the 26th, every energy of the army was bent. Such a change of base, in the presence of a powerful enemy, is one of the most difficult undertakings in war, but I was confident in the valor and discipline of my brave army, and knew that it could be trusted . . . to fight the series of battles now inevitable, whether retreating from victories or marching through defeats; and, in short, I had no doubt whatever of its ability, even against superior numbers, to fight its way through to the James and get a position whence a successful advance upon Richmond would be again possible.

In other words, McClellan planned to retreat, fighting off Lee as he went, to a point about twenty miles southeast of Richmond. At Harrison's Landing the army would be relatively safe. Not only was the ground well-suited to defensive deployment, but there the army would have the close support of the navy. Moreover, the army would be in union with its supplies. From this base, after suitable preparations, McClellan planned to renew his efforts against the Confederate capital. He was certain that Washington would now understand that he had been right all along, that the Confederates outnumbered him badly, and that the success of the campaign depended on his being given strong reinforcements.

In order for McClellan to effect the evacuation of White House and lay the groundwork for the army's retreat, the Confederates north of the river had to be kept occupied for another day. Fitz John Porter had to fight a second battle. During the early morning hours of June 27, McClellan had Porter retreat about six miles down the river to a position near Gaines's Mill. This placed him across the river from the Union's main body, with the advantage of good bridge connections.

Before noon, according to Northern soldier John W. Urban, "everything was in readiness to receive the enemy, every man and every gun being in position." Somewhat incongruously, enterprising young newsboys chose this moment to circulate among the soldiers with the latest editions from New York and Philadelphia, and the white sheets blossomed everywhere.

The line formed a two-mile semicircle along the bank of a small creek that was fringed with woods. The terrain over which the Confederates were obliged to approach, says Urban, "was made up of beautiful green meadows, large fields of waving grain, several swamps and ravines . . . and a strip of wood . . . opposite to the Union position."

Fitz John Porter describes his thoughts as the battle loomed:

I had reason to believe that the enemy largely outnumbered me. . . . Though in a desperate situation, I was not without strong hope of some timely assistance from the main body of the army. . . .

But Confederate General "Prince John" Magruder was still putting on his act in the Richmond defenses, making McClellan believe that his small army was a large one that might roll forward along its whole line at any moment. Throughout the morning, McClellan could not be certain on which side of the river the real attack would be made.

The afternoon began. The men in Fitz John Porter's lines found the summer sun becoming oppressive, with the breeze being barely strong enough to stir the army's flags. But the discomfort soon became a minor consideration. Writes Union trooper F. Colburn Adams:

The clouds of dust that roll up all along our front, added to the noise of artillery and the tramp of horsemen, tell us that the enemy is advancing to the attack. Now we see the top of his banners over the hill in front of our centre, then suddenly he appears full in view . . . and comes sweeping forward. . . . [A] fire so terrible that it makes the very ground tremble, opens all along the line.

It was General A. P. Hill's troops that attacked first. "These gallant masses," says an unidentified Confederate officer, "rushed forward with thundering hurrahs upon the musketry of the foe. . . . Whole ranks went down under that terrible hail. . . ." Adds a correspondent for the Richmond Whig:

It was absolutely necessary that we should carry their line, and . . . regiment after regiment, and brigade after brigade was successively led forward. Still, our repeated charges, gallant and dashing though they were, failed to accomplish the end. . . . Thus for more than two mortal hours the momentous issue stood trembling in the balance.

As they met the Confederate charges, the Federals accompanied their gunfire with "defiant cheers." However, as Union trooper Adams explains, the defense line's losses were heavy, especially in the center and on the left:

The slaughter at these points is sad to contemplate. The enemy's batteries have literally rained shot, shell, and case ["case" being canister and grapeshot] into our ranks, and our men have fallen like grass before the mower's scythe. . . . The reserves have nearly all been brought up and are engaged at various points. . . .

One of these reserves was John W. Urban, who joined the line at a point that had just seen some desperate hand-to-hand fighting:

Some of the dead had their heads broken in by blows from butts of rifles, and others lay dead with bayonets thrust through them, the weapon having been left sticking in their bodies. Some of the wounded begged piteously to be helped to the rear. . . .

Again in Adams's words:

There is a limit to human endurance; and our troops are beginning to show it. . . . Our shattered lines now begin to waver . . . and General Porter finds that his position is so critical as to need reinforcements from the south side of the river.

General Henry W. Slocum's division, sent by McClellan, reached Porter about 4:00 P.M. But the Confederate attack, begun by A. P. Hill, now included Longstreet, Jackson, and D. H. Hill. Porter was outnumbered by some 20,000 men. About 4:30, according to Adams:

A terrible cannonade . . . breaks forth [on the right]. . . . It is the thunder of Stonewall Jackson's artillery that we hear. . . . Porter again calls for reinforcements, and reports his condition as critical in the extreme.

Porter's men, without further reinforcements, somehow managed to hold their ground for nearly two hours longer. Then the Confederate brigades of General John B. Hood and Colonel E. M. Law hurled themselves against the line's left center. Says the Richmond Whig's *correspondent:*

The charge was made under the most galling fire I ever witnessed. . . . A ravine deep and wide yawned before us, while on the other side of the crest of the almost perpendicular bank a breastwork of logs was erected, from behind which the dastard invaders were pouring murderous volleys upon our troops.

Adds the Reverend John S. Hutchinson, chaplain of a Confederate unit that helped support this assault:

The roar of the musketry was incessant; the ground fairly trembled under the thunder of the cannon; the cloud of smoke and dust was almost blinding. . . . Our line of advance was marked by piles of dead and wounded; streams of bleeding men were pouring to the rear. . . . On before us rushed the brave Texans [Hood's brigade], yelling and shouting as they advanced. The fiery storm of shot and shell poured destruction into these ranks, but there was no halt. . . .

The assault broke through, and the Confederates at last had the advantage. Relates Union trooper Adams:

The whole line soon falls back in some disorder to a high ridge about three-quarters of a mile in the rear, which overlooks Alexander's Bridge. . . . The enemy . . . pauses. . . . The . . . dust and smoke . . . almost obscures the enemy's line on our centre and left. But Jackson's artillery is still thundering on our right, telling us that there the battle is still raging in all its fury. . . .

We have lost . . . twenty guns, and the ground is strewn with small arms, clothing, and indeed everything our soldiers find to be an encumbrance. We have also left the enemy all our dead and the greater part of our severely wounded.

It is [past] seven o'clock now. . . . The . . . heavens are overspread with crimson light, and lurid shadows are playing over the battlefield, now giving a strange and weird effect to the enemy's line, then lighting up and giving a clearer outline to the features of the dead and the wreck of the field.

Again the enemy pushes through the meadow and up the hill, and the battle is renewed. Officers turn instinctively and cast ominous glances over that long log-way leading to Alexander's Bridge, and impatiently ask, "Where are the reinforcements?" If they are not here soon, all is lost.

But listen. There is great shouting and cheering over there. They are coming at last. The head of the column is full in sight, coming at a double-quick, pushing the [battle's] stragglers aside as it sweeps along, and making the very woods resound with cheers. There is [General William H.] French and [General Thomas F.] Meagher, both at the head of their brigades, the latter in his shirt-sleeves, calling to his men and encouraging them to hasten forward. . . .

The sight of these two brigades sweeping up the slope . . . and the cheerfulness with which they advance to the front . . . and engage the enemy, revives the drooping spirits of the exhausted troops, reanimates them, and gives them new courage. Men who have thrown away their guns . . . pick up others and fall in, ready to renew the fight.

This cheering and shouting takes the enemy by surprise. He sees that our line has found new energy; and he knows that we have been reinforced, but not to what extent. He hesitates, then advances with a degree of caution uncommon with him.

The advance was soon halted. Lee's regiments, though they had won the day, were disorganized and decimated. The last charge alone had cost Lee more than a thousand men. Laments an unnamed member of Hood's brigade:

It was indeed a sad sight to look at the old regiment . . . gathered around their tattered colours. I could not realize that this little band of fifty or sixty men was the Fourth Texas. . . . Out of five hundred and thirty men who went into the fight, there were two hundred and fifty-six killed, wounded, or missing, while many were completely broken down, and nearly everyone was struck or grazed.

Again in the words of Union trooper Adams:
 . . . night closes on the scene now, and the clash of arms ceases. The ruddy glare has gone from the dread scene of battle, and dusky shadows are struggling with the veil of smoke that hangs like a funeral pall overhead, giving a dim and misty outline to the configuration of the two armies.

Fitz John Porter's battered, bone-tired, and powder-blackened regiments soon began withdrawing across the river to join McClellan's main body. Adams says they were met with a painful scene:
 The wounded from the battlefield, to the number of several thousand, had been brought over and laid in rows on the ground so thick that it was with difficulty you could pick your way through them. . . . Now and then one, in seeing a passer-by, would raise his head and inquire how the battle had resulted. Another would request him to tell somebody to bring him a drink of water.

General McClellan's headquarter tents were all struck [in preparation for the retreat to the James], and the general was laying down under a booth made of the branches of trees, worn out with fatigue, for he had not slept for forty-eight hours and had been almost constantly in the saddle. Generals Franklin, Porter, Sumner, and Heintzelman soon joined him, and remained in consultation until nearly eleven o'clock.

An hour and a half later, at 12:20 A.M., McClellan wrote a telegraphic report of the day for Washington. He disclaimed all responsibility for the repulse, with its heavy casualties, and insisted that "very large" reinforcements must be sent him at once:
 Had I twenty thousand, or even ten thousand fresh troops to use tomorrow, I could take Richmond; but I have not a man in reserve, and shall be glad to cover my retreat and save the material and personnel of the army. . . . I have lost this battle because my force was too small. . . . I feel too earnestly tonight. I have seen too many

dead and wounded comrades to feel otherwise than that the government has not sustained this army.

In closing, McClellan went so far as to accuse Secretary of War Edwin Stanton of having done his best to sacrifice the army (an accusation meant also for Lincoln's eyes), but Washington's supervisor of military telegrams deleted the bitter words before releasing the message.

Lincoln had long considered McClellan's lack of numbers "a curious mystery." Current records indicated there were well over 100,000 Federals on the Peninsula. Lincoln had also felt from the start that McClellan was altogether too ready to accept as gospel the reports he got concerning the numbers under Lee. But now the President was deeply worried. Having no way of knowing that McClellan was actually stronger than Lee, he had no choice but to reply that reinforcements would be sent as fast as possible and that McClellan should concentrate on saving the army.

It wasn't until sunrise of the day following the battle that the last of Fitz John Porter's troops crossed Alexander's Bridge, destroying it behind them. McClellan's entire army was now on the Richmond side of the river. This made Confederate General "Prince John" Magruder and his inferior force very nervous. But McClellan's thoughts were wholly concerned with flying to Harrison's Landing. All of that day, June 28, was spent in furious preparations for the retreat. Enlisted man Warren Goss says that working parties were assigned to the destruction of stores for which there was no wagon space:

. . . some of our officers, high in rank, set an unselfish example by destroying their personal baggage. . . . Tents were cut and slashed with knives; canteens punched with bayonets; clothing cut into shreds; sugar and whiskey overturned on the ground, which absorbed them. Some of our men stealthily imitated mother earth as regards the whiskey.

Up to this point the Confederates were ignorant of McClellan's intentions. Writes General Lee:

. . . the bridges over the Chickahominy in rear of the enemy were destroyed, and their reconstruction impracticable in the presence of his whole army and powerful batteries. We were therefore compelled to wait until his purpose should be developed.

Adds D. H. Hill, one of the generals who had fought against Fitz John Porter:

While we were lying all day idle on the 28th, unable to cross the Chickahominy, the clouds of smoke from the burning [stores] in the Federal camps, and the frequent explosions of magazines indicated a retreat; but [General W. H. C.] Whiting kept insisting . . . that all this was but a *ruse de guerre* of McClellan preparatory to a march upon Richmond.

I made to him some such reply as that once made to General Longstreet, when a cadet at West Point, by Professor Kendrick. The professor asked Longstreet, who never looked at his chemistry, how the carbonic acid of commerce was made. Longstreet replied, "By burning diamonds in oxygen gas."

"Yes," said Professor Kendrick, "that will do it; but don't you think it would be a *leetle* expensive?"

"Don't you think," I said to Whiting, "that this *ruse* of McClellan is a leetle expensive?"

The old West Point yarn had a very quieting effect upon his apprehensions.

Returning to the Union lines and Warren Goss:

Early on the morning of the 29th the work of destruction was complete, our picket line was [called in], and with faces that reflected the gloom of our hearts we turned our backs upon Richmond and started upon the retreat. The gloom was rather that of surprise than of knowledge, as the movement was but slightly understood by the mass of the army, or for that matter by most of the officers.

Warren Goss was one of the soldiers of the army's rear guard, whose duty it was to fight off the Confederates of the Richmond lines who marched in pursuit. Goss continues:

About nine o'clock, line of battle was formed near Allen's farm. Occasionally the report of a sharpshooter's rifle was heard in the woods. Some of the men took advantage of such shade as was afforded by scattering trees and went to sleep. All were suddenly brought to their feet by a tremendous explosion of artillery. . . . This attack was, after some sharp fighting, repelled; and, slinging knapsacks, the march was again resumed over the dusty roads. It was scorching hot when we arrived at Savage's Station. . . .

The Battle of Savage's Station.

This point along the south side of the Chickahominy had been serving as a Union depot. It was connected with White House by railroad. Goss says that here, too, a great destruction of supplies was effected:

Immense piles of flour, hard bread in boxes, clothing, arms, and ammunition were burned, smashed, and scattered. Two trains of railroad cars, loaded with ammunition and other supplies, were here fired, set in motion toward each other, and under a full head of steam came thundering down the track like flaming meteors. When they met in collision, there was a terrible explosion. Other trains and locomotives were precipitated [into the Chickahominy] from the demolished Bottom's Bridge. . . .

Here, awaiting the approach of the enemy, we halted, while wagons of every description passed over the road on the retreat. It was now five o'clock in the afternoon . . . when dense clouds of dust . . . warned us of the approach of our antagonists. Soon they advanced from the edge of the woods and opened fire from the whole mass of their artillery. Our guns responded. For nearly an hour . . . the air vibrated with the artillery explosions. Then the infantry became engaged. . . . Even after the shadows of night covered the scene with their uncertain light, the conflict went on, until nine o'clock, when to the deep-toned Union cheers there were no answering high-pitched rebel yells. . . .

Turning their backs [that same night] upon the battlefield and [a previously established] hospital camp of twenty-five hundred sick and wounded, who were abandoned to the enemy, the troops resumed their march. The long trains, of five thousand wagons and two thousand five hundred head of beef, had by this time crossed White Oak Swamp [up ahead]. The defile over which the army passed was narrow, but it possessed the compensating advantage that no attack could be made on the flank because of the morass on either side. As fast as the rear-guard passed, trees were felled across the road to obstruct pursuit.

Among the Confederates from the Richmond lines who had followed the Federals was artilleryman Robert Stiles (adjutant of the Richmond Howitzers):

. . . the main thing that struck us was the immense quantity of abandoned stores and equipment, indicating how abundant had been the supply of the Federal forces and how great the demoralization of their retreat. Near Savage Station there must have been acres covered by stacks of burning boxes of bacon, crackers, and desiccated vegetables—"desecrated vegetables" our boys called them.

To us poorly equipped and half-starved rebels it was a revelation. Here and elsewhere we picked up a few rations and a few choice equipments of various kinds, but had really neither time nor taste for plunder.

There were other mementoes of their stay and of their hasty departure . . . not quite so attractive or appetizing—the ghastly leavings of numerous field hospitals; pale, naked corpses and grotesque piles of arms and legs.

At one of these hospital stations we found an Irishman, whom we at first thought dying, as perhaps he was; but a swallow or two of [whiskey] revived him. . . . He seemed to grasp the situation perfectly, and upon someone asking if the apparent flight might not after all be a trap—

"Be dad!" said he. "An' ef it's a thrap, thin shure an' Little Mac's lost the thrigger [i.e., the trigger of the trap]!"

Demoralization among the retreating Federals wasn't so great as Robert Stiles believed. The men in the combat columns, in fact, had developed a good morale. There was a strong degree of demoralization

only in the great wagon train the combat columns were protecting.
As explained by civilian observer Samuel Wilkeson, writing for the
New York Tribune:

Huddled among the wagons were 10,000 stragglers—for the credit
of the nation be it said that four-fifths of them were wounded, sick,
or utterly exhausted. . . . The confusion of this herd of men and
mules, wagons and wounded, men on horses, men on foot, men by
the roadside, men perched on wagons, men searching for water, men
famishing for food, men lame and bleeding, men with ghostly eyes
looking out between bloody bandages that hid the face—turn to some
vivid account of the most pitiful part of Napoleon's retreat from
Russia, and fill out the picture. . . .

McClellan's rear guard troops, following in the wagon train's wake,
completed their crossing of White Oak Swamp on the morning of
June 30. Destroying a key bridge behind them, they emerged into
country that "began to change from swamp and wood to cultivated
fields." In these fields, along the rim of the swamp, the Federals set
up a strong defense line that faced in the direction from which they
had come.

General Lee's main columns, having crossed the Chickahominy,
had joined the pursuit. Jackson and D. H. Hill approached through
the swamp, while Longstreet and A. P. Hill, accompanied by Lee
and President Davis, used roads that swung around the swamp's
southern side. The left of the Union line faced the troops that Lee
was leading in person, while the right faced the demolished bridge
that was in the path of Jackson and D. H. Hill.

Among the Union officers at the bridge, where General William
Franklin commanded, was trooper F. Colburn Adams:

About 11 o'clock the enemy suddenly appeared in the woods on
the opposite bank. . . . We could distinctly see the gunners busy
among their batteries, preparing for the work of death. . . . Our
artillery line was formed. . . . Both armies stood now for some time
in silence, as if watching each other and hesitating as to which should
begin the work of death first.

An open field intervened between the two lines, and on a bit of
rising ground . . . stood the house General McClellan had used
for his headquarters [during the previous day, and until early in
the morning of the present one]. The owner's wife, a smart, talkative
woman with strong Southern sympathies, had made herself very un-

comfortable at the presence of so many soldiers about her premises, and had several times remonstrated against the liberties they took with her fruit trees. She had also expressed great anxiety as to who was to compensate her for the loss of her fences and crop.

The Confederate artillery answered that question, I think, in a rather summary manner. . . . A little after 12 o'clock they opened along their whole line with a crash that made the very earth tremble. . . . The house settled to the ground as if it had been cut suddenly from its foundation, and the fruit trees around it were splintered to pieces. The enemy evidently thought General McClellan still occupied the house. . . . A number of orderlies around the house probably led to the error.

The woman was safely distant when the shells came, but her husband was not. He was unwilling to leave his chickens and ducks unprotected from Union appetites. Losing a leg to a shell, he quickly bled to death.

With General Franklin's infantrymen hugging the ground, his artillerists returned the fire. Men on both sides of the stream later called the duel the worst they had ever experienced. Stonewall Jackson, in chief command of the Confederate attack at this point, allowed Franklin's fire to keep him at bay, making no determined effort to ford the stream. In this campaign, Jackson was showing little of the initiative that had made him famous. Writes D. H. Hill:

I think that an important factor in this inaction was Jackson's pity for his own corps, worn out by long and exhausting marches, and reduced in numbers by its numerous sanguinary battles. He thought that the garrison of Richmond ought now to bear the brunt of the fighting.

On the Union left, where Generals Samuel Heintzelman and Edwin Sumner commanded, midafternoon saw a furious attack launched by Longstreet and A. P. Hill. The battle that developed is thus described by an unnamed Southern correspondent:

The thunder of the cannon, the crackling of the musketry from thousands of combatants, mingled with screams from the wounded and dying, were terrific to the ear and to the imagination.

In a battle that saw a number of daring attacks and counterattacks, one assault, says the Union's Warren Goss, was "unusual in the his-

*tory of war." It was made by the Confederates on an artillery battery
and its supporting infantry in the lines of General George McCall.
Goss relates:*

In one dense mass, without order, a perfect mob of desperate
men . . . shouting, screaming—on they came. . . . Vainly the artillery of the Federals tore great gaps and paths through this torrent
of men. . . . Closing up their shattered ranks, on they came. . . .

An acquaintance who . . . took part as an artillerist told me
afterwards that the enemy had advanced so near when the last order
was given to fire that he was obliged to discharge the rammer from
his gun as well as the shot. . . .

In the artillerist's own words (as quoted by Goss):

Our sergeant shouted to the boys as the rebs came yelling like
mad upon us, "Don't run from them!"

I thought to myself, "I ain't going to git from no such ragged
fellows as they be."

One of them shot my hoss, and I punched [a hole in] him with a
bayonet. Another reb came up yelling, "Surrender, you durned
Yanks, to the Sixtieth Virginia!" Whereupon a big gunner knocked
him over the head with his rammer.

*Suddenly there was hand-to-hand fighting everywhere. Muskets were
swung as clubs, pistols were fired point-blank, and swords flashed
and clanged. In some of the bayonet encounters, writes Goss, "men
fell mutually pierced." The Confederates "bayoneted and shot the
horses, and overturned the guns." The Federals soon fell back.*

*Other parts of the battlefield saw Confederate attacks nearly as
fierce as this one. Goss says that many of the prisoners taken by the
Federals were found to be "under the influence of stimulants."*

It was current talk at that time—to account for the desperate,
reckless charges made during the day—that the Confederates were
plied with whiskey. I am not of that opinion. . . .

*The Battle of Glendale (or Frayser's Farm) continued until well
after dark. Writes Southerner D. H. Hill:*

It was a critical day for both commanders, but especially for
McClellan. . . . Escape seemed impossible for him, but he *did* escape, at the same time inflicting heavy damage upon his pursuers. . . . General Lee reported: "Many prisoners, including a gen-

eral of division, McCall, were captured, and several batteries, with some thousands of small-arms, were taken." But as an obstruction to the Federal retreat, the fight amounted to nothing.

About midnight, the first Federal units began withdrawing from the field. Again in Goss's words:

By daylight, began our march to Malvern, the pioneers felling trees in the rear. Acres and acres of waving grain, ripe for the reapers, were seen on every side. The troops marched through the wheat, cutting off the tops and gathering them into their haversacks, for, except in more than ordinarily provident cases, they were out of rations and hungry, as well as lame and stiff from marching.

The bands, which had been silent so long before Richmond, here began playing patriotic airs, with a very inspiring effect.

As they neared James River and caught sight of our gunboats, a cheer went up from each regiment. About eleven o'clock in the morning they took position on the Malvern plateau [joining units that had arrived earlier]. . . . Our stragglers, their courage revived by sight of the gunboats, came up the hill, seeking their regiments. One squad . . . had their haversacks filled with honey, and bore marks of a battle with bees.

. . . long lines of men with dusty garments and powder-blackened faces climbed the steep Quaker Road. Footsore, hungry, and wearied, but not disheartened, these . . . men took their positions and prepared for another day of conflict. The private soldiers were quick to perceive the advantages which the possession of Malvern Hill gave us. . . . [My friend] Wad Rider . . . said, "Satan himself couldn't whip us out of this!"

As soon as it was in position near the north front of the hill, our regiment was given the order, "In place—rest." And in a few minutes the men were asleep, lying beside their muskets.

. . . skirmishing began along the new line. Some of [our] troops, while going up the hill to take their positions . . . were fired upon by the enemy's batteries. Small parties [of Confederates] advanced within musket shot, evidently reconnoitring our position. . . . Shells from our gunboats on the James came hoarsely spluttering over the heads of our troops.

These conditions continued on through the noon hour, with the Federal batteries on Malvern Hill adding to the shellfire as Lee's

*main columns drew closer. Stonewall Jackson and D. H. Hill found
themselves personally threatened. Says Hill:*

I saw Jackson helping with his own hands to push [Captain
James] Reilly's North Carolina battery farther forward. It was soon
disabled, the woods around us being filled with shrieking and exploding shells. I noticed an artilleryman seated comfortably behind
a very large tree, and apparently feeling very secure. A moment later
a shell passed through the huge tree and took off the man's head.

*Hill and his units soon reached the edge of the woods that over-
looked the open area that was to be the battlefield:*

My five brigade commanders and myself now made an examination of the enemy's position. He was found to be strongly posted on
a commanding hill, all the approaches to which could be swept by
his artillery and were guarded by swarms of infantry, securely sheltered by fences, ditches, and ravines.

*Most of the Federals had a clear view across the fields toward the
woods where the Confederates were massing. One of the keener observers was Captain William B. Weeden, stationed with an artillery
battery on the left:*

It was a fine afternoon, hot but tempered by a cooling breeze.
The soldiers waited. . . . Action might begin at any moment; and
between 2 and 3 o'clock it did begin. Out of the woods, puffs of
smoke from guns, and nearer, light wreaths from their [bursting]
shells, lent new colors to the green of woods and fields and the deep
blue sky. . . .

The woods swarmed with butternut coats and gray. These colors
were worn by a lively race of men, and they stepped forward briskly
[into the fields], firing as they moved. The regimental formations
were plainly visible, with the colors flying. . . .

In this first heavy skirmish . . . the . . . brunt of the blow fell
upon Colonel [James] McQuade's 14th New York. . . . The New
Yorkers began to give ground. . . . But only for a moment. The
men stiffened up to the color line, charged forward with a cheer, and
drove back the enemy.

Adds the Union's Fitz John Porter:

The spasmodic, though sometimes formidable attacks . . . at

different points along our whole front, up to about 4 o'clock, were presumably demonstrations or feelers, to ascertain our strength, preparatory to their engaging in more serious work. An ominous silence . . . now intervened. . . .

Lee's main attack wasn't launched until about five-thirty. To his disappointment, it developed in a piecemeal fashion. One of the first brigades to advance was that of Colonel John B. Gordon (just recently promoted from regimental commander):

Isolated from the rest of the army and alone, my brigade moved across this shell-ploughed plain toward the heights, which were perhaps more than half a mile away. Within fifteen or twenty minutes the centre regiment, Third Alabama . . . had left more than half of its number dead and wounded along its track, and the other regiments had suffered almost as severely. One shell had killed six or seven men in my immediate presence. My pistol, on one side [of my body], had the handle torn off; my canteen, on the other, was pierced, emptying its contents—water merely—on my trousers; and my coat was ruined by having a portion of the front torn away. . . .

At the foot of the last steep ascent . . . I found that McClellan's guns [because of the elevation of their muzzles] were firing over us; and as any further advance by this unsupported brigade would have been not only futile but foolhardy, I halted my men and ordered them to lie down and fire upon McClellan's standing lines of infantry. . . . In vain I looked behind us for the promised support. Anxiously I looked forward, fearing an assault upon my exposed position. . . . As a retreat in daylight promised to be almost or quite as deadly as had been the charge, my desire for . . . darkness . . . can well be imagined.

In this state of extreme anxiety, a darkness which was unexpected and terrible came to me alone. A great shell fell, buried itself in the ground, and exploded near where I stood. It heaved the dirt over me, filling my face and ears and eyes with sand. I was literally blinded. . . . [T]houghts never ran more swiftly through a perplexed mortal brain. Blind! Blind in battle! . . . [W]hat was I to do? . . . The blindness, however, was of short duration. The delicate and perfect machinery of the eye soon did its work. . . .

Large bodies of troops had been sent forward, or rather led forward, by that intrepid commander, General [D. H.] Hill. . . . In the hurry and bustle . . . coming as they did from different directions, there was necessarily much confusion, and they were subjected to the same destructive fire through which my troops had previously passed.

Writes General Lee:

D. H. Hill . . . engaged the enemy gallantly . . . but a simultaneous advance of the other troops not taking place, he found himself unable to maintain the ground he had gained. . . . Jackson sent to his support his own division, and that part of [General Richard S.] Ewell's which was in reserve; but owing to the increasing darkness and the intricacy of the forest and swamp, they did not arrive in time to render the desired assistance.

But, says Hill, some of the other troops approached as he fell back:

I never saw anything more grandly heroic than the advance after sunset of the nine brigades under Magruder's orders. Unfortunately, they did not move together, and were beaten in detail. As each brigade emerged from the woods, from fifty to one hundred guns opened upon it, tearing great gaps in its ranks; but the heroes reeled on—and were shot down by the [infantry supports] at the guns, which a few squads reached. . . . It was not war—it was murder.

Northerner Warren Goss takes up:

Night came, yet the fight went on. . . . The lurid flashes of artillery . . . the crackle of musketry, with flashes seen in the distance like fireflies; the hoarse shriek of the huge shells from the gunboats . . . made it a scene of terrible grandeur. The ground in front . . . was literally covered with the dead and wounded. At nine o'clock the sounds of the battle died away, and cheer after cheer went up from the victors on the hill.

Thus, on July 1, 1862, ended seven days of almost continual fighting. The casualty count in killed, wounded, captured, and missing was, for the Federals, nearly 16,000; and for the Confederates, over 20,000.

Malvern Hill staggered Lee's army. Explains Adjutant Robert Stiles, of the Richmond Howitzers:

The effect of these repeated bloody repulses can hardly be conceived. . . . The demoralization was great, and the evidences of it palpable everywhere. The roads and forests were full of stragglers. Commands were inextricably confused, some, for a time, having actually disappeared. Those who retained sufficient self-respect and sense of responsibility to think of the future were filled with the deepest apprehension. I know that this was the state of mind of some of our strongest and best officers. . . .

Stonewall Jackson, at least, was calm. At the battle's close, he returned to his headquarters and went to sleep. Soon, however, three of his generals came with the intention of telling him that if McClellan should decide to attack in the morning they would be too weak to offer resistance. Says Jackson's medical director, Dr. Hunter McGuire:

It was difficult to wake General Jackson, as he was exhausted and very sound asleep. I tried it myself, and after many efforts, partly succeeded. When he was made to understand what was wanted, he said: "McClellan and his army will be gone by daylight," and went to sleep again.

Jackson was right, of course. McClellan considered Malvern Hill not so much a victory as another escape from disaster. Whereas the Confederates feared that he would take advantage of their defeat and march upon Richmond, McClellan had no thought but to continue his retreat to Harrison's Landing. There the James was wider, which would facilitate the navy's protective operations. Moreover, the army could be deployed on the river's very bank, making it immune to enemy encirclement.

The march was begun as soon as the battle ended, with only the rear guard, commanded by Colonel William W. Averell, still on Malvern as a foggy dawn broke. Writes Averell:

Our ears had been filled with agonizing cries from thousands before the fog was lifted, but now our eyes saw an appalling spectacle upon the slopes down to the woodlands half a mile away. Over five thousand dead and wounded men were on the ground, in every attitude of distress. A third of them were dead or dying, but enough were alive and moving to give to the field a singular crawling effect.

The retreat from victory caused some of McClellan's officers to protest in high anger. As for the enlisted men, Warren Goss says they did "a deal of growling . . . but most of them seemed to think Little Mac knew what he was about. . . ."

It began to rain during the march, and on their arrival at the landing the tired and hungry men were obliged to set up their camps in "great fields of mud." All was well, however, when McClellan praised them for their heroism during the "change of base." Said he: "Your conduct ranks you among the celebrated armies of history." This was enough to earn him louder cheers than ever.

One officer, the Frenchman Regis de Trobriand, felt that the chief reason the army deserved praise was that it had managed to survive, "not allowing itself to be destroyed by Robert E. Lee, nor by George B. McClellan."

President Lincoln, who had been hoping almost desperately for a strong upswing in the news from the Peninsula, got instead a request from McClellan for 100,000 reinforcements! The outcome of the campaign was a terrible blow to the burdened President. He later admitted to a friend: "I was as nearly inconsolable as I could be and live."

Lincoln himself came in for much of the blame for McClellan's failure. Some people felt that he should have removed McClellan from command at an early date. Others were convinced that he had crippled the campaign by withholding McDowell—though even with another corps McClellan would have considered his strength inferior to that of Lee. Most Democrats, of course, continued to support McClellan, attributing the fiasco entirely to administration mismanagement.

It was now nearly a year since McClellan had been summoned to Washington and had become the Union's Young Napoleon. He had begun this career with exceptional promise, creating a splendid army. But he seemed to be psychologically unable to use the army with boldness and dispatch. It is probable that the reason he was so ready to believe the wildly exaggerated Pinkerton reports on Confederate numbers was that they gave him an excuse to proceed with extreme caution. Tragically, he doubtless sacrificed more of his devoted troops by being cautious than he would have lost in the most daring assault up the Peninsula and into the Richmond defenses.

McClellan's plan to strengthen his army for a new advance upon Richmond came to nothing. He continued to insist that Lee had 200,000 men, and Lincoln and Stanton could not provide him the kind of reinforcements he requested. As his hopes for lavish support deteriorated, McClellan wrote his wife: "I am sick and weary of all this business. I am tired of serving fools."

The Union, of course, held many people who felt that McClellan himself was the situation's greatest fool. In the words of Republican editor Horace Greeley:

Never before did an army so constantly, pressingly need to be re-inforced—not by a corps, but by a leader; not by men, but by a man.

A month after Malvern Hill, McClellan got orders from Washington to put his troops aboard transports for shipment northward. This evacuation filled the Union with gloom, and stirred extravagant joy in the Confederacy. Says Virginia's John Minor Botts, the persecuted loyalist:

Nothing occurred during the whole war so much to give new life, spirit, energy, and courage to the Confederate army and people as this untoward retreat of McClellan from the Peninsula. . . .

9

SECOND BULL RUN

Even while McClellan's army *of the Potomac was fighting its way through the Seven Days, a new Federal army was forming between Washington and Richmond. Named the Army of Virginia, and numbering about 50,000 men, it was a consolidation of the units that had been operating individually around Washington and in the Shenandoah Valley. Its commander was Major General John Pope, who had been called from the war's Western theater, where, the previous spring, he had made a reputation for himself by capturing Island Number Ten in the Mississippi. Unfortunately, Pope got off on the wrong foot with his new troops. In a proclamation dated July 14, 1862, he told them:*

Let us understand each other. I have come to you from the West, where we have always seen the backs of our enemies; from an army . . . whose policy has been attack, and not defence. . . . I presume that I have been called here to pursue the same system, and to lead you against the enemy. It is my purpose to do so, and that speedily. . . . I desire you to dismiss from your minds certain phrases which I am sorry to find much in vogue amongst you. I hear constantly of "taking strong positions and holding them," of "lines of retreat," and of "bases of supplies." Let us discard such ideas. . . . Let us study the probable lines of retreat of our opponents, and leave our own to

John Pope.

take care of themselves. . . . Success and glory are in the advance. Disaster and shame lurk in the rear. Let us act on this understanding, and it is safe to predict that your banners shall be inscribed with many a glorious deed. . . .

Pope's words were hardly inspirational. Instead of comparing the new army unfavorably with another army, he would have done better to describe it as being made up of a fine-looking bunch of men with an obvious potential for success. He seemed to be trying to shame the army into a good performance.

The proclamation offended not only Pope's troops; it was construed as disparagement by McClellan's Army of the Potomac (at this time encamped at Harrison's Landing after the Seven Days).

As for the Confederates, they laughed when the story spread that Pope had added that from then on his headquarters would be in the saddle. "It is strange," they said, "that a general should have his headquarters where his hindquarters ought to be." (Pope, incidentally, later denied having made such a statement.)

Writes Confederate General Longstreet:

Pope was credited with . . . expressions such as that he . . . hoped in Virginia to see the faces of the rebels, as in the West he had been able to see only their backs. When General Lee heard of these strange utterances, his estimate of Pope was considerably lessened. . . . For centuries there has been among soldiers a maxim: "Don't despise your enemy." General Pope's words would seem to indicate great contempt for his enemy.

Few armies in history were less deserving of contempt than the Confederates under Lee. Modestly numbered and sparely equipped, they had just bested the greatest army the Federal government had ever assembled.

Little time was granted to Lee and his men for resting on their laurels. Pope loomed in the north even before McClellan began to retire in the east. Actually, McClellan was a part of the new threat. He was expected to reinforce Pope by way of the Chesapeake and Potomac. Such a union would give the Federals a powerful advantage, so Lee had to act quickly; he had to go against Pope before McClellan's move was completed.

First to see action on the new field was Stonewall Jackson. On August 9, he clashed sharply but inconsequentially with a part of Pope's army at Cedar Mountain, north of the Rapidan River, about halfway between Washington and Richmond (westward, however, of the direct line). Jackson was soon joined by General Lee with Longstreet and his corps. This gave the Confederates a numerical edge. According to an Alabama officer, William C. Oates:

. . . Pope . . . retreated. . . . And thus the braggart who had "never seen the rebels except their backs" was exhibiting to the rebels that interesting part of his own anatomy.

Pope set up a defense line just north of the Rappahannock. He did not hesitate to skirmish with the Confederates now, for his position was a strong one. Expecting reinforcements to arrive shortly, he felt fairly secure.

Says Robert L. Dabney, who served for a time as Stonewall Jackson's chief of staff and became one of his first biographers:

While the enemy was thus deluded . . . General Jackson was preparing, under the instructions of the Commander-in-Chief, for the most adventurous and brilliant of his exploits. This was no less than to separate himself from [Longstreet] . . . pass around Pope to the westward, and place his corps between him and Washington City, at Manassas Junction. . . .

General Lee's purpose in sending Jackson on this mission was to confuse Pope and draw him northward from his strong position into a situation where he would be vulnerable. Lee planned to follow Jackson with Longstreet's corps in time to support him in a new confrontation. Robert Dabney goes on:

Having made a hasty and imperfect issue of rations, Jackson disembarrassed himself of all his trains save the ambulances and the carriages for the ammunition, and left Jeffersonton [a village in front of Pope's lines] early on the morning of August 25. Marching first westward [and then swinging northward], he crossed the . . . Rappahannock, passed the hamlet of Orleans, and paused at night, after a march of twenty-five miles, near Salem. . . . Many of [his troops] had no rations, and subsisted upon the green corn gathered along the route. . . .

As the weary column approached the end of the day's march, they found Jackson, who had ridden forward, dismounted and standing upon a great stone by the roadside. His . . . cap was lifted from his brow . . . and his blue eye . . . returned the rays of the evening [sun] with almost equal brightness. His men burst forth into their accustomed cheers . . . but . . . he sent an officer to request that there should be no cheering, inasmuch as it might betray their presence to the enemy. They at once repressed their applause. . . . But as they passed him, their eyes and gestures . . . silently declared what their lips were forbidden to utter.

Jackson turned to his staff . . . and said: "Who could not conquer, with such troops as these?"

. . . On the morning of the 26th, he turned eastward and, passing through the Bull Run Mountains at Thoroughfare Gap, proceeded to Bristoe Station . . . by another equally arduous march. At Gainesville [on the way to Bristoe Station] he was joined by Stuart with his cavalry. . . . The corps of Jackson had now marched fifty miles in two days. The whole army of Pope [still on the line of the Rappahannock] was . . . between it and its friends. They had no supplies whatever. . . .

But near at hand was Manassas Junction, a lightly guarded Union depot. That night Jeb Stuart's horsemen, together with some foot troops, were sent to take it. Jackson's main body followed the next morning. In the words of Confederate Lieutenant John Hampden Chamberlayne:

Upon reaching Manassas Junction, we met a [Federal] brigade, the First New Jersey—which had been sent from Alexandria [near Washington]. . . . They were fools enough to send a flag demanding our surrender at once. Of course, we scattered the brigade, killing and wounding many. . . . At the Junction was a large depot of stores. . . . [C]ollected . . . in the space of a square mile [was] an amount and variety of property such as I had never conceived of. . . .

'Twas a curious sight to see our ragged and famished men helping themselves to every imaginable article of luxury or necessity, whether of clothing, food, or what not. For my part, I got a toothbrush, a box of candles, a quantity of lobster salad, a barrel of coffee, and other things. . . .

Our men . . . had brought no wagons, so we could carry little away of the riches before us. But the men could eat for one meal at least. . . . To see a starving man eating lobster salad and drinking Rhine wine, barefooted and in tatters, was curious.

A South Carolinian, J. F. J. Caldwell, noted something else that was curious: ". . . elegant . . . linen handkerchiefs were applied to noses hitherto blown with the thumb and forefinger. . . ."

Lieutenant Chamberlayne adds that

The whole thing was incredible. . . . At nightfall, fire was set to the depot, storehouses, the loaded trains, several long empty trains, sutlers' houses, restaurants—everything.

"The glare of our big bonfire," writes another of Jackson's men, "lighted up the country for miles. . . ."

Even some of General Pope's troops saw the red glow. The Federal columns had started northward that day, their advance making contact, at Bristoe Station, with Jackson's rear guard.

Turning to the story of the campaign as recorded by Northern soldier Warren Goss:

Jackson did not care to stay at Manassas waiting for Pope, his command being separated from the rest of Lee's army. He therefore retired . . . on the night of the 27th, to the old battleground of Bull Run, where he first showed his ability as a commander, and where he gained the sobriquet of "Stonewall."

. . . on the 28th Pope did not know, practically, where his own

Confederates marching against Pope.

forces were, or those of the enemy who had so manoeuvred as to mislead, elude, and confuse him. His divisions, scattered by contradictory and confusing orders, were held so loosely in hand, and were so isolated from each other, that so far as exercising control over them was concerned, it would almost have been as well for him to have been in the West, where he came from, as in Virginia.

Pope now outnumbered Lee, having been reinforced by Fitz John Porter and Samuel Heintzelman of McClellan's army. The Federal total was about 70,000. Stonewall Jackson had about 25,000, while Lee was approaching with 30,000 more under Longstreet.

By this time Jackson had taken up a position along the bed of an unfinished railroad at the northwestern edge of the old Bull Run battlefield. He was about seven miles east of Thoroughfare Gap in the Bull Run Mountains, through which he expected Lee and Longstreet to issue. That evening (the twenty-eighth) Jackson deliberately revealed his position to Pope by attacking a Federal column that was passing him by. The Federals responded with spirit, and the fight continued until about nine o'clock.

Pope ordered his other columns to converge on the spot, his chief concern being that Jackson might get away. Jackson, of course, planned to stay where he was. His defense line extended along the unfinished railroad for about two miles. In front of the line was an expanse of woods in which Jackson placed large bodies of skirmishers.

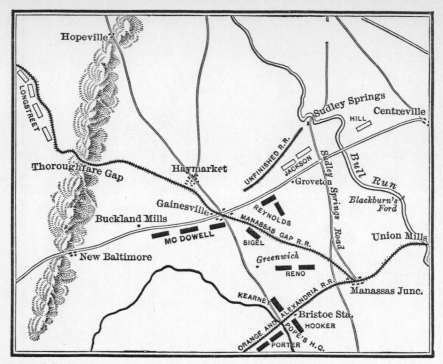

Second Bull Run: Situation on morning of August 28. Jackson is shown at unfinished railroad, while Longstreet approaches Thoroughfare Gap. Scattered Federal units are shown as black rectangles.

The Federals began their attack on the skirmishers at daybreak, August 29, advancing with "bands playing, flags flying, and their artillery . . . slowly firing. . . ." The struggle with the skirmishers lasted all morning, with additional blue columns arriving on the field from time to time. Many of the Federals, says Warren Goss,

. . . came upon the rusty remains of guns, bayonets, weather-beaten fragments of gun carriages and equipments, and the bleaching skulls and bones of their comrades who had perished on the field the year before—the first sacrifices to the blunders of the war.

Early afternoon arrived. In the words of D. H. Strother, of Pope's headquarters:

. . . the general and staff [were] grouped around a large pine tree which stood solitary on the crest of an open hill, overlooking our whole line of battle. The summit immediately in our front was occupied by a line of [our] batteries, some thirty or forty pieces, blazing and fuming like furnaces. . . . The dry grass which covered

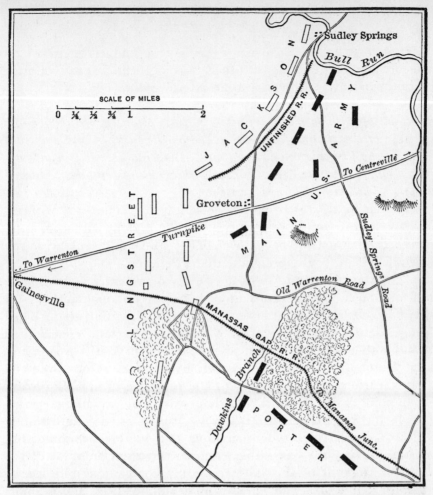

Second Bull Run: Situation at midday on August 29. Main Federal army faces Jackson at unfinished railroad. Longstreet is coming into position on Federal flank. Federals under Porter (bottom of map) remain inactive.

. . . [a hill on the left] had taken fire and was burning rapidly, occasionally obscuring that portion of the field with its smoke. . . .

The enemy's position can only be known by the smoke of his guns, for all his troops and batteries are concealed by the wood. . . . He fights stubbornly, and has thus far resisted all our efforts to dislodge him. . . . The shot and shells of the enemy directed at the batteries in our front render this position rather uncomfortable, as they are continually screeching over our heads or plowing the gravelly surface with an ugly rasping whir. . . .

Adds General Pope:

From 1:30 to 4 o'clock P.M., very severe conflicts occurred repeatedly all along the line, and there was a continuous roar of artillery and small arms, with scarcely an intermission.

Thus far, Jackson's main defense line was altogether intact. Some spots, in fact, were only lightly touched by the fury. In one such spot was a young Virginian named Allen C. Redwood. He tells what happened when, separated from his own unit, he accidentally wandered among a battalion of Louisianans:

The major . . . attached my person. . . . "Better stay with us, my boy; and if you do your duty I'll make it right with your company officers when the fight's over. They won't find fault with you when they know you've been in with the Pelicans."

. . . The command was as unlike my own as it was possible to conceive. Such a congress of nations only the cosmopolitan Crescent City [New Orleans] could have sent forth, and the tongues of Babel seemed resurrected in its speech. English, German, French, and Spanish, all were represented, to say nothing of Doric brogue and local "gumbo." There was, moreover, a vehemence of utterance and gesture curiously at variance with the reticence of our Virginians.

In point of fact, we burned little powder that day, and my promised distinction as a Pelican . . . was cheaply earned. The battalion did a good deal of counter-marching, and some skirmishing, but most of the time we were acting as support to a section of [artillery]. . . . The tedium of this last service my companions relieved by games of "seven up," with a greasy, well-thumbed deck, and in smoking cigarettes, rolled with great dexterity between the deals. Once, when a detail was ordered to go some distance under fire to fill the canteens of the company, a hand was dealt to determine who should go. . . .

Our numerous shifts of position completely confused what vague ideas I had of the situation, but we must have been near our extreme left . . . and never very far from my own brigade, which was warmly engaged that day. . . .

It was against the Confederate left that General Pope, late in the afternoon, ordered a heavy attack. At the same time, Fitz John Porter, who was stationed about two miles from the main army's left, was supposed to march against Jackson's right; but Porter was unable to make his attack, for Longstreet's columns, having passed through

Thoroughfare Gap early in the day, were now on this section of the field.

The first Federal unit to form for the attack on Jackson's left was General Cuvier Grover's brigade, of Joe Hooker's division. The order "Fix bayonets!" sounded up and down the lines. Writes Henry N. Blake, who took part in the attack as a captain with the Eleventh Massachusetts:

. . . the soldiers, led by their brave general, advanced upon a hidden foe through tangled woods which constantly interfered with the formation of the ranks. . . . The rebel skirmishers were driven in upon their reserve behind the . . . unfinished railroad, [where] detachments from five brigades were massed in three lines. . . .

The awful volleys [from the Confederates] did not impede the storming party that pressed on over the bodies of the dead and dying; while the thousands of bullets which flew through the air seemed to create a breeze that made the leaves upon the trees rustle, and a shower of small boughs and twigs fell upon the ground. . . .

The railroad bank was gained, and the column, with cheers, passed over it and advanced over the groups of the slain and mangled rebels who had rolled down the declivity. . . . The horse of General Grover was shot upon the railroad bank while he was encouraging the men to go forward, and he had barely time to dismount before the animal, mad with pain, dashed into the ranks of the enemy. . . .

The forces sometimes met face to face, and the bayonet and sword . . . were used with deadly effect in several instances. . . . In one company . . . a son was killed by the side of his father, who continued to perform his duty with the firmness of a stoic. . . .

The Federals broke the second defense line and swept toward the third. Victory, says Blake,

appeared to be certain, until the last [Confederate] support, that had rested upon their breasts on the ground, suddenly rose up and delivered a destructive volley which forced the brigade, that had already lost more than one-third of its number in killed and wounded, to retreat.

The retreat was made "under a fire of grape and canister, which was added to the musketry." One of the Confederates in the third line was later to say of Grover's attack: "They did it so splendidly that we couldn't help cheering them. It made me feel bad to fire on such brave fellows."

Now General Pope ordered the woods bombarded in preparation for an attack by Phil Kearny's division. Told that the woods was filled with the wounded of both sides, Pope answered, "And yet the safety of this army and the nation demands their sacrifice, and the lives of thousands yet unwounded."

According to D. H. Strother, of Pope's staff:

The artillerymen worked with a fiendish activity, and the sulphurous clouds which hung over the field were tinged with a hot coppery hue by the rays of the declining sun. Meanwhile, Kearny had gone in, and the incessant roar of musketry resembled the noise of a cataract.

Relates an officer on the Confederate side, Edward McCrady, Jr., of General Maxcy Gregg's South Carolina brigade:

Our men fell fast around us. . . . The enemy . . . compelled us, step by step, to yield . . . the position . . . which we had maintained all day. But we would not give it up without a desperate struggle. Now again, the same hand-to-hand fight we had with Grover we renewed with Kearny. We were not, however, entirely without help. General [L. O'Brien] Branch came to our assistance with one of his regiments, and . . . with coat off, personally took part in the affray. With his aid we made a stand. . . .

On our left . . . the enemy . . . was . . . repulsed, and those who had pressed . . . us back . . . now hesitated and commenced to yield. We pressed them, in our turn. They broke and fell back in disorder. I recollect that as they did so, they left a mule which, notwithstanding all the turmoil, was quietly cropping a green blade, here and there, in the bloodstained grass around him.

As Kearny was stopped, the Federal division under General Isaac I. Stevens came forward to renew the attack. Gregg's South Carolinians were now on the verge of exhaustion, their ears numbed by the din and their eyes blurred by the smoke. Their hearts fell when they heard the distant cheering of the advancing Federals. At that moment General Gregg was approached by an officer sent by division commander A. P. Hill, who wanted to know whether Gregg could hold. Gregg immortalized himself by replying that his ammunition was exhausted but that he thought he could hold with the bayonet.

Again in the words of Southerner Edward McCrady, Jr.:

We could hear the enemy advancing [through the woods], and

had not a round with which to greet them, but must wait the onslaught with only our bayonets. . . . They had nearly reached the
railroad . . . when a shout behind [us] paralyzed us with dread.
Was [this] . . . an unseen movement to our rear? Terror stricken,
we turned; when lo! there were our friends, coming to our assistance. . . . [W]ith a wild Confederate yell [they] rushed upon Stevens as he was in the confusion of crossing [the railroad] to our attack. The Federals halted, turned, and fled, our friends crossing the
railroad and pursuing them.

*For a time during these late afternoon attacks, Jackson's left was
folded back; but the Federals were unable to hold their advantage.
According to Southern Lieutenant John Hampden Chamberlayne:*
    When the sun went down, their dead were heaped in front of the
incomplete railway; and we sighed with relief, for Longstreet could
be seen coming into position on our right. . . . But the sun went
down so slowly.

*While setting up his lines, Longstreet was opposed by three brigades
under General John P. Hatch. The Union's D. H. Strother, who saw
the action from afar, describes it as "a beautiful pyrotechnical
display."*
    The sparkling lines of musketry shone in the darkness like fire-
flies in a meadow, while the more brilliant flashes of artillery might
have been mistaken for swamp meteors. The show continued for an
hour, the advancing and receding fires indicating distinctly the surge
of the battle tide. . . . It seemed at length that the fire of the enemy's line began to extend and thicken, while ours wavered and fell
back. . . . Between eight and nine o'clock it ceased entirely. . . .

*Pope had expected to destroy Jackson's corps that afternoon. Even
as it was, the Union general somehow concluded that he had won
a considerable victory. He thought it likely that the Confederates
would retreat before he could renew his attack the next day.
Strangely enough, he refused to believe that Longstreet's entire corps
was on the field, choosing to think instead that only a small part of
the corps had arrived.*
    That evening, according to Union soldier Warren Goss:
    . . . as soon as the fighting ceased, many sought without orders
to rescue comrades lying wounded between the opposing lines. There

seemed to be a mutual understanding between the men of both armies that such parties were not to be disturbed in their mission of mercy. . . . Blankets attached to poles or muskets often served as stretchers. . . . Vehicles of various kinds were pressed into service.

The removal of the wounded went on during the entire night, and tired soldiers were roused from their slumbers by the plaintive cries of wounded comrades passing in torturing vehicles. In one instance, a Confederate and a Union soldier were found comforting each other on the field. They were put into the same Virginia farmcart and sent to the rear, talking and groaning in fraternal sympathy. . . .

The condition of Pope's army on Saturday, August 30, was such that a more cautious general would have hesitated before giving battle. His men were exhausted by incessant marching and fighting; thousands had straggled from their commands; the men had had but little to eat for two days previous; the horses of the artillery and cavalry were broken down from being continually in harness for over a week, and from want of forage.

But Pope believed . . . that the enemy were demoralized, while in fact their lines held the railroad embankment as a fortress. . . . At an early hour Pope ordered a reconnoissance made in his front. At this time the enemy, in readjusting their lines, had withdrawn their troops from some of the contested ground of the day previous. Pope interpreted this movement to mean that the enemy were in full retreat. . . .

The general worsened his view of the situation by persisting in his belief that the bulk of Longstreet's corps was still at a safe distance. Consequently Pope's orders, issued at noon, were that Jackson be pursued and pressed vigorously all day!

As it turned out, the fight began very much like that of the day before, the Federals going against the woods in front of the unfinished railroad.

Says General Longstreet, whose corps was linked to Jackson's right and was angled forward in such a way as to overlook Pope's left:

. . . a considerable force . . . began to attack . . . the whole of Jackson's line. . . . Pope . . . was ignoring me entirely. His whole army seemed to surge up against Jackson as if to crush him with an overwhelming mass. . . . It was a grand display of a well-organized attack. . . .

Lee at first withheld Longstreet from the action, choosing to let Pope wear himself down against the "stone wall." But Jackson soon had to call up his reserves. Writes Lieutenant Robert Healy, of the Fifty-fifth Virginia:

. . . we received urgent orders to reinforce a portion of our line . . . which was about to give way. We proceeded at double-quick. . . . The troops occupying this place had expended their ammunition and were defending themselves with rocks . . . which many were collecting and others were throwing. . . . We had ammunition—twenty rounds to the man—and we attacked the enemy and drove them headlong . . . [until] recalled. . . .

In Jackson's words:

As one line was repulsed, another took its place. . . . So impetuous and well sustained were these onsets as to induce me to send to the commanding general for reinforcements. . . .

Lee now ordered Longstreet to Jackson's support. Longstreet relates:

To retire from my advanced position . . . and get [around the rear] to Jackson would have taken an hour and a half. I had discovered a prominent position [on Pope's left] that commanded a view of the great struggle, and . . . I quickly ordered out three batteries, making twelve guns.

Lieutenant William H. Chapman's Dixie Battery of four guns was the first to report, and was placed in position to rake the Federal ranks that seemed determined to break through Jackson's lines. In a moment a heavy fire of shot and shell was being poured into the thick columns of the enemy, and in ten minutes their stubborn masses began to waver and give back. For a moment there was chaos; then order returned, and they reformed. . . .

Meanwhile my other eight pieces reported to me, and from the crest of the little hill the fire of twelve guns cut them down. As the cannon thundered, the ranks broke, only to be formed again with dogged determination. A third time the batteries tore the Federals to pieces, and as they fell back under this terrible fire, I sprung everything to the charge.

One of John Hood's brigades led the advance, with its colors, touched by the evening sun, "showing red against the azure sky." Other units, giving "exultant yells," quickly followed.

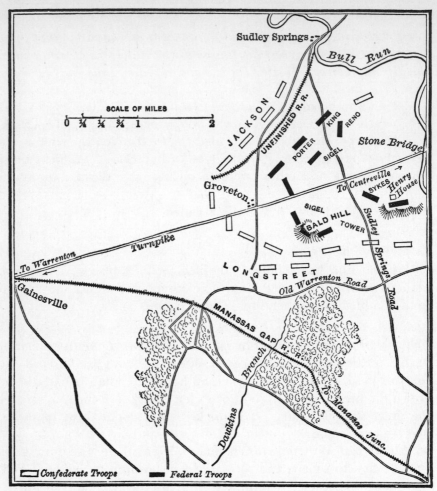

Second Bull Run: the Union retreat.

Writes the Union's Rufus R. Dawes, on the field as a major in the Sixth Wisconsin Volunteers:

We could see regiment after regiment of the enemy . . . form-ing into line of battle as they advanced. . . . The solid shot and shell struck around us and whizzed over us. Occasionally a horse would be killed . . . and one man's head was carried away entirely. . . . The rebel musketry fire was pouring . . . upon our men, who were closing together and rallying under the attack. Regiments would sweep splendidly forward into the front line, fire a crashing volley . . . and then [fight] with great energy. But they quickly withered away until there would appear to be a mere company crowding around the colors. The open fields were covered with wounded and stragglers, going to the rear.

Jackson's line joined Longstreet in the attack. The whole formed a great semicircle that pressed the Federals back across the old battle-field toward the Stone Bridge, where the Warrenton Turnpike crossed Bull Run (scene of the great rout of the first battle).

"As far as the eye could reach," says one Confederate officer, "the long lines of our army . . . were breaking over the plain in pursuit."

Adds Alexander Hunter, a Virginian with Hood's Division:

It was late in the evening, and . . . from all directions came the warring sound of cannon and musketry. . . . How hot it was! The clothes damp with perspiration, the canteens empty, throats parched with thirst, faces blackened by powder, the men mad with excitement.

Troops on both sides recognized spots on the battlefield where they had fought the year before. The Federals made their strongest stand on the Henry House Hill, and guns crashed over the grave of the aged Judith Henry, who had died in the first battle. This time her house was left a complete ruin.

The Union's Rufus Dawes relates that:

Regiments moved steadily . . . to the rear. The batteries moved also in retreat. A rebel line in our front rose up from the ground and advanced slowly after us. It was a strange sight—our blue line slowly retreating, and the long gray line slowly and quietly following. When we halted . . . the rebels halted and lay down on the ground.

It was growing dark [under skies turning cloudy and beginning to dispense a misty rain]. There was still a heavy roll of musketry to our left, and some sharp firing on our right. By nine o'clock, all had died away. About ten o'clock General Philip Kearny came up in rear of our regiment, which now lay . . . near the stone bridge over Bull Run. He informed us that our brigade was to be the rear guard of the army, which was in full retreat. We had not before suspected the real extent of the disaster.

Says General Longstreet:

. . . we had the field. Pope was across Bull Run [on the side toward Washington] and the victorious Confederates lay down on the battleground to sleep, while all around were strewn thousands—friend and foe—sleeping the last sleep together.

Pope stopped at Centreville, about twenty miles west of Washington. He was joined there by two more of McClellan's corps, those of Edwin Sumner and William Franklin.

Though now heavily outnumbered, Lee crossed Bull Run the day after the battle and sent Jackson on a northerly flanking maneuver in an effort to disrupt Pope's communications with the capital. On September 1, in a heavy rainstorm, Jackson encountered a part of the Federal force at Chantilly, just north of Centreville. Jackson was repulsed, but not until Generals Phil Kearny and Isaac Stevens had been killed. The next day Pope sought the security of the strong defenses around Washington.

The casualty figures for this campaign are variously given. They seem to have been somewhere around 15,000 for the Federals and 10,000 for the Confederates (both figures, as usual, representing a total of the killed, wounded, captured, and missing). Lee gave permission for the Federals to collect their wounded from the fields of Bull Run. These men were scattered everywhere, on the ground and also in buildings and tents. An unnamed soldier with a group in one of the tents was later to write:

There were six of us . . . and we six had had seven legs amputated. Our condition was horrible in the extreme. Several of us were as innocent of clothing as the hour we were born. Between our mangled bodies and the rough surface of the board floor there was a thin rubber blanket. To cover our nakedness, another blanket. . . . Between us and the fierce heat of that Virginia sun there was but the poor protection of the thin tent-cloth. There were plenty of flies to pester us and irritate our wounds. Our bodies became afflicted with loathsome sores, and—horror indescribable!—maggots found lodgings in wounds and sores, and we were helpless. . . .

A very few attendants had been detailed to stay behind with us when it was apparent we must fall into the enemy's hands, but they were entirely inadequate in point of numbers to minister to our wants. Heat and fever superinduced an awful thirst, and our moans were for water, water; and very often there was none to give us water.

The Union rescue operation is described by Warren Goss:

The ambulances, too few for the occasion, were supplemented by hacks and carriages of every description, brought from Washington. The tender hand of woman was there to alleviate distress; and the picture of misery was qualified by the heroic grit of those who suffered.

Thus ended another campaign in which Lee and his ragged, ill-equipped, and outnumbered army had enjoyed a signal triumph. Again a Union general had been made to look foolish. "Pope," said one Confederate soldier, "has found lines of retreat *and has not seen the* backs *of Lee, Longstreet, Stonewall Jackson, and their men."*

Lee had every reason to be pleased with the situation. In the words of Edward Pollard, the Southern editor and historian: "Now the war was transferred from the gates of Richmond to those of Washington."

The capital was the scene of great agitation over the nearness of the enemy. Pollard claims, with considerable justification, that the Confederates had risen so much in Northern opinion "that no project was thought too extravagant, or enterprise too daring, for the troops of Lee and Jackson." But Washington's fears were groundless. Lee and Jackson had no intention of attacking the city. They hadn't the power.

As for the Federal troops, they were dispirited but not robbed of their confidence. They had fought well, and they knew it. They blamed their defeat on the way they were led. In a letter written as the campaign closed, Captain William T. Lusk, of New York, lamented:

Men show themselves in a thousand ways incompetent, yet still they receive the support of the Government. . . . The battle comes; there is no head on the field; the men are handed over to be butchered. . . . The army finds that nothing has been learned. New preparations are made, with all the old errors retained. New battles are prepared for, to end in new disasters. Alas, my poor country!

10

ANTIETAM

DURING POPE'S CAMPAIGN, George B. McClellan's authority declined sharply. Overall control of the Union armies in Virginia was in the hands of Major General Henry W. Halleck, operating from Washington in cooperation with Lincoln and Stanton. (Halleck had recently been appointed "to command the whole land forces of the United States, as general-in-chief.") McClellan wasn't officially deprived of his title as commander of the Army of the Potomac, but his numbers melted away under his orders from Halleck to reinforce Pope's Army of Virginia. Now, as Pope fell from grace, McClellan came to the fore again. His talents were needed to rescue the situation, to merge the Virginia armies into a revitalized Army of the Potomac. Writes Union soldier Warren Goss:

Two days after our second defeat at Bull Run, while yet the roads were crowded with stragglers, and despondency overshadowed all, McClellan reassumed command of the army. It was the morning of September 2d, 1862, and reorganization began at once. . . . In no direction was the ability of McClellan so conspicuous as in organizing. Even before the soldiers knew he was again in command, they began to detect a new influence around them.

But McClellan's schedule was quickly upset. On September 3 General Lee began marching northward to the Potomac River, Maryland's southwestern border. His plan of the moment was unknown to the Federals, but they had a pretty good idea of his general intentions. Explains Northern news correspondent Charles Coffin:

It was universally believed in the South that the sympathies of the people of Maryland were with the Confederacy. . . . It was believed that if General Lee were to cross the Potomac and enter that state thousands of young men would flock to his ranks; that Baltimore would welcome him with open arms; and that the possible result might be the capture of Washington or a movement into Pennsylvania. . . .

. . . a movement [into Maryland] would terrify the Northern States [and strengthen the sentiment, already considerable, for settling the war in a manner agreeable to the South]. If he could fight another battle and win a great victory north of the Potomac, England and France would [be likely to] recognize the Confederacy and break the blockade. The soldiers were ready and eager to invade the North. Had they not driven McClellan from Richmond? Had they not defeated the combined armies of McClellan and Pope?

McClellan takes up:

The Army of the Potomac was thoroughly exhausted and depleted by its desperate fighting and severe marches in the unhealthy regions of the Chickahominy and . . . during the Second Bull Run campaign. Its [wagon] trains, administration services, and supplies were disorganized or lacking. . . . The divisions of the Army of Virginia were also exhausted and weakened, and their trains were disorganized and their supplies deficient. . . . Had General Lee remained in front of Washington, it would have been the part of wisdom to hold our own army quiet until its pressing wants were fully supplied. . . . But as the enemy maintained the offensive . . . it became necessary to meet him at any cost, notwithstanding the condition of the troops. . . .

McClellan wrote his wife:

Again I have been called upon to save the country. . . . I still hope for success, and will leave nothing undone to gain it. . . . It makes my heart bleed to see the poor, shattered remnants of my noble Army of the Potomac . . . and to see how they love me even now. I hear them calling out to me as I ride among them, "George, don't leave us again!"

As McClellan's various units began making their way out of Washington for the march against Lee, an officer of the Twentieth Massachusetts Infantry, Francis W. Palfrey, noted that the city and its environs "presented singular sights."

The luxury and refinements of peace contrasted sharply with the privations and squalor of war. There are few prettier suburban drives than those in the neighborhood of Washington, and no weather is more delightful than that of late summer there. . . . As the shadows lengthened in the golden afternoon, well-appointed carriages rolled along those charming drives, bearing fair women in cool and fresh costumes; and by their side the ragged, dusty, sunburnt regiments from the Peninsula trudged along. . . . The carriages returned to their stables, the fair ladies returned to the enjoyment of every pleasure that Washington could confer; but the Army of the Potomac moved steadily northward, to bivouac under the stars or the clouds, and to march again in its tatters through the dust and the sunshine, through the rain and the mud.

Lee wasted no time entering Maryland, the men being in high spirits as the bold move was made. Relates Henry Kyd Douglas, of Stonewall Jackson's staff:

On the 5th of September [we] crossed the Potomac at White's Ford, a few miles beyond Leesburg. The passage [through the shallow waters] of the river by the troops, marching in fours, well closed up—the laughing, shouting, and singing, as a brass band in front played "Maryland, My Maryland," was a memorable experience.

The Marylanders in the corps [since earlier in the war] imparted much of their enthusiasm to the other troops; but we were not long in finding out that if General Lee had hopes that the decimated regiments of his army would be filled by the sons of Maryland, he was doomed to a speedy and unqualified disappointment. However, before we had been in Maryland many hours, one enthusiastic citizen presented Jackson with a gigantic gray mare. . . . Yet the present proved almost a Trojan horse to him, for the next morning when he mounted his new steed and touched her with his spur, the . . . undisciplined beast reared straight into the air, and . . . threw herself backward, horse and rider rolling upon the ground. The general was stunned and severely bruised. . . .

Early that day the army went into camp near Frederick, and Generals Lee, Longstreet, Jackson, and for a time Jeb Stuart, had their headquarters near one another in Best's Grove. Hither in crowds came the good people of Frederick, especially the ladies. . . . General Jackson, still suffering from his hurt, kept to his tent, busying himself with maps and official papers, and declined to see visitors. Once, however, when he had been called to General Lee's tent, two young girls waylaid him, paralyzed him with smiles and embraces and questions, and then jumped into their carriage and drove off rapidly, leaving him there, cap in hand, bowing, blushing, and speechless. But once safe in his tent, he was seen no more that day.

The Federals, whom the geography of the situation had placed north of the Potomac when they set out, were at this time some miles southeast of Frederick. Writes the French officer, Regis de Trobriand:
The army advanced slowly and with caution. In this, General McClellan did not depart from his usual habits, but here the circumstances demanded prudence. The Confederates menaced Baltimore as well as Washington. While endeavoring to divine their intentions, it was necessary for him to cover the two cities. . . .

Lee's army numbered about 55,000 men. McClellan's strength was building toward 90,000; but information he got from his cavalry scouts convinced him he was outnumbered: "The last reports . . . are that the enemy have 110,000. . . . I must watch them closely and try to catch them in some mistake. . . ."
The Federals in the ranks were not altogether clear as to what was happening. They knew only one thing for certain: They had covered a lot of miles since the previous spring. Said a letter written by Chaplain A. M. Stewart, of the Pennsylvania Volunteers:
If marching and countermarching, assuming new positions, changing base, with multiplied strategy, will suffice to catch those rascally secesh, we'll have them, certainly, and that soon.

In another letter, Chaplain Stewart pondered the morality of appropriating the fruits and vegetables of Maryland's farmers:
During the past six months our regiment has been almost entirely confined to strong, coarse army grub—hard crackers, salt pork

and beef, with coffee, and occasionally rice, beans, and fresh beef. In consequence of such a diet so long continued, when the Peninsula was abandoned scurvy had become quite common. . . . Montgomery County, Maryland . . . abounded in apple, pear, and peach orchards . . . also with cornfields. . . . These . . . were the very things needed to give proper tone to the system. . . .

. . . our boys have been in possession of no money for long months—scarcely a copper among a hundred. . . . Nor has the quartermaster the authority to purchase and distribute [the farm products] as rations. . . . If taken without pay . . . the owners . . . will be left in want and to suffer. . . .

Scenes . . . like the following have not been unfrequent of late. It may be prefaced that the young men of our regiment are in every possible way kind and obliging to their chaplain [having even given him the honorary title of "Doctor of Divinity"]. One of them, brave and generous, from a dozen bloody battlefields, lately visited my humble bunk. . . .

"Doctor," says the young veteran, "will you accept half a dozen beautiful ripe peaches?" at the same time producing the delicious-looking and fragrant-smelling fruit.

"O, what beautiful peaches! Why, where, and how did you obtain them?"

With a peculiarly knowing look and tone, as the peaches are laid beside me, he replies, "Ask no questions, Doctor, for conscience' sake."

Another comes with the salutation, "Doctor, will you accept these two roasting ears? They are very good, and nicely cooked."

"Roasting ears, my dear young friend, are great favorites with me."

And still another—"Doctor, here is a big boiled potato. . . . See how it laughs through a dozen cracks in its bursted skin."

"Much obliged. Very fond of a good potato."

Though personally I have pulled no roasting ears, shaken no apple tree, plucked no peaches, nor turned up a single potato hill, yet . . . these things have been taken and eaten, the owners uncompensated. . . .

Not all of the Federals were as poor as Chaplain Stewart's Pennsylvanians. Many paid for the foodstuffs and other things they acquired.

As for Lee's troops, many of them also paid as they went. It was Lee's intention that the sellers be given their choice of accepting either U.S. Treasury notes or Confederate currency, but numerous Unionists were forced to take "the damn Rebel issue."

An unnamed private in the Confederate army recorded this example of foraging on the march:

The men had not a mouthful to eat, and squads from the different companies obtained permission to forage for themselves and comrades. I was on one of these details. Leaving the road and striking across the fields, we entered into a yard in the center of which stood a fine brick mansion. We knocked at the door; there was no response; and then after waiting awhile we entered and found to our astonishment that it was deserted. The inmates had fled in anticipation of a battle. . . .

Not an article had been carried off; the parlor door was open; there stood the piano; the pictures depended from the wall; the curtains hung as gracefully as if some hand had just arranged their folds. We entered the dining room; there rested the cat on the window sill; everything seemed so natural it was difficult to realize that the hostess would not enter and welcome us in a few moments.

We had no time to linger. . . . Beside, we had come to get something to eat, and not to make any voyage of discovery. So finding nothing in the pantry nor in the kitchen, we went to the spring and filled our canteens with water, then to the dairy at the foot of the hill, and discovered several buckets and cans of milk which had been placed there last night. . . .

We [emptied our canteens of water and filled them] with the lacteal fluid; and noticing the loft, a room over the dairy, we climbed up, and found it a perfect storeroom. Several barrels were on stands, and on investigating the contents of one, it was found to be cider; and then the canteens were emptied of milk and filled with the juice of the apple. An exclamation from one of the party brought us over to him, and he showed us a barrel of apple brandy. That cider in the canteens was soon poured on the floor, and the apple jack took its place.

An animated discussion took place. The whole squad, except the sergeant, wanted to carry the barrel and leave everything else behind; but then came the difficulty about obeying orders. The discussion waxed high, and to end the matter the sergeant stove in the head of the barrel with the butt of his musket, and the precious liquid that would have made glad, for a time at least, the whole brigade, poured in a useless stream upon the floor.

In the room were half a dozen tubs of apple butter, which we

confiscated for the use of our comrades. . . . Starting toward the reflected steel that flashed in the sunlight like a beacon to the mariner,
showing us where our troops were marching, we hurried after, and
soon caught up with them.

I will drop for a second the character of a veracious chronicler,
and not mention how many lips were glued long and lovingly to the
mouths of those canteens. The owner's health was honestly drank,
however. . . .

*Because Maryland had fewer Southern sympathizers than antici-
pated, the Confederates were unable to get supplies in the quantities they needed. Shoes remained a desperate want. Some of the
troops were without blankets. Comfort at night for most depended
upon their having a piece of canvas or some other water-repellent
material to roll in. The private of the apple brandy tells of his situation when "some thieving Reb" made off with his oilcloth:*

I had no blanket. . . . As a makeshift, I begged a newspaper, a
copy of the New York *World,* and lay on that; and, as it kept the
moistened earth from my person, it answered quite well. . . . I
would fold it up with great care every morning. But one night it
rained, and there was nothing left of it. Anyway, I have always had a
tender feeling for the New York *World* ever since.

*The same Southern private wrote graphically of another problem he
and his comrades had to contend with, that of body lice. The vermin,
actually, were a common problem in both armies, but they appear to
have been especially annoying to the Confederates during the invasion of Maryland:*

These insects, which in camp parlance were called "graybacks,"
first made their appearance in the winter of 1861. At first the soldier
was mortified, and felt almost disgraced at discovering one of these
insects on his person . . . and energetic efforts were made to hide
the secret and eliminate the cause. At first the soldier used to steal
out companionless and alone, and hide in the woods and bushes,
with as much secretness and caution as if he were going to commit
some fearful crime. Once hid from the eyes of men, he would pursue
and murder the crawling insects with a vengeful pleasure, thinking
that now he would have peace and comfort of mind. . . . On his
stealthy way back he would be sure to run in on a dozen solitary in-

dividuals, who tried to look unconcerned, as if indeed they were in the habit of retiring in the dim recesses of the forest for private meditation.

The satisfaction he felt would not last long. In a day or two his body would be infested again. . . . It was simply impossible to exterminate them. . . . Once lodged in the seams of the clothing, they remained until time moldered the garments. You might scald, scour, scrub, cleanse, rub, purify, leave them in seathing liquid, or bury the raiment in the ground; but it was wasted labor, for the insects seemed to enjoy the process, and increased and multiplied under it.

On this march, particularly, when the troops had no change of clean clothes for weeks, the soldiers were literally infested with them. Many used to place their under raiment, during the night, in the bottom of some stream, and put a large stone to keep them down. In the morning they would hastily dry them, and get a temporary relief. Every evening in Maryland, when the army halted and bivouacked for the night, hundreds of the soldiers could be seen sitting on the roads or fields, half denuded, with their clothes in their laps, busily cracking, between the two thumb-nails, these creeping nuisances.

The "good people of Frederick" who came out to Lee's camp and enthused over his presence were not in the majority. On September 10, when the army marched through the town, the citizens who lined the streets to watch were "decidedly cool." All, however, were fascinated. One woman, a staunch Unionist whose name survives only as "Kate," left these impressions in a letter intended for a friend in Baltimore:

I wish, my dearest Minnie, you could have witnessed the transit of the Rebel army through our streets. . . . Their coming was unheralded by any pomp and pageant whatever. . . . Instead came three long dirty columns that kept on in an unceasing flow. I could scarcely believe my eyes.

Was this body of men, moving . . . along with no order, their guns carried in every fashion, no two dressed alike, their officers hardly distinguishable from the privates—were these, I asked myself in amazement, were these dirty, lank, ugly specimens of humanity, with shocks of hair sticking through the holes in their hats, and the dust thick on their dirty faces, the men that had coped and encountered successfully and driven back again and again our splendid legions . . . ?

I must confess, Minnie, that I felt humiliated at the thought that this horde of ragamuffins could set our grand army of the Union at defiance. Why, it seemed as if a single regiment of our gallant boys in blue could drive that dirty crew into the river without any trouble!

. . . I wish you could see how they behaved. A crowd of boys on a holiday don't seem happier. They are on the broad grin all the time. O, they are so dirty! I don't think the Potomac River could wash them clean. And ragged! There is not a scarecrow in the corn-fields that would not scorn to exchange clothes with them. . . .

I saw some strikingly handsome faces though, or rather they would have been so if they could have had a good scrubbing. They were very polite, I must confess. . . . Many of them were bare-footed. Indeed, I felt sorry for the poor misguided wretches, for some of them limped along so painfully, trying hard to keep with their comrades.

But I must stop. I . . . hope [this] will reach you safely. Write to me as soon as the route is open.

Kate never received an answer to this letter, for it never reached Minnie. It was intercepted by the Confederates, who read it with enjoyment and preserved it for the record.

Henry Kyd Douglas, in writing of Stonewall Jackson's passage through Frederick, sets something straight:

Just a few words here in regard to Mr. [John Greenleaf] Whittier's touching poem, "Barbara Frietchie." An old woman by that . . . name did live in Frederick . . . but she never saw General Jackson, and General Jackson never saw Barbara Frietchie. I was with him every minute of the time he was in that city. . . . Mr. Whittier must have been misinformed as to the incident.

On the march that day . . . we entered each village . . . before the inhabitants knew of our coming. In Middletown two very pretty girls, with ribbons of red, white, and blue floating from their hair, and small Union flags in their hands, rushed out of a house as we passed, came to the curbstone, and with much laughter waved their flags defiantly in the face of the general.

He bowed and raised his hat, and, turning with his quiet smile to his staff, said: "We evidently have no friends in this town."

And that is about the way he would have treated Barbara Frietchie!

William Miller Owen, an officer with one of Lee's artillery units, tells of another incident concerning a Southerner's reaction to a Union sympathizer:

On a small gallery [i.e., on a front porch passed by the Confederate marchers] stood a buxom young lady with laughing black eyes, watching the scene before her. On her breast she had pinned a small flag, the "stars and stripes." This was observed, and some soldier sang out, "Look h'yar, miss; better take that flag down; we're awful fond of charging breast-works!"

Lee's columns were moving westward to the passes through Maryland's South Mountain, with Stonewall Jackson looking southwestward toward the northern end of Virginia's Shenandoah Valley. As explained by Regis de Trobriand, of McClellan's army:

When the Confederates invaded Maryland, their line of retreat and their base of supplies were necessarily transferred to the valley of the Shenandoah. At the point where that river empties into the Potomac, we had, at Harper's Ferry [which place had been retaken after its abandonment to the Confederates at the war's beginning], a corps of nine thousand men . . . [the corps being supported by] a brigade of two thousand men at Martinsburg. . . . These troops barred the way [to and] from the valley. . . . General Lee . . . found it necessary . . . to detach a considerable portion of his force to reduce Harper's Ferry. . . .

However, McClellan, on arriving at Frederick, [came] to the knowledge of the movements of his adversary by a happy chance, which . . . delivered into his hands a copy of a dispatch addressed to the generals of his enemy.

This dispatch was one composed by Lee, and it outlined his whole plan of action, explaining how he had divided his army. The paper was found, wrapped around some cigars, on an abandoned Confederate campground. The mystery of how this highly confidential document arrived in such an unlikely situation was never solved.

"Here is a paper," said the jubilant McClellan, "with which, if I cannot whip Bobbie Lee, I will be willing to go home!"

But instead of pressing forward at once, McClellan waited until the next morning, September 14. He encountered strong opposition at the South Mountain passes, and spent all day and part of the night fighting his way through. When the last of the Confederates finally fell back, it was too late for the Federals to save Harpers Ferry (some

*miles to the south) from Jackson. But McClellan got the idea that he
had won a glorious victory. He wrote his wife:*

Every moment adds to its importance. . . . How glad I am for
my country that it is delivered from immediate peril! . . . If I can
believe one-tenth of what is reported, God has seldom given an army
a greater victory than this.

*By telegram, McClellan enthused so convincingly to Washington
that a delighted Lincoln replied: "God bless you, and all with you.
Destroy the rebel army if possible."*

*Actually, the main battle had not yet been fought. McClellan
was delayed long enough at South Mountain for Lee to begin setting
up a defense line to the west, behind Antietam Creek at Sharpsburg.*

Writes Confederate General James Longstreet:

On the forenoon of the 15th, the blue uniforms of the Federals
appeared among the trees that crowned the heights on the eastern
bank of the Antietam. The number increased, and larger and larger
grew the field of blue until it seemed to stretch as far as the eye
could see; and from the tops of the mountains down [through the
farmlands] to the edges of the stream gathered the great army of Mc-
Clellan. It was an awe-inspiring spectacle as this grand force settled
down in sight of the Confederates, then shattered by battles and scattered by long and tiresome marches.

*In recent days, the Confederate army had been much reduced by
straggling—perhaps mostly on the part of men without shoes, who
found Maryland's macadam roads severely punishing.*

"Fortune," says the Union army's Regis de Trobriand,

was not yet weary of offering to McClellan favorable opportu-
nities. . . . Here again she put into his hands all the good cards. She
brought him, with more than eighty thousand men, in front of an
enemy compelled to accept battle with . . . forty thousand. . . .

*McClellan spent September 15 and 16 preparing his attack. His de-
liberateness enabled Lee to assemble all of his forces except three divisions lingering at Harpers Ferry (to the south) to tie up the loose
ends of the capture—and even they would arrive on the field in time
to share in the fighting.*

*The evening of the sixteenth saw some skirmishing as Joe Hooker
swung around the Confederate left, where Jackson commanded, in
preparation for his part in the attack.*

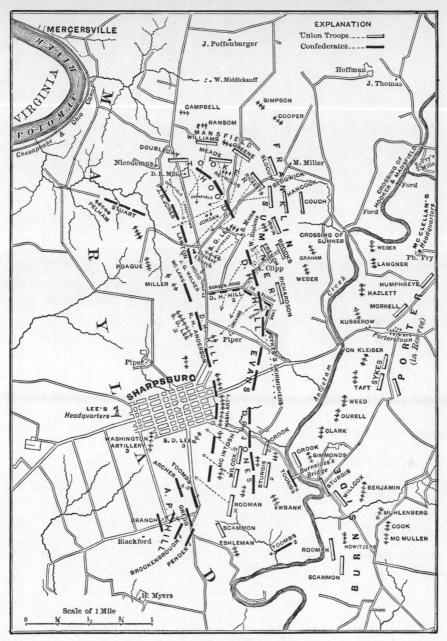

The Battle of Antietam.

A Confederate volley at South Mountain.

Writes Union officer Francis Palfrey:
The night before the battle passed quietly, except for some alarms on Hooker's front; and most of the men in both armies probably got a good sleep. The morning broke gray and misty, but the mists disappeared early. . . .

Confederate brigade commander John B. Gordon, who was stationed near the center of Lee's line and had an excellent view of "both armies and the entire field," tells how the battle began:
On the elevated points beyond the narrow valley the Union batteries were rolled into position, and the Confederate heavy guns unlimbered to answer them. For one or more seconds, and before the first sounds reached us, we saw the great volumes of white smoke rolling from the mouths of McClellan's artillery. The next second brought the roar of the heavy discharges and the loud explosions of hostile shells in the midst of our lines. . . . The Confederate batteries promptly responded.

. . . while the artillery of both armies thundered, McClellan's compact columns of infantry fell upon the left of Lee's lines [scene of "the cornfield" and "the Dunkard Church"] with the crushing weight of a landslide. . . . Pressed back . . . the Southern troops, enthused by Lee's presence, re-formed their lines, and, with a shout

Antietam: Federals shelling Lee's lines.

as piercing as the blast of a thousand bugles, rushed in counter-charge upon the exulting Federals [and] hurled them back in confusion. . . .

Again and again . . . by charges and counter-charges, this portion of the field was lost and recovered, until the green corn that grew upon it looked as if it had been struck by a storm of bloody hail. . . . From sheer exhaustion, both sides, like battered and bleeding athletes, [at length] seemed willing to rest. General Lee took advantage of the respite and rode along his lines. . . .

Lee's counterpart on the Union side remained at his headquarters at a country home behind his right wing. McClellan rarely appeared at the front during a battle. He did not lack courage, but it pained him acutely to see his beloved army bloodied.

Charles Coffin, of the Boston Journal, *spent some time at McClellan's headquarters that morning:*

The general was sitting in an arm-chair in front of the house. His staff were about him; their horses . . . were hitched to the trees and fences. Stakes had been driven in the earth in front of the house, to which were strapped the headquarters telescopes. . . . The panorama included fully two-thirds of the battlefield. . . .

About 10:30 A.M. the telescopes were swung from the Confederate left toward the center, where a new Federal attack was developing against several brigades stationed along a sunken road. Lee had anticipated this attack, and had told the brigade commanders that the center must stand firm at all costs. John B. Gordon, whose brigade occupied an advanced position, promised, "These men are going to stay here, General, till the sun goes down or victory is won."

The day was clear and beautiful [Gordon relates]. . . . The men in blue filed down the opposite slope, crossed the little stream . . . and formed in my front, an assaulting column four lines deep. . . . The brave Union commander, superbly mounted, placed himself in front, while his band in rear cheered them with martial music. . . . As we stood looking upon that brilliant pageant, I thought . . . "What a pity to spoil with bullets such a scene of martial beauty!" But . . . Mars is not an aesthetic god. . . .

Every act and movement of the Union commander . . . clearly indicated his purpose to discard bullets and depend upon bayonets. He essayed to break through Lee's centre by the crushing weight and momentum of his solid column. . . . In a few minutes they were within easy range of our rifles. . . . Now the front rank was within a few rods of where I stood. It would not do to wait another second, and with all my lung power I shouted "Fire!"

My rifles flamed and roared in the Federals' faces. . . . The entire front line, with few exceptions, went down in the consuming blast. The gallant commander and his horse fell in a heap . . . the horse dead, the rider unhurt. Before his rear lines could recover from the terrific shock, my exultant men were . . . devouring them with successive volleys. Even then these stubborn blue lines retreated in fairly good order. . . .

The result . . . of this first effort to penetrate the Confederate centre did not satisfy the intrepid Union commander. Beyond the range of my rifles he reformed his men into three lines, and on foot led them to the second charge, still with unloaded guns. This advance was also repulsed; but again and again did he advance in four successive charges in the fruitless effort to break through my lines with the bayonets.

Finally his troops were ordered to load. He drew up in close rank and easy range, and opened a galling fire upon my line. . . . The first volley . . . sent a ball . . . through the calf of my right leg. On the right and the left my men were falling . . . like trees in a hurricane. . . . Higher up in the same leg I was again shot; but still no bone was broken. I was able to walk along the line and give encouragement to my resolute riflemen. . . .

At one point Gordon came upon an elderly man and his son lying side by side on the ground:

The son was dead, the father mortally wounded. The gray-haired hero called me and said, "Here we are. My boy is dead, and I shall go soon. But it is all right."

When Gordon himself was hit a third time, the ball "tearing . . . the tendons and mangling the flesh" of his left arm, his men urged him to go to the rear:

I could not consent to leave them in such a crisis. . . . I had a vigorous constitution, and this was doing me good service.

A fourth ball ripped through my shoulder. . . . I could still stand and walk, although the shocks and loss of blood had left but little of my normal strength.

I remembered the pledge to the commander that we would stay there till the battle ended or night came. I looked at the sun. It . . . seemed to stand still. I thought I saw some wavering in my line, near the extreme right; and Private Vickers, of Alabama, volunteered . . . to go quickly and remind the men of the pledge to General Lee. . . . He bounded away . . . but he had gone less than fifty yards when he fell, instantly killed by a ball through his head.

I then attempted to go myself, although I was bloody and faint, and my legs did not bear me steadily. I had gone but a short distance when I was shot down by a fifth ball which struck me squarely in the face and passed out, barely missing the jugular vein. I fell forward and lay unconscious with my face in my cap; and it would seem that I might have been smothered by the blood running into my cap . . . but for the act of some Yankee who . . . had at a previous hour . . . shot a hole through the cap, which let the blood out.

I was borne on a litter to the rear. . . .

Gordon would be seven months recovering; but this remarkable leader's role in the war was far from over.

Among the men on the Union side who fought at the sunken road was Lieutenant A. H. Nickerson:

It seemed that everybody near me was killed. A waif of a boy named Johnny Cummins . . . though his arm was broken by a rifle ball . . . would not leave me. Handing me his musket, he said, "Do the shooting, lieutenant, and I'll furnish the cartridges."

. . . I used all the cartridges he had; and as I was putting down [through the muzzle] the twelfth and last, I felt the whiz of a bullet that came very close to me and drove the splinters from a little sapling . . . on my right rear. I saw the tall Confederate who had apparently paid me the compliment as he slowly put down his gun and looked to see if he had hit me. Then he dropped down, and was evidently reloading his piece. I could see the crown of his hat, in which I thought about four inches of his head might be exposed. . . . I drew as close a bead as I could. . . . A little cloud of dust flew up from the edge of the bank as I fired, and the man's head, unconsciously popping up, showed me that I had missed him.

I looked around for Cummins, but he had disappeared. A dead soldier lay across my feet, and stooping down, I hastily drew a cartridge from his box, bit off the end, poured in the powder, and forced the bullet in. It proved to be an elongated bullet . . . unfitted for a smoothbore musket. When it was [rammed] about halfway down it turned in the barrel and there stuck.

My adversary raised and very deliberately drew a bead on me. I knew that I was gone. . . . Had I tried to run away I should certainly have been shot in the back. . . . All the while . . . I was trying to force the bullet in my musket home. My arm was upraised in this position when my Confederate antagonist fired. I felt the sharp jab of the bullet, a blur about the eyes, and the warm blood running down my right side as that arm fell helpless. His shot had . . . struck the shoulder joint, and . . . came out between the shoulder and elbow.

Upon orders from his commanding officer, Nickerson went to the rear. Presently meeting his black servant, a youth named Joe White, he was taken to an emergency hospital in nearby Keedysville, one set up in a church:

The operating surgeons were in their shirtsleeves, which were rolled up, leaving their bare arms exposed and covered with blood, giving them the appearance of a bevy of butchers in a Chicago abattoir. While sitting awaiting the surgeon, every few minutes an attendant would bring past me, to the open window, an arm, a leg, or a mangled hand, which he pitched into a little trench dug under the window for the purpose.

Pretty soon a young surgeon came up, and, grabbing me by the shoulder, said . . . "Shoulder smashed?"

A sickening feeling came over me as I replied that it certainly would be [now] if it were not [before].

"Bring this man some whisky," said he, as I reeled in my seat.

A glass of whisky . . . did not seem to affect me any more than would so much water, the pain was so intense. Then the young surgeon thrust his finger into the hole where the bullet had entered, and with his other forefinger plunged into the place of its exit he rummaged around for broken bones, splinters, etc., until I swooned away. . . .

Fortunately I knew no more about what transpired until I found myself [with arm intact and shoulder bandaged] . . . under the trees outside, and Joe fanning me with his old slouched hat.

At the sunken road, things were going badly for the Confederates. Some of the attacking Federals had swung around the position's right flank and subjected it to an enfilading fire. The defenders fell by scores, and the survivors staggered back.

This part of the action was watched with keen interest by those at Union headquarters across the Antietam. Writes D. H. Strother, formerly of Pope's staff and now on McClellan's:

As the smoke and dust disappeared, I was astonished to observe our troops moving along the front and passing over what appeared to be a long, heavy column of the enemy without paying it any attention whatever. I borrowed a glass from an officer, and discovered this to be actually a column of the enemy's dead and wounded lying along a hollow road—afterward known as Bloody Lane. Among the prostrate mass I could easily distinguish the movements of those endeavoring to crawl away from the ground; hands waving as if calling for assistance, and others struggling as if in the agonies of death.

I was standing beside General McClellan during the progress and conclusion of this attack. The studied calmness of his manner scarcely concealed the underlying excitement, and when it was over he exclaimed, "By George, this is a magnificent field, and if we win this fight it will cover all our errors and misfortunes forever!"

As for errors—this assertion by Federal newsman Charles Coffin tells the story:

Just here McClellan lost a great opportunity. It was the plain dictate of common sense that then was the time when [his reserves]

Burnside's attack across Antietam Creek.

should have been . . . thrown like a thunderbolt upon the enemy. It was so plain that the rank and file saw it. . . . The moment had come for dividing Lee's army at its center and crushing it back upon the Potomac in utter rout.

McClellan's reason for not committing his reserves was that he was saving them for a possible defensive emergency. He did not know that he had Lee outnumbered 2 to 1. In a telegram to Washington at 1:20 P.M., he reported, "I have great odds against me."

Thus far, little had been heard from McClellan's left, where Ambrose Burnside commanded. It was Burnside's mission to force his way across the Antietam and attack the troops under Longstreet on Lee's right, southeast of Sharpsburg.

D. H. Strother, of Union headquarters, says that McClellan had begun to ask with impatience, "What is Burnside about? Why do we not hear from him?"

Strother goes on:

During the morning [McClellan had] sent several messengers to hasten his movements; but we only heard vaguely that he . . . could not carry the bridge. . . . At length, about four o'clock in the afternoon, the cumulating thunder on the left announced that Burnside's advance had at last commenced. . . . The advance was distinctly visible from our position, and the movement of the dark columns, with arms and banners glittering in the sun, following the double line of skirmishers, dashing forward at a trot, loading and firing alternately as they moved, was one of the most brilliant and exciting exhibitions of the day.

Though his position in Lee's lines forbade him a sight of this action, General John G. Walker could tell what was happening. He writes that the sounds of the action indicated

that the Federal left had forced a crossing of the Antietam, and that it must be perilously near our only line of retreat to the Potomac. . . . Could it be that A. P. Hill had come up [from Harpers Ferry] and had been repulsed? If so, we had lost the day. . . .

Soon the sound of musketry, which had almost ceased, roared out again with increased volume, indicating that fresh troops had been brought up, on one side or the other. For thirty minutes the sound of the firing came steadily from the same direction; then it seemed to recede eastward, and finally to die away almost entirely.

We knew then that Hill *was* up; that the Federals had been driven back, and that the Confederate army had narrowly escaped defeat.

During the confusion of Burnside's retreat, groups of Federals were left behind. David L. Thompson, an enlisted man from New York, lingered to aid some wounded comrades gathered in a hollow, and he soon found himself cut off from his regiment:

There was nothing to do but lie there and await developments. Nearly all the men in the hollow were wounded, one man . . . frightfully so, his arm being cut short off. He lived a few minutes only. All were calling for water, of course, but none was to be had.

We lay there . . . perhaps an hour. . . . During that hour . . . we had time to speculate on many things—among others, on the impatience with which men clamor, in dull times, to be led into a fight.

We heard all through the war that the army "was eager to be led against the enemy." It must have been so, for truthful correspondents said so, and editors confirmed it. But when you came to hunt for this particular itch, it was always the next regiment that had it.

The truth is, when bullets are whacking against tree trunks and solid shot are cracking skulls like eggshells, the consuming passion in the breast of the average man is to get out of the way. Between the physical fear of going forward and the moral fear of turning back, there is a predicament of exceptional awkwardness. . . .

The introspective Thompson and his comrades were soon rounded up by the Confederates. Thompson's time in custody was to be short. Within a few weeks, an exchange of prisoners would make him "again legally and technically food for powder."

Antietam's fighting was about over. The long day was coming to a close. Says Federal newsman Charles Coffin:

The sun went down, the thunder died away, the musketry ceased, bivouac fires gleamed out as if a great city had lighted its lamps.

The smoke from the campfires merged with the great pall left by the battle, and the illuminations were overmatched in several places by burning farm buildings and the bright embers of burned haystacks. From all parts of the field, with its orange-hued shadows, came "the wailing cries of the wounded." As usual, the facilities for caring for these men were inadequate.

Even as the wounded agonized, some of the men in both camps sang around their fires. On the Union side, one of the songs went as follows:

> *Do they miss me at home? Do they miss me?*
> *'Twould be an assurance most dear*
> *To know that this moment some loved one*
> *Were saying, "I wish he were here,"*
> *To feel that the group at the fireside*
> *Were thinking of me as I roam;*
> *Oh, yes, 'twould be joy beyond measure*
> *To know that they miss me at home.*

The day had been extraordinarily costly for both sides. It would, indeed, become known as "the bloodiest day of the war." The Confederates had suffered about 11,000 casualties; and the Federals, as the attackers, had suffered some 12,000. The Confederates, in particular, could not afford such losses. Writes James Longstreet:

It was heart-rending to see how Lee's army had been slashed by the day's fighting. . . . We were so badly crushed that at the close of the day ten thousand fresh troops could have come in and taken Lee's army and everything it had. But McClellan did not know it. . . .

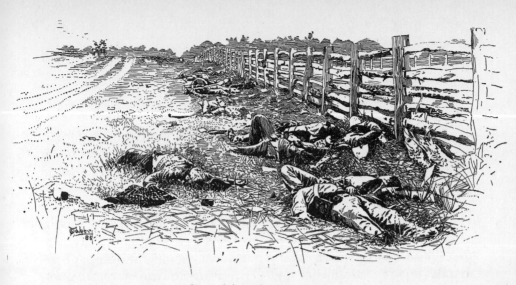

Casualties of Antietam.

McClellan wrote his wife:

The general result was in our favor. . . . I hope that God has given us a great success. . . . Those in whose judgment I rely tell me that I fought the battle splendidly, and that it was a masterpiece of art.

Others felt differently. Newsman Coffin criticizes:

The battle was in the main fought by divisions—one after another. There was no concerted action, no hammering along all the line at the same time. Heavy blows were given, but they were not followed up.

Most of the soldiers on both sides at last settled down to "sleep and forgetfulness and refreshment."
General McClellan was among the wakeful:

The night brought with it grave responsibilities. Whether to renew the attack on the 18th, or to defer it, even with the risk of the enemy's retirement, was the question before me. After a night of anxious deliberation and a full and careful survey of the situation and condition of our army, the strength and position of the enemy, I concluded that the success of an attack on the 18th was not certain.

Union officer Regis de Trobriand laments:

Thus the whole of the 18th passed away, and McClellan was unable to come to the resolution to profit by this last opportunity offered him by fortune. He had asked for fifteen thousand men from Washington, and he was waiting for them!

Always reinforcements; reinforcements *quand même!*

Adds Union General Jacob D. Cox:

. . . McClellan estimated Lee's troops at nearly double their actual numbers. . . . I do not doubt that most of his subordinates discouraged the resumption of the attack, for the rooted belief in Lee's preponderance of numbers had been chronic in the army during the whole year.

That belief was based upon the inconceivably mistaken reports of the secret service organization, accepted at headquarters, given to the War Department at Washington as a reason for incessant demands [for] reinforcements, and permeating downward through the whole organization till the error was accepted as truth by officers and men, and became a factor in their morale which can hardly be overestimated.

The result was that Lee retreated unmolested on the night of the 18th, and that what might have been a real and decisive success was a drawn battle in which our chief claim to victory was the possession of the field.

According to Confederate General John Walker:

. . . a little after sunrise . . . the entire Confederate army had safely recrossed the Potomac at Shepherdstown. . . . I was among the last to cross. . . . As I rode into the river I passed General Lee, sitting on his horse in the stream, watching the crossing of the wagons and artillery. Returning my greeting, he inquired as to what was still behind. There was nothing but the wagons containing my wounded, and a battery of artillery, all of which were near at hand; and I told him so.

"Thank God!" I heard him say as I rode on.

11

A NEW CAUSE
AND A NEW CAPTAIN

G ENERAL MC CLELLAN WAS *well satisfied with what he had accomplished. Three days after the battle, he wrote his wife:*

Our victory was complete, and the disorganized rebel army has rapidly returned to Virginia, its dreams of invading Pennsylvania dissipated forever. I feel some little pride in having, with a beaten and demoralized army, defeated Lee so utterly and saved the North so completely.

The people of the Union, who had followed the progress of the campaign with anxiety, were happy to learn that Lee's army had been turned back, but they would have been even happier to learn that it had been destroyed.

Lincoln was gloomy over Lee's escape. But, as it turned out, Antietam enabled the President to make a momentous move. For months he had been contemplating the issuance, as a war measure, of a proclamation of emancipation for the South's slaves. This had to be done, he believed, for these reasons: to placate the faction of his political support that was demanding such a move; to give the war a new meaning for Northerners in general, who were frustrated with the way things were going; and to diminish the threat of foreign intervention. The European nations, he reasoned, would have grave

*doubts about moving to an open alliance with the South if she were
made to appear as though fighting chiefly for the preservation of
slavery. England and France had freed their slaves, peaceably, some
years before.*

*Lincoln had been on the point of issuing the proclamation two
months earlier, but had been advised by his cabinet to wait until he
had a victory behind him—otherwise, said Secretary of State William Seward, the proclamation would seem like "our last shriek, on
the retreat."*

*General McClellan's role in the matter was a curious one. As a
Democrat (one with rising presidential aspirations), he was opposed
to "forcible abolition." The war, he said, had been launched to save
the Union, not to subjugate the South. Only "armed forces and political organizations" ought to be dealt with. But it was precisely
McClellan's way of dealing with the enemy's armed forces on the
Peninsula that had brought the Northern cause to such a state that
the proclamation seemed necessary. Now, oddly enough, it was Mc-
Clellan's success at Antietam that made the measure possible.*

*On September 23, 1862, Northern newspapers published the pre-
liminary proclamation. It said, in part:*

That on the first day of January, in the year of our Lord one thousand eight hundred and sixty-three, all persons held as slaves within
any State, or designated part of a State, the people whereof shall then
be in rebellion against the United States, shall be then, thencefor-
ward, and forever free. . . .

*As will be noted, only the Confederacy was affected. It would re-
main for the Thirteenth Amendment to the Constitution, ratified in
1865, to free the slaves "within the United States, or any place subject to their jurisdiction."*

*When the proclamation was made official on the date specified, it
inspired no sudden renewal of the North's war spirit. The anti-
slavery people were encouraged, but many others viewed the measure with grave unease or with angry disapproval. Some ridiculed it as
being unenforceable. The South, of course, was infuriated by this
"triumph of the Abolition party," and vowed greater exertions
toward independence. Lincoln himself could only hope that he had
done the right thing:*

We are like whalers who have been long on a chase. We have at
last got the harpoon into the monster, but we must now look how
we steer, or with one flop of his tail he will send us all into eternity.

Among the European nations, the proclamation had its effect. Not that anti-Unionism was killed. Lincoln's blockade, after all, was hurting Europe's economies. Besides, the aristocratic ruling classes would have been pleased to see America's democratic experiment permanently disrupted. Anti-Union statesmen, however, were impeded not only by the proclamation's moral implications but also by the public support the document gained. This extended even to people thrown out of work for lack of the South's cotton. Said a "letter to the editor" published in London's venerable Gazette:

We English have to open our eyes to the fact that the war in America has resolved itself into a war between freedom and slavery. . . . There is now no "medium" course. Slavery or freedom must prevail. . . . Providence declares, as plainly as the handwriting on the wall: "Choose you this day which you will serve."

Up to this time the Negroes aiding the Union cause were chiefly seamen, laborers, and servants. But now, says Horace Greeley of the New York Tribune, *the government began "the regular, authorized, avowed employment of blacks in the Union armies—not as menials, but as soldiers." Black regiments were formed both in the North and in Southern areas occupied by Union troops.*

Among the whites in the Union armies, the Emancipation Proclamation kindled feelings of a mixture similar to that revealed by the Northern public. At one extreme was vehement opposition; at the other, firm approval. Regis de Trobriand saw the war as profoundly changed:

It was no longer a question of the Union *as it was* that was to be re-established. It was the Union *as it should be*—that is to say, washed clean from its original sin, regenerated on the baptismal font of liberty for all. . . . We were no longer merely the soldiers of a political controversy. . . . We were now the missionaries of a great work of redemption, the armed liberators of millions. . . . The war was ennobled; the object was higher.

General McClellan did not see it that way. As early as September 25, 1862 (eight days after the Battle of Antietam), he wrote his wife that he did not expect to continue in his job much longer, that his self-respect was suffering at serving such an administration. The preliminary draft of the Emancipation Proclamation was only part of the trouble. He had expected Antietam to advance his prestige to a point where he would no longer be "interfered with" by Secretary Stanton and General Halleck, but this hadn't happened.

McClellan felt no compulsion to press into Virginia after Lee. He committed himself to "the work of reorganizing, drilling, and supplying the army."

Regis de Trobriand takes up the narrative:

The fine days of October . . . slipped away without any indication on the part of General McClellan of any intention to profit by them. More than a month had passed since the Battle of Antietam, and the army was immovable. It was impatient at this long inaction. The country was astonished at it. Everywhere it was asked, "What is McClellan doing?"

What was he doing? Nothing. What did he wish to do? Keep us in Maryland, perhaps winter there—who knows? Ever since the 23d of September he had recommenced his eternal refrain by demanding reinforcements, and . . . more reinforcements! While waiting for them, he announced his intention of remaining where he was, *in order to attack the enemy in case he should again cross the Potomac. . . .*

October 1, the President visited the army. Without doubt, he returned to Washington convinced of the necessity of issuing positive orders to overcome the persistent inertia of the general, for on the 6th he sent him a formal order "to cross the Potomac and give battle to the enemy, or drive him south."

. . . The reply was that the army could not be moved in the condition in which it was. It needed so many tents, so many shoes, so many uniforms, such and such supplies and equipments, etc. And twenty other pretexts.

"It was my duty," writes McClellan of these days, "to be prepared for all emergencies."

Many of McClellan's problems of preparation were real enough; and Lincoln understood this. But he knew also that Lee had even greater problems. In a letter to McClellan dated October 13, the President said:

You remember my speaking to you of what I called your overcautiousness? Are you not over-cautious when you assume that you cannot do what the enemy is constantly doing? Should you not claim to be at least his equal in prowess, and act upon the claim?

*Even as Lincoln chided McClellan for his excessive caution, the Con-
federates completed another act of daring. As recorded by Southern
writer Edward Pollard:*

. . . Gen. Lee [had] ordered the famous cavalry commander Gen.
Stuart to cross the Potomac . . . to reconnoitre the Federal positions, and, if practicable, to enter Pennsylvania, and do all in his
power to impede and embarrass the military operations of the enemy. The order was executed with skill, address, and courage. Gen.
Stuart . . . passed through Maryland, occupied Chambersburg
[Pennsylvania], and destroyed a large amount of public property,
making the entire circuit of Gen. McClellan's army, and thwarting
all the arrangements by which that commander . . . reported his
capture certain.

*Shortly after Stuart's feat, Lincoln was asked by a group of asso-
ciates what he thought of McClellan now. Lincoln answered, "When
I was a boy we used to play a game, 'three times round and out.'
Stuart has been round him twice. If he goes round him once more,
gentlemen, McClellan will be out!"*

Again in the words of Union officer Regis de Trobriand:

Nothing was done [about advancing southward]. One pretext
disposed of, McClellan found another. And so the days ran on, and
the army did not move. Sometimes the impatience of the President
was expressed in biting irony. Here is one of his dispatches, dated
October 25:

"I have just read your dispatch about sore-tongued and fatigued
horses. Will you pardon me for asking what the horses of your army
have done since the Battle of Antietam that fatigues anything?"

And then McClellan complained that the services of his cavalry
had been disparaged [a charge to which Lincoln replied with a qualified apology]. Afterwards [McClellan] wished to know what should
be done to protect Maryland when he went into Virginia. He advised this; he objected to that. . . . As a last resort, McClellan discovered that it was necessary to fill up the old regiments [with re-
placements] before putting them in the field.

If the matters concerned had not been so grave, it would have
been equal to any comedy. But the country was not in the humor to
laugh at jokes, especially when it did not understand them. It saw
only the incomprehensible inaction of the Army of the Potomac, and
was indignant at it. McClellan's friends endeavored to throw the re-

sponsibility on the President, on General Halleck, on the Secretary of War. The partisans of the Government saw only in the delay . . . McClellan [being] conformable to his antecedents. It was full time to put an end to the false situation. The patience of everyone was exhausted.

On October 27 the President wrote categorically to the recalcitrant general: "And now I ask a distinct answer to the question—Is it your purpose not to go into action again till the men now being drafted . . . are incorporated in the old regiments?"

On this occasion the general replied . . . at last that he was about to move [his advance units having already crossed the Potomac]. The next day, the 28th, we broke camp. . . . The same day we crossed the Potomac at White's Ford. . . . The troops were full of ardor and good spirits. The water was cold and the atmosphere was not warm, but the comical incidents of the passage spread good humor over all, and gave rise to a great deal of laughter. Moreover, we stopped near the ford, and the campfires quickly dried the shoes and wet trousers. . . .

On October 31, we took the road to Leesburg. We supposed that the whole army must have crossed the Potomac [by this time]. It was a mistake. With his accustomed slowness, McClellan took five days for that operation [McClellan himself says he took a week!], which was accomplished only on the 2d of November. . . . At nightfall [of November 3] we stopped at Mount Gilliat. . . . The next day's march took us to Millville. . . . On the 5th we passed through Middle[burg] and White Plains, to camp near Salem; and on the 6th we arrived a few miles from Waterloo. . . .

It was now piercing cold. . . . The night was really glacial. Happily, fuel was plentiful. The great fires lighted on all sides continued to blaze until morning. Then [on November 7] the snow began to fall, at first in light flakes and soon in a thick whirlwind, whipped by continual squalls. The trees groaned, the ground trembled, and the men shivered.

No forward movement was made that day. In the evening, De Trobriand had reason to consult with a superior officer, General George Stoneman, and there was "something indefinable in the manner of the general and his staff" that made De Trobriand think that the army's advance had been suspended. "Why? I could not imagine. But there was something new in the air. . . ."

What had happened was that General C. P. Buckingham, of the

War Department, had made a special trip down from Washington (arriving in the middle of the snowstorm), and instead of going to see the army's commander, had gone into consultation with a subordinate, Ambrose Burnside.

General McClellan tells what followed:

Late at night I was sitting alone in my tent, writing to my wife. All the staff were asleep. Suddenly someone knocked upon the tent-pole, and, upon my invitation to enter, there appeared Burnside and Buckingham, both looking very solemn. I received them kindly and commenced conversation upon general subjects in the most unconcerned manner possible.

After a few moments, Buckingham said to Burnside, "Well, general, I think we had better tell General McClellan the object of our visit."

I very pleasantly said that I should be glad to learn it. Whereupon Buckingham handed me the . . . orders of which he was the bearer. . . . I saw that both—especially Buckingham—were watching me most intently. . . .

I read the papers with a smile, immediately turned to Burnside, and said, "Well, Burnside, I turn the command over to you."

They soon retired. . . .

Again alone, with the snow whipping against his tent and his candle-light fitful, McClellan added the story of the visit to his wife's letter:

Of course I was much surprised; but as I read the order . . . I am sure that not the slightest expression of feeling was visible on my face. . . . They have made a great mistake. Alas for my poor country! I know in my inmost heart she never had a truer servant. . . . Do not be at all worried—I am not. I have done the best I could for my country. To the last I have done my duty as I understand it.

Though he wanted to leave quickly, McClellan heeded Burnside's plea that he stay on for a few days to help make the transition smoother. Burnside had accepted the command with reluctance; he did not feel adequate to the job.

After Burnside was oriented, all that remained for McClellan to do was to make a final appearance before the troops. According to an unnamed eyewitness:

As General McClellan, mounted upon a fine horse, attended by a retinue of fine-looking military men, riding rapidly through the ranks, gracefully recognized and bid a farewell to the army, the cries and demonstrations of the men were beyond bounds—wild, impassioned, and unrestrained. Disregarding all military forms, they rushed from their ranks and thronged around him with the bitterest complaints against those who had removed from command their beloved leader.

Not all of the soldiers reacted in this way. Many had become disillusioned with McClellan and were glad to see him go. Others accepted the change "for better or for worse."

North and South, the dismissal stirred earnest discussion. Some of the Confederates expressed relief, for they believed that McClellan was finally ready to make a determined assault upon Richmond. General Lee, on the other hand, was said to be sorry to see McClellan go, since he was a gentleman who fought "by the rules of civilized warfare." Northern opinion was sharply divided, with party lines much in evidence. There was rejoicing among Republicans who had been demanding McClellan's removal for months. Some of these people had continued to denounce McClellan as a traitor—which he certainly wasn't. Many of the general's Democratic friends saw the dismissal as a political act, one by which Lincoln hoped to destroy his value to the party—a view with scant evidence to support it.

At any rate, says De Trobriand, "It was finished. The military career of General McClellan had come to an end." De Trobriand saw the whole case of the controversial commander in simple terms: "His misfortune, and that of the country, was his sudden elevation to a position to which his ability was not equal."

An editorialist for the New York Times *expressed it this way:*

The sole defeat of General McClellan has been that he lacked motive power. . . . That overcautious disposition was noticed long ago, but there was a fond hope that experience would cure it. Experience—and that too of the hardest sort—has not cured it. It has been demonstrated to be an inseparable part of General McClellan's nature. It is the presence of this fatal quality alone . . . that reconciles us . . . to the displacement of a commander otherwise so competent.

12

FREDERICKSBURG

I N THE . . . FALL OF 1862 [writes Confederate General James
Longstreet] a distance of not more than thirty miles lay between
the Army of the Potomac and the Army of Northern Virginia. . . .
The Federal army was encamped around Warrenton, Virginia [north
of the Rappahannock River], and was soon divided [by General Burn-
side] into three grand divisions, whose commanders were Generals
Sumner, Hooker, and Franklin. Lee's army was on the opposite side
of the Rappahannock River, divided into two corps, the first commanded by myself and the second commanded by . . . Stonewall
Jackson. At that time the Confederate army extended from Culpeper
Court House . . . across the Blue Ridge. . . to Winchester. . . .

About the 18th or 19th of November, we received information
through our scouts that Sumner, with his grand division of more
than thirty thousand men, was moving [southeastward] toward
Fredericksburg [this being the opening act in another Federal drive
upon Richmond]. . . . On receipt of the information, two of my
divisions were ordered [by Lee] down to meet him. We made a forced
march and arrived on the hills [south of] Fredericksburg . . . on
the afternoon of the 21st. Sumner had already arrived, and his army
was encamped on Stafford Heights, overlooking the town from the
[northeast side of the Rappahannock]. . . .

The Union camp at Warrenton.

About the 26th or 27th it became evident that Fredericksburg would be the scene of a battle, and we advised the people who were still in the town to prepare to leave. . . . The evacuation . . . by the distressed women and helpless men was a painful sight.

Adds Southern artilleryman Robert Stiles (the Richmond Howitzer adjutant):

I never saw a more pitiful procession than they made trudging through the deep snow . . . little children tugging along with their doll babies . . . women so old and feeble that they could carry nothing and could barely hobble themselves. There were women carrying a baby in one arm, and its bottle, its clothes, and its covering in the other. Some had a Bible and a toothbrush in one hand, a picked chicken and a bag of flour in the other.

Most of them had to cross a creek swollen with winter rains, and deadly cold with winter ice and snow. We took the battery horses down and ferried them over, taking one child in front and two behind, and sometimes a woman or a girl on either side with her feet in the stirrups, holding on by our shoulders. Where they were going we could not tell, and I doubt if they could.

James Longstreet goes on to explain:

Very soon after I reached Fredericksburg the remainder of my corps arrived from Culpeper Court House, and as soon as it was

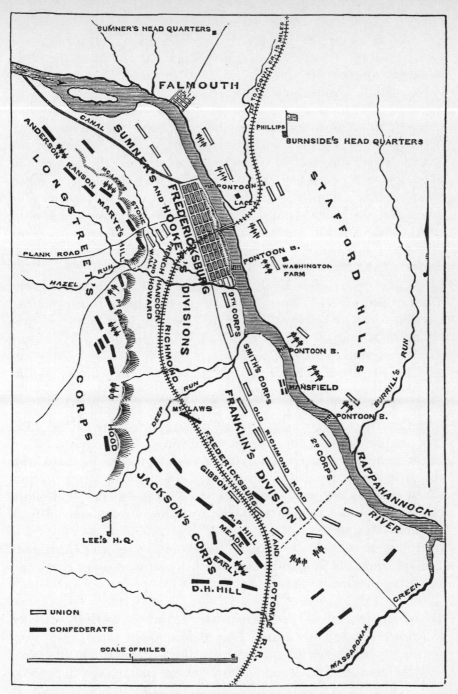

The Battle of Fredericksburg.

known that all the Army of the Potomac was in motion for the pro-
spective scene of battle Jackson was drawn down from the Blue
Ridge. In a very short time the Army of Northern Virginia was face
to face with the Army of the Potomac.

*The heights occupied by the two armies, however, were separated by
both the town and the river. In numbers, the Confederates again
were inferior. Burnside had well over 100,000 men, while Lee had
about 78,000. This time, though, the Confederate lack was not a
handicap. Lee's position, stretching for six miles from Taylor's Hill
across Marye's Heights and Telegraph Hill and on through Hamil-
ton's Crossing, was a very strong one. And Lee planned to await
Burnside's attack, which had to be made across the river, and then,
on one flank, through the town, and on the other flank, over a wide
plain, both approaches being commanded by Confederate artillery
fire. Lee had plenty of time to dig in, for Burnside's crossing of the
river was delayed by the failure of his pontoon boats to arrive from
the northward on schedule.*

   Says an unnamed Union soldier:

   The narrow river brought the outposts of the armies within
speaking distance; and conversations, jokes, newspapers, and tobacco
were exchanged by the pickets of the two armies until prohibited.
The Confederate pickets are said to have repeatedly remarked, "Before you 'un Yanks can get to Richmond you 'uns will have to get up
Early, go up a Longstreet, get over the Lee of a Stonewall, and climb
two Hills."

   I never heard them say anything so allegorical as that, but while
on picket one said to me, "Why don't you 'uns come over and fight
we 'uns? We want yer to!"

   It was quite cold, and many of the rebel pickets wore [captured]
Federal overcoats, and when not on duty occupied holes excavated
in the banks opposite us.

*Writes Confederate General Lafayette McLaws, who had charge of
the pickets on the banks nearest Fredericksburg:*

   Two or three evenings previous to the Federal attempt to cross
. . . we were attracted by one or more of the enemy's bands playing.
. . . A number of their officers and a crowd of their men were about
the band, cheering their national airs—the "Star Spangled Banner,"
"Hail Columbia," and others once so dear to us all. It seemed as if

they expected some response [to these airs] from us; but none was given until, finally, [the Union musicians] struck up "Dixie," and then both sides cheered, with much laughter.

Among the men of both armies, of course, the impending battle stirred feelings of apprehension. On the evening of December 10, having learned that things would begin the next day, William T. Lusk, the captain from New York, wrote his mother:

I have heretofore . . . been singularly exempt from the accidents of war. . . . But if in His wisdom it seemeth best this time to take my life, then, my dear mother, recognize in it only the Hand of the Inevitable. . . . But I am not given to entertaining forebodings. . . . I prefer to think of the time when we all will return home, the laurel won. . . . Think of the stories I would have to tell. I believe that . . . the next generation will be better when they hear the story of the present. And another generation still, when the dimness of time shall have enhanced the romance, will dearly love to hear the tale of the Great Rebellion. . . .

Relates the Union's Regis de Trobriand:

The night was full of suppressed agitation. . . . The fires remained burning longer than usual. In different directions was heard the rolling of wagons . . . and cannon. . . . Confused noises indicated the march of regiments changing position. Their bayonets flashed through the obscurity, lighted up by the bivouac fires.

We were awakened at daybreak by the sound of . . . cannon. Everyone was quickly on foot. . . . At half-past seven our division was . . . behind the Stafford Hills, which were crowned by a hundred and forty-five pieces of artillery. Under their protection, and favored by a thick fog, three [pontoon] bridges were commenced in front of the city, and two more one or two miles further down. The latter, intended for the Left Grand Division, were finished without much opposition. But work on the others was stopped by the deadly fire of the Mississippi sharpshooters.

Pennsylvania's Chaplain A. M. Stewart says that the Federal batteries

were keeping up a continuous and tremendous cannonade in order to drive back the rebels and protect the pontoons. The rebel sharpshooters persisted in firing from the windows and roofs of the houses in Fredericksburg upon our bridgebuilders, by which quite a

Union guns opening on the town of Fredericksburg.

number of them were killed and wounded. Our commanders, becoming at length weary with such an uncivil sort of process, ordered our batteries to open upon the city.

Confederate General McLaws avers:

It is impossible fitly to describe the effects of this iron hail hurled against the small band of defenders and into the devoted city. The roar of the cannon, the bursting shells, the falling of walls and chimneys, and the flying bricks and other material dislodged from the houses by the iron balls and shells, added to the fire of the infantry from both sides and the smoke from the guns and from the burning houses, made a scene of indescribable confusion, enough to appall the stoutest hearts!

Adjutant Robert Stiles, of the Richmond Howitzers, takes up:

During the bombardment I was sent into Fredericksburg with a message for General [William] Barksdale. As I was riding down the street that led to his headquarters, it appeared to be so fearfully swept by artillery fire that I started to ride across it, with a view of finding some safer way of getting to my destination, when, happen-

ing to glance beyond that point, I saw walking quietly and uncon-
cernedly along the same street I was on, and approaching General
Barksdale's headquarters from the opposite direction, a lone woman.
She apparently found the projectiles which were screaming and exploding in the air, and striking and crashing through the houses, and
tearing up the streets, very interesting—stepping a little aside to in-
spect a great gaping hole one had just gouged in the sidewalk, then
turning her head to note a fearful explosion in the air.

I felt as if it really would not do to avoid a fire which was merely
interesting . . . to a woman; so I stiffened my spinal column as well
as I could and rode straight down the street toward headquarters
and the self-possessed lady; and having reached the house I rode
around back of it to put my horse where he would at least be safer
than in front. As I returned on foot to the front, the lady had gone
up on the porch and was knocking at the door.

One of the staff came to hearken, and on seeing a lady, held up
his hands, exclaiming in amazement, "What on earth, madam, are
you doing here? Do go to some safe place, if you can find one!"

She smiled and said, with some little tartness, "Young gentleman,
you seem to be a little excited. Won't you please say to General
Barksdale that a lady at the door wishes to see him?"

The young man assured her General Barksdale could not possibly see her just now; but she persisted. "General Barksdale is a
Southern gentleman, sir, and will not refuse to see a lady who has
called upon him."

Seeing that he could not otherwise get rid of her, the General
did come to the door, but actually wringing his hands in excitement
and annoyance. "For God's sake, madam, go and seek some place of
safety. I'll send a member of my staff to help you find one."

She again smiled gently—while old Barksdale fumed and almost
swore—and then she said quietly, "General Barksdale, my cow has
just been killed in my stable by a shell. She is very fat, and I don't
want the Yankees to get her. If you will send someone down to
butcher her, you are welcome to the meat."

*On the Union side, thousands watched the bombardment with fasci-
nation. Explains Regis de Trobriand:*

The artillery not being able to dislodge [the sharpshooters] from
the houses . . . two Massachusetts regiments and one Michigan, who
had volunteered for the dangerous work, were sent over in the pontoon boats. In spite of a terrible fire, they succeeded in landing . . .

and soon swept before them the Mississippians. . . . These bridges were then finished without hindrance, and our heads of columns began to occupy the city. . . .

Southerner Robert Stiles, the adjutant who had encountered the brave lady, says that the Twenty-first Mississippi was the last regiment to leave, and that

The last detachment was under the command of Lane Brandon . . . my *quondam* classmate at Yale. . . . In skirmishing with the head of the Federal column . . . Brandon captured a few prisoners and learned that the advance company was commanded by [a captain named] Abbott, who had been his chum at Harvard Law School when the war began. He lost his head completely. He refused to retire before Abbott. He fought him fiercely and was actually driving him back. In this he was violating orders and breaking our plan of battle. He was put under arrest, and his subaltern brought the command out of town.

Buck Denman . . . a Mississippi bear hunter and a superb specimen of manhood, was color sergeant of the Twenty-first. . . . He was rough as a bear in manner, but withal a noble, tender-hearted fellow and a splendid soldier.

The enemy, finding the way now clear, were coming up the street, full company front, with flags flying and bands playing, while the great shells from the [Federal] siege guns were bursting over their heads and dashing their hurtling fragments after our retreating skirmishers.

Buck was behind the corner of a house, taking sight for a last shot. Just as his fingers trembled on the trigger, a little three-year-old fair-haired baby girl toddled out of an alley accompanied by a Newfoundland dog, and gave chase to a big shell that was rolling lazily along the pavement, she clapping her little hands and the dog snapping and barking furiously at the shell.

Buck's hand dropped from the trigger. He dashed it across his eyes to dispel the mist and make sure he hadn't passed over the river and wasn't seeing his own baby girl in a vision. No—there is a baby, amid the hell of shot and shell; and here come the enemy. A moment, and he has grounded his gun, dashed out into the storm, swept his great right arm around the baby, gained cover again, and, baby clasped to his breast and musket trailed in his left hand, is trotting after the boys up to Marye's Heights.

The town's invaders soon began settling in. According to Federal newsman Charles Coffin:

There were stringent orders against plundering; but . . . the soldiers . . . appropriated to their own use whatever pleased their fancy. They cooked bacon and eggs, made hotcakes in the kitchens, eating them with sugar and molasses. They carried mattresses and beds into the streets, spreading them upon the sidewalks for a luxurious night's repose; dressed themselves in old-fashioned, antiquated clothes; danced and sang, and played upon the pianos. I saw a soldier throw away his cap and put on a tall hat . . . his comrades making fun of him for wearing a "stovepipe" hat.

A Confederate correspondent was later to report that these Yankees and other arrivals devoured everything in the town that was edible and perpetrated "every conceivable injury that devilish malice or thieving lust could invent."

"On the 12th," says the Union's De Trobriand, "the different corps continued to cross the Rappahannock. . . ."

Adds a New York chaplain, A. H. Lung:

The rebels occasionally opened their batteries from the mountain, to which ours replied from Stafford Heights on the other side. The musket firing between skirmishers at times was very brisk. The day was mostly spent, however, in getting our men in position and [studying] the strongholds of the enemy. . . .

The surgeons of our corps selected for a hospital a large massive stone building. . . . The building was elegantly furnished with paintings, pictures, drawings, mirrors, and with other things to correspond. It was owned by a wealthy old secesh bachelor of a literary stamp. But a sudden change came over the spirit of his dreams. Nearly one hundred of his slaves had run away, and he was put under arrest and sent up toward the North Star. Union officers fed their horses from his crib, slept on his bed, eat [sic] from his table, read his library books, sat in his chairs, smoked his segars, and drank his sugar and coffee from his china cups.

That night, says a London Times *correspondent who was in Lee's lines:*

. . . as the pickets of the two armies were stationed within a hundred yards of each other, the Confederates could hear the earnest and impassioned speeches of Federal orators rousing the spirit of their troops and making vehement appeals to the sanctity of the "old flag."

"The old flag is played out!" shouted the Confederates in reply.

"Somehow," remarked one of the Confederates to me, "there must be a want of grit among the Yankees, otherwise they wouldn't want all this talking to."

The same narrator goes on to say that the sky that night was host to a superb performance of the aurora borealis, "accepted by the Confederates as the cross outlined on the sky was accepted by Constantine— [as a sign] of assured victory."

On the morning of December 13, writes Southerner James Longstreet:

The valley, the mountaintops, everything was enveloped in the thickest fog, and the preparations for the fight were made as if under cover of night. . . . Suddenly, at 10 o'clock, as if the elements were taking a hand in the drama about to be enacted, the warmth of the sun brushed the mist away and revealed the mighty panorama in the valley below. Franklin's 40,000 men, reinforced by two divisions of Hooker's grand division, were in front of Jackson's 30,000 [the Confederate right wing]. The flags of the Federals fluttered gayly, the polished arms shone brightly in the sunlight, and the beautiful uniforms of the buoyant troops gave to the scene the air of a holiday occasion. . . . About the city [which lay in front of the Confederate left wing] . . . a few soldiers could be seen, but there was no indication of the heavy masses that were concealed by the houses.

The Federals looking toward the Confederate lines got only a limited impression of pageantry. Regis de Trobriand says that the heights were "covered with retrenchments and bristling with cannon."

I confess it. After having long examined with the aid of a field glass that formidable arc . . . I thought involuntarily of the gladiators of old, entering into the amphitheatre. *Ave, Caesar! Morituri te salutant!* If we had had there our Caesar, we also would have been able to exclaim, "Those about to die salute thee!"

The Southern troops found encouragement in the strength of their position. In Jackson's lines, however, a curious concern existed. Confederate officer Fitzhugh Lee explains:

Jackson . . . appeared that day . . . in a bright new uniform which replaced his former dingy suit, having actually exchanged his faded old cap for another which was resplendent in gold lace. . . .

It was a most remarkable metamorphosis of his former self, and his men did not like it, fearing, as some of them said, that "Old Jack would be afraid of [soiling] his clothes and would not get down to his work."

The work of all was about to begin. In the words of Walter H. Taylor, of General Lee's staff:

And now, as the command is given to the Federal troops to advance, a new interest, a spirit of intense excitement, is added to the scene; and as the whole line of blue—solid and regular, bristling with the glittering bayonets—moves steadily forward, accompanied by the deafening roar of the artillery . . . men hold their breath and realize that war is indeed as glorious as it is terrible. The Federal soldiers advanced right gallantly to the desperate work assigned them. . . . The cool, steady veterans of Lee . . . made terrible havoc in the ranks of the assailing columns. . . .

Especially effective on the Confederate right at this time were the guns managed by young John Pelham of Jeb Stuart's horse artillery.

The Union division of General George G. Meade managed to break through Jackson's advanced line, but the success was only temporary. Meade was pushed back, his formations in disarray.

James Longstreet says that the Federals attacking on the Confederate left (Edwin Sumner's command) swarmed out of Fredericksburg "like bees out of a hive." These men were stopped by heavy fire from behind a long stone wall in front of Marye's Heights.

Union Chaplain A. H. Lung, whose post was at the hospital set up in the rich bachelor's stone home (behind the center of the Federal lines), could stand at the door and see almost the whole field:

The battle raged like a fierce storm; sometimes on our extreme right, sometimes to the left, and then in front. Our men made several desperate charges at an immense sacrifice, without success. The enemy's superior position and impregnable works rendered them superior in power. . . . The deathly missiles rained down from the hills amid the smoke and thunder of booming cannon, carrying death through our ranks and drenching the field with blood.

Union General Darius N. Couch describes the scene on the Federal right as he viewed it from the steeple of the Fredericksburg court-house:

. . . the whole plain was covered with men, prostrate and dropping, the live men running here and there, and in front closing upon each other [to form lines of battle], and the wounded coming back. The commands seemed to be mixed up. I had never before seen fighting like that—nothing approaching it in terrible uproar and destruction. There was no cheering on the part of the men, but a stubborn determination to obey orders and do their duty. I don't think there was much feeling of success. As they charged, the artillery fire would break their formation and they would get mixed. Then they would close up, go forward, receive the withering infantry fire, and . . . fight as best they could. And then the next brigade coming up in succession would do its duty, and melt like snow coming down on warm ground.

The battle was going so badly for Burnside's forces that the London newsman in Lee's lines believed he was witnessing "a memorable day to the historian of the Decline and Fall of the American Republic."

A Confederate artillerist on Marye's Heights who helped throw back several attacks says that the Federals came on bravely but that "no troops on earth" could withstand the kind of fire they were getting. "Spotting the fields in our front we could detect little patches of blue—the dead and wounded. . . ."

One of the wounded was Colonel Edward E. Cross, of New Hampshire. He tells how he was hit:

. . . I was near my colors. A twelve-pounder shell . . . burst right in front of me. One fragment struck me just below the heart, making a bad wound. Another blew off my hat. Another small bit entered my mouth and broke out three of my best jaw-teeth, while the gravel, bits of . . . earth, and minute fragments of shell covered my face with bruises. I fell insensible, and lay so for some time, when another fragment of shell, striking me on the left leg, below the knee, brought me to my senses. My mouth was full of blood, fragments of teeth, and gravel; my breastbone almost broken in; and I lay in mud two inches deep. . . .

Dead and wounded lay thick around. One captain . . . was gasping in death within a foot of my head, his bowels all torn out. The air was full of hissing bullets and bursting shells. . . . Two lines [of the Union attack] passed over me, but soon they swayed back, trampling on the dead and dying. Halting about thirty yards in the rear, one line laid down and commenced firing. Imagine the situation. Right between two fires. . . . I covered my face with both hands . . . expecting every moment my brains would spatter the ground. But they didn't. . . . The end of my days was reserved for another, and I hope more fortunate, occasion.

The battle had its lighter moments. Writes Union General William F. Smith:

During the afternoon, hearing some heavy musketry firing in my front, I went to ascertain the cause, and while riding along behind a regiment lying with their faces to the ground, a round shot [i.e., a cannonball] struck the knapsack of a soldier, and . . . sent a cloud of underclothes into the air, and high above them floated a scattered pack of cards. The soldier, hearing the shouts of laughter, turned over to see what was the matter, and when he saw the mishap which had befallen him made a feeble effort to join in the laugh.

"On all sides," says another witness, "could be heard the cry, 'Oh, deal me a hand!' "

By this time, of course, the Federal hospitals were hubs of bloody activity. Chaplain Lung relates:

The hospital [in the stone mansion] was in range of the enemy's fire, and at times the shells screamed fearfully over us and around us. Fragments flew into the door. A poor soldier had just reached the steps from the field with a wound in his arm when a shell dashing at his feet most shockingly mangled his right leg. This lad, twenty minutes before, stood in the ranks full of bravery and life. Now with broken arm and gory leg he sits sighing and weeping with pain. A little while afterward and we find this young warrior lying in the chamber upon a bunch of straw with only one leg and one arm. Such are the fortunes of war.

The wounded came rapidly in from the field, some on foot and alone, some supported on either side by fellow-soldiers, some in clusters of two, three, and four, all wounded and clutching to each other; some borne on stretchers, some carried on the back of a fellow-soldier or brother, and some in the ambulances. . . . We stored these unfortunate creatures away as best we could. They lay scattered here and there all over the yard, in the corn-house, smoke-house, and slave shanties. In the hospital, we filled the rooms below and above, and many were carried into the cellar. . . .

In every possible conceivable way, men are wounded. I saw one man with gun in hand, walking with a firm step and a cheerful countenance, having been struck by a piece of shell in the forehead, laying bare the brain so I could see every pulsation. It is really surprising how soon one becomes accustomed to these scenes of suffering, so that broken bones and mangled limbs can be attended to with untrembling nerve. I was busily engaged nearly all day in the amputating room, where feet, legs, arms, and fingers were cut off.

Toward the end of the day, says Northerner Regis de Trobriand, a new horror afflicted the battlefield:

The cannonade had set the high grass on fire at several points, and the flame, quickened by light currents of air, extended rapidly on all sides. Despairing cries were heard. They were the unfortunate wounded left lying on the ground and caught by the flames. Through the smoke, they were seen exerting themselves in vain efforts to flee, half rising up, falling back overcome by pain, rolling on their broken limbs, grasping around them at the grass red with their blood, and at times perishing in the embrace of the flames.

Writes a Northern newsman, "M.H." of the Cincinnati Commercial:

It was with a deep sense of relief that I saw the sun go down, and felt that in a little while darkness would put an end to the unequal combat. But . . . there was severe fighting even after dark, and the sparkle of musketry made a fine display. Then the big rebel rifled cannon ceased to mark time, the sputter and crackle of small arms ceased on the centre, Franklin and Jackson's guns throbbed heavily a few times on the left, and all was still. . . .

Many of the Federals dropped to the ground to rest on their arms where they had been standing, the weather having turned mild enough so that they could do this without serious discomfort.
Union officer D. Watson Rowe says of those on the right who withdrew into Fredericksburg:

Some sat on the curbstones, meditating, looking gloomily at the ground. Others lay on the pavement, trying to forget the events of the day in sleep. There was little said; deep dejection burdened the spirits of all.

Some of the troops on the field were shifted during the night. Captain John W. Ames later recorded that the brigade he belonged to made its way among "many dead horses . . . and many more dead men."

Here stood a low brick house [Ames adds] with an open door . . . from which shone a light, and into which we peered when passing. Inside sat a woman, gaunt and hard-featured, with crazy hair . . .

still sitting by a smoking candle, though it was nearly two hours past midnight. But what woman could sleep . . . alone in a house between two hostile armies—two corpses lying across her doorsteps, and within, almost at her feet, four more! So with wild eyes and face lighted by her smoky candle, she stared across the dead barrier into the darkness outside with the look of one who heard and saw not. . . .

Ambulances and stretcher-bearers moved about the field—staying close, however, to the Union lines, for no truce existed. D. Watson Rowe says that after the din of the day, the noises made by the ambulances and their horses seemed oddly subdued:

The stretcher-bearers walked silently toward whatever spot a cry or a groan of pain indicated an object of their search. . . . The cries . . . borne through the haze . . . from every direction . . . expressed every degree and shade of suffering, of pain, of agony: a sigh, a groan, a piteous appeal, a shriek, a succession of shrieks, a call of despair, a prayer to God, a demand for water, for the ambulance, a death rattle. . . .

To the Federals who glanced toward the heights occupied by Lee's army, the bivouac fires seemed to mingle with the stars. Union officer Francis Palfrey was aware that "the Confederates had had a day of such savage pleasure as seldom falls to the lot of soldiers, a day on which they saw their opponents doing just what they wished them to do. . . ."

But the Confederates had not come out of the battle unhurt. Lee lamented the death of many brave men, including a number of fine officers; and caring for his wounded had crowded the hours of his surgeons and also of such volunteers as Mrs. Martha Stevens, who stayed at her endangered house on the field and, running out of bandages,"tore from her person most of her garments" for this use.

The final casualty count would reveal a loss of a little over 5,000 men for the Confederates and well over 12,000 for the Federals.

It wasn't known on the night of December 13 that the battle was over. Burnside wanted to renew the attack in the morning. His generals, however, opposed the idea.

Again in Regis de Trobriand's words:

We displayed a bold front to the end. During two days we kept our position in line of battle in front of our adversaries, who made no movement to take the offensive. Only during the night . . . the picket lines being close together, the firing of the skirmishers caused frequent alarms. They were usually brought on by the marauders seeking to strip the dead, or by some brave men who, under cover of the darkness, ventured outside of the lines to give water to the wounded and bring them in on their backs. . . .

Finally, in the afternoon of the 15th . . . a suspension of hostilities was concluded for two hours. Officers with details of men without arms, carrying litters, were sent immediately upon the ground between the lines. . . . I will never forget the joy of the wounded when they were brought into our lines. One of them cried out, trying to raise himself on his litter, "All right now! I shall not die like a dog in the ditch!" Another said to the men carrying him, while two great tears ran down his hollow cheeks, "Thanks, my friends. Thanks to you, I shall see my mother again."

The dead were hideous—black, swollen, covered with clotted blood, riddled with balls, torn by shells. The rebels, poorly clothed, had left them neither shoes, nor trousers, nor overcoats. . . .

At nine o'clock in the evening the order came to fall back in silence to the bridges. During the night the whole army repassed the Rappahannock . . . and the next day we returned to our old camps [around Stafford Heights]. . . .

The Confederates held their position. General Barksdale, however, was instructed to move his brigade down from Marye's Heights in order to reoccupy Fredericksburg.

And what had happened to Mississippi bear hunter Buck Denman and the little girl he had rescued?

Robert Stiles explains:

. . . behind that historic stone wall [in front of Marye's Heights] and in the lines hard by, all those hours and days of terror was that baby kept, her fierce nurses taking turns patting her, while the storm of battle raged and shrieked, and at night wrestling with each other for the boon and benediction of her quiet breathing under their blankets. Never was baby so cared for. They scoured the countryside for milk, and conjured up their best skill to prepare dainty viands for her little ladyship.

When the struggle was over, and the enemy had withdrawn to his strongholds across the river, and Barksdale was ordered to reoccupy the town, the Twenty-first Mississippi . . . was given the place of honor in the van, and led the column. There was a long halt, the brigade and regimental staff hurrying to and fro—the regimental colors could not be found. Denman stood about the middle of the regiment, baby in arms. Suddenly he sprang to the front. Swinging her aloft above his head, her little garments fluttering like the folds of a banner, he shouted, "Forward, Twenty-first! Here are your colors!" And without further order, off started the brigade toward the town, yelling as only Barksdale's men could yell.

They were passing through a street fearfully shattered by the enemy's fire, and were shouting their very souls out—but let Buck himself describe the last scene in the drama: "I was holding the baby high . . . with both arms, when above all the racket I heard a woman's scream. The next thing I know I was covered with calico, and she fainted on my breast. I caught her before she fell, and laying her down gently, put her baby on her bosom. She was most the prettiest thing I ever looked at, and her eyes were shut. And—and—I hope God'll forgive me, but I kissed her just once."

No sublime experiences lightened the hearts of the Federals across the river. New Yorker William Lusk expressed the general mood in a letter to his mother written on December 16:

Gone are the proud hopes, the high aspirations that swelled our bosoms a few days ago. Once more unsuccessful, and only a bloody record to show our men were brave. . . . [The army] has strong limbs to march and meet the foe, stout arms to strike heavy blows, brave hearts to dare—but the brains, the brains! Have we no brains to use the arms and limbs and eager hearts with cunning? Perhaps Old Abe has some funny story to tell appropriate to the occasion.

On the contrary, the despairing President sent the troops a message of consolation and encouragement. He lamented their losses, praised their courage, and attributed their lack of success to accidental causes.

Union soldier Jesse Young (transferred east after Shiloh, and, in spite of his youth, promoted to lieutenant) writes that Lincoln's message stirred "an undercurrent of comment and criticism." Young heard an officer say:

"Our failure was an accident, was it, Mr. President? The Lord deliver us from any more such accidents! The worst accident that has befallen us is to have a commander at our head who is not able to lead us to victory. Little Mac would never have dreamed of hurling men against such a stronghold when nothing was to be gained by it but certain defeat."

"O, no," said another. "Little Mac would have kept you ditching till the ditches were your graves. He did not know when to order his army forward into the works of the enemy, and Burnside did not know when to call them back from inevitable disaster."

. . . The army had lost heart and hope and confidence—not in itself or in its cause, but in its leader. . . . And in moody, surly, and ominous silence, mingled with occasional low growls of discontent, and with many doubtful shakes of the head, and a good deal of anxiety for the future . . . the heartsick army settled down into winter quarters.

13

MURFREESBORO

SINCE THE *Battle of Shiloh, Tennessee, on April 6 and 7, 1862, the war's Western theater had seen no clashes of like magnitude. This is not to say that significant developments were lacking. At the end of April, a Federal naval squadron under Flag Officer David G. Farragut captured New Orleans, at the mouth of the Mississippi. This was a vital step in the Union's effort to gain control of the whole length of the river and thus split the Confederacy in two. In June, a flotilla moving down the river from the north took Memphis, Tennessee. By July 1 the Confederates were left with only one major river port: Vicksburg, Mississippi.*

The Western land war—in which present Federal aims were the capture of Vicksburg and the conquest of Tennessee—had included battles at Iuka and Corinth, Mississippi, and at Perryville, Kentucky, the first occurring in September and the last two in October. Perryville brought an end to a serious Confederate counterthrust (led by General Braxton Bragg) into Union-controlled territory.

Toward the close of the year, as explained by Confederate historian Edward Pollard, "Grant was moving from West Tennessee into Mississippi, while a strong detached force under Sherman was organizing for a separate expedition down the Mississippi River against Vicksburg." But the scene of the war's next major battle was central Tennessee. Here, about thirty miles apart, the Union's Army

Braxton Bragg.

of the Cumberland, under General William S. Rosecrans, confronted the Army of Tennessee, under Braxton Bragg. Pollard continues:

The . . . Federal army . . . maintained itself . . . at Nashville. . . . Rosecrans determined . . . to advance [southeastward] from Nashville. He prepared to force the passage of Stones River, north of Murfreesboro. . . . The Confederate army was collected in and around Murfreesboro.

Says Union General Philip H. Sheridan (later of cavalry fame, but now commander of an infantry division):

Slight skirmishes took place frequently during this period, and now and then heavy demonstrations were made . . . by reconnoitring parties from both armies, but none of these ever grew into a battle. These affairs sprung from the desire of each side to feel his antagonist, and had little result beyond emphasizing the fact that behind each line of pickets lay a massed and powerful army busily preparing for the inevitable conflict. . . .

But according to David Urquhart, an officer on Braxton Bragg's staff, the Confederates in Murfreesboro had other things on their minds as well:

Social recreation . . . at this time was at its zenith. Christmas was approaching. The young officers of our army were all bent on fun and gayety. Invitations were out for a ball on the day after Christmas.

Urquhart adds that these same days saw the wedding of Confederate cavalry commander John H. Morgan:

. . . [The] marriage ceremony was performed at the house of the bride. General Bragg and his staff, with a few of Morgan's comrades, were gathered as witnesses in the front parlor. General [Leonidas] Polk, Bishop of Louisiana, performed the ceremony and gave the blessing.

About a week later, Morgan left his bride to take his horsemen on a raid against the Federal railway system in Kentucky.

In the Union camps, the enlisted men were not aware of the plans of their commander, Rosecrans, and many hoped that the army was settled for the winter. This hope, however, diminished as a result of something done by the quartermaster department. In the words of private soldier R. B. Stewart:

Until now we had been using the Sibley tent, a tent large and comfortable enough for camp purposes, but hard to manage and heavy to transport, and when our wagons got behind, as they often did for days together, we had to do the best we could, with only the heavens above us for shelter.

One day there was issued to each one about two yards square of heavy cotton, with buttons and button-holes along three sides, and small loops of cord along the other. We were . . . informed that henceforth these were to be our burden by day and our shelter by night, and [being white] they might answer for flags of truce in a time of need. . . . [W]e folded them away for whatever emergency they might happen to suit.

It was the morning after Christmas, 1862, when orders came to . . . draw three days' rations and be ready to march at a moment's notice. . . . We were hardly fairly started before it began to rain, and to rain only as it can rain in that Southern country. Soon the earth was all mud beneath us, the heavens all dark above us, while sounds that were not thunder gave us a hint of business before us. We tramped on and on, encountering nothing worse than the enemy's pickets, who retreated slowly over the hills.

In the evening we halted near Nolensville. The rain had ceased to pour, but fog was settling heavily and night was near at hand. We

were wet and tired and hungry. There was an abundance of good
cedar rails nearby, and soon roaring, fragrant fires gave us what cheer
they could. Hot coffee, crackers, and pork soon helped to modify the
situation. . . .

When we began preparations for the night, our minds went out to
our squares of muslin. If ever they might be useful, now was the time.
We unfolded them carefully, spread them out gently, and studied
their anatomy. Evidently they were constructed with reference to each
other. They seemed to be social in their nature, and must somehow
go together. . . . We went to work and buttoned two pieces together, then stretched them over a ridge-pole made of a cedar rail, and,
with pegs through the loops, made them fast to the ground. We now
had a shelter about four feet high, long enough and wide enough for
two persons. The idea thus far developed seemed to strike us favor-
ably, and we wondered if they would shed the rain.

We paired off, selected our ground, pitched our united squares,
and in a little while the evening gloom was all lighted up by the
snowy whiteness of our shelter tents. Spreading our blankets and putting our knapsacks under our heads, with jest and joke we took possession of our strange new quarters. When all seemed to be settling
down into the quiet of the night, some sleepless fellow stuck his head
out and began to bark. Soon another followed, then another. The
idea was swiftly contagious, and in a few minutes the whole camp
sounded like a vast dog convention, where all kinds of dogs were barking for a prize.

The shape of the tent, the way of getting into it, and all the surroundings gave to someone the idea of a dog kennel, and he felt constrained to bark. The tents were henceforth christened "dog tents,"
which in a little while degenerated into "pup tents," and by this name
they were ever after known. It rained during the night, and . . . we
were dry in the morning. . . . The man who invented the "dog
tent" ought to have a monument.

The next day we reached Triune, the enemy contesting every inch
of the way, and sometimes making our further progress doubtful.
[Especially effective during these delaying actions was the work of the
Confederate cavalrymen under General Joseph Wheeler.] Finding
the little village almost deserted, we took possession of such livestock
and provisions as we could conveniently carry along, and the next day
being the Sabbath we rested from all our labors and feasted upon the
spoils.

Early on Monday we took up our burdens, and leaving the good road to go its own way to the right, we struck across lots. Through cedar forests and dismal swamps we plodded patiently along, stimulated by the occasional booming of cannon far off to our left and front. We knew that the other divisions of the army were somewhere . . . forcing their way along, but we did not know where they were. But as to that, we did not know where we were ourselves. Night found us joining them . . . a few miles north of Murfreesboro. It now became evident that unless Bragg should keep [falling back] . . . traveling faster than we, there was going to be trouble pretty soon. . . .

We all felt exceedingly homesick that night as we lay under the clouds and in the mud. But we still had some hope that the situation was not so serious as it seemed to be—that Mr. Bragg would think better of it and get out of our way before it would be forever too late. . . . Thinking a great many thoughts about home and the morrow, we dropped off at last into a restless sleep.

Morning dawned cloudy and cold. We ate our breakfast in silence, rolled up our blankets, and patiently waited for orders. Rumors and reports of what had taken place the day before were plenty, but none of them very encouraging except to those who were longing for a fight, and that class was not conspicuous. We lay under arms all day and made but little change in our position. At irregular intervals, somewhere in front of us, cannon kept thundering away, not as in battle, but as though searching for a foe. All day long, regiments of other divisions kept marching past us . . . disappearing in the woods and dark thickets of cedar. In the evening came our turn to move, and we marched to the right, through woods and across fields until we came to the Franklin Pike. Here we formed the extreme right of the line of battle. . . .

Explains the Union's Phil Sheridan:

The enemy under Bragg lay between us and Stones River in order of battle. . . . [T]he two armies were in close proximity, and . . . Rosecrans intended to attack by throwing his left on the enemy's right. . . . Bragg . . . planned to swing his left on our right by an exactly similar manoeuvre. . . . The conceptions in the minds of the two generals were almost identical. . . .

Union soldier R. B. Stewart continues:

Night came on clear, cold, and frosty, almost too cold for sleep, and we were allowed no fires. We made our beds among the rocks and under the cedar branches. . . . The morning of December 31, 1862,

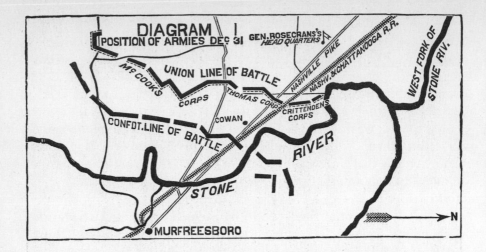

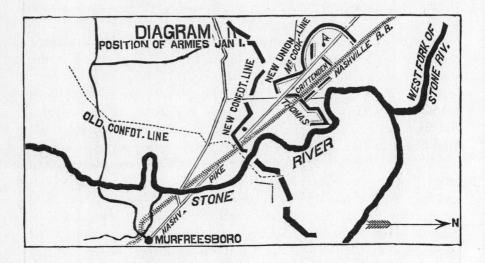

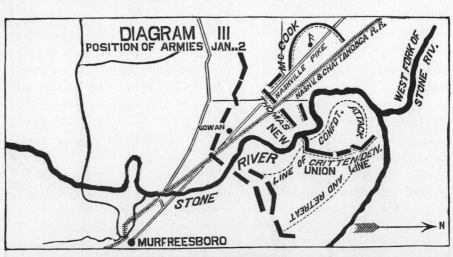

The Battle of Murfreesboro.

came on with a cloudless sky and a ringing, frosty air. With the first streak of dawn we were all up and lively, with fires kindled, coffee boiling, and meat frying on the coals. The night had passed without any alarm, and the early light revealed no signs of an approaching storm.

But a storm—one of Confederate making—was near indeed. "Bragg took the initiative," says Phil Sheridan, "beginning his movement about an hour earlier than the time set by Rosecrans, which gained him an immense advantage. . . ." Part of the advantage, of course, was that Rosecrans' attack plan was thwarted. Bragg's attack was launched by General William J. Hardee's corps.

R. B. Stewart, in his position on the Union right, where General Alexander McCook commanded, was one of the first to come under fire:

Just as I had taken my meat and coffee from the fire and was sitting down on a cold rock to eat my breakfast, a few shots rang through the woods in front. We had hardly time to be alarmed before others followed, and we heard bullets singing uncomfortably near and saw the pickets rushing in, followed by a line of gray, yelling and shooting like demons. . . . Dropping our pots and pans, leaving our haversacks and blankets, we snatched up our cartridge-boxes and rushed for our guns. . . . We stood to deliver [one round of] fire and say good morning, then took to our heels and ran. But not all of us. Some fell right there. Many lingered too long with their breakfast dishes. But most of us ran.

Our way was through [a] cornfield. The stalks were yet thickly standing. The ground was frozen and rough. I could hear the bullets striking the stalks. I could hear them strike a comrade as he ran. Then there would be a groan, a stagger, and a fall. I could hear the wild yelling behind, and the roar of guns [i.e., artillery pieces] that were now getting into action. I saw, by a backward glance, a gray mass covering all the ground where our camp had so lately been. I saw the fields . . . filling up with regiments and columns and armies of gray. . . . I felt as though I would like to be all legs, with no other purpose in life but to run.

At the lower side of the field was a high rail-fence. No fence ever stood so much in my way. I could not get to it for the crowd that was ahead of me. We all wanted to get over it first. But many never got over it at all. None of us sat on the top rail to rest. Some tumbled off and ran no further.

Philip H. Sheridan.

There was an old house a little way ahead. I reached it safely, and, sheltered behind its big chimney, reloaded and fired, and loaded again. I do not know that I hurt anybody. I am not sure that I shot at anybody in particular, but it was a good thing to do. It made me feel better. My fingers were so cold that I could hardly handle the cartridges, but they very soon warmed up to the work.

A team of battery-horses came dashing along without riders, and, passing between two gate-posts, one of them struck a post and was killed.

By this time we were so scattered and mingled that hardly two of a company were together, and there did not seem to be anyone to give us a word of command. It was a plain case of "everyone for himself, and the devil take the hindmost."

The pursuit had now somewhat slackened and the noise behind us was not so furious, but we continued our retreat until we crossed the small creek about one mile from where we started. Here we seemed to be at a distance safe enough to stop and breathe and gather ourselves together. The flag was still with us, and one or two of our regimental officers made it a rallying point.

Writes Union staff officer G. C. Kniffin, who was with General Rosecrans near his headquarters behind the lines when the battle began:

Suddenly the woods on the right . . . appeared to be alive with men wandering aimlessly in the direction of the rear. The roar of artillery grew more distinct, mingled with the continuous volleys of musketry.

The rear of a line of battle always presents the pitiable spectacle of a horde of skulkers, men who, when tried in the fierce flame of battle, find, often to their own disgust, that they are lacking in the element of courage. But the spectacle of whole regiments of soldiers flying in panic to the rear was a sight never seen by the Army of the Cumberland except on that occasion.

Captain [Elmer] Otis [of the Fourth U.S. Cavalry], from his position on the extreme right dispatched a messenger, who arrived breathless to inform General Rosecrans that the right wing was in rapid retreat. The astounding intelligence was confirmed a moment later by a staff-officer from McCook. . . .

Rosecrans responded with confidence to a situation fast growing desperate: "All right—we will rectify it." Told of the death of Joshua W. Sill, one of Phil Sheridan's brigade commanders, he replied, "Never mind. Brave men must die in battle. We must seek results." Already in the saddle for some time, Rosecrans would spend the day there, a striking picture of courageous leadership. Among those who accompanied him was an unnamed correspondent for the Cincinnati Commercial:

. . . the General . . . galloped into the field, followed by his staff and escort. He . . . galloped to the left and sent forward [Colonel John] Beatty's brigade. Moving down to the extreme left he was discovered by the enemy, and a full battery opened upon him. Solid shot and shell stormed about us furiously. The General himself was unmoved by it, but his staff generally were more sensitive. The inclination to dodge was irresistible. Directly one poor fellow of the escort was dismounted, and his horse galloped frantically over the fields. The General directed . . . his chief of artillery to post a battery to shell the enemy, waiting to see it done. . . .

Through these moments, Phil Sheridan's division was vitally engaged in trying to stem the foe's advance. The diminutive Sheridan would come out of the battle with a reputation as an especially vigorous and capable commander. General Lovell H. Rousseau, sent with his reserves into the cedar thickets where Sheridan was fighting, was later to say:

I knew it was hell in there before I got in, but I was convinced of it when I saw Phil Sheridan, with hat in one hand and sword in the other, fighting as if he were the devil incarnate, or had a fresh indulgence from Father Tracy [Rosecrans' chaplain] every five minutes.

It was to be said by others that if Sheridan needed indulgence for the fury of his deeds, he needed it also for the nature of some of his words.

As for Rosecrans and his perilous travels: The Cincinnati Commercial's correspondent writes that the party soon came under "another blizzard, with an interlude of Minies [rifle bullets],* which whistled about. . . ."

The shifting scene of the battle [the correspondent goes on] now carried the General back to the centre of the field. The enemy were streaming through the woods a few hundred yards in front. The forest was populous with them. Our batteries were dashing across the plain with frightful vehemence, wheeling into position and firing with terrific rapidity. The rebel artillery played upon us remorselessly, tear-

---

* Properly "Minié balls," but written variously by the war's recorders.

ing men and horses to pieces. The sharpshooters were still more vicious. A flight of bullets passed through the staff.

I heard an insinuating thud! and saw a poor orderly within sabre-distance topple from his saddle and tumble headlong to mother earth. One convulsive shudder, and he was no more. His bridle-hand clutched the reins in death. A comrade loosened his grasp, and his faithful gray stood quietly. . . .

Another bullet went through the jaw of Lieut. Benton's beautiful chestnut. Smarting with pain, he struck violently with his hoofs at the invisible tormentor. . . .

One or two other horses were hit, and the [General's] cavalcade rushed from that line of fire to another, just in time to be splashed with mud from the spat of a six-pound shot. It seemed that there was not a square yard on the field free from fire. The rattle of musketry and roar of artillery was deafening. Still the General charged through it as if it had been harmless rain. It was wonderful that he escaped. . . .

Galloping down again to the extreme front, an officer in range with the General was suddenly dismounted. A round shot struck his horse squarely on the thigh, knocking him a rod, and tumbling the rider all in a heap over the soil.

Pushing out to the cedar forest where [General James S.] Negley's gallant division was struggling against great odds, trusty Sheridan was met, bringing out [and falling back with] his tried division in superb order. . . . The . . . enemy was dreadfully punished. Still they came on like famished wolves, in columns, by divisions. . . .

Conspicuous among the Confederate leaders who enhanced their reputations during these assaults was the courageous and resourceful General Patrick R. ("Pat") Cleburne. The men of his division performed many valiant deeds. An example is given by a Confederate staff officer, James D. Porter:

The Seventeenth Tennessee, Col. A. S. Marks . . . [found barring its way] a battery of four guns. . . . Colonel Marks said, "Boys, do you see that battery? It is ours, is it not?" The regiment rushed upon it, drove back its support, and took the guns. But the gallant colonel fell, maimed for life.

Up to this time the Confederates had kept the advantage. The Federal right, hinging on a brigade in the center (that of Acting General

William B. Hazen) which had fought fiercely and had managed to stand fast, had swung back two or three miles.

"At 12 o'clock," says Southerner David Urquhart, "we had a large part of the field, with many prisoners, cannon, guns, ammunition, wagons, and the dead and wounded of both armies."

Adds Confederate General Bragg: "These important successes and results had not been achieved without heavy sacrifices on our part, as the resistance of the enemy, after the first surprise, was most gallant and obstinate."

Returning to the Union side and to the Cincinnati Commercial's correspondent:

The enemy had compelled us to change front completely. Gen. Rosecrans himself executed it at awful personal hazard. There was not a point in the very front of battle which he did not visit. Taking advantage of a commanding crest . . . he posted the batteries; and some twenty or thirty guns opened with prodigious volume. Solid shot and shell crashed through the populous forest in a tumult of destructive fury. The cloud of smoke for some minutes completely enveloped the gunners and obscured them from view.

Now then, we charge. Down through the field and across the road, the General in the lead. Bitterly whistled the leaden hail. A soldier falls dead under the very hoofs of the Commander's horse.

"Advance the line! Charge them!"

And our gallant lads, fired with the wild enthusiasm of the moment, madly push up the hill. The forests are splintered with the furious volumes of fire. . . . Yon line of gray and steel halts, staggers, reels.

"There they go!" shouts the gallant leader. "Now drive them home!"

Great God, what tumult in the brain! Sense reels with the intoxicating frenzy. There was a line of dead blue-coats where the charge was so gallantly made. But the corpses of the foe were scattered thickly through those woods.

This was an isolated charge, not a general one. All along the new line, however, the Federals rallied strongly. The Confederate surge was stopped. Fresh attacks were turned back.

Writes an unnamed correspondent for the Chattanooga Daily Rebel:

Gen. [John C.] Breckinridge, who held our right, [on the other side] of Stones River, and who had not been previously engaged, was now ordered across, with a view of relieving our wearied columns. . . . [Two] brigades . . . were formed and sent forward. They imitated the coolness and courage of their predecessors, going forward with the utmost alacrity and firmness. They met the same tempest of shell, grape, canister, and musketry, and recoiled.

This attack was made against the angle in the Federal line—against the "hinge" upon which the right wing had swung backward. Two more Confederate brigades came across the river, and the attempt was repeated. In the words of Union staff officer G. C. Kniffin:
   . . . the gallantry of this advance is indescribable. . . . The Confederates had no sooner moved into the open field from the cover of the river bank than they were received with a blast from the artillery. [They] plucked the cotton from the boles at their feet and stuffed it in their ears. Huge gaps were torn in the Confederate line at every discharge. The Confederate line staggered forward half the distance across the fields, when the Union infantry added minie-balls to the fury of the storm. Then the Confederates wavered and fell back. . . .

The Union's Phil Sheridan takes up:
   . . . I was ordered by Rosecrans to prepare to make a charge should the enemy again assault us. In anticipation of this work I massed my troops in close column. The expected attack never came, however, but the shot and shell of a furious cannonade told with fatal effect upon men and officers as they lay on their faces hugging the ground.

The torments of this trying situation were almost unbearable, but it was obvious to all that it was necessary to have at hand a compact body of troops to repel any assault the enemy might make pending the reconstruction of the extreme right of our line, and a silent determination to stay seemed to take hold of each individual soldier.

Nor was this grim silence interrupted throughout the cannonade, except in one instance, when one of the regiments broke out in a lusty cheer as a startled rabbit in search of a new hiding-place safely ran the whole length of the line on the backs of the men.

While my troops were still lying there, General Rosecrans, with a part of his staff and a few orderlies, rode out on the rearranged line to supervise its formation and encourage the men, and in prosecution of these objects moved around the front of my column of attack, within range of the batteries that were shelling us so viciously. As he passed to the open ground on my left, I joined him.

The enemy, seeing this mounted party, turned his guns upon it, and his accurate aim was soon rewarded, for a solid shot carried away the head of Colonel [Julius P.] Garesché, the chief-of-staff, and killed or wounded two or three orderlies. Garesché's appalling death stunned us all, and a momentary expression of horror spread over Rosecrans' face; but at such a time the importance of self-control was vital, and he pursued his course with an appearance of indifference. . . .

Rosecrans shortly met General Thomas L. Crittenden, who later recorded:

. . . I saw the stains of blood on his breast, and exclaimed, "Are you wounded, General?"

"Oh, no," said he. "That is the blood of poor Garesché, who has just been killed."

Relates Union newsman "Wapello" of the Louisville Journal, *who had watched the last two Confederate attacks from the busy lines of General Lovell Rousseau:*

. . . the army was saved. The terrific firing ceased, the smoke quickly rolled away, and the sun shone out bright and clear on the scene that was lately so shrouded. . . . How still everything was! Everybody seemed to be holding his breath. . . .

General Rousseau and his staff galloped forward to the ground the rebels had advanced over. Their dead lay there in frightful heaps, some with the lifeblood not yet all flowed from their mortal wounds, some propped upon their elbows and gasping their last.

The flag of [an] Arkansas regiment lay there on the ground beside its dead bearer. Every depression in the field was full of wounded who had crawled thither to screen themselves from the fire, and a large number of prisoners came out of a little copse in the middle of the field and surrendered themselves to General Rousseau in person. . . .

As the rebel line rolled back through the woods, General Rousseau ordered his right wing to charge their left flank. . . . The regulars advanced gallantly into the cedars . . . and inflicted heavy loss on the retreating foe, but they also suffered greatly. . . . The rebels continued their flight . . . [and] our troops were recalled. . . .

The indomitable Confederates returned to mass in front of the Union center "with banners flying" as though planning another attack, but they retired when greeted by an outburst of fire.

The day ended with the Southern army holding most of the ground it had taken in the morning. "Both armies," says Confederate General Bragg, "exhausted by a conflict of full ten hours' duration, rarely surpassed for its continued intensity and heavy losses sustained, sunk to rest with the sun. . . ."

Adds David Urquhart, of Bragg's staff:

A bitter cold night was now on us. . . . The sheen of a bright moon revealed the sad carnage of the day, and the horrors of war became vividly distinct. That night General Bragg again made his headquarters at Murfreesboro, whence he gave orders for the care of the wounded. All the churches and public buildings were turned into hospitals. He announced to Richmond by telegraph: "God has granted us a Happy New Year."

The viewpoint of the Chattanooga Daily Rebel's *correspondent was not quite so positive. He says that the victory was*

glorious and complete as far as it went, but it was not consummate. We thought at one time that the Yankees were as good as routed, but it appears they were not. We thought they would skedaddle that night, but they did not.

It was a long night for Union soldier R. B. Stewart and his comrades:

What was left of our brigade was sent back to the right and rear to guard against cavalry and give warning of any danger. . . . We had nothing to eat. Our blankets were giving comfort to the enemy, and we were allowed no fires . . . and we felt gloomy and doubtful and miserable enough. We had time to think over the events of the day, to count up the missing, and wonder what was their fate; to think of our homes, so many of them soon to be clouded with sorrow. There was no chance for sleep and no occasion for motion, so we just sat and waited, and watched the old year out and the new one in. When morning came, it brought us a little comfort in the softer atmosphere and pleasant sunshine, but no breakfast.

On some parts of the field the hungry men, allowed fires with the coming of daylight, began to cut steaks from the dead horses.

Action that day was confined to skirmishing, artillery exchanges,

Union troops at Murfreesboro: watching the old year out and the new
one in.

*and encounters between Confederate cavalry units and the troops in
the Union rear. Southern General John A. Wharton and his horsemen met their match in a detachment of Michigan engineers and
Ohio infantrymen entrenched along the road to Nashville. Repelled
in several assaults, the Confederates had the audacity to send in a demand for surrender. The affair reportedly ended when the Federals
sent back the reply, "We don't surrender much."*

*The night of January 1, 1863, and the following morning passed
with no major developments. But then, says Southerner David
Urquhart:*

At about noon General Bragg determined to dislodge the force
[that threatened him from a hill] on his right . . . and our best
troops were carefully selected. . . . A gun fired by one of our batteries at 4 o'clock was the signal for the attack. After a fierce fight we
carried the hill. The orders were to take its crest, and there remain
entrenched. General Breckinridge endeavored to execute this order,
but the commanders of the brigades engaged could not restrain the
ardor of their men, who pushed on beyond support. The Federal
batteries that had been massed on the other side of the stream now
opened on them. . . .

The fire was murderous. Writes Southerner L. D. Young, who was on the field as a lieutenant of infantry:

While lying on the ground momentarily . . . a shell exploded right in the middle of the company, almost literally tearing it to pieces. When I recovered from the shock, the sight I witnessed was appalling. Some eighteen or twenty men hurled in every direction, including my dear friend, Lieut. George Burnley. . . . But these circumstances were occurring every minute now. . . .

Union General Rosecrans was "as usual . . . in the midst of the fray, directing the movement of troops and the range of batteries." He soon ordered a counterattack. With a resounding cheer, the infantry lunged forward. Relates R. B. Stewart:

Down through the open fields we rushed, keeping in as good order as possible. Cannon thundered before us, to the right of us, and behind us. Shells shrieked over us, and, bursting, scattered their fragments through our ranks. But it was "close up," "guide right," and still forward until Stones River was reached, and we paused for a moment on its bank. A part of the line passed over, and the Southern ranks were broken. They fell back . . . and the battle ended. . . .

Bragg's brigades had been severely handled. In a period of about an hour they had suffered about 2,000 casualties. Laments David Urquhart: ". . . the news of this disastrous charge, led by the elite of the Confederate army, cast a gloom over all."

Again in the words of Unionist R. B. Stewart:

At night we rested where our work ended, but to most of us there was no rest. There was comfort in the thought that our defeat had turned to victory—that we who had fared so badly under the first stroke of the enemy were permitted to lay the last stroke on his back. All night long the rain poured down as though it would wash away every stain of blood. All night long we listened to the cries of the wounded where they lay upon the field. All night long the ambulances were busy gathering in the sheaves of this fearful harvest. All night long we waited and watched and wondered if the battle were really over. The morning came, dark and damp and gloomy. . . .

It rained all day, with the two armies lying before each other, the pickets exchanging shots, and, in the afternoon, a sharp skirmish occurring. That night, says Union General Phil Sheridan,

Bragg retired from Murfreesboro. . . . General Rosecrans occupied Murfreesboro on the 4th and 5th. . . . The enemy in retiring did not fall back very far—only behind Duck River to Shelbyville and Tullahoma—and but little endeavor was made to follow him. Indeed, we were not in condition to pursue, even if it had been the intention at the outset of the campaign.

As soon as possible after the Confederate retreat I went over the battlefield to collect such of my wounded as had not been carried off to the South, and to bury my dead. In the cedars and on the ground where I had been so fiercely assaulted when the battle opened on the morning of the 31st, evidences of the bloody struggle appeared on every hand in the form of broken firearms, fragments of accoutrements, and splintered trees. The dead had nearly all been left unburied, but as there was likelihood of their mutilation by roving swine, the bodies had mostly been collected in piles at different points and inclosed by rail fences. The sad duties of interment and of caring for the wounded were completed by the 5th. . . .

During the engagement there had been little straggling [in my division], and my list of missing was small and legitimate. Still, it was known that a very few had shirked their duty, and an example was necessary. Among this small number were four officers who, it was charged, had abandoned their colors and regiments. When their guilt was clearly established . . . I caused the whole division to be formed in a hollow square . . . and had the four officers marched to the centre, where, telling them that I would not humiliate any officer or soldier by requiring him to touch their disgraced swords, I compelled them to deliver theirs up to my colored servant, who also cut from their coats every insignia of rank. Then, after there had been read to the command an order from army headquarters dismissing the four from the service, the scene was brought to a close by drumming the cowards out of camp. . . .

My effective force in the Battle of Stones River was 4,154 officers and men. Of this number I lost 1,633 killed, wounded and missing, or nearly 40 per cent. . . . The ratio of loss in the whole of Rosecrans' army was also high, and Bragg's losses were almost equally great. Rosecrans carried into the action about 42,000 officers and men. He lost 13,230, or 31½ per cent. Bragg's effective force was 37,800 officers and men. He lost 10,306, or nearly 28 per cent.

Though our victory was dearly bought, yet the importance of gaining the day at any price was very great. . . . Nashville was firmly established as a base for future operations, Kentucky was safe from the possibility of being again overrun; and Bragg, thrown on the defensive, was compelled to give his thoughts to the protection of the interior of the Confederacy and the security of Chattanooga, rather than indulge in schemes of conquest. . . .

14

LINCOLN TURNS
TO HOOKER

January, 1863, *found Burnside's Army of the Potomac and Lee's Army of Northern Virginia in winter quarters at Fredericksburg. The Confederates occupied the hills they had defended so well during the battle of December 13, while the Federals were encamped across the river on the heights and plains below the town of Falmouth.*

Says Federal newsman Charles Coffin:

All the surrounding forests had disappeared, built into huts, with chimneys of sticks and mud, or [cut for burning] in the stone fireplaces constructed by the soldiers, who also built mud ovens and baked their beans and bread. The winter was severe, the snow deep. The soldiers were discouraged. They knew that they had fought bravely but that there had been mismanagement and inefficient generalship. Homesickness set in and became a disease.

Matters weren't helped by the fact that men wounded in the battle were still dying. Relates Lieutenant Jesse Young:

One of the most affecting scenes of camp life . . . was a funeral which occurred one wintry day. . . . [A] burial party, formed of the company to which the dead soldier had belonged, with other comrades from the regiment, lovingly bore or followed his body to the grave that had been dug not far away . . . on a neighboring hill. Through the snow and the slush, led by the band which played . . . a dead march . . . with melting and penetrating effect, the boys marched out and reverently stood by the open grave.

No chaplain was then serving with the regiment, and there was no burial service read; but, as the boys stood in silence at the side of the pit that had been dug, one of them, with tremulous utterance, began to sing,

> Rock of ages, cleft for me,
> Let me hide myself in thee.

Soon another voice chimed in with the first, and then another joined, until, by the time the closing stanza of the glorious old hymn had been reached, all the boys, in the cold bleak January weather, with uncovered heads and tearful eyes, with tenderness and pathos, thinking of the dear ones far away and wondering whose turn next would come to die of sickness or wounds, in the camp or hospital or on the field, were singing,

> While I draw this fleeting breath,
> When my eyes shall close in death,
> When I rise to worlds unknown
> And behold thee on thy throne,
> Rock of ages, cleft for me,
> Let me hide myself in thee.

But the camp's atmosphere wasn't wholly one of sadness and discouragement. Many of the men raised their spirits by finding ways to entertain themselves. Again in Young's words:

As one means of recreation and sport, a minstrel troupe was organized in the regiment, and often in the evening the camp resounded with the sound of fiddle, banjo, and bones, while the air reechoed with the stale jokes which Christie and his fellow-minstrels were just then retailing on the stage throughout the land.

As for the Confederates encamped on the heights across the Rappahannock: Artilleryman Robert Stiles says that their spare-time pursuits included organized snowball battles:

These contests were unique in many respects. In the first place, here was sport, or friendly combat, on the grandest scale, perhaps, known in modern times. Entire brigades lined up against each other for the fight. And not the masses of men only, but the organized military bodies—the line and field officers, the bands and the banners, the generals and their staffs, mounted as for genuine battle.

There was the formal demand for the surrender of the camp, and the refusal, the charge, and the repulse; the front, the flank, the rear attack. And there was intense earnestness in the struggle—sometimes limbs were broken and eyes, at least temporarily, put out; and the camp equipment of the vanquished was regarded as fair booty to the victors. . . .

One would have supposed these veteran troops had seen too much of the real thing to seek amusement in playing at battle.

Little rancor existed among the pickets on opposite sides of the river. Southerner Stiles noted with amusement that they kept up a lively commerce by means of toy sailboats:

The communication was almost constant, and the vessels many of them really beautiful little craft, with shapely hulls, nicely painted; elaborate rigging, trim sails, closed decks, and perfect-working steering apparatus. The cargoes, besides the newspapers of the two sides, usually consisted on our side of tobacco and on the Federal side of coffee and sugar; yet the trade was by no means confined to these articles, and on a sunny, pleasant day the waters were fairly dotted with the fairy fleet. Many a weary hour of picket duty was thus relieved and lightened, and most of the officers seemed to wink at the infraction of military law, if such it was. A few rigidly interdicted it, but it never really ceased.

According to John B. Gordon (the Southern brigade commander who was wounded five times at Antietam), some of the fraternization between the pickets was more personal:

[A] Confederate officer of pickets . . . asked the Union lieutenant [on the opposite shore] if he would not come over after dark and go with him to a farmhouse near the lines, where certain Confederates had invited the country girls to a dance. The Union officer hesitated, but the Confederate insisted and promised to call for him in a boat after dark and to lend him a suit of citizen's clothes, and pledged his honor as a soldier to see him safely back to his own side before daylight the next morning.

The invitation was accepted, and at the appointed hour the Confederate's boat glided silently to the place of meeting on the opposite bank. The citizen's suit was a ludicrous fit, but it served its purpose. The Union soldier was introduced to the country girls as a new recruit just arrived in camp. He enjoyed the dance, and, returning with his Confederate escort, was safely landed in his own lines before daylight.

During the weeks since the battle, General Burnside, eager to redeem himself, had been involved with plans for a new offensive. But the plans hadn't been divulged to the troops, and nothing that happened in camp revealed that a movement was pending. Indeed, writes Regis de Trobriand,

A few indications . . . rather denoted the contrary. For instance, the ladies were allowed passes to visit the army, which was only permitted . . . when active hostilities were suspended for some time. General [David B.] Birney had been allowed . . . to go to Washington to [fetch] Mrs. Birney, who was accompanied by quite a party of Philadelphians—ladies, sisters, or relatives of officers of his staff. They arrived at his headquarters on the 13th [of January], where everything was ready to receive them; and for three days there was nothing but gayety, rides on horseback and drives in carriages, collations, reviews, music, and improvised dances by moonlight.

Suddenly, however, the ladies were sent away. Burnside was ready to move. He planned to make a rapid march up the river and cross over by means of pontoon bridges, thus flanking Lee and obliging him to come out of his strong defenses and fight in the open.

When the Federals got their orders, says Samuel Fiske, a volunteer from New England:

Excitement took the place of the quiet that had reigned in our midst for a month. Hearts beat high with hope and patriotic ardor, and [in others] spirits sank in dismay at the thought of approaching danger. . . . Some left couches of sickness, roused to new strength at the call to arms. Some, who had been perfectly well, paled into sudden sickness at the same prospect and came sneaking round the surgeons' tents and crawling into hospitals.

The movement, Fiske goes on to explain, began on Tuesday morning, January 20:

. . . camps were broken up . . . knapsacks packed; and soon long lines of troops were in motion over hill and dale all around. . . .

The roads for miles were choked with supply wagons, ammunition trains, and rumbling batteries. All was noise, confusion, and utmost activity. Trumpets sounded, drums beat, whips cracked, mules squealed, and teamsters cursed. In short, all things showed that a vast army was on the move.

The fords selected by Burnside for the crossing, eight or ten miles above the Union camp, were soon reached. As the day closed, Burnside informed the troops they were "about to meet the enemy once more" and that "the auspicious moment had arrived to strike a great and mortal blow to the rebellion. . . ."

Writes a correspondent for the New York Times, *William Swinton (later the author of a widely acclaimed history of the Army of the Potomac):*

We were sitting, the editor-in-chief of the *Times* and the present writer, in our tent at headquarters that evening, looking forward to a start on horseback for the scene of operations before daylight the following morning. About nine o'clock a light, ominous pattering was heard on the canvas roof. "It is rain!" was the exclamation, and, looking out from the tent, the heavens showed all the signs of a terrible storm. . . .

It was a wild Walpurgis Night, such as Goethe paints in the "Faust" while the demons held revel in the forest of the Brocken. . . . Yet was there hard work done that fearful night. One hundred and fifty pieces of artillery were to be planted [to cover the crossing] in the position selected for them by Gen. [Henry J.] Hunt, Chief of Artillery. . . . The pontoons, also, were drawn nearer toward the river.

But it was dreadful work. The roads, under the influence of the rain, were becoming shocking. And by daylight, when the boats should all have been on the banks, ready to slide down into the water, but fifteen had been gotten up—not enough for one bridge, and five were wanted!

. . . The utmost effort was put forth to get pontoons enough into position to construct a bridge or two. Double and triple teams of horses and mules were harnessed to each pontoon-boat. It was in vain. Long powerful ropes were then attached to the teams, and one hundred and fifty men were put to the task on each boat. The effort was but little more successful. They would founder through the mire for a few feet—the gang of Lilliputians with their huge-ribbed Gulliver—and then give up breathless.

Night arrived, but the pontoons could not be got up. The rebels had discovered what was up, and the pickets on the opposite bank called over to ours that they "would come over tomorrow and help us build the bridge."

That night the troops again bivouacked in the same position in the woods they had held the night before. . . . Many had brought their shelter tents; and making a floor of spruce, hemlock, or cedar boughs, and lighting huge campfires, they enjoyed themselves as well as the circumstance would permit. On the following morning a whisky ration, provided by the judicious forethought of Gen. Burnside, was on hand for them.

Thursday morning saw the light struggling through an opaque envelope of mist, and dawned upon another day of storm and rain. It was a curious sight presented by the army as we rode over the ground, miles in extent, occupied by it. One might fancy some new geologic cataclysm had overtaken the world, and that he saw around him the elemental wrecks left by another Deluge.

An indescribable chaos of pontoons, wagons, and artillery encumbered the road down to the river—supply wagons upset by the roadside, artillery stalled in the mud, ammunition trains mired by the way. Horses and mules dropped down dead, exhausted with the effort to move their loads through the hideous medium. One hundred and fifty dead animals, many of them buried in the liquid muck, were counted in the course of a morning's ride. . . .

It was now no longer a question of how to go on; it was a question of how to get back. That night . . . the three days' cooked rations which the men had taken in their haversacks . . . would give out; and the other six days' provisions were in the supply trains, which stuck fast in the mud miles behind. Indeed, the rations had already, in many cases, given out, and boxes of hard crackers were brought up on mules or carried on men's shoulders.

Union soldier Warren Goss concludes the story of this "mud campaign":

. . . the next morning the army wretchedly began its return to camp. Some ironically offered to get into the boats and row them to camp through the mud. . . . Finally the army began to corduroy the road [i.e., to cover the worst spots with logs laid side by side] . . . and with laughter and jest, and oath and execration, it floundered back to its camps; but not until the enemy had facetiously put up a big placard on the opposite shore which read: BURNSIDE STUCK IN THE MUD.

Said General Lee in a letter to his wife written on January 29:

The storm has culminated here in a deep snow, which does not improve our comfort. It came particularly hard on some of our troops whom I was obliged to send some eleven miles up the Rappahannock to meet a recent move of General Burnside. Their bivouac in the rain and snow was less comfortable than at their former stations, where they had constructed some shelter.

General Burnside's designs have apparently been frustrated, either by the storm or by other causes; and on last Saturday he took a special steamer to Washington to consult the military oracles at the Federal seat of Government. Sunday I heard of his being closeted with President Lincoln, Secretary Stanton, and General Halleck. I suppose we shall have a new programme next week.

What happened was that Burnside was replaced as commander of the Army of the Potomac. Warren Goss writes that

. . . the appointment of General Joseph Hooker . . . came to gladden us like the sudden appearance of the sun in cloud-darkened skies. . . . Hooker had been identified with the battles and history of this army from the beginning, and by his dashing bravery had won the sobriquet of "Fighting Joe." It was the general feeling among the rank-and-file that he was more likely to err from over-rashness and daring than to fail by over-caution.

The President had not promoted him to these high duties without misgivings. He had been an outspoken, unsparing critic of his superiors, and it remained to be seen if this spirit of insubordination would not react against him, and whether or not he would bear the ordeal of a command from which no commander had as yet escaped unscathed.

In a private letter addressed to him . . . with his usual sense, quaint humor, and fatherly kindness, Mr. Lincoln said: "I have heard, in such a way as to believe it, of your recently saying that both the army and the government needed a dictator. Of course, it was not for this, but in spite of it, that I have given you the command. Only those generals who gain successes can set up dictators. What I now ask of you is military success, and I will risk the dictatorship. . . . Beware of rashness, but with energy and sleepless vigilance go forward and give us victories."

Federal newsman Charles Coffin takes up:

How should General Hooker cure homesickness which had become a disease? Officers and men alike had an intense longing for home. When he took command of the army, desertions were at the rate of two hundred a day. Two thousand nine hundred and twenty-two officers and eighty-two thousand men were reported absent, with or without leave! It was in itself a great army. We are not to think that they were all deserters. By far the larger number were absent on leave, but, once home, had not returned.

"What word of encouragement can you give us?" asked a company of ladies of President Lincoln.

"I have no word of encouragement for you," he said. "The military situation is far from bright, and the country knows it. The fact is, the people have not yet made up their minds that we are at war. They have not buckled down to the determination to fight this war through. They have got it into their heads that they are going to get out of this fix, somehow, by strategy . . . and no headway will be made while this state of mind lasts. . . ."

. . . They were plain words. General McClellan had talked about strategy and strategic movements, and the people somehow thought that by some great, brilliant movement—by getting on the flank or the rear of the Confederate army—General Lee might be manoeuvred out of Fredericksburg, and finally out of Richmond, and that would be the end of the rebellion. President Lincoln knew better.

General Hooker saw that the first thing to be done was to cure the homesickness. The surgeons and physicians had no medicine in their chests to cure the disease. A sight of home, a look into the faces of loved ones, a clasp of the hand, the kiss, the welcome of father, mother, wife, or sister was the only medicine.

Although so many were absent, the first order which General Hooker issued provided that one brigade commander, one field officer, two line officers of a regiment, and two men out of every hundred might be absent at one time, not exceeding ten days to the near States and fifteen days for States farther away. . . .

The soldiers were informed that if they did not return on the day fixed they would be court-martialed. If they did not return, their regiment could have no more furloughs. It touched their honor. If they did not return, none of their comrades could go home.

Officers had been running up to Washington. The hotels were full of those who ought to have been at Falmouth [with the army]. "Officers visiting Washington without permission will be dismissed [from] the service," was the order of the War Department.

During the bright winter days the soldiers went through their drills and manoeuvres. The bands played stirring tunes. The inspector kept close watch of their arms and equipments and clothing. The surgeons were careful of the health of the army. The men on furlough returned with bright faces. Stragglers were brought back to their regiments. The army . . . became larger day by day. Homesickness disappeared. Wherever General Hooker rode he was welcomed with a cheer.

The troops had another way of showing their approval. A little song they made up included the line: "Joe Hooker is our leader; he takes his whisky strong. . . ."

Charles Coffin continues:

The cavalry of the Army of the Potomac had been of little account. General Hooker saw, and the Government saw, that the cavalry must be increased; that men on horseback are the "eyes of the army," seeing what the enemy is doing or about to do. New regiments were organized, the horses exercised, and the men drilled. . . .

While General Hooker was getting the Union army under discipline and curing the homesickness, General Lee was filling his army up with new conscripts [the South having been obliged to establish a draft system while the North was still only thinking about such a step]. The Confederate Government did not organize new regiments, but put new men into the ranks with soldiers who had been in a score of battles. The new men soon became as brave and steady as they. It was a much better plan than that adopted by the Union Government—the raising of new regiments.

But other advantages on the Southern side were few. In the first place, the new conscripts would not increase Lee's strength against Hooker. Lee was obliged to provide troops from his army for duty in other areas. In the end, he would have to face Hooker with fewer men than he had employed against Burnside. At present, says Southern General Fitzhugh Lee:

General Lee was surrounded by embarrassments. . . . The troops were scantily clothed, rations for men and animals meager. The shelters were poor, and through them broke the snows, rains, and winds. He could not strike his enemy, but must watch and be patient. . . .

Union Lieutenant Jesse Young avers that General Hooker soon had the Army of the Potomac so well trained and so completely equipped

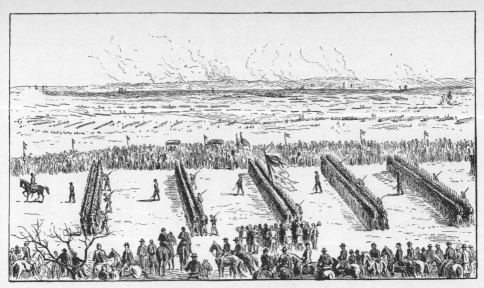

The grand review at Falmouth.

that it was really what he claimed it to be, "the finest army on the planet."

A grand review was arranged in early April, and President Lincoln, his wife, his son Tad, and others from Washington were present. In Young's words:

On a spacious plain . . . where ample room was afforded for maneuvering the troops, the display was made. Many miles of marching were necessary in order that all the army should be marshalled at one point, as their camps were scattered over a large extent of country. . . .

From far and wide they came, their bands of music mingling in patriotic strains in the glowing buoyant air; the generals in splendid uniforms and showily mounted on prancing horses who seemed to enjoy the display as much as their riders; the artillery coming into line with the precision of machinery, at a gallop; the cavalry dashing across the plains; the staff officers gayly loping their horses hither and thither with their orders and messages; and, in brief, the whole mechanism of an army, handled with skill, ease, grace, and military pomp, amid intense enthusiasm and ardor.

At last the whole army stood in line of battle—General Hooker, with the President and other noted visitors . . . in the midst of a brilliantly dressed body of officers, posted in front of the center of the line. When the troops had presented arms, and the banners had drooped, and the bands had united in a piercing blast of music, the commanding general and troops passed in review, proud, hopeful, exultant, confident in their leader, and believing in their beloved President, "Father Abraham."

During that visit the President made a hasty visit to many of the camps . . . galloping from one encampment to another, greeted with hearty cheers, showing his long, ungainly, awkward figure to poor advantage on horseback, making a very brief address now and then to the boys, and leaving his image—the picture of patience, fidelity, political shrewdness, and indomitable gentleness and human kindness—indelibly printed in their hearts.

By this time General Hooker was fairly bursting with confidence. "My plans are perfect," he told a group of his officers, "and when I start to carry them out, may God have mercy on General Lee, for I will have none." He also prefaced many of his statements with, "When I get to Richmond. . . ."

President Lincoln found Hooker's attitude depressing. The general seemed altogether too cocky. Said Lincoln: "The hen is the wisest of all of the animal creation, because she never cackles until the egg is laid."

15

CHANCELLORSVILLE

Late April, 1863, *found General Hooker ready to launch his "perfect" plans against Lee. While a part of the army, under General John Sedgwick, demonstrated against Lee's front at Fredericksburg, the main body, commanded by "Fighting Joe" himself, was to march up the Rappahannock on a flanking maneuver that would bring it down behind Lee's left. At the same time, the Union cavalry corps was to operate against Lee's communications with Richmond. Hooker had more reason for confidence than he knew: To oppose his army of about 130,000 men, Lee had only about 60,000.*

The story of the flanking expedition is begun by Union soldier Warren Goss:

On the morning of April 27th, the divisions of the army, followed by pack-mules, and the men laden like pack-mules, with rations for eight days—salt pork, hard bread, salt, sugar, and coffee—broke camp and went marching up the northern banks of the Rappahannock, often making wide detours behind the hills to conceal the movement, as far as practicable, from the vigilant foe. . . . The next morning the [expedition] crossed the Rappahannock by a pontoon bridge constructed on light canvas boats, twenty-seven miles above, at Kelly's Ford. . . .

The columns soon reached [the Rapidan River]. . . . The water

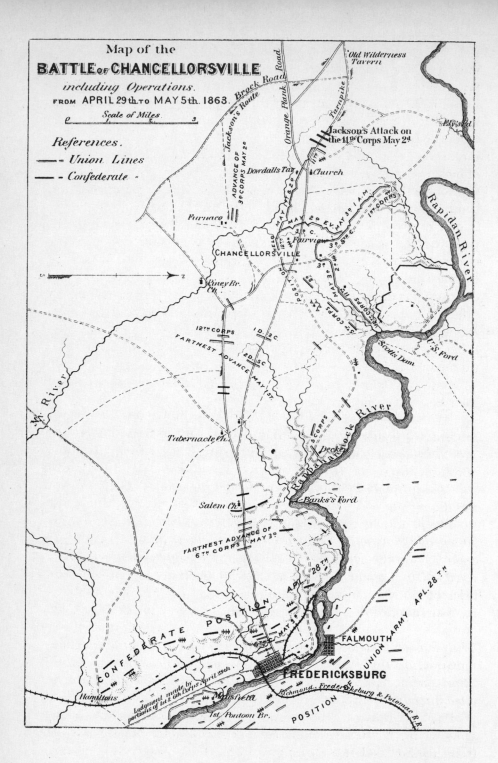

Map of the
BATTLE OF CHANCELLORSVILLE
including Operations.
FROM APRIL 29th TO MAY 5th. 1863.

Scale of Miles

References.
— Union Lines
— Confederate "

was rapid, and at first glance it seemed impracticable—in view of the heavy baggage of sixty pounds carried by each man—to cross by fording; but the men stripped, and, bearing their baggage aloft on their heads, or on bayonets, waded shoulder-deep the swift-running river. One who had been carried away by the current and was picked up by the cavalry, stationed below, said to [me], "Old Joe Hooker thought of most everything, but forgot to give us swimming lessons!"

Bonfires were kindled on the banks, and the crossing was continued all night. To say that the men were in good spirits would but faintly express their good humor and hilarity. Every hardship, impediment, or accident was surmounted with laughter and joke; for the rank-and-file, acute judges of military movements, recognized in the march they were making one of those battles with legs, which are often equivalent to a victory. They humorously congratulated each other that they had a commander at last who knew how to use their legs as well as their arms. They recognized that they were doing a big thing, or, as one of them said, "Going to give the rebs an awful thump on the flank."

At the fords they captured some prisoners, who joked them on their heavy luggage.

"When you 'uns capture we 'uns, you 'uns don't get much but a reb. But if we 'uns capture you 'uns, we 'uns get a heap of truck."

"We've got eight days' rations to last us to Richmond," said one of our men in response.

"You 'uns will need to carry a year's rations before you get thar!" was the retort.

The point of concentration [Chancellorsville] was reached on the afternoon of April 30, and so far the movement was a grand success. . . . In the evening . . . amid enthusiastic cheers, Hooker arrived and took up his quarters at Chancellor House, an old-fashioned brick building with massive pillars extending from the ground to the roof, surrounded by its rude Negro cabins.

The mansion's civilian occupants, protesting at the Yankee invasion, remained on the property. Some of the passing Federals saw, on an upper porch, "quite a bevy of ladies" who "scolded audibly and reviled bitterly."

Hooker [Goss continues] issued a glowing proclamation to his army, saying, "The enemy must either ingloriously fly or come out from behind his defences and give us battle upon our own ground, where certain destruction awaits him."

Joseph Hooker.

The Chancellor House.

"And everyone repeated," adds *Regis de Trobriand, " 'He is in our power!' Nobody doubted that, before two days, all our past reverses would be effaced by the annihilation of Lee's army."*

General Lee, though well aware of the great odds against him, had no intention of "ingloriously flying." He had already sent one division, that of General Richard H. Anderson, toward Chancellorsville.

Lee relates:

The enemy in our front near Fredericksburg continued inactive [after crossing the Rappahannock as though to attack], and it was now apparent that the main attack would be made upon our flank and rear. It was therefore determined to leave sufficient troops to hold our lines, and with the main body of the army to give battle to the approaching column.

Early's division . . . and Barksdale's brigade . . . with part of the reserve artillery . . . were intrusted with the defense of our position at Fredericksburg; and at midnight on the 30th, General McLaws marched . . . toward Chancellorsville. General Jackson followed at dawn next morning. . . .

Returning to the Union side and Warren Goss:

The plateau at Chancellorsville is hemmed in by a region covered with a dense growth of dwarfed pines and scrub oaks, intertwined and interlaced by a profusion of vines, creepers, and briars. The distance . . . to Fredericksburg was about ten miles, with two excellent roads; and on both sides of these roads, a few miles from the plateau, were open spaces on which to deploy troops, and where the Union army could avail itself of its superiority in artillery. . . .

. . . [On May 1] Hooker gave orders to advance and form line of battle. . . . The passage through the tangled thickets broke up companies and regiments into crowds. Men were separated from their commands and absolutely lost in the woods. They were in inextricable confusion, but almost out of the thickets . . . when they struck the enemy's advance. . . .

. . . there was no reason why we could not have continued the march, as the army was almost out of the hindering thickets. The general line was a good one. . . . There was absolutely every reason for desiring to get out of the Wilderness, and none for remaining in it. [The Wilderness, a local name raised to prominence in this campaign, was to become even better known later in the war.]

It was then . . . that Hooker issued that inexplicable order for the army to fall back to Chancellorsville. . . .

Officers and men received the order with mingled incredulity and astonishment, and the phlegmatic [senior corps commander, General Darius] Couch was so overwhelmed with a sense of its folly that he . . . remonstrate[d]. But Hooker adhered doggedly to his resolution; and, followed step-by-step by the enemy, our army fell back to . . . the plateau at Chancellorsville.

General Lee, now before the Federals in force, spent the rest of the day feeling their lines. He writes:

. . . the enemy had assumed a position of great natural strength, surrounded on all sides by a dense forest filled with a tangled undergrowth, in the midst of which breastworks of logs had been constructed, with trees felled in front, so as to form an almost impenetrable abatis. . . . It was evident that a direct attack upon the enemy would be attended with great difficulty and loss, in view of the strength of his position and his superiority of numbers. It was therefore resolved to endeavor to turn his right flank and gain his rear, leaving a force in front to hold him in check and conceal the movement.

According to James Power Smith, aide-de-amp to Stonewall Jackson, Lee's plan was developed in the dead of the night, while the Confederate troops were asleep on the ground:

Sometime after midnight I was awakened by the chill of the early morning hours, and, turning over, caught a glimpse of a little flame on the slope above me, and, sitting up to see what it meant, I saw, bending over a scant fire of twigs, two men seated on old cracker boxes and warming their hands over the little fire. I had but to rub my eyes and collect my wits to recognize the figures of Robert E. Lee and Stonewall Jackson.

Again in Lee's words:

The execution of this plan was intrusted to Lieutenant General Jackson with his three divisions [about 28,000 men]. The commands of General McLaws and Anderson [less than 20,000 men in total] . . . remained in front of the enemy. Early on the morning of the 2d, General Jackson marched by the Furnace and Brock roads, his movement being effectually covered by Fitzhugh Lee's cavalry, under General Stuart in person.

Explains Union division commander General Abner Doubleday:

As soon as Jackson was en route, Lee began to demonstrate against our centre and left, to make Hooker believe the main attack was to be there, and to prevent him from observing the turning column in its progress toward [our] right. . . . In spite of every precaution, Jackson's column . . . was seen to pass over a bare hill . . . and its numbers were pretty accurately estimated. . . . It is always pleasant to think your adversary is beaten, and Hooker thought . . . Jackson might be retreating on Gordonsville. It was evident enough that he was either doing that or making a circuit to attack [our right].

Regis de Trobriand adds that

. . . he continued to march with impunity along our front the greater part of the day. When at last, in the afternoon, our division was sent to cut him in two, we were only able to reach his rear guard, which merely hastened his march.

Stationed on the Union right was the Eleventh Corps, under General Oliver O. Howard. Hooker says that this corps "was posted to meet a front attack from the south, but was in no condition for a flank attack from the west." Earlier in the day, Hooker had dispatched a message to Howard, telling him to be alert for a flank attack—just in case. Howard claimed later that the message did not reach him, but there seems to be evidence that it did. At any rate, Howard knew that the Confederates were on the move, but did not consider his troops to be in danger. As a result, says Warren Goss:

About sundown [many of] the soldiers of the Eleventh Corps, with stacked arms, were boiling their coffee, smoking their pipes, lounging in groups, and playing cards among the baggage wagons, pack-mules, and teamsters, when rabbits, deer, and other game driven by Jackson's advance came into our lines. Some of the men were chasing the rabbits with shouts of laughter, and all were unprepared, when a few shots were heard . . . and Jackson's men . . . burst upon them like a clap of thunder from a cloudless sky. . . .

Everything was in confusion. No change of front was possible, and the officers, isolated from the rank-and-file, could not rally them. The impetuosity of Jackson's attack was terrible. A soldier of the Eleventh Corps said afterwards to me, "It was a perfect whirlwind of men. The enemy seemed to come from every direction."

Writes Confederate soldier John O. Casler, who made the attack with a pioneer unit whose job it was to help keep the artillery rolling:

We ran through the enemy's camps. . . . Tents were standing and camp-kettles were on the fire, full of meat. I saw a big Newfoundland dog lying in one tent as quietly as if nothing had happened. We had a nice chance to plunder their camps and search the dead, but the men were afraid to stop, as they had to keep with the artillery and were near a good many officers who might whack them over the head with their swords if they saw them plundering. But the temptation was too great, and sometimes they would run their hands in some of the dead men's pockets as they hurried along, but seldom procured anything of value.

The Union's Abner Doubleday relates:

The constantly increasing uproar, and the wild rush of fugitives past the Chancellorsville House told Hooker what had occurred and roused him to convulsive life. His staff charged on the flying crowd, but failed to stop them, and it became necessary to form a line of fresh troops, for Jackson in his onward march was sweeping everything before him. It was not easy to find an adequate force for this emergency, for the whole line was now actively engaged [its south and east being demonstrated against by Lee]. . . . Fortunately, [General Hiram G.] Berry's division was held in reserve and was available. They were true and tried men, and went forward at once to the rescue.

"The division," says Regis de Trobriand, "supported by [General William] Hays' brigade of the Second Corps, advanced with a firm and steady step, cleaving the multitude of disbanded men as the bow of a vessel cleaves the waves of the sea."

These Federals, aided by a number of artillery batteries, managed to check Jackson on his left and in his center. In the path of his right, some twenty artillery pieces were positioned by General Alfred Pleasonton. As the Confederates came through the woods in the gathering dusk, writes Pleasonton's aide-de-camp, Clifford Thomson, the general rode from gun to gun, instructing the crews "to aim low, not to get excited, to make every shot tell."

. . . the enemy could be seen forming line of battle in the edge of woods now in our front. They were scarcely two hundred yards distant; yet such was the gloom that they could not be clearly distinguished. General Pleasonton was about to give the order to fire

Federal reserves arrive amid confusion of Howard's rout.

when a sergeant at one of the guns said, "General, aren't those our troops? I see our colors in the line."

This was true, for where he pointed our colors could be seen—trophies picked up on the field. General Pleasonton turned to me and said, "Mr. Thomson, ride out there and see who those people are."

For myself, I was not at all curious about "those people," being perfectly willing to wait till they introduced themselves. Riding out between our guns, I galloped to within thirty or forty yards of them. All along the line they cried out to me, "Come on! We're friends!" It was quite dark and I could not make out their uniforms; but I could see three of our flags, and these caused me to hesitate. I came to a halt, peering into the darkness to make sure, when a bullet whistled by me; and then came the "rebel yell."

The line charged up the hill toward our guns, and I led it! Lying down upon my horse's neck, I gave him the spur; and the yells of the "Johnnies" . . . further stimulated him, so that we got over the ground in a lively manner. But with the report of the first shot fired at me General Pleasonton had opened fire, and those twenty-two guns belched forth destruction at a fearfully rapid rate. Although lying down on my horse, I kept an eye on the guns and guided my horse between the flashes; and in less time than it takes to tell it I was on the safe side of them.

It was load and fire at will for some minutes. The enemy was mowed down in heaps. They could make no headway against such a cyclone, and ran back down the slope to the cover of the woods. But still the canister was poured into them, and a second attempt to charge the guns failed. . . . Old artillery officers have informed me that they never before heard such rapid firing. . . . The roar was a continuous one, and the execution terrific.

After it had ceased, I rode up to General Pleasonton and said, "General, those people out there are rebels!"

There was a grave twinkle in his eye as he held out his hand and replied, "Thomson, I never expected to see you again. I thought if they didn't kill you I should; but that was no time to stop for one man."

I should have agreed with him more cordially if that one man had been somebody else.

Stonewall Jackson was at this time with the troops on the left of his attack. Relates his aide-de-camp, James Power Smith:

Division commanders found it more and more difficult as the twilight deepened to hold their broken brigades in hand. . . . General Jackson . . . ordered A. P. Hill's division, his third and reserve line, to be placed in front. While this change was being effected, impatient and anxious, the general rode forward on the turnpike [that led toward Chancellorsville], followed by two or three of his staff and a number of couriers and signal sergeants. He . . . came upon a line of the Federal infantry lying on their arms. Fired at by one or two muskets . . . he turned and came back toward his line, upon the side of the road to his left.

As he rode near to the Confederate troops, just placed in position and ignorant that he was in the front, the left company began firing . . . and two of his party fell from their saddles dead. . . . Spurring his horse across the road to his right, he was met by a second volley from the right company. . . . Under this volley . . . the general received three balls at the same instant. One penetrated the palm of his right hand. . . . A second passed around the wrist of the left arm and out through the left hand. A third ball passed through the left arm halfway from shoulder to elbow. The large bone of the upper arm was splintered to the elbow joint, and the wound bled freely.

His horse turned quickly from the fire, through the thick bushes, which swept the cap from the general's head and scratched his forehead, leaving drops of blood to stain his face. As he lost his hold upon the bridle-rein, he reeled from the saddle and was caught by the arms of Captain [R. E.] Wilbourn. . . . Laid upon the ground, there came at once to his succor General A. P. Hill and members of his staff. The writer reached his side a minute after, to find General Hill holding the head and shoulders of the wounded chief. Cutting open the coatsleeve from wrist to shoulder, I found the wound in the upper arm, and with my handkerchief I bound the arm above the wound to stem the flow of blood.

Couriers were sent for Dr. Hunter McGuire, the surgeon of the corps and the general's trusted friend, and for an ambulance. Being outside of our lines, it was urgent that he should be moved at once. With difficulty, litter-bearers were brought from the line nearby, and the general was placed upon the litter and carefully raised to the shoulder, I myself bearing one corner. A moment after, artillery from the Federal side was opened upon us. Great broadsides thundered over the woods. Hissing shells searched the dark thickets through, and shrapnel swept the road along which we moved.

Two or three steps farther, and the litter-bearer at my side was struck and fell; but, as the litter turned, Major Watkins Leigh, of Hill's staff, happily caught it. But the fright of the men was so great that we were obliged to lay the litter and its burden down upon the road. As the litter-bearers ran to the cover of the trees, I threw myself by the general's side and held him firmly to the ground as he attempted to rise. Over us swept the rapid fire of shot and shell, grape-shot striking fire upon the flinty rock of the road all around us, and sweeping from their feet horses and men of the artillery just moved to the front.

Soon the firing veered to the other side of the road, and I sprang to my feet, assisted the general to rise, passed my arm around him, and with the wounded man's weight thrown heavily upon me, we forsook the road. Entering the woods, he sank to the ground from exhaustion; but the litter was soon brought, and again rallying a few men, we essayed to carry him farther, when a second bearer fell at my side. This time, with none to assist, the litter careened, and the general fell to the ground with a groan of deep pain. Greatly alarmed, I sprang to his head, and, lifting his head as a stray beam of moonlight came through the clouds and leaves, he opened his eyes and wearily said, "Never mind me, Captain; never mind me."

Raising him again to his feet, he was accosted by Brigadier General [William D.] Pender: "Oh, General, I hope you are not seriously wounded. I will have to retire my troops to reform them, they are so much broken by this fire."

But Jackson, rallying his strength, with firm voice said, "You must hold your ground, General Pender. You must hold your ground, sir!" and so uttered his last command on the field.

Again we resorted to the litter, and with difficulty bore it through the bush, and then under a hot fire along the road. Soon an ambulance was reached, and stopping to seek some stimulant at Chancellor's (Dowdall's Tavern), we were found by Dr. McGuire, who at once took charge of the wounded man. Passing back over the battlefield of the afternoon, we reached . . . the field-hospital of our corps under Dr. Harvey Black. Here we found a tent prepared; and after midnight the left arm was amputated near the shoulder, and a ball taken from the right hand.

Soon after Jackson's wounding, the firing at the front had ceased on both sides. But the night's action wasn't over. Jackson's attack had, at one point, penetrated far enough to sever the contact of a large part of General Daniel Sickles' Third Corps with the rest of Hooker's army; and Sickles decided to make an attempt to push through the interposed Confederates and restore his communications.

. . . at eleven o'clock [says Northerner Warren Goss] while darkness enshrouded the thickets, his men cautiously advanced. The mournful notes of the whippoorwill, the crackling of the underbrush beneath the feet of stealthily advancing men, the low-toned command, alone broke the silence. Peering into the darkness, halting here and there to catch the faintest sound, the advancing line suddenly encountered the enemy. . . .

A blinding flash illumined the darkness, and the terrible discharge of musketry resounded through the woods. The foes charged each other with mutual yells, cheers, and shouts; and the Union artillery . . . advanced into the thickets and opened within a hundred yards of the enemy's lines. The dark wood was now lit up with lurid flashes of artillery and the firefly sparkle of rifles. . . . The deep tones of the cannon marked time to the incessant roll of musketry. . . .

The impossibility of giving orders in the darkness, among the tangled thickets, soon produced its effects. Brigades were broken into regiments, regiments into companies, and these into smaller groups, while friend and foe seemed confusedly playing a sanguinary game of hide-and-seek. In this manner prisoners on each side were captured. Friends encountered each other as enemies, and each mistook foes for friends. A comrade who participated [and at one time found himself with a group that had been cut off from its regiment] . . . afterwards related the following incident:

". . . There were six of us; and Matt Jenkins, a little corporal with a big voice, was the ranking man of the squad. We had lost the p'ints of the compass as completely as if there were none, though there was no mistaking where the fight was. We were cautiously groping through the brushwood, where the occasional flash of musketry only made us all the blinder, when a blaze and the roar of a volley on our front showed us that we had encountered an enemy. Their shot, however, had pattered all around without injuring any of us.

"Our little corporal, with his big voice, which sounded for all the world like a major general's, shouted out: 'Reserve your fire, men!' and then gave orders to Captain *this* and Major *that* and Colonel *someone else,* as if he was in command of a brigade.

" 'Thunder!' said someone in the party we had encountered. 'You needn't make all that fuss. We'll surrender!'

"And then," said my informant with a chuckle, "about twenty of *our own company,* including the captain, came in and surrendered to Matt Jenkins!"

Among the Union officers who helped to keep the attack moving by means of cool leadership was Regis de Trobriand:

The moon was hidden; we could not see ten steps. Around me, men fell or disappeared. The part of the wood where we were had become the focus to which all the firing converged. The bullets struck the trees all around us. Shells crossed their sparks from all directions and filled the air with the noise and flash of their bursting. The groans of the wounded, the orders of the officers, the oaths of the soldiers, the whistling of the balls, the roaring of the conical projectiles, the crackling of the branches, the rolling of the fusillade, the thunder of the artillery—everything united in a concert infernal. . . .

With a handful of men who still followed me, I turned my steps towards a point where the firing seemed to have ceased. All at once I felt the ground moving under my feet, and cries issuing from it. It was a [shallow] square hole, from which the dirt had been taken out, without doubt, for the intrenchments. Five or six poltroons had lain down there flat on the ground, literally packed like sardines in a box. We passed over them and continued our advance.

In the end, General Sickles achieved his breakthrough. His communications with Hooker were restored.

The battle [writes Warren Goss] gradually died away, only blazing out here and there fitfully as little squads encountered each other in the tangled wilderness. It was past midnight. The moon now shone brightly. . . .

Adds Union Lieutenant Jesse Young:

. . . exhausted, anxious, and terror-stricken, the soldiers sought respite in sleep. Wounded men groaned here and there in the underbrush, surgeons went to work to relieve their distress, nurses and hospital stewards cared for all who could be reached; but multitudes lay bleeding and dying between the lines where no help could be afforded them.

According to Goss:

Sunday morning, May 3, the situation was by no means discouraging, but for the incomprehensible mental torpor of the Union commander. We were not able to see anywhere evidence of a master mind during the conflict which followed. We still held the point where the roads converged at Chancellorsville, but our position promised more for offensive than defensive battle.

We had seventy-five thousand men posted between the [divided] wings of the Confederate army, who did not number forty-five thousand [in total]; and from these converging roads as a pivot, we could have directed a terrible blow upon either one or the other of these severed wings of the enemy before they could be united. . . .

. . . the Sixth Corps, under Sedgwick, still confronted the rebel position at Fredericksburg. . . . When disaster fell on the Eleventh Corps, Hooker ordered Sedgwick to seize the heights and advance [toward Chancellorsville] by the plank road with his twenty-two thousand men to deliver him from the clutches of the Confederate devilfish which was crushing him in its embrace.

General Sedgwick, who had received the order from Hooker late Saturday night, had begun maneuvering his troops into position at once, and was ready to move against Jubal Early's lofty works by

Sunday morning—even as the fight between Hooker and Lee's two wings was beginning anew.

Among those with Sedgwick was the contemplative chaplain from Pennsylvania, A. M. Stewart:

As the sun of that beautiful Sabbath morning arose in its glorious beauty; and as final preparations were being made for a desperate and determined assault upon the rebel works, I rode back through the old city, and found it almost wholly deserted of its inhabitants, the doors and windows all open. The desolate quietness was almost painful. Passing on the lower skirts of the city, a long and beautifully shaded gravel carriage-way was seen, leading to a fine old and retired mansion. Riding along it to the dwelling, a strange, poetic, and fairy-like scene presented itself.

The grounds and gardens were beautifully laid out and adorned with a great variety of ornamental trees and shrubbery, all now budding into leaf and bloom. Through the branches of these, hundreds of birds were carolling forth their morning songs—joyous as though no war had ever desolated our sin-cursed earth. Woodbines, honeysuckles, and roses, in their May freshness twined over the arbors, colonnades, and porticos; yet was there no sound of human voice or footsteps.

Had superstition been a ruling feeling, it might have been taken for a place enchanted. The front door of the capacious old mansion stood open. I entered, and the sound of my footsteps and voice echoed strangely through the empty halls. The so late proud and luxuriant occupants all gone. . . .

On the old stone steps I sat me down and tried to realize that it was the Sabbath—read a chapter, sang a psalm, and offered up a prayer for the speedy approach of peace founded upon righteousness. . . .

About 11 A.M. all was in readiness for a final and desperate assault upon the rebel strongholds. A scene of terrible grandeur immediately ensued. . . . An open field, some fifty rods across, lay between our now marshalled and devoted columns and the rebel works. The ground rises gradually at an elevation of some eight or ten degrees, till it reaches the front line of rebel intrenchments, or rifle pits. Behind and more abruptly rising above this is a second line of earthen defences; and finally, on the top of the ridge, their intrenched batteries.

Our regiment was on the left, and supporting the assaulting column. At the signal to move, the soldiers raised a general cheer and started off at double-quick, up and across the open ground. In an instant the whole rebel works were in a blaze of fire, with a cloud of smoke; and from them a rain of leaden death was poured upon our advancing columns, and the earth strewn with the wounded and the dying, even as grass before the scythe of the mower. Yet on they pressed at a brisk run, with fixed bayonets, and none waiting to fire a gun.

The flag of each regiment was proudly carried in front by its sturdy standard-bearer. When one of these fell, the emblem was snatched up by another, and still borne on. Still onward pressed the columns, each seemingly intent to be ahead and enter first the rebel works. Every yard of advance was strewn with the fallen. It was a moment of unutterable excitement. A lifetime seemed compressed into a few minutes.

The first line of earthworks was reached. Our soldiers now—without any special attention to military order, the stronger having gotten ahead—scrambled as a flock of sheep up and over the embankment and bounded into the ditch, bayonetting or capturing its rebel occupants. Then with a shout the second line was similarly carried in triumph; and finally, accompanied with tremendous cheers from the whole corps, the upper tier of works, with their batteries, which had made such havoc in our ranks, were taken at the point of the bayonet.

As soon as the old Stars and Stripes were seen to wave over the highest rampart, both officers and privates seemed wrought up to the highest possible human excitement. The feelings of many seemed too deep and strong even for cheers, yet scarcely an eye was dry.

I rode on horseback with our regiment till the last works were stormed and the firing ceased. Then, giving my horse in charge of a wounded soldier, I turned back over the field of mutilation and death. What a price at which to purchase a few earthen ditches! . . .

For hours I busied myself in bringing into a right position this arm broken and bent under the fallen body; straightening that mangled leg; binding up the fractured head; tying a handkerchief or canteen cord above some jetting artery; turning into a more easy position this poor fellow whose fountain of life was fast oozing out from a fatal wound; and all the while speaking such words of comfort, direction, and encouragement as the occasion and case suggested.

During the morning I had obtained two bottles of wine. . . . Having these in my pockets, a few spoonfuls were poured into the mouths of those seeming most faint. Thus over twenty were refreshed before all was gone.

So calmly did many of our dear young men lie in their last sleep that not a few were taken hold of in order to arouse and assist, before becoming convinced that they were dead.

This daring, bloody, and successful assault upon the rebel works, the most prominent point of which was called Marye's Heights, was made about 11 A.M. on the Sabbath! What a business for God's holy day of rest!

Back at the Virginia estate that Chaplain Stewart had visited earlier, the "quiet grandeur and solemn silence were all gone."

This old mansion became a large hospital. The halls within were filled, and the grass plots without were covered with wounded, mutilated, and dying men.

The Federals paused for some time to reorganize. Then they hurried after the retreating foe, who, says the chaplain,

. . . had taken the plank road leading to Chancellorsville, distant about ten miles. There Hooker's and Lee's armies were, at the same time, engaged in a fierce and bloody struggle.

Actually, the struggle at Chancellorsville was already about over. It had begun early, with the separated Confederate wings assuming the offensive and striving to make contact with each other as they pressed forward. General Hooker, in spite of his great numerical superiority, remained on the defensive, thinking chiefly in terms of protecting his line of retreat to the Rappahannock.

Colorful Jeb Stuart was now in command of Jackson's corps. According to Heros von Borcke, a Prussian who served in the battle as a Confederate staff officer:

Stuart was all activity, and wherever the danger was greatest there was he to be found, urging the men forward and animating them by the force of his example. The shower of missiles that hissed through the air passed round him unheeded; and in the midst of the hottest fire I heard him, to an old melody, hum the words, "Old Joe Hooker, get out of the Wilderness."

After a raging conflict, protracted for several hours, during which the tide of battle ebbed and flowed on either side, we succeeded in taking the advanced works and driving the enemy upon their third line of intrenchments, of a still stronger character than those before it. This partial success was only gained with a sad sacrifice of life, while countless numbers were seen limping and crawling to the rear. . . .

Riding to the front, I was hailed by a young soldier whose boyish looks and merry songs on the march had frequently attracted my attention and excited my interest, and who was now leaning against a tree, the lifeblood streaming down his side from a mortal wound and his face white with the pallor of approaching death.

"Major," said the poor lad, "I am dying, and I shall never see my regiment again; but I ask you to tell my comrades that the Yankees have killed but not conquered me."

When I passed the place again, half an hour afterwards, I found him a corpse.

On the Union side, Regis de Trobriand penciled notes about the bloodshed even as the battle raged:

The wounded are continually passing through our lines. One of them, half naked, is as black as a Negro. He runs shrieking towards the ambulances. It is an artilleryman, wounded by the explosion of a caisson. . . . A lieutenant of the Third Maine is cut in two by a shell bursting in his body—legs thrown to one side, the trunk to the other. . . . General Berry has just been killed near us.

According to General Hooker's second-in-command, Darius Couch:

Upon the south porch of [the Chancellor House], General Hooker stood leaning against one of its pillars, observing the fighting, looking anxious and much careworn. . . . I doubt if any orders were given by him to the commanders on the field, unless, perhaps, to "retire when out of ammunition."

Says Hooker himself:

I was standing on [a] step of the portico . . . the cannon-balls reaching me from both the east and the west, when a solid shot struck the pillar near me, splitting it in two and throwing one half longitudinally against me, striking my whole right side, which soon turned livid. For a few moments I was senseless. . . .

Word flew around that Hooker had been killed, and General Couch was one of the first to hear it:

I was at the time but a few yards to his left, and, dismounting, ran to the porch. The shattered pillar was there, but I could not find him or anyone else. Hurrying through the house, finding no one, my search was continued through the back yard. All the time I was thinking, "If he is killed, what shall I do with this disjointed army?"

Passing through the yard I came upon him, to my great joy, mounted and with his staff also in their saddles. Briefly congratulating him on his escape . . . I went about my own business. This was the last I saw of my commanding general in front. The time, I reckon, was from 9:15 to 9:30 A.M. . . . He probably left the field soon after his hurt, but he neither notified me of his going, nor did he give any orders to me whatever. . . . It was not then too late to save the day. . . . But it is a waste of words to write what might have been done.

About this time Jeb Stuart's troops were gladdened by a new development. Writes staff officer Heros von Borcke:

. . . we had news from General Lee, informing us that, having been pressing steadily forward . . . [with the attack's right wing], he had now . . . reached our right. . . . I was at once despatched by Stuart to the Commander-in-Chief to report the state of affairs and obtain his orders for further proceedings. I found him . . . looking as calm and dignified as ever, and perfectly regardless of the shells bursting round him and the solid shot ploughing up the ground in all directions.

General Lee expressed himself much satisfied with our operations and intrusted me with orders for Stuart directing a general attack with his whole force, which was to be supported by a charge of Anderson's division [of Lee's wing]. . . .

With renewed courage and confidence our three divisions [those under Stuart] now moved forward upon the enemy's strong position on the hills, encountering, as we emerged from the forest into the open [area] opposite the plateau of Chancellorsville, such a storm of canister and bullets that for a while it seemed an impossibility to take the heights in the face of it.

Suddenly we heard to our right, piercing the roar and tumult of the battle, the yell of Anderson's men, whom we presently beheld hurled forward [by Lee] in a brilliant charge, sweeping everything before them. Short work was now made of the Federals, who, in a few minutes, were driven from their redoubts, which they abandoned in disorderly flight, leaving behind them cannons, small arms, tents, and baggage in large quantities, besides a host of prisoners. . . .

A more magnificent spectacle can hardly be imagined than that which greeted me when I reached the crest of the plateau and beheld, on this side, the long lines of our swiftly advancing troops stretching as far as the eye could reach, their red flags fluttering in the breeze and their arms glittering in the morning sun; and farther on, dense and huddled masses of the Federals flying . . . towards the United States Ford [on the Rappahannock], whilst high over our heads flew the shells which our artillery were dropping amidst the crowd of the retreating foe. The Chancellorsville House had caught fire, and was now enveloped in flames. . . .

By this time, the female occupants of the house had been evacuated. Explains one of Hooker's staff officers:

They were taken away . . . after the firing became very hot. One of the ladies fainted. It was a forlorn sight to see that troupe passing through our lines at such a time.

From his elevated spot on the Southern side, Von Borcke noted that the battlefield's flames were not confined to the Chancellorsville House:

The woods had caught fire in several places from the explosion of shells—the flames spreading principally, however, over a space of several acres in extent where the ground was thickly covered with dry leaves; and here the conflagration progressed with the rapidity of a prairie fire, and a large number of Confederate and Federal wounded thickly scattered in the vicinity, and too badly hurt to crawl out of the way, met a terrible death.

Adds the Union's Warren Goss:

One of the wounded narrated to me . . . afterwards, how he watched the flames and counted the moments when it would strike him, when the progress of the flames were arrested by a little stagnant pool of water.

A comrade . . . afterwards related the following:

"I was among the wounded [near one of the woods fires]. . . . [U]sing my musket for a crutch, I began to pull away the burning brushwood, and got some of them out. I tell you, it was hot! Them pines was full of pitch and rosin, and made the fire as hot as a furnace.

"I was working away, pulling out Johnnies and Yanks, when one of the wounded Johnnies . . . toddled up and began to help. . . .

The underbrush crackled and roared, and the poor devils howled and shrieked when the fire got at them.

". . . by and by another reb—I guess he was a straggler—came up and began to help too. . . . We were trying to rescue a young fellow in gray. The fire was all around him. The last I saw of that fellow was his face. . . . His eyes were big and blue, and his hair like raw silk surrounded by a wreath of fire. . . . I heard him scream, 'O, Mother! O, God!' It left me trembling all over like a leaf.

"After it was over, my hands were blistered and burned so I could not open or shut them; but me and them rebs tried to shake hands. . . ."

Von Borcke concludes his observations on Hooker's retreat:

The flight and pursuit took the direction of United States Ford as far as about a mile beyond Chancellorsville, where another strong line of intrenchments offered their protection to the fugitives, and heavy reserves of fresh troops opposed our further advance.

General Lee takes up:

[Our] troops, having become somewhat scattered by the difficulties of the ground and the ardor of the contest, were immediately reformed preparatory to renewing the attack. . . . Our preparations were just completed when further operations were arrested by intelligence received from Fredericksburg. . . . The success of [Union General Sedgwick at Marye's Heights] enabled him . . . to come [toward] our rear at Chancellorsville by the plank road . . . his progress being gallantly disputed by the brigade of General [Cadmus M.] Wilcox. . . . General Wilcox fell back slowly until he reached Salem Church, on the plank road, about . . . [six miles from Chancellorsville].

Information of the state of affairs in our rear having reached Chancellorsville, as already stated, General McLaws, with his three brigades and one of General Anderson's, was ordered to reinforce General Wilcox. He arrived at Salem Church early in the afternoon. . . .

One of the Union officers with Sedgwick at Salem Church was Huntington W. Jackson, who writes:

Lee had met with such complete success in his attack upon Hooker that he felt he could well spare these troops and not suffer. . . . The fight [that developed at the church] was very severe in the thick woods, and for a time was waged with varying success. The crest of the woods and a little schoolhouse near the church were gained, and once it was thought they could be held; but the enemy, in superior numbers, pressed on, and the ground and the church were left in their possession. The contest did not last long, but nearly 1500 were killed and wounded. . . .

It [had been] understood throughout the Sixth Corps that as soon as it should become engaged with the enemy Hooker would immediately attack in his [own] front and prevent any reinforcements from being sent against Sedgwick. . . . [T]he sound of Hooker's guns were eagerly listened for. No sound would have been more welcome. But . . . [at length] the feeling became widely prevalent that the Sixth Corps would be compelled to take care of itself.

The fighting at Salem Church was over for May 3; and that night both sides slept on their arms.

"In the meantime," says General Lee,

the enemy had so strengthened his position near Chancellorsville that it was deemed inexpedient to assail it with less than our whole force, which could not be concentrated until we were relieved from the danger that menaced our rear. It was accordingly resolved still further to reinforce the troops in front of General Sedgwick, in order, if possible, to drive him across the Rappahannock. Accordingly, on the 4th, General Anderson was directed to proceed with his remaining three brigades to join General McLaws [at Salem Church].

By thus further reducing his forces at Chancellorsville—forces that had been thin to begin with—Lee showed a splendid contempt for his adversary.

"Hooker remained inactive," writes Federal officer Huntington Jackson. "With a force greatly in excess of the enemy in his front, he made no effort to relieve Sedgwick from his perilous position."

Again in Lee's words:

Anderson reached Salem Church about noon, and was directed to gain the left flank of the enemy and effect a junction with Early [already positioned there]. McLaws' troops were disposed as on the previous day, with orders to hold the enemy in front. . . . The attack did not begin until 6 P.M., when Anderson and Early moved forward and drove General Sedgwick's troops rapidly before them . . . in the direction of the Rappahannock. . . .

Return of the vanquished army to its abandoned camp at Falmouth.

The next morning it was found that General Sedgwick had made good his escape and removed his bridges. . . . But as General Sedgwick had it in his power to recross, it was deemed best to leave General Early, with his division and Barksdale's brigade, to hold our lines . . . McLaws and Anderson being directed to return to Chancellorsville.

They reached their destination during the afternoon, in the midst of a violent storm which continued throughout the night and most of the following day.

Preparations were made to assail [Hooker's] works at daylight on the 6th; but, on advancing our skirmishers, it was found that under cover of the storm and darkness of the night he had retreated over the river.

Dejected at having suffered yet another defeat, and "wondering when this cruel war would be over," the Federals marched through the rain and mud to their old winter camp.

Thus [says Warren Goss] ended the campaign which Hooker opened as with a thunderbolt from the hand of Mars, and ended as impotently as an infant who has not learned to grasp its rattle.

Ironically, even Hooker's cavalry corps, sent toward Richmond to disrupt Lee's communications, had largely bungled its mission.

Northerner Regis de Trobriand tells of the campaign's casual-

ties: *"The victory cost the enemy only thirteen thousand men; defeat cost us seventeen thousand."*

Hooker's second-in-command, Darius Couch, meditates upon his chief's great failure:

As to the charge that the battle was lost because the general was intoxicated . . . he probably abstained from the use of ardent spirits when it would have been far better for him to have continued in his usual habit in that respect. . . .

In looking for the causes of the loss of Chancellorsville, the primary ones were that Hooker expected Lee to fall back without risking a battle. Finding himself mistaken, he assumed the defensive and was outgeneraled and became demoralized by the superior tactical boldness of the enemy.

Asked at a later date what had happened to him at Chancellorsville, Hooker replied, "Well, to tell the truth, I just lost confidence in Joe Hooker."

When President Lincoln got word from Hooker that he had withdrawn his troops from the south side of the Rappahannock and had them "safely encamped" in their old positions, he groaned, "My God, my God, what will the country say?"

The answer came quickly, with a new round of lamentations and complaints being showered upon Washington. Above the rumble rose the ringing plea: "Abraham Lincoln, give us a man!"

Southern hopes soared anew, and General Lee was lionized. Says editor and historian Edward Pollard: "He had won one of the most remarkable victories on record. . . . Chancellorsville must ever remain the masterpiece of his military life."

However, Pollard continues:

While the great victory . . . was causing joy and congratulation throughout the Confederacy, Gen. Stonewall Jackson lay dying at a small farmhouse a few miles from where he had led his last and most famous attack. No one had supposed that his wounds would prove mortal. . . . But . . . an attack of pneumonia . . . supervened. . . .

By this time the news of Jackson's prostration had reached the Union camp, where the reaction was mixed; Stonewall had many admirers among his enemies. General Oliver Howard, whose corps Jackson scattered with his flank attack, took a practical view, saying later:

. . . providentially for us, it was the last battle that he waged against the American Union. . . . Jackson stood head and shoulders above his confreres, and . . . General Lee could not replace him.

Among those at Jackson's bedside around noon on Sunday, May 10, was Dr. Hunter McGuire, who relates:

His mind . . . began to fail and wander, and he frequently talked as if in command upon the field, giving orders in his old way; then the scene shifted, and he was at the mess table, in conversation with members of his staff; now with his wife and child [who were present also in reality]; now at prayers with his military family.

Occasional intervals of return of his mind would appear, and during one of them I offered him some brandy and water; but he declined it, saying, "It will only delay my departure and do no good; I want to preserve my mind, if possible, to the last."

About half-past one he was told that he had but two hours to live, and he answered again, feebly but firmly, "Very good; it is all right."

A few moments before he died he cried out in his delirium, "Order A. P. Hill to prepare for action! Pass the infantry to the front rapidly. Tell Major Hawks—" then stopped, leaving the sentence unfinished.

Presently a smile . . . spread itself over his pale face, and he said quietly, and with an expression as if of relief, "Let us cross over the river and rest under the shade of the trees."

16

LEE INVADES PENNSYLVANIA

THE CLOSE of the Battle of Chancellorsville [writes Northern General Abner Doubleday] found the Union army still strong . . . and ready, as soon as reinforcements and supplies arrived, and a brief period of rest and recuperation ensued, to take the field again. To resist the effects of this defeat [on the public] and recruit our armies required, however, great determination and serious effort on the part of the Administration; for a large and powerful [peace] party still clogged and impeded its efforts. . . .

Our army, however, at the end of May [1863] was still formidable in numbers and too strongly posted to be effectually assailed. . . . The rebels had obtained a triumph rather than a substantial victory at Chancellorsville. It was gained, too, at a ruinous expense of life; and when the battle was over they found themselves too weak to follow up our retreating forces. . . .

The resources of the Davis Government in men and means were limited, and it was evident that . . . prolonged defensive warfare . . . would ultimately exhaust the seceding States without accomplishing their independence. . . . The situation in Vicksburg [on the Mississippi River] was becoming alarming. . . . It was essential

. . . to counterbalance the impending disaster in the West by some brilliant exploit in the East. [Some Southern strategists, in fact, felt that such an exploit would save the Western situation by drawing large numbers of Federal troops eastward.]

There was perhaps another reason for [a] great forward movement, founded on the relation of the Confederacy to the principal European powers. England still made a pretense of neutrality, but the aristocracy and ruling classes sided with the South. . . . The rebels were fighting us [in part] with English guns and war material furnished by blockade runners. . . . The French Government was equally hostile to us, and there was hardly a kingdom in Europe which did not sympathize with the South. . . .

The [overseas] agents of the Confederate Government stated in their official dispatches that if General Lee could establish his army firmly on Northern soil England would at once acknowledge the independence of the South; in which case ample loans could not only be obtained on Southern securities, but a foreign alliance might be formed, and perhaps a fleet furnished to reopen the Southern ports.

While thus elated by hopes of foreign intervention, the Confederate spies and sympathizers who thronged the North greatly encouraged the Davis Government by their glowing accounts of the disaffection there, in consequence of the heavy taxation rendered necessary by the war, and by the unpopularity of the draft which would soon have to be enforced as a defensive measure. They overrated the influence of the *Copperhead* or anti-war party, and prophesied that a rebel invasion would be followed by outbreaks in the principal cities which would paralyze every effort to reinforce the Federal forces in the field.

These reasons would have been quite sufficient of themselves to induce Lee to make the movement, but he himself gives an additional one. He hoped by this advance to draw Hooker out, where he could strike him a decisive blow and thus ensure the permanent triumph of the Confederacy. He was weary of all this marching, campaigning, and bloodshed, and was strongly desirous of settling the whole matter at once.

Having been reinforced after the Battle of Chancellorsville . . . he determined to advance. On May 31st, his force, according to rebel statements, amounted to . . . 68,352 . . . ready for duty. Recruits, too, were constantly coming in from the draft, which was rigidly enforced in the Southern States.

Adds Southern General Fitzhugh Lee:

Among the results to be reached by a march to Pennsylvania was the relief of the Confederate commissariat. Indeed, when [requisitioned] for a supply of rations, the commissary general is reported to have said, "If General Lee wants rations, let him seek them in Pennsylvania."

One of the Union newspaper correspondents who covered this campaign was Charles Coffin, of the Boston Journal. *He tells how things began:*

General Hooker, at Fredericksburg, the first week in June received positive information that Lee was breaking up his camp and that some of his divisions were moving towards Culpeper [about thirty miles to the northwest]. . . .

. . . intelligence was received that Stuart had massed the Rebel cavalry . . . [near Culpeper]. . . . General Pleasonton, commanding the [Union] cavalry, was sent with his entire force to look into the matter. He fell upon Stuart on the 9th of June on the broad, open plains along the Rappahannock. A desperate battle ensued [the Battle of Brandy Station]. . . . The object of the attack was accomplished . . . Lee's movement unmasked.

. . . Lee's advanced divisions reached Winchester [in the Shenandoah Valley], attacked General [Robert H.] Milroy, captured the town, the cannon in the fortifications, and moved on to the Potomac.

Fitzhugh Lee explains:

There was nothing now for the Union commander to do except to keep interposed between his enemy and Washington. . . . The movement of the Army of the Potomac depended on that of the Army of Northern Virginia. As Lee proceeded north, so did Hooker on parallel lines.

Newsman Coffin was also on the move:

Hastening to Pennsylvania, I became an observer of the great events which followed. . . . Harrisburg was a Bedlam when I entered it on the 15th of June. The railroad stations were crowded with an excited people—men, women, and children—with trunks, boxes, bundles; packages tied up in bed-blankets and quilts; mountains of baggage—tumbling it into the cars, rushing here and there in a frantic manner; shouting, screaming, as if the Rebels were about to dash into the town and lay it in ashes. . . .

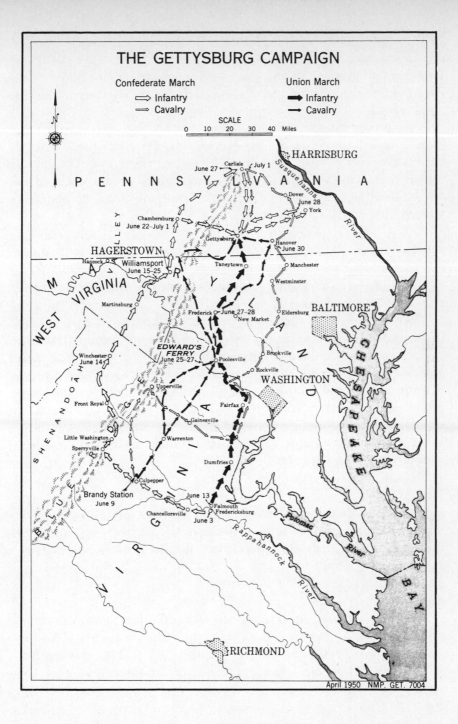

THE GETTYSBURG CAMPAIGN

Confederate March
⇨ Infantry
⇒ Cavalry

Union March
➡ Infantry
→ Cavalry

SCALE
0 10 20 30 40 Miles

HARRISBURG

P E N N S Y L V A N I A

Carlisle
June 27   July 1

Dover
June 28
York

Chambersburg
June 22–July 1

Gettysburg

Hanover
June 30

HAGERSTOWN

Hancock
Williamsport
June 15–25

Taneytown

Manchester

Martinsburg

Frederick
June 27–28
New Market

Westminster

Eldersburg

BALTIMORE

M A R Y L A N D

EDWARD'S
FERRY
June 25–27

Poolesville

Brookville

Winchester
June 14

Rockville

WASHINGTON

WEST
VIRGINIA

VIRGINIA

Upperville

Fairfax

Front Royal

Gainesville

Little Washington

Warrenton

Sperryville

Dumfries

Culpepper

Brandy Station
June 9

June 13

Chancellorsville   Falmouth
June 3   Fredericksburg

Rappahannock River

Potomac River

CHESAPEAKE

B A Y

V I R G I N I A

RICHMOND

Susquehanna River

SHENANDOAH

BLUE

M A R Y L A N D

April 1950 NMP. GET. 7004

The merchants were packing up their goods. . . . At the State House, men in their shirtsleeves were packing papers into boxes. Every team, every horse and mule and handcart in the town were employed.

. . . a steady stream of teams [came] thundering across the bridge [that spanned the Susquehanna River]—farmers from the Cumberland Valley, with their household furniture piled upon the great wagons peculiar to the locality; bedding, tables, chairs, their wives and children perched on the top, kettles and pails dangling beneath; boys driving cattle and horses. . . .

Various communities of the region saw the Negro residents move out en masse. This included the town of Gettysburg, about forty miles southwest of Harrisburg. A white citizen, Tillie Pierce, then a young girl, later recounted:

They regarded the Rebels as having an especial hatred toward them, and believed that if they fell into their hands annihilation was sure. . . . I can see them yet; men and women with bundles as large as old-fashioned feather ticks slung across their backs, almost bearing them to the ground. Children, also, carrying their bundles and striving in vain to keep up with their seniors. The greatest consternation was depicted on all their countenances as they hurried along, crowding and running against each other in their confusion, children stumbling, falling, and crying.

Mothers, anxious for their offspring, would stop for a moment to hurry them up, saying, "Fo' de Lod's sake, you chillen, cum right long quick! If dem Rebs dun kotch you, day tear you all up." These terrible warnings were sure to have the desired effect; for, with their eyes open wider than ever, they were not long in hastening their steps.

Again in Coffin's words:

General Lee was greatly in need of horses, and his cavalrymen, under General [Albert G.] Jenkins, ravaged the Cumberland Valley. A portion visited Chambersburg; another party, Mercersburg; another, Gettysburg, before any infantry entered the state.

Adds the Union's Abner Doubleday:

Jenkins was at the head of 2,000 cavalry, and soon became a terror to the farmers in that vicinity by his heavy exactions, in the way of horses, cattle, grain, etc. It must be confessed he paid for what he took in Confederate scrip, but as this paper money was not worth ten cents a bushel, there was very little consolation in receiving it. His followers made it a legal tender at the stores for everything they wanted.

Having had some horses stolen, he sternly called on the [Chambersburg] authorities to pay him their full value. They did so without a murmur—in Confederate money. He pocketed it with a grim smile, evidently appreciating the joke.

He boasted greatly of his humanity and his respect for private property, but if the local papers are to be believed, it must be chronicled . . . that he seized a great many Negroes, who were tied and sent south as slaves.

Newsman Coffin soon left Harrisburg to go to meet the Army of the Potomac, on his way detouring eastwardly to pay a visit to Baltimore:
. . . I found the Marylanders . . . barricading the streets. . . . Colored men were impressed to construct fortifications. . . . They went to work singing their *Marseillaise,* "John Brown's Body."
. . . I heard the song sung by a thousand voices. . . . Twenty-six months before, Massachusetts troops had fought their way through the city [then in the grip of proslavery mobs]; now the colored men were singing of John Brown amid the cheers of the people!

General Hooker waited in front of Washington till he was certain of Lee's intentions [the information being gained by Pleasonton's cavalry during a series of engagements with Jeb Stuart], and then by a rapid march pushed on to Frederick.

During this march, says Lieutenant Jesse Young:
The hearty greeting given to the soldiers . . . gladdened the army. In Virginia the Army of the Potomac was considered a ruthless invader. . . . Now, however, the atmosphere rang with cheers; the Stars and Stripes were everywhere floating on the breeze; men, women, and children vied with each other in their exhibitions of loyalty and zeal. . . .

As [our] division marched along, [we] passed by a country schoolhouse in a little grove at a crossroad. The teacher, hearing the music of the [division's] band at a distance, and expecting the arrival of troops, had dismissed the school to give them a sight of the soldiers.

The boys and girls, before the troops came in sight, had gathered bunches of wild flowers and platted garlands of leaves and secured several tiny flags. And now, as General [Andrew A.] Humphreys rode up in front of the schoolhouse, a little girl came forth and presented him with a bouquet, which he acknowledged with gracious courtesy.

Then the group of assembled pupils began to sing, as they waved their flags and garlands in the air. The song made a tumult in every soldier's heart . . . and many strong men wept as they looked on the scene and thought of their own loved ones far away in their Northern homes, and were inspired with newborn courage and patriotism. . . .

This is the song which rang forth . . . from that country schoolhouse . . . :

> Yes, we'll rally round the flag, boys, we'll rally once again,
>   Shouting the battle cry of Freedom;
> We'll rally from the hillside, we'll gather from the plain,
>   Shouting the battle cry of Freedom!
>
> We are springing to the call of our brothers gone before,
>   Shouting the battle cry of Freedom;
> And we'll fill the vacant ranks with a million freemen more,
>   Shouting the battle cry of Freedom!
>
> We are marching to the field, boys, we're going to the fight,
>   Shouting the battle cry of Freedom;
> And we bear the glorious stars for the Union and the right,
>   Shouting the battle cry of Freedom!
>
> The Union forever; hurrah, boys, hurrah!
>   Down with the traitors, up with the stars,
> While we rally round the flag, boys, rally once again,
>   Shouting the battle cry of Freedom!

By this time, writes newsman Coffin:

Lee's entire army was across the Potomac. . . . General Hooker asked [Washington] that the troops at Harper's Ferry might be placed under his command, that he might wield the entire available force and crush Lee. This was refused, whereupon he informed the War Department that . . . he wished to be relieved of the command of the army. The matter was laid before the President, and his request was granted. General [George G.] Meade was placed in command; and what was denied to General Hooker was substantially granted to General Meade—that he was to use his best judgment in holding or evacuating Harper's Ferry!

George G. Meade.

. . . It was a dismal day at Frederick when the news was promulgated that General Hooker was relieved of the command. Notwithstanding the result at Chancellorsville, the soldiers had a good degree of confidence in him. General Meade was unknown except to his own corps. . . . He commanded a division at Antietam and Fredericksburg, and the Fifth Corps at Chancellorsville.

General Meade cared but little for the pomp and parade of war. His own soldiers respected him because he was always prepared to endure hardships. They saw a tall, slim, gray-bearded man wearing a slouch hat, a plain blue blouse, with his pantaloons tucked into his boots. He was plain of speech and familiar in conversation. . . .

I saw him soon after he was informed that the army was under his command. . . . It was in the hotel at Frederick. He stood silent and thoughtful, by himself. Few of all the noisy crowd around knew of the change that had taken place. The correspondents of the press knew it long before the corps commanders were informed of the fact. No change was made in the machinery of the army, and there was but a few hours' delay in its movement.

Lee's infantry columns were now in Pennsylvania, some at Chambersburg and Fayetteville, twenty to twenty-five miles westward from Gettysburg; others had gone about thirty miles north of the town to Carlisle; and still others had headed toward York, a similar distance in a northeasterly direction from the town. Gettysburg was then only another Pennsylvania community, its role in the campaign undeveloped.

The entire North, according to Abner Doubleday, was by this time in a state of "wild commotion."

. . . people began to feel that the boast of the Georgia Senator [Robert] Toombs, that he would call the roll of his slaves at the foot of Bunker Hill monument, might soon be realized.

The cavalry units attached to the Confederate columns kept active; and Private James H. Hodam, of the Seventeenth Virginia regiment, later recorded:

Near Gettysburg, we captured the camp and equipage of a force of Pennsylvania militia, and after an exciting chase of several miles our regiment succeeded in picking up over 300 of the "band-box boys," as we called them. . . .

While returning from escorting a lot of prisoners to the rear, I met a large party of prisoners hurrying by [on their way to join the others in the rear], while a short distance behind them a little drummer boy was trying to keep up. He was bareheaded, wet, and muddy, but still retained his drum.

"Hello, my little Yank; where are you going?" I said.

"Oh, I am a prisoner and am going to Richmond," he replied.

"Look here," I said, "you are too little to be a prisoner; so pitch that drum into that fence-corner, throw off your coat, get behind those bushes, and go home as fast as you can."

"Mister, don't you want me for a prisoner?"

"No."

"Can I go where I please?"

"Yes."

"Then you bet I am going home to mother!"

Saying this as he threw his drum one way and his coat another [and became, in appearance, a civilian], he disappeared behind a fence and some bushes; and I sincerely hope he reached home and mother.

Writes Southerner John B. Gordon (now, incidentally, a general):

The Valley of Pennsylvania . . . was delightful to look upon. . . . Its broad grain fields, clad in golden garb, were waving their welcome to the reapers and binders. Some fields were already dotted over with harvested shocks. . . . On every side, as far as our alert vision could reach, all aspects and conditions conspired to make this fertile and carefully tilled region a panorama both interesting and enchanting. It was a type of the fair and fertile Valley of Virginia at its best, before it became the highway of armies and the ravages of war had left it wasted and bare. This melancholy contrast . . . brought to our Southern sensibilities a touch of sadness.

Robert Stiles, of the Richmond Howitzers, found even the towns comparable to those in Virginia:

One bright day toward the end of June, our column was passing through the main street of such a town, when, being very thirsty, I rode up to the front fence of a house . . . and asked an elderly lady sitting in the porch if I might get a drink of water from the well. She courteously gave permission and I entered the yard, got a delicious drink of water, thanked her, and was in the act of leaving, when the old lady . . . very pleasantly asked if I wouldn't take a seat and rest a little. I thanked her, stepped up on the porch and sat down, and we soon got into a friendly and pleasant conversation. . . .

Before I left, the old lady asked me if I had ever seen Stonewall Jackson, and upon my responding that I had, she said quietly, but with the deepest feeling, that she expected to see him soon, for if anyone had ever left this earth who had gone straight to Heaven it was he.

This was almost too much, and I said to her, "Madam, who on earth are you, and where did you come from?"

She said she was born in the Valley of Virginia and had been brought to this country when a girl. I could not forbear kissing her hand as I departed, and told her I felt sure she would get There, and I hoped we would meet in that blessed country where there would be no more wars nor separations between God's dear children.

Again in the words of General Gordon:

. . . the orders from General Lee for the protection of private property and persons were of the most stringent character. . . . I resolved to leave no ruins along the line of my march through Pennsylvania; no marks of a more enduring character than the tracks of my soldiers along its superb pikes. . . .

Going into camp in an open country and after dark, it was ascertained that there was no wood to be had for even the limited amount of necessary cooking, and I was appealed to by the men for permission to use a few rails from an old-fashioned fence near the camp. I agreed that they might take the top layer of rails, as the fence would still be high enough to answer the farmer's purpose.

When morning came, the fence had nearly all disappeared, and each man declared that he had taken only the top rail! . . . It was a case of adherence to the letter, and neglect of the spirit; but there was no alternative except good-naturedly to admit that my men had gotten the better of me that time.

On Sunday, June 28, the general led his brigade into the city of York:
A committee, composed of the mayor and prominent citizens, met my command . . . before we reached the corporate limits, their object being to make a peaceable surrender. . . . They returned, I think, with a feeling of assured safety. The church bells were ringing, and the streets were filled with well-dressed people. The appearance of these churchgoing men, women, and children . . . strangely contrasted with that of my marching soldiers. Begrimed as we were, from head to foot, with the impalpable gray powder which rose in dense columns from the macadamized pikes and settled in sheets on men, horses, and wagons, it is no wonder that many of York's inhabitants were terror-stricken as they looked upon us. . . .

Confederate pride, to say nothing of Southern gallantry, were subjected to the sorest trial by the consternation produced among the ladies of York. In my eagerness to relieve the citizens from all apprehension, I lost sight of the fact that this turnpike powder was no respecter of persons, but that it enveloped all alike—officers as well as privates. . . .

Halting on the main street, where the sidewalks were densely packed, I rode a few rods in advance of my troops in order to speak to the people from my horse. As I checked him and turned my full dust-begrimed face upon a bevy of young ladies very near me, a cry of alarm came from their midst. But after a few words of assurance from me, quiet and apparent confidence were restored.

I assured these ladies that the troops behind me, though ill-clad and travel-stained, were good men and brave; that beneath their rough exteriors were hearts as loyal to women as ever beat in the breasts of honorable men; that their own experience and the experience of their mothers, wives, and sisters at home had taught them how painful must be the sight of a hostile army in their town; that . . . both private property and non-combatants were safe. . . .

Even while Gordon was making his speech, the Union's General Meade was assigning his columns to routes out of Frederick. The town lay some thirty miles south of Gettysburg.

Writes newsman Coffin:

All Sunday the army was passing through Frederick. It was a strange sight. The churches were open, and some of the officers and soldiers attended service. . . . The stores also were open, and the town was cleaned of goods—boots, shoes, needles, pins, tobacco, pipes, paper, pencils, and other trifles which add to a soldier's comfort. Cavalry, infantry, and artillery were pouring through the town, the bands playing and the soldiers singing their liveliest songs. . . . The lines of march were like the sticks of a fan, Frederick being the point of divergence.

Only now did General Lee learn, through a scout, that the Federals had crossed the Potomac and were hot on his trail. He had been under the impression they were still abreast of Washington. His lack of day-to-day information arose from the fact that his army's eyes and ears, Jeb Stuart, having taken advantage of an order too generally worded, was on another grand circuit of the foe and had no opportunity to send dispatches.

When Lee learned what the Federals were doing, he sent word for his scattered columns to converge west of Gettysburg. First to arrive in the area was A. P. Hill's advance.

Explains Southern General Fitzhugh Lee:

Lee was rapidly concentrating. . . . On the 30th, [General J. Johnston] Pettigrew, commanding a brigade of [General Henry] Heth's division, Hill's corps, was directed to march to Gettysburg to get shoes for the barefooted men of the division, but returned the same evening without them and reported that Gettysburg was occupied by the Federal cavalry, and that drums were heard beating on the other side of the town. So Heth told Hill if he had no objection he would take his whole division there the next day . . . to which Hill replied, "None in the world."

. . . Heth . . . reached McPherson's Heights, one mile west of

Gettysburg, at 9 A.M. on July 1st, deployed two brigades on either side of the road and advanced on the town. Promptly [a] few sputtering shots, which first announced the skirmish line's opening, told him that [General John]Buford's dismounted cavalry were blocking the way.

These "few sputtering shots" between Heth and Buford were the precursors of a battle that was to decide the fate of the United States and was thus to have a profound influence on the course of world events.

17

GETTYSBURG

W HEN THE BATTLE OF GETTYSBURG—*destined to last through
the first three days of July, 1863—began about a mile west of
the town as a skirmish between advance units of the two armies, General Meade was at Taneytown, a dozen miles to the south, and General
Lee was coming eastward from Chambersburg. Neither commander
selected the battlefield, but each was drawn into assembling his full
strength there. (Meade's Army of the Potomac numbered perhaps
85,000 or 90,000 men of all arms, while Lee's Army of Northern Virginia probably totaled about 75,000.) The columns of the armies
were at varying distances out, the Federals to the southwest, south,
and southeast; and the Confederates to the west, north, and northeast.*

Says Union General Abner Doubleday of the opening skirmish:
As the rebels had had several encounters with militia, who were
easily dispersed, they did not expect to meet any serious resistance at
this time, and advanced [upon John Buford's dismounted cavalry]
confidently and carelessly. Buford gave way [toward Gettysburg]
slowly, taking advantage of every accident of ground to protract the
struggle. After an hour's fighting he felt anxious, and went up into
the steeple of the Theological Seminary [just west of the town] from
which a wide view could be obtained, to see if the First Corps was in

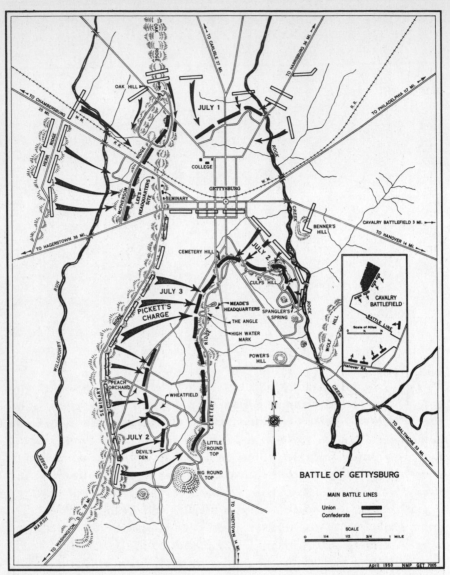

BATTLE OF GETTYSBURG

sight. One division of it was close at hand, and soon [General John F.] Reynolds, who had preceded it, climbed up into the belfry to confer with him there and examine the country around.

. . . there are two roads coming into Gettysburg from the west. . . . Each is intersected by ridges running north and south. On that nearest to the town . . . is . . . [the] Theological Seminary. A small stream of water called Willoughby Run winds between the next two ridges. The battle on the first day was principally fought on the heights on each side of this stream.

The troops under Reynolds, with Doubleday second-in-command, re-
lieved Buford's hard-pressed cavalrymen. Recognized as a key posi-
tion at this time was McPherson's Woods, just east of Willoughby
Run. Doubleday goes on:

Both parties were now trying to obtain possession of the woods.
[General James J.] Archer's rebel brigade, preceded by a skirmish
line, was crossing Willoughby Run to enter them on one side as the
Iron Brigade [a battle-hardened unit of Federals famed for their exploits and their black slouch hats] went in on the other.

General Reynolds was on horseback in the edge of the woods,
surrounded by his staff. He felt some anxiety as to the result, and
turned his head frequently to see if [enough of] our troops would be
up in time. While looking back in this way, a rebel sharpshooter shot
him through the back of the head, the bullet coming out near the
eye. He fell dead in an instant without a word.

I felt the great loss the country had sustained in his death, and
lamented him as almost a lifelong companion, for we were at West
Point together, and had served in the same regiment . . . upon first
entering service. . . . When quite young we had fought in the same
battles in Mexico.

I had little time, however, to indulge in these recollections. The
situation was very peculiar. The rebel left . . . had driven in [our
right] . . . and our left . . . had charged into the woods . . .
swept suddenly and unexpectedly around the right flank of Archer's
brigade, and captured a . . . part of it, including Archer himself.

The fact is, the enemy were careless and underrated us. . . . The
Iron Brigade [however] . . . were recognized at once by their old
antagonists. Some of the latter were heard to exclaim, "There are
those damned black-hatted fellows again! 'Taint no militia. It's the
Army of the Potomac." Having captured Archer and his men, many
of the Iron Brigade kept on beyond Willoughby Run and formed
on the heights on the opposite side.

The command now devolved upon me, with its great responsibilities. The disaster on the right required immediate attention, for
the enemy, with loud yells, were pursuing [part of General Lysander]
Cutler's brigade toward the town. I at once ordered my reserve . . .
to advance against their flank.

Two of Cutler's regiments that were still at the front joined this ef-
fort. The Confederates, taking cover in a railroad cut, were soon
almost wholly encircled; and "the greater number gave themselves

up as prisoners, and the others scattered over the country and escaped."

The action lulled, but only so that its intensity could be increased, for fresh troops were coming up on both sides. Abner Doubleday, while reforming and strengthening his line, found a moment
to devote to the captured General Archer, whom he had known at
West Point.

"Good morning, Archer!" he said. "How are you? I am glad to
see you!"

Archer scowled back, "Well, I am not glad to see you, by a
damned sight!"

The Federal reinforcements, according to correspondent William
Swinton of the New York Times, were "in the highest spirits."

One of the brigades . . . under command of Colonel Roy Stone,
had been assigned to a position where it came under a heavy artillery
fire; and as the troops took their post Colonel Stone remarked, "We
have come to stay." This went quickly through the brigade, the men
adopting it as a watchword—"We have come to stay!" And a very
large part of them never left that ground.

Along with the fresh arrivals on the Union side was a Gettysburg
civilian named John Burns. Writes Sergeant George Eustice, who
was at the front with the Seventh Wisconsin Volunteers:

It must have been about noon when I saw a little old man coming up in the rear. . . . I remember he wore a swallow-tailed coat
with smooth brass buttons [presumably an ancient military jacket,
for he was a veteran of the War of 1812]. He had a rifle on his shoulder. We boys began to poke fun at him . . . as we thought no civilian in his senses would show himself in such a place.

Finding that he had really come to fight, I wanted to put a car-
tridge-box on him. . . . Slapping his pantaloons-pocket, he replied,
"I can get my hands in here quicker than in a box. I'm not used to
them new-fangled things."

In answer to the question what possessed him to come out there at
such a time, he replied that the rebels had either driven away or
milked his cows, and that he was going to be even with them. About
this time the enemy began to advance. Bullets were flying thicker
and faster, and we hugged the ground. . . . Burns got behind a tree
and surprised us all. . . . He was as calm and collected as any veteran on the ground.

We soon had orders to get up and move about a hundred yards to the right, when we were engaged in one of the most stubborn contests I ever experienced. . . . I never saw John Burns after our movement to the right . . . and only know that he was true blue and grit to the backbone, and fought until he was three times wounded.

The Union's Eleventh Corps, under Oliver Howard, arrived on the field about 1:00 P.M. Overall command devolved upon Howard by reason of seniority. He simply left the fighting on the left to Doubleday, while assigning his own divisions to the right. It became necessary to extend the right around to the north of the town, for Confederate General Richard Ewell's divisions had become a threat from that direction.

It was Ewell's arrival that decided the issue, for the Confederates were now superior in numbers. Ewell attacked in an arc that started on Doubleday's right and embraced the whole of Howard's line. One of the decisive charges was led by General John B. Gordon:

With a ringing yell, my command rushed upon the line posted to protect the Union right. Here occurred a hand-to-hand struggle. That protecting Union line once broken left my command not only on the right flank but obliquely in rear of it. Any troops that were ever marshalled would, under like conditions, have been as surely and swiftly shattered. There was no alternative for Howard's men except to break and fly, or to throw down their arms and surrender. Under the concentrated fire from front and flank, the marvel is that any escaped.

In the midst of the wild disorder in his ranks, and through a storm of bullets, a Union officer was seeking to rally his men for a final stand. He, too, went down, pierced by a Minié ball. Riding forward with my rapidly advancing lines, I discovered that brave officer lying upon his back, with the July sun pouring its rays into his pale face. He was surrounded by the Union dead, and his own life seemed to be rapidly ebbing out.

Quickly dismounting and lifting his head, I gave him water from my canteen, asked his name and the character of his wounds. He was Major General Francis C. Barlow, of New York, and of Howard's corps. The ball had entered his body in front and passed out near the spinal cord, paralyzing him in legs and arms. Neither of us had the remotest thought that he could possibly survive many hours. I summoned several soldiers who were looking after the wounded, and directed them to place him upon a litter and carry him to the shade in the rear.

(Unknown to Gordon, Barlow made a complete recovery. A year later, Barlow learned that a Confederate General J. B. Gordon had been killed in a battle near Richmond. This was actually a kinsman of the Gordon of Gettysburg, but Barlow naturally assumed it was the same man. Nearly fifteen years later, Barlow and Gordon met in Washington, D.C. Gordon asked, "Are you related to the Barlow who was killed at Gettysburg?" Barlow replied, "I am the man, sir. Are you related to the Gordon who killed me?" Said Gordon: "I am the man, sir!" A lifetime friendship resulted.)

The collapse of Howard's forces left Doubleday's right flank exposed, and, suffering heavy casualties, he soon had to yield. Now the entire Union line was driven back toward Gettysburg and the fields on its flanks. This brought the right of the advancing Confederate line under punishing artillery fire from batteries stationed southwest of town, on Seminary Ridge. Writes Union cannoneer Augustus Buell:

. . . for seven or eight minutes ensued probably the most desperate fight ever waged between artillery and infantry at close range without a particle of cover on either side. They gave us volley after volley . . . and we gave them double-canister as fast as we could load. . . . How those peerless cannoneers sprang to their work! . . . The very guns became things of life . . . . Every man was doing the work of two or three. . . .

Up and down the line, men reeling and falling; splinters flying from wheels and axles where bullets hit; in rear, horses tearing and plunging, mad with wounds or terror; drivers yelling, shells bursting; shot shrieking overhead, howling about our ears or throwing up great clouds of dust where they struck; the musketry crashing . . . bullets hissing, humming, and whistling everywhere; cannon roaring, all crash on crash, and peal on peal; smoke, dust, splinters, blood; wreck and carnage indescribable. . . . Every man's shirt soaked with sweat, and many of them sopped with blood from wounds not severe enough to make such bulldogs let go—bareheaded, sleeves rolled up, faces blackened. . . .

Out in front of us an undulating field, filled almost as far as the eye could reach with a long, low, gray line creeping towards us, fairly fringed with flame. . . . For a few moments the whole Rebel line . . . seemed to waver. . . . But their second line came steadily on, and . . . Orderly Sergeant [John] Mitchell . . . gave the order to limber to the rear. . . .

Among the units waiting in reserve positions behind the Confederate attack was a regiment of Jenkins' cavalry, one of the members of which was Private James Hodam (the trooper who had earlier freed the Union drummer boy):

Soon the "rebel yell" could be distinguished in the mighty roar, and conveyed to us the gratifying intelligence that our boys were getting the best of the fight; and a signal officer of a station nearby soon verified the fact that the enemy was retreating from every position. Then the welcome order came for us to quickly advance to the front . . . and we spurred our horses along the road for Gettysburg. Through the timber, across a small stream—and the battlefield was before us in all its horrors and excitement.

In our front were open fields and orchards, and a little further on, the town. Many pieces of artillery [had] occupied the high ground to our right, but their thunder was silenced now, while the heaps of dead and dying . . . told how the boys in blue had bravely stood by their guns. A little beyond, to judge from the windrows of dead, a Union regiment had been blotted out. Along the road the blue and gray veterans lay thickly. . . . Dashing forward, we came up with our infantry, driving Howard's corps through the town.

Many of Gettysburg's citizens had remained in their homes. Some took to their cellars as the action approached, while others peered from windows and doorways.

"As we passed through the streets," says Abner Doubleday, "pale and frightened women came out and offered us coffee and food, and implored us not to abandon them."

Far from gaining protection, the residents were obliged to aid scores of the soldiers, many of them bloody with wounds, who entered the houses looking for places to hide from the enemy. Odd corners of attics, cellars, and backyard sheds were quickly filled.

Southern artilleryman Robert Stiles takes up:

My gun had come . . . into battery in the outskirts of the town. No enemy was in sight in our front. . . . At this moment little George Greer, a chubby boy of sixteen, rode on by, further into the town. . . . I shouted a caution to him as he passed, but on he went, disappearing in the smoke and dust ahead. In a few moments a cloud of blue coats appeared in the street in front of us, coming on . . . at a run.

I was about to order the detachment to open fire, when . . . back of the men in blue I noticed little Greer, leaning forward over the neck of his horse, towering above the Federals, who were on foot; and with violent gesticulations and in tones not the gentlest, ordering the "blue devils" to "double-quick to the rear of that piece," which they did in the shortest time imaginable. There must have been over fifty of them.

I am aware this statement sounds incredible, but the men had thrown away their arms and were cowering . . . in the streets and alleys.

In a moment the Confederates were in the houses, "racing through them from cellar to attic," on a hunt for Federals. Union newsman Charles Coffin later learned the following story from one of the homeowners:

Among those who sought shelter in the houses was [a] Colonel Wheelock. . . . He . . . [was] followed by Confederate soldiers and an officer who demanded his sword.

"I'll not surrender my sword to a rebel," was the reply.

"Surrender your sword, or I will shoot you."

"Shoot! I'll not surrender it," again the defiant reply from Wheelock, who opened his vest, waiting for the fatal shot.

A girl sprang between them—Miss Carrie Shead—who seized the sword, bore it away, and secreted it. His sword safe, Colonel Wheelock became a submissive prisoner.

(Taken to a Confederate camp outside the town, Wheelock managed to escape during the night; and after the three-day battle ended he went back to the Shead house and retrieved his sword.)

The retreating Federals, their ranks drastically thinned, streamed south of Gettysburg to the hill that held the town's cemetery, where a new line was formed under cover of artillery fire.

Relates Confederate horseman James Hodam:

Our lines were re-formed, skirmishers advanced beyond the town to the south and east, while our regiment engaged in gathering up the prisoners. It was now about four o'clock, and the enemy's fire ceased for a short time. . . . My captain sent me forward to our skirmish line to locate the battery that had so fiercely shelled us.

While returning, the enemy began a brisk fire from several guns. A shell exploded just in front of me, and just over a woman as she ran across the street. She disappeared in a cellar, unhurt.

Then came a blinding flash in my face, and the next thing I realized was being carried to the sidewalk by three or four infantrymen. My horse had been killed by a piece of shell, but I escaped with a few bruises and a general shaking up.

"Late in the afternoon," says Confederate General Gordon,

. . . when the firing had greatly decreased along most of the lines, General Ewell and I were riding through the streets of Gettysburg. In a previous battle he had lost one of his legs, but prided himself on the efficiency of the wooden one which he used in its place. As we rode together, a body of Union soldiers, posted behind some buildings and fences on the outskirts of the town, suddenly opened a brisk fire. A number of Confederates were killed or wounded, and I heard the ominous thud of a Minié ball as it struck General Ewell, at my side.

I quickly asked, "Are you hurt, sir?"

"No, no," he replied, "I'm not hurt. . . . It don't hurt a bit to be shot in a wooden leg."

General Lee had reached the scene and was in command during the rout of the Federals. With his binoculars, he watched them form their new line on Cemetery Hill. According to General James Longstreet:

He sent orders to Ewell to follow up the success if he found it practicable, and to occupy the hill on which the enemy was concentrating. As the order was not positive, but left discretion with General Ewell, the latter thought it better to give his troops a little rest. . . .

The attack was not continued. "Both Hill and Ewell," says Abner Doubleday, "had received some stunning blows during the day, and were disposed to be cautious." This caution was ever after to be a topic for speculation among students of the battle. The possibility exists that a continuation of the attack, even with weakened and disorganized forces, would have driven the Federals from the vital

high ground while they were still off balance, thus changing the bat-
tle's outcome. Lee is reputed to have said later: "If I had had Stone-
wall Jackson at Gettysburg, I would have won that fight; and a com-
plete victory there would have given us Washington and Baltimore,
if not Philadelphia, and would have established the independence
of the Confederacy."

That evening, according to Northerner Warren Goss, the tri-
umphant Confederates

. . . were scattered through the village, pillaging its houses,
buying out its stores and people with Confederate money. . . . The
women remaining in town were doing their best to propitiate the
rebel soldiers with the best they could give them of eatables and
drinkables. The chivalrous Southerners had struck a bonanza. . . .
They were feasting and rejoicing in a land of milk and honey.

During the last hours of daylight, both sides were joined by new
columns. The concentration of the Confederate forces was now
about complete, while the Federals still had substantial numbers on
the way. That evening the bivouac fires of the two armies were a
scant mile apart.

Abner Doubleday's division was encamped on Gettysburg's ceme-
tery, at the arched gateway of which was the following sign: ALL PER-
SONS FOUND USING FIREARMS IN THESE GROUNDS WILL BE PROSECUTED
WITH THE UTMOST RIGOR OF THE LAW.

Says Doubleday:

We lay on our arms that night among the tombs . . . so suggestive of the shortness of life and the nothingness of fame; but the
men were little disposed to moralize on themes like these, and were
too much exhausted to think of anything but much-needed rest.

General Meade arrived from Taneytown sometime after midnight;
and, accompanied by a party that included General Oliver Howard,
he rode along the lines under a bright moon. Said Howard: "I am
confident that we can hold this position." Meade replied: "I am glad
to hear you say so, for it is too late to leave it."

The Union lines were taking the shape of a fishhook, one three
miles long. The shank was on Cemetery Ridge, which ran in a north–
south direction between Cemetery Hill, just south of the town, and
Little Round Top and Big Round Top, about two miles below. The
hook, the convex side of which faced the town, began at Cemetery

Confederate victims of the battle's first day.

Hill, ran a half mile eastward to Culp's Hill, then continued another half mile southeastward to Spangler's Spring.

As for the Confederates, they were obliged to set up a larger fishhook running parallel to that of the Federals. Ultimately five miles long, this line was a mile from the Federal line at some points, and considerably closer at others. The shank ran north–south on Seminary Ridge, southwest of the town; the hook ran eastward through the town, then southeastward around Culp's Hill and Spangler's Spring.

The Confederates, with the smaller army, had the longer line to fill. Moreover, they were going to have to operate on exterior lines of communication—that is, on the outside of their fishhook. The Federals, on the other hand, could look forward to operating on compact interior lines of communication. It was going to be relatively easy for them to shift troops from point to point along the inside of their fishhook as the situation required.

General Lee, of course, was aware of the disadvantages he faced. But, according to the Union's Warren Goss:

The temper of his army was such, and its confidence in its ability to defeat the Yankees at all times and under all circumstances so great, that Lee himself, with all his equipoise of character, caught something of this overconfidence.

General Longstreet, whom Lee called his "old war horse," was very much opposed to engaging Meade in his strong position, advising that he be flanked out of it—that the Confederate army maneuver so as to interpose itself between the Federals and Washington. But Lee was adamant: "No, the enemy is there, and I am going to attack him there."

Warren Goss relates that

The early morning hours of July 2d were cloudy, and a heavy vapor overhung the valley. By ten o'clock the threatening clouds vanished and the green meadows were bathed in sunlight. . . . Cattle were grazing in the fields below; the shrill crowing of chanticleer was heard from neighboring farmyards; tame pigeons cooed on the hillside; and birds sang among the trees.

The crest [that held our troops], as far as the eye could see, glittered with burnished arms. On our [regiment's] right was the cemetery with its white monuments, among which shone the burnished brass pieces of artillery and the glittering bayonets of the infantry. Beyond this were seen the spires of the town; while . . . to the . . . rear was Culp's Hill. Running across our front, obliquely, was the Emmitsburg road, while farther beyond was Seminary Ridge, on which the enemy was posted. On our left, over a mile distant, rose the sugar-loaf summits of the Round Tops. . . . Occasionally a lightning-like glimmer on the opposite hills showed the reflection from the burnished arms of the enemy. . . . With a glass, the rebel soldiers . . . could be distinctly seen.

The Federals, Goss goes on to explain, were troubled by what was coming:

To the observant eye there was perceptible beneath the mask of rough humor and careless indifference an undercurrent of anxiety and gloomy foreboding. The look of earnestness which gathers on soldiers' faces before a battle was, perhaps, now deepened by the thought that the impending battle was to be fought on our own soil, and of the consequences if we met defeat. . . . The general feeling was well expressed by a sergeant of a Pennsylvania regiment who said, "We've got to fight our best today or have these rebs for our masters!"

Daniel E. Sickles.

View of the Union lines on July 2.

General Lee's plans called for Longstreet to deliver a smashing blow against the Union left, which lay in the vicinity of the Round Tops. At the same time, Ewell was to make a supporting attack on the Union right—on the "hook" going rearward from Cemetery Hill over Culp's Hill to Spangler's Spring. Ewell was to begin his move when he heard Longstreet open with his artillery.

Noon came and went, and the only action on the field was between the skirmishers out ahead of the lines on both sides. Longstreet, reluctant to make the attack in the first place, was having trouble getting his troops into position.

Meanwhile, General Daniel Sickles, who commanded on the Union left, where Longstreet was about to attack, decided to move his troops forward from Cemetery Ridge a good half mile to a position he considered more advantageous.

Among the men under Sickles was Lieutenant Jesse Young:

It was a brilliant sight—the march of the Third Army Corps . . . from its place in the line of battle near Little Round Top . . . to occupy a new position . . . in their front. Battle flags waved above the heads of the gallant soldiers; the bright gleam of their muskets flashed along their extended line; aides were to be seen galloping in every direction to execute the orders for the advance; bugles sounded out their stirring blasts, indicating the will of the corps commander, Major General Sickles. . . . [T]he rapid "crack! crack!" of muskets . . . all along the skirmish line afforded signs of fast-approaching battle. . . .

It is half past three o'clock in the afternoon, and suddenly a cannon shot is heard, followed by another, a sign that something is going to happen. General Sickles has been . . . away to the rear . . . and the noise of the artillery brings him galloping to his corps, with General Meade following close behind. . . . It seems that Sickles has gone out far beyond the point that Meade had intended as the line of battle. . . .

As the two generals sat on their horses for a moment . . . it could be clearly seen that both were in deep concern. Finally, after some discussion, Sickles said, "Well, general, I will withdraw and resume my former position back yonder if you give the command." General Meade, rightly divining the movement then in progress on the part of the enemy, said, "The Confederates will not let you withdraw now."

And the words were hardly out of his lips when an exploding shell in the air almost over their heads showed that the battle was begun. In five minutes the batteries on both sides, which had been wheeling into position, were belching forth round shot and shell against each other, and the attack of the rebels against the Union left flank was begun in earnest.

Since parts of Sickles' line were only thinly manned, Meade sent at once for reinforcements. (Only now, incidentally, were the last of Meade's troops—the Sixth Corps under John Sedgwick—arriving at Gettysburg. After about thirty-five miles of forced marching over hot and dusty roads, these men were thinking chiefly in terms of coffee and rest. They took up a reserve position.)

Three obscure spots, in addition to Little Round Top, were to be made famous that afternoon: a peach orchard, a wheatfield, and a modest height that held a jumble of giant boulders. The last, appropriately named Devil's Den, marked the extreme left, or southernmost point, of the new Union line. It lay out in front of Little Round Top, across a scrub-covered and rock-strewn valley.

On moving his line forward, General Sickles had forsaken Little Round Top and its neighbor Big Round Top, the latter still farther to the left, or the south. Logically, the left of Sickles' line should have embraced both. Little Round Top was the more important position, for it could be ascended by horse-drawn artillery; Big Round Top was too steep and rocky for this.

The beginning of the battle found Meade's artillery chief, Henry J. Hunt, making an inspection of the guns that had been set up at Devil's Den. He had walked across the rugged little valley, leaving his horse tied to a tree near the Round Tops. He found the guns well posted, but not adequately supported:

. . . I left to seek infantry supports, very doubtful if I would find my horse, for the storm of shell bursting over the place was enough to drive any animal wild. On reaching the foot of the cliff [at the edge of Devil's Den], I found myself in a plight at once ludicrous, painful, and dangerous. A herd of horned cattle had been driven into the valley between Devil's Den and Round Top, from which they could not escape. A shell had exploded in the body of one of them, tearing it to pieces; others were torn and wounded. All were stampeded and were bellowing and rushing in their terror, first to one side and then to the other, to escape the shells that were bursting over them and among them.

Cross I must, and in doing so I had my most trying experience of that battlefield. Luckily the poor beasts were as much frightened as

I was, but their rage was subdued by terror, and they were good enough to let me pass through scot-free, but badly demoralized. However, my horse was safe, I mounted, and in the busy excitement that followed almost forgot my scare. . . .

As soon as Longstreet's attack commenced, General [Gouverneur K.] Warren was sent by General Meade to see to the condition of the extreme left. The duty could not have been intrusted to better hands. Passing along the lines, he found Little Round Top, the key of the position, unoccupied except by a signal station. The enemy [a part of John Hood's division] at the time lay concealed, awaiting the signal for assault, when a [cannon] shot fired in their direction caused a sudden movement on their part which, by the gleam of reflected sunlight from their bayonets, revealed their long lines outflanking the position. Fully comprehending the imminent danger, Warren sent to General Meade for a division. The enemy [however] was already advancing. . . .

Warren himself says that the Confederates were "shouting in the most confident tones."

While I was still all alone with the signal officer, the musket balls began to fly around us, and he was about to fold up his flags and withdraw, but remained at my request and kept waving them in defiance. Seeing [Federal reinforcements for the main battle line] going out on the Peach Orchard road [just north of Little Round Top], I rode down the hill. . . .

Warren happened to ride toward the point in the long column occupied by the brigade of General Stephen H. Weed. By a fortunate coincidence, these were troops who knew Warren well, for he had commanded them himself until a few months earlier, at which time he was made the army's chief engineer.

One of the men who noted Warren's approach was Captain Porter Farley of Colonel Patrick H. ("Paddy") O'Rorke's regiment:

He came from the direction of the hilltop. His speed and manner indicated unusual excitement. Before he reached us he called out to O'Rorke to lead his regiment that way, up the hill. O'Rorke answered him that General Weed had gone ahead and expected this regiment to follow him.

"Never mind that," answered Warren. "I'll take the responsibility."

. . . O'Rorke turned the head of the regiment to the left, and
. . . led it diagonally up the eastern slope of Little Round Top.
Warren rode off, evidently bent upon securing other troops.

General George Sykes, commander of the entire column of reinforce-
ments, aided Warren by turning back the other regiments of Weed's
brigade. Sykes, previously aware of the threat to the Federal left, had
already sent General Strong Vincent's brigade on the same mission.

Returning to Paddy O'Rorke's regiment and narrator Porter
Farley:

Some of the guns of [Lieutenant Charles E.] Hazlett's battery
broke through our files before we reached the hilltop, amid the
frantic efforts of the horses, lashed by the drivers, to pull their heavy
pieces up that steep acclivity. A few seconds later the head of our
regiment reached the summit of the ridge, war's wild panorama
spread before us, and we found ourselves upon the verge of battle. . . .

There was no time for tactical formation. Delay was ruin. . . .
The bullets flew in among the men the moment the leading company mounted the ridge; and, as not a musket was loaded, the natural
impulse was to halt and load them. But O'Rorke permitted no such
delay. Springing from his horse, he threw the reins to the sergeant-
major. His sword flashed from its scabbard into the sunlight; and
calling, "This way, boys!" he led the charge over the rocks, down the
hillside, till he came abreast the men of Vincent's brigade, who were
posted in the ravine to our left.

Joining them, an irregular line was formed, such as the confusion
of the rocks lying thereabout permitted; and this line grew and was
extended toward the right as the successive rearward companies [the
remainder of Weed's brigade] came upon the scene of action. There
[we loaded our muskets, and] while some were partly sheltered by
the rocks and others stood in the open, a fierce fight went on with an
enemy among the trees and underbrush. Flushed with the excitement of battle and bravely led, they pushed up close to our line.

By this time some of the Confederate troops fighting farther back had
gained a hold on the height that held Devil's Den. This meant that
the defenders of Little Round Top had to contend not only with the
foe in their immediate front but also with sharpshooters who had
taken up positions among the Den's boulders.

Writes Union Private Theodore Gerrish, of Vincent's brigade:

General Weed . . . ran up to speak with Hazlett as the latter, begrimed with powder, was working at a gun. Weed was shot down by a sharpshooter. While his lips, moving in death, seemed to speak some message, gallant Hazlett stooped down to catch it, when he too was shot and fell dead upon the lifeless form of his commander. Vincent . . . sprang upon a rock to cheer on his brave Michiganders. . . . His voice rang out . . . and his sword glistened above his head as he too fell, pouring out his blood in a crimson baptism upon the rock. . . .

Again in the words of Porter Farley of Paddy O'Rorke's regiment:

The steadfastness and valor displayed on both sides made the result for some few minutes doubtful; but a struggle so desperate and bloody could not be a long one. The enemy fell back. A short lull was succeeded by another onslaught, which was again repelled. . . . Of our regiment, eighty-five enlisted men and six officers had been wounded. Besides these, twenty-six . . . had fallen dead. . . . O'Rorke was among the dead. Shot through the neck, he had fallen without a groan, and we may hope without a pang.

The Confederates, having themselves suffered severely, made no more attacks at this point. But now two regiments (the Fifteenth and Forty-seventh Alabama) moved upon the defense line's extreme left flank—the left flank, in fact, of the whole Union army. Holding this position was the Twentieth Maine, the regiment of Vincent's brigade to which Private Gerrish belonged:

It was a most critical moment. If that line was permitted to turn the Federal flank, Little Round Top was intenable, and with this little mountain in the Confederates' possession, the whole position would be intenable. It was a most fortunate fact for the Union cause . . . that in command of the Twentieth Maine was [Colonel Joshua L. Chamberlain], a man equal to the emergency in which he was placed. . . .

The Federal line was near the crest. . . . The conflict opened . . . [with] fire flashing out from behind the trees and rocks. The sharp report of rifles rang along the hillside; bullets whistled through the air and buried themselves in the trees or struck the rocks, only to glance off . . . to lodge elsewhere. Men began to shout with excitement. Others were shot, and then laid them down to die, or staggered weak and bleeding to the rear. . . .

As the moments passed, the conflict thickened. The cartridge boxes were pulled around in front and left open; the cartridges were torn out and crowded into the smoking muzzles of the guns with a terrible rapidity. The steel rammers clashed and clanged in barrels heated with burning powder. The rifles were aimed with deadly precision upon the gray forms before them. And thus the work went on, and many a Federal and Confederate bit the dust. O, how fast they went down!

One company lost many of its bravest men. . . . Sergeant Steele staggered up to his gallant captain, with a large hole in his breast, and exclaimed, "I am going, captain."

"My God, sergeant!" cried the captain, who sprang forward to support him; but too late—the sergeant was dead at his feet. . . .

Not only on the crest of the hill among the bluecoats was blood running in little rivulets and forming crimson pools, but in the gray ranks of the assailants there had also been a fearful destruction.

This is confirmed by Southerner William C. Oates, commander of the Fifteenth Alabama:

. . . Captain Brainard . . . in leading his company forward, fell, exclaiming, "O, God, that I could see my mother!" and instantly expired. Lieutenant John A. Oates, my dear brother, succeeded to the command of the company, but was pierced through by a number of bullets and fell mortally wounded. Lieutenant Cody fell mortally wounded; Captain Bethune and several other officers were seriously wounded; while the carnage in the ranks was appalling.

I again ordered the advance. . . . I passed through the line waving my sword, shouting, "Forward, men, to the ledge!" and was promptly followed by the command in splendid style. . . . The Twentieth Maine was driven back from this ledge, but not farther than to the next ledge on the mountainside. . . . I, with my regiment, made a rush forward from the ledge. . . . The Maine regiment charged my line, coming right up in a hand-to-hand encounter. . . . A Maine man reached to grasp the staff of [our] colors, when Ensign Archibald stepped back and Sergeant Pat O'Connor stove his bayonet through the head of the Yankee, who fell dead. . . .

There never were harder fighters than the Twentieth Maine men and their gallant colonel. . . . My position rapidly became untenable. . . . My dead and wounded were then nearly as great in number as those still on duty. They literally covered the ground. The blood stood in puddles in some places on the rocks; the ground was soaked with the blood of as brave men as ever fell on the red field of battle. . . .

. . . I . . . did not undertake to retire in order. I . . . had the officers and men advised the best I could that when the signal was given . . . everyone should run in the direction from whence we came. . . . I found the undertaking to capture Little Round Top too great for my regiment unsupported [the Forty-seventh Alabama having fallen back]. . . . When the signal was given we ran like a herd of wild cattle. . . . As we ran, a man . . . who was to my right and rear had his throat cut by a bullet, and he ran past me breathing at his throat and the blood spattering. His windpipe was entirely severed. . . .

The Federals gave a wild yell and pursued for a short distance "like avenging demons." They returned to their lines with many prisoners. Little Round Top was now secure, and Meade's fears for his left flank were eased.

But the situation was very much up in the air along the Federal defense line under Dan Sickles (now reinforced by units from other corps) that stretched northwestward from Devil's Den through the Wheatfield and the Peach Orchard, then ran for a distance northeastward along the Emmitsburg road. An overall depiction of this fighting is given by Confederate General John B. Gordon. Though on another part of the field at this time, he could hear the action and see its smoke, and he soon learned its details from participants:

On . . . opposite hills, Lee and Meade, surrounded by staff and couriers and with glasses in hand, are surveying the intervening space. Over it the flying shells are plunging, shrieking, bursting. The battered Confederate line staggers, reels, and is bent back before the furious blast. The alert Federals . . . rush through this thin and wavering line. Instantly, from the opposite direction, with deafening yells, come the Confederates in countercharge, and the brave Federals are pressed back. . . .

The Confederate banners sweep through the riddled Peach Orchard; while . . . on the gory Wheatfield the impacted forces are locked in deadly embrace. Across this field in alternate waves rolls the battle's tide, now from the one side, now from the other, until the ruthless Harvester piles his heaps of slain thicker than the grain shocks gathered by the husbandman's scythe. Hard by is Devil's Den. Around it and over it the deadly din of battle roars. The rattle of rifles, the crash of shells, the shouts of the living and groans of the dying convert that dark woodland into a harrowing pandemonium.

The Union's Lieutenant Jesse Young was a witness to one of the battle's sidelights:

The Irish Brigade, with their emerald flag and the insignia of Erin in golden characters upon it waving above them, was advancing to go into battle in the region of the Devil's Den. Before they ventured into the actual battle they halted. The priest who was their chaplain stood on a rock high above the field, where he could be seen by the whole command, and, with the bullets flying about him and with the awful battle raging in his front, he pronounced absolution in behalf of his kneeling constituents. For a moment they bowed there while the priest commended their souls to the mercy of God, and then, with a united and terrible shout they dashed forward into the bloody field. . . .

Relates a Union staff officer, Captain Don Piatt, who was in the thick of the fight:

The air was filled with smoke and the interchanging fires of artillery and musketry. The shouts of both armies were almost deafening. . . . I trust in God I may never again be called to look upon such scenes. . . . Col. Thomas W. Egan . . . was charging with his command when a ball from the enemy pierced the heart of his mare, who sank under him. . . . The poor brute that I was riding had two minie balls buried in him—one in the shoulders, the other in the hip —and was so frantic with pain that he . . . wellnigh [broke] my neck in his violent fall. My sword was pitched a dozen yards from me. . . .

Col. A. V. H. Ellis, of the 124th New York . . . was riding at the head of his regiment, waving his sword in the air and shouting to his men—his orange blossoms, as he called them, the regiment having been raised in Orange County, New York—when a bullet struck him in the forehead. He was borne to the rear, his face covered with blood and the froth spirting from his mouth. He died in a few moments. . . .

. . . I was within a few feet of General Sickles when he received the wound by which he lost his leg. . . . [A] terrific explosion seemed to shake the very earth. This was instantly followed by another equally stunning, and the horses all began to jump. I instantly noticed that General Sickles' pants and drawers at the knee were torn clear off to the leg, which was swinging loose. . . .

As he attempted to dismount, he seemed to lose strength, and half fell to the ground. He was very pale and evidently in most fearful pain as he exclaimed excitedly, "Quick! Quick! Get something and tie it up before I bleed to death."

. . . He was carried from the field . . . coolly smoking a cigar. . . . His leg was amputated within less than half an hour after his receiving the wound.

As evening came, the fight "grew hotter and hotter." But the Confederates were gaining the advantage. Soon the Federals began to fall back toward their original position on Cemetery Ridge. Says Jesse Young:

Against [our] weakened, struggling lines . . . in the advancing twilight, regiments of heroic Confederates were pressing with eager yells, trampling the wounded Union men under their feet as they pressed on. . . . It was impossible to maintain regimental lines; yet the soldiers . . . were firing as fast as they could while falling back.

Young saw the Confederates score a direct hit on a Union artillery battery:

The caisson was set on fire, and in a moment, with all its stock of ammunition, it exploded. . . . [T]here flashed for a single instant against the sky the sight of wheels, limbs of horses and of men, pieces of timber, and scores of exploding shells, all inextricably interwoven into a spectacle of horror. . . . Then the smoke covered the scene. . . .

It seemed to Young at this point that "all hope of victory was taken away," and that "the Union was being destroyed forever."

On the Confederate side, elation was high. Writes Longstreet's chief of artillery, E. Porter Alexander:

. . . I believed that Providence was indeed "taking the proper view" and that the war was very nearly over. Every battery was limbered to the front. . . .

An artillerist's heaven is to follow the routed enemy, after a tough resistance, and throw shells and canister into his disorganized and fleeing masses. . . . There is no excitement on earth like it. . . . Now we saw our heaven just in front and were already breathing the very air of victory. . . . The ground was generally good, and pieces and caissons went at a gallop, some cannoneers mounted, and some running by the sides. . . .

But we only had a moderately good time with Sickles' retreating corps after all. They fell back upon fresh troops. . . .

Among these troops were elements of John Sedgwick's Sixth Corps, now at least partly rested after their recent arrival at Gettysburg. The corps' familiar flag, just barely visible against the dimming sky, was a heartening sight to the Federals who were reeling back in disorder. Jesse Young rejoices:

The day was not lost, then, after all! . . . Still, the battle was not over yet. Off to the left . . . the glorious Pennsylvania Reserves could be heard cheering and shouting . . . in [a] magnificent charge down from the ridge. . . . Hancock the Magnificent [i.e., General Winfield Scott Hancock, a senior corps commander], one of the most inspiring figures that ever roused and led men on any battlefield, was to be seen riding up and down the field, planting batteries, marshalling the reinforcements as they arrived, filling in the broken line, and aiding in the repulse of the advancing Confederates. . . . [The enemy's] line, it is true, was thin by this time, and was not well reinforced; but it made up in courage and spirit what it lacked in weight, and actually penetrated through the Union ranks at one point.

These Confederates were soon thrown back by a fresh line of Federals urged on by General Meade in person. Darkness was now settling over the bloody field, and the Confederate assault was everywhere collapsing. Finally, says Young, "the awful din of battle" was replaced by "something like . . . quiet. . . ."

Though the Confederates had gained control over much of the disputed ground, the outcome was that the Federals were back in their true position on Cemetery Ridge, with the all-important Little Round Top firmly in their hands. "When the battle . . . was over," writes James Longstreet, "General Lee pronounced it a success . . . but we had accomplished little toward victorious results."

As for the support attack Lee had ordered Richard Ewell's corps to make on the Federal right: After a late start, it precipitated several hours of savage fighting. Confederate General Harry T. Hays and his "Louisiana Tigers" actually broke through the defense line on East Cemetery Hill, but they were soon driven back. When the fighting ended for the night, however, other Confederate units remained in a lodgment they had gained in the works on the lower slopes of Culp's Hill and at Spangler's Spring.

Returning to the day's main battlefield and to Confederate artillery chief E. Porter Alexander:

It was evident that we had not finished the job, and would have to make a fresh effort in the morning. The firing had hardly ceased when my faithful little darkey, Charlie, came up hunting for me, with a fresh horse, affectionate congratulations on my safety, and, what was equally acceptable, something to eat. Negro servants hunting for their masters were a feature of the landscape that night.

I then found General Longstreet . . . and got orders for the morning. They were, in brief, that our present position was to be held and the attack renewed as soon as [General George E.] Pickett arrived [from Chambersburg, his division having been assigned to guard Longstreet's supply trains]. . . .

There was a great deal to do meanwhile. Our sound horses were to be fed and watered, those killed and disabled were to be replaced from the wagon teams, ammunition must be replenished, and the ground examined and positions of batteries rectified. But a splendid moon made all comparatively easy, and greatly assisted, too, in the care of the wounded, many of whom, both our own and the enemy's, lay about among our batteries nearly all night. . . .

On the Union side, General Meade assembled his corps commanders for a council of war. Lee's plan to renew the attack the next day was anticipated, and the decision was that the Union line be maintained as it was (except for adjustments to make it stronger) and the attack awaited.

The dawn of July 3 had barely arrived before the Union's Twelfth Corps, under General Henry W. Slocum, was heavily engaged with the Confederates lodged at Culp's Hill and Spangler's Spring. The fighting continued for much of the morning, with Ewell's men at last falling back.

In the meantime, the Confederates in front of Cemetery Ridge were making the final preparations for their new attack. Again in artillery chief Alexander's words:

Early in the morning General Lee came around, and I was then told that we were to assault [the Union center], which lay rather to our left. This necessitated a good many changes of our positions, which the enemy did not altogether approve of, and they took occasional shots at us, though we shifted about as inoffensively as possible and carefully avoided getting into bunches. . . .

Pickett's division had arrived, and his men were resting and eating. . . . About 11, some of Hill's skirmishers and the enemy began fighting over a barn between the lines, and gradually his artillery and the enemy's took part, until over a hundred guns were engaged, and a tremendous roar was kept up for quite a time. But it gradually died out, and the whole field became as silent as a churchyard. . . . The enemy, aware of the strength of his position, simply sat still and waited for us.

It had been arranged that when the infantry column was ready, General Longstreet should order two guns fired by the Washington Artillery. On that signal, all our guns were to open on Cemetery Hill and the ridge extending toward Round Top, which was covered with batteries. I was to observe the fire and give Pickett the order to charge. I accordingly took position, about 12, at the most favorable point, just on the left of the line of guns, and with one of Pickett's couriers with me.

Alexander shortly received a note from Longstreet in which the general said that if the artillery fire should prove insufficiently demoralizing to the enemy he would prefer that Pickett should not be advised to charge. Alexander was startled at having been given so much discretion at this critical moment in the battle. He wrote back that if there was any alternative to the attack, which was certain to prove costly, it ought to be considered at once, before a great deal of irreplaceable ammunition was spent. Longstreet merely sent another note directing that if the artillery fire had the desired effect the attack was to go forward.

Says Alexander:

I hardly knew whether this left me discretion or not, but at any rate it seemed decided that the artillery must open. I felt that if we went that far we could not draw back, but the infantry must go too. . . .

At exactly 1 o'clock by my watch the two signal guns were heard in quick succession. In another minute every gun was at work.

Writes an unnamed participant on the Union side:

The storm broke upon us so suddenly that [numbers of] soldiers and officers who leaped, as it began, from their tents or from lazy siestas on the grass were stricken in their rising with mortal wounds and died, some with cigars between their teeth, some with pieces of food in their fingers, and one at least—a pale young German from Pennsylvania—with a miniature of his sister in his hands. . . . As . . . I groped through this tempest of death for . . . shelter . . . an old man, a private in a company belonging to the 24th Michigan, was struck, scarcely ten feet away, by a cannonball which tore through him, extorting such a low, intense cry of mortal pain as I pray God I may never again hear.

The start of the cannonade found correspondent Samuel Wilkeson, of the New York Tribune, *along with other newsmen and a number of staff officers, behind the lines seeking relief from the July sun "in the shadow cast by the tiny farmhouse . . . which General Meade had made his headquarters."*

Every size and form of shell known to British and to American gunnery shrieked, whirled, moaned, whistled, and wrathfully fluttered over our ground. . . . They burst in the yard—burst next to the fence on both sides, garnished as usual with the hitched horses of aides and orderlies. The fastened animals reared and plunged with terror. Then one fell, then another. . . . Through the midst of the storm . . . an ambulance, driven by its frenzied conductor at full speed, presented to all of us the marvellous spectacle of a horse going rapidly on three legs. A hinder one had been shot off at the hock.

The farmhouse took several hits, and General Meade "found it necessary temporarily to abandon the place."

Warren Goss was among the Federals who were hugging the ground in the front lines. He and his comrades "were sheltered behind a stone wall surmounted by a post and rail fence which was struck, splintered, and crushed."

Right, left, and rear of us, caissons were exploded; scudding fragments of wheels, woodwork, shell and shot [were] sent a hundred feet into the air, like the eruption of a volcano. . . . When a caisson was exploded, yells of exultation were heard along the whole rebel lines. . . .

If a constellation of meteoric worlds had exploded above our heads, it would have scarcely been more terrible than this iron rain of death. . . . Over all these sounds were heard the shrieks and groans of the wounded and dying. . . .

Cemetery Hill and Ridge were ploughed and furrowed. . . .

The flowers in bloom upon the graves at the Cemetery were shot away. Tombs and monuments were knocked to pieces, and ordinary gravestones shattered in rows.

By this time, of course, the Federals were returning the fire. To the Confederates it seemed that the whole of Cemetery Ridge was ablaze with muzzle blasts. Writes Lieutenant G. W. Finley, of Lee's infantry:

. . . the most terrific cannonade any of us had ever experienced was kept up, and it seemed as if neither man nor horse could possibly live under it. Our gunners stood to their pieces and handled them with such splendid courage as to wake the admiration of the infantry crouching on the ground behind them. . . . Our loss was considerable under this storm of shot and shell. Still there was no demoralization of our men in line. They waited almost impatiently for the order to advance, as almost anything would be a relief from the strain upon them.

"Before the cannonade opened," says Confederate artilleryman Alexander,

I had made up my mind to give Pickett the order to advance within fifteen or twenty minutes after it began. But when I looked at the full development of the enemy's batteries, and knew that his infantry was generally protected from our fire by stone walls and swells of the ground, I could not bring myself to give the word. It seemed madness to launch infantry into that fire, with nearly three-quarters of a mile to go at midday under a July sun.

I let the 15 minutes pass, and 20, and 25, hoping vainly for something to turn up. Then I wrote to Pickett: "If you are coming [forward] at all you must come at once, or I cannot give you proper support; but the enemy's fire has not slackened at all; at least eighteen guns are still firing from the cemetery itself."

Five minutes after sending that message, the enemy's fire suddenly began to slacken, and the guns in the cemetery limbered up and vacated the position. We Confederates often did such things as that to save our ammunition for use against infantry, but I had never before seen the Federals withdraw their guns simply to save them up for the infantry fight. So I said, "If he does not run fresh batteries in there in five minutes, this is our fight."

I looked anxiously with my glass, and the five minutes passed without a sign of life on the deserted position, still swept by our fire, and littered with dead men and horses and fragments of disabled carriages. Then I wrote Pickett urgently: "For God's sake, come quick. The eighteen guns are gone; come quick, or my ammunition won't let me support you properly."

When Alexander's first note reached him, Pickett had just finished writing a letter to his sweetheart, his Sally "of the sunset eyes," a letter he intended to give to Longstreet to mail, in case he was killed. He was, indeed, standing with Longstreet when the courier came up. In a subsequent letter to Sally, Pickett says that he read the note, then handed it to Longstreet and asked if he should obey its summons:

He looked at me for a moment, then held out his hand. Presently clasping his other hand over mine without speaking, he bowed his head upon his breast. I shall never forget the look in his face nor the clasp of his hand when I said: "Then, General, I shall lead my division on." I had ridden only a few paces when I remembered your letter and . . . scribbled in a corner of the envelope, "If Old Peter's nod means death, then good-by and God bless you, little one," turned back and asked the dear old chief if he would be good enough to mail it for me. . . . I saw tears glistening on his cheeks and beard. The stern old war-horse, God bless him, was weeping for his men. . . .

Again in Alexander's words:

. . . Pickett's division swept out of the wood and showed the full length of its gray ranks and shining bayonets—as grand a sight as ever a man looked on. Joining it on the left, Pettigrew [i.e., Heth's division under a substitute commander, Heth having been wounded] stretched farther than I could see.

Additional troops were forming in the rear. All told, the assault force and its reserves probably numbered nearly 15,000 men. The move from the wood had carried the advance units through the long line of artillery pieces. As the attack began to swing forward, covering a front two-thirds of a mile wide, the Federals on the ridge across the valley raised the cry, "Here they come! Here comes the infantry!"

Relates Confederate Lieutenant Finley:

. . . the fatal field was before us. Where I marched, through a wheatfield that sloped gently toward the Emmitsburg road, the position of the Federals flashed into view. Skirmishers lined the fences along the road, and back of them, along a low stone wall or fence, gleamed the muskets of the first line. . . . As we came in sight, there seemed to be a restlessness and excitement along the enemy's lines, which encouraged some of us to hope they would not make a stubborn resistance. Their skirmishers began to run in. . . .

Longstreet's artillery chief turned to a new task:

. . . I rode down the line of guns, selecting such as had enough ammunition to follow Pickett's advance, and starting them after him as fast as possible. . . . Meanwhile, the infantry had no sooner debouched on the plain than all the enemy's line [of artillery], which had been nearly silent, broke out again. . . . The eighteen guns were back in the cemetery, and a storm of shell began bursting over and among our infantry. All of our guns—silent as the infantry passed between them—reopened over their heads when the lines had got a couple of hundred yards away. . . .

But as our supporting guns advanced, we passed many poor, mangled victims [of the Federal artillery fire]. . . . I remember one with the most horrible wound that I ever saw. We were halted for a moment by a fence, and as the men threw it down for the guns to pass, I saw in one of the corners a man sitting down and looking up at me. A solid shot had carried away both jaws and his tongue. I noticed the powder smut from the shot on the white skin around the wound. He sat up and looked at me steadily, and I looked at him until the guns could pass; but nothing, of course, could be done for him.

Union observer Warren Goss says that the Confederates

. . . came on in magnificent order, with the step of men who believed themselves invincible. . . . A light wind sprang up, and the smoke of their guns drifted over the valley towards the cemetery. For a moment it threatened to obscure the charging columns from the sight of those who were about to encounter them in the grapple of death. . . . It was but for a moment. The smoke drifted lazily away to the westward, revealing to us the gray lines steadily advancing. . . .

Solid shot ploughs huge lanes in their close columns. As the enemy approach still nearer, shells burst upon their compact masses. Their shattered lines do not waver, but steadily closing up the gaps of death, come on in magnificent order. With banners waving, with steady step, they sweep on like an irresistible wave of fate. . . .

The Union soldiers on Cemetery Ridge clutch their muskets. . . . On each face rests grim resolve and the nervous pallor of suspense. . . . On come the rebel lines with bayonets glistening. . . . Now the Union guns open with canister at close range upon this line of human targets. . . . As they come on, they leave behind them a trail of dead and dying, like a swath from the scythe of a mower.

Now they are at . . . musket range, and from behind the stone wall a wave of flame, perceivable even in this noonday light, springs from the muzzles of the line of Union muskets. Volley after volley is poured in with deadly effect upon them.

By this time, two regiments of Vermonters who occupied Cemetery Ridge to the left of the zone under assault had swung down the slope and were firing through the growing pall of smoke and dust into Pickett's right flank. At the same time Pettigrew (supported by two brigades under Isaac Trimble), advancing abreast of Pickett's left, was being punished in a similar way by some Ohio troops on his left flank. The fire on the attack force as a whole was coming from three directions.

Confederate Lieutenant Finley depicts the moment:

Men were falling all around us, and cannon and muskets were raining death upon us. Still, on and up the slope toward that stone fence our men steadily swept, without a sound or a shot, save as the men would clamor to be allowed to return the fire that was being poured into them.

This clamor was interpreted by some of the Federals as a collective cry of despair. A true moan from many throats was "distinctly to be heard amid the storm of battle" toward the assault's left, where artillery bursts caused "arms, heads, blankets, guns, and knapsacks" to be tossed into the air.

The smoke and dust had thickened, and the Confederates were mere gray shadows. But now, says Warren Goss:

They return our fire and rush upon the wall. As they are about to close in upon us they are met by a volley. On they come. . . . The shock is terrible, and its full strength falls upon [General Alexander S.] Webb's brigade. Our men are shot with the rebel muskets touching their breasts. A fierce encounter now takes place. Great God! The line at the stone wall gives way!

George E. Pickett.

Federals firing from stone wall as Pickett charges.

The Confederates reached the line at one spot only, at a small clump of trees they had been using as a landmark. Just behind the Union front at this spot was a young staff officer, Frank Aretas Haskell, who was appalled to see some of Webb's men retreating toward him:

My sword that had always hung idle by my side, the sign of rank only, in every battle, I drew, bright and gleaming, the symbol of command. . . . [A]s I met the tide of those rabbits, the damned red flags of the rebellion began to thicken and flaunt along the wall. . . . I ordered those men to halt and face about and fire, and they heard my voice and gathered my meaning and obeyed my commands. On some unpatriotic backs, of those not quick of comprehension, the flat of my sabre fell, not lightly; and at its touch their love of country returned, and with a look at me as if I were the destroying angel, as I might have become theirs, they again faced the enemy.

At the same time, as Northerner Goss explains,

The heroic rebel, General [Lewis A.] Armistead, determined to conquer or die, waving his hat on the point of his sword, jumps the wall, followed by his men, rushes forward and seizes a Union battery. Troops are now rushing in upon them from every side. . . . Armistead falls mortally wounded among the artillery he has captured. . . .

Near him lies our young and heroic [Lieutenant Alonzo H.] Cushing, who, while mortally wounded, has fired his only serviceable gun, exclaiming, "Webb, I will give them one more shot!"

. . . Groups of Federals are surrounded by Confederates—Confederates surrounded by Federals. Shots, shrieks, imprecations, shouts and yells; fierce calls for surrender, with defiant answers; all mingle together in a devilish uproar of sounds. Men fight with clubbed muskets, rifles, pistols, bayonets, and color staffs.

General Hancock, in top command at the critical spot, was shot from his horse at this time. Though the wound was severe (his thigh had been deeply punctured), he remained on the field. Hancock and the Confederate General Armistead had been friends before the war. Armistead died requesting that Hancock be given his personal effects for delivery to his family.

Along its entire front, the great Confederate effort was now spent. No matter that two fresh brigades were coming across from Lee's lines; they would accomplish nothing. No matter that Jeb Stuart (finally back with Lee) had been sent around behind the Union army to cooperate with the assault; Stuart was even then commencing a clash with Meade's cavalry that he would not win—thanks in part to a daring young Federal officer named George Armstrong Custer.

Union newsman Charles Coffin describes the final moments of Pickett's attack:

The lines waver. The soldiers of the front rank look round for their supports. They are gone—fleeing over the field, broken, shattered, thrown into confusion by the remorseless fire. . . . The lines have disappeared like a straw in a candle's flame. The ground is thick with dead, and the wounded are like the withered leaves of autumn. Thousands of Rebels throw down their arms and give themselves up as prisoners. How inspiring the moment! How thrilling the hour! It is the high-water mark of the Rebellion—a turning point of history and of human destiny!

To the Union soldiers on the ridge, it was simply a great success— something they were unaccustomed to. According to Jesse Young:

Cheer after cheer rose from the triumphant boys in blue, echoing from Round Top, reechoing from Cemetery Hill, resounding in the vale below, and making the very heavens throb. . . .

Of the original number of Confederates (approximated at close to 15,000), perhaps half made the retreat. Pickett himself escaped unhurt; Pettigrew was wounded; Trimble was wounded and captured.

Writes General Longstreet:

As they came back, I fully expected to see Meade ride to the front and lead his forces to a tremendous countercharge. . . . The Federals were advancing a line of skirmishers which I thought was the advance of their charge. As soon as the line of skirmishers came within reach of our guns, the batteries opened again and their fire seemed to check at once the threatened advance. After keeping it up a few minutes the line of skirmishers disappeared, and my mind was relieved of the apprehension that Meade was going to follow us.

General Lee came up as our troops were falling back and encouraged them as well as he could; begged them to re-form their ranks and reorganize their forces, and assisted the staff officers in bringing them all together again. It was then he used the expression that has been mentioned so often: "It was all my fault; get together, and let us do the best we can toward saving that which is left us."

As our troops were driven back from the general assault, an attack was made on my extreme right by several squadrons of cavalry, which succeeded in breaking through our line of pickets. They were met by a counter-move . . . and driven back. . . .

"The battle was now over," says Northerner Jesse Young, "but nobody knew it." He goes on:

. . . thousands of men were lying unattended, scattered over the field, mingled with broken gun carriages, exploded caissons, hundreds of dead and dying horses, and other ghastly debris of the battlefield. At once the poor victims of shot and shell nearest our lines were brought in; others farther out were in due time reached. . . .

It was possible, as night came on, to make a bit of a fire here and there in the rear and boil water for a cup of coffee, which was a boon to be grateful for. While the boys sat or lay on the ground, eating a bite of hard-tack, and eagerly, in their hunger, devouring the succulent salt pork, which was about the only nourishment to be secured, relays of men with stretchers, and hundreds of others helping the wounded to walk to the rear, passed . . . with their bloody freight, now and then a groan or a suppressed shriek telling the story of suffering and heroic fortitude.

"Listen, boys!" was the shout of one of [the] men, as they lay on the ground. . . . "The fight must be over. Listen! There is a band in the rear beginning to tune up. . . ."

It was a sight and a situation long to be remembered. The field was covered with the slain; the full moon looked down with . . . softened luster on the field . . . trodden down for miles by the two great armies; surgeons were cutting off limbs, administering whisky, chloroform, and morphine to deaden pain; hundreds of men were going back and forth . . . [taking] to the rear . . . the mangled bodies of the wounded; and . . . the survivors . . . in the two armies were waiting to see what would come on the morrow—when suddenly a band of music began to play in the rear of the Union line of battle, down somewhere on the Taneytown road. . . .

Down the valley, and up the hill, and over the field, into the ears of wounded and dying men, and beyond our line into the bivouac of the beaten enemy, the . . . tune was borne on the evening breezes. . . . "Home—Sweet, Sweet Home" was the tender air. . . .

Among the Confederates, there was deep dejection over Pickett's repulse. That night even General Lee, well known for his equanimity, was heard to lament, "Too bad! Too bad! Oh, too bad!"

An artilleryman from Louisiana, Napier Bartlett, says that many of the men, afraid for their dream of liberty, were moved to tears. However, he adds,

. . . when we were permitted at length to lie down under the caissons, or in the fence corners, and realized that we had escaped the death that had snatched away so many others, we felt too well satisfied at our good fortune—in spite of the enemy still near us—not to sleep the soundest sleep it is permitted on earth for mortals to enjoy.

Returning to the Union lines and Jesse Young:

The next morning was the Fourth of July, but it seemed at the time to those who were at Gettysburg a somber and terrible national anniversary, with the indescribable horrors of the field, as yet hardly mitigated by the work of mercy, before the eye in every direction. The army did not know the extent of the victory; the nation did not realize as yet what had been done. The armies were still watching each other, although the Confederates had withdrawn from the town of Gettysburg and concentrated their troops on Seminary Ridge.

The people in the village came out of their cellars and other places of refuge, and as the day broke upon them opened their doors. They had been under a reign of terror [though only one citizen, a young woman named Jennie Wade, had been killed—a stray bullet having entered the kitchen of her home]. . . . Now, as they came out of doors, they cherished new hopes, for they could see no rebel soldiers. . . . It is almost daybreak, and some of the citizens venture to stand out on the pavements to watch for the development of events. . . .

They see a squad of men coming toward them down the main street . . . bearing a banner. It is too dark at first to tell whether they wear the blue or the gray. . . . The watchers hold their breath in suspense, until in a moment the dawning light reveals to their longing eyes the glorious flag which the advancing troops are carrying, the Stars and Stripes, torn with the marks of battle, stained with blood, but wreathed and crowned with victory. . . .

But . . . among the troops themselves, that Fourth of July, 1863 . . . was a wretched, dismal, and foreboding day, a day of uncertainty and suspense for both armies, which still faced each other. Each . . . was watching to find out what the other would do. Neither Meade nor Lee, just at that time, was anxious to bring about a renewal of the fight, and the time was occupied in caring for the wounded and burying the dead.

On the Confederate side, some of the dead had been lying unburied since the first day's fighting (the army being too shorthanded under the press of events to spare a sufficiency of burial parties). The morning of the Fourth found artilleryman Robert Stiles and his unit shifted to one of the worst parts of the field:

. . . the dead bodies of men and horses had lain there putrefying under the summer sun for three days. The sights and smells that assailed us were simply indescribable—corpses swollen to twice their original size, some of them actually burst asunder with the pressure of foul gases and vapors. I recall . . . the shocking distension and protrusion of the eyeballs of dead men and dead horses. Several human or inhuman corpses sat upright against a fence, with arms extended in the air and faces hideous with something very like a fixed leer, as if taking a fiendish pleasure in showing us what we essentially were and might at any moment become.

Again in Northerner Young's words:

A heavy rainstorm set in about noon, which made the roads and fields in the course of a few hours a sea of mud. . . . When the day was over, the soldiers, anxiously and in discomfort, lay . . . on the soaking earth, trying almost in vain to keep up the smoldering fire at their bivouacs. And then, when the night had gone and Sunday morning arrived, July 5, there was news indeed. Before daylight the rumors spread far and wide, and they were verified by [orders for the] advance of the skirmish lines all along our front—"The rebels have retreated back toward the Cumberland Valley!"

Southern artilleryman E. Porter Alexander says that the retreat, during which the army was short of horses (so many having been killed in the battle) and was encumbered by thousands of wounded men, was made "in a pouring rain and over roads that were almost gulfs of mud." He adds:

Providence had evidently not yet taken a "proper view of the situation." We had not finished the war, but had to go back to Virginia and start afresh.

Casualty totals for the three days of fighting were appalling. The vanquished army lost about 20,000 in killed, wounded, captured, and missing; the victors lost even more—about 23,000.

General Meade was satisfied with what had been accomplished. Though the Confederate army was still intact, he believed that the

Battle of Gettysburg was (as Northern newspapers proclaimed) "A Great and Glorious Victory for the Potomac Army." President Lincoln, however, felt strongly that the victory should be followed by an all-out effort to destroy Lee's army as it retreated. When Meade announced that his aim was merely "to drive from our soil every vestige of the presence of the invader," Lincoln cried, "My God, is that all?"

That was indeed all. Meade followed Lee cautiously, well aware that the Army of Northern Virginia was a highly dangerous instrument even when its edges were blunted; and the Confederates crossed the Potomac safely on the night of July 13.

Lincoln soon softened toward Meade, grateful after all that Lee's alarming invasion of the North had been turned back. But later the President told Meade somewhat ruefully that his pursuit of the Confederates reminded him ever so much of "an old woman trying to shoo her geese across a creek."

18

THE SIEGE
OF VICKSBURG

THE SELFSAME DAYS *of July, 1863, that saw the war in the East reach a climax at Gettysburg saw a climax of similar consequence in the war's Western theater. Since the preceding December, General Grant, as commander of the Army of the Tennessee, had been actively occupied with efforts against Vicksburg, Mississippi, the last great river port in Confederate hands. Its capture would lead quickly to Federal control of the full length of the river, which would split the Confederacy in two, denying the East the cattle, grain, and other supplies it needed from the West, which embraced Texas, Arkansas, and the greater part of Louisiana. At the same time, the Federals would gain a convenient highway for further operations. Winning the Mississippi was the chief goal of the Union forces in the West.*

Grant's earliest move had been to send the wing of his army commanded by W. T. Sherman down the river from Memphis in boats while he himself led an overland expedition toward Vicksburg's rear. The venture failed, with Sherman being brought up short before the Confederate defenses at Chickasaw Bluffs, just north of the objective, and with Grant being stopped, far to the northeast, through the disruption of his supply lines by Confederate cavalry units, some of them under General Nathan Bedford Forrest, whose raids and other exploits were fast making him famous.

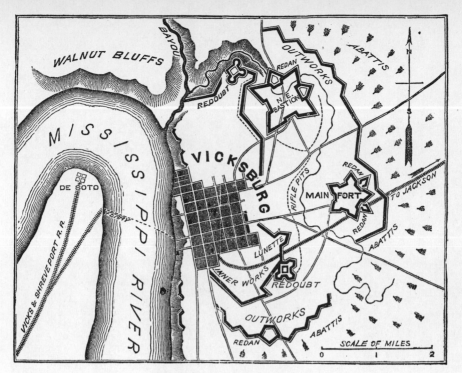

Vicksburg and its defenses.

By the end of January, 1863, Grant was operating from the Mississippi at Young's Point, about ten miles upstream from Vicksburg. The general had the aid of a strong fleet, well equipped with iron-clad gunboats, under Admiral David Dixon Porter (son of the daring and colorful Commodore David Porter, hero of the War of 1812).

Located on a set of bluffs on the Mississippi's eastern bank, Vicksburg was nearly impregnable. It discouraged all Federal thoughts of assaulting it frontally (from the river), and its northern flank was protected by a great area of wet bottomland.

The Federals failed not only in their attempts to get through the flanking swamps but also to bypass the city through similar bottomland across the river, on the western, or Louisiana shore. The Louisiana efforts involved the laborious digging of canals for Porter's vessels, the idea being to get them, along with the troops, safely around Vicksburg's guns and into a position where the city might be approached from the south. One by one, the various ventures had to be abandoned.

In Grant's words:

The long, dreary, and—for heavy and continuous rains and high

David D. Porter.

water—unprecedented winter was one of great hardship to all engaged about Vicksburg. . . . Troops could scarcely find dry ground on which to pitch their tents. Malarial fevers broke out among the men. Measles and smallpox also attacked them. . . . Visitors to the camps went home with dismal stories to relate. . . . Because I would not divulge my ultimate plans to visitors, they pronounced me idle, incompetent, and unfit to command men in an emergency, and clamored for my removal. . . . I took no steps to answer these complaints, but continued to do my duty, as I understood it, to the best of my ability. . . . With all the pressure brought to bear upon them, both President Lincoln and General Halleck stood by me. . . . I had never met Mr. Lincoln, but his support was constant.

Lincoln had actually become a shade unsure of Grant but continued to be impressed by his quiet, unremitting resolve. It was at this time (according to Albert D. Richardson, of the New York Tribune) *that the Lincoln anecdote about Grant's drinking was born. When one of Grant's detractors complained that Grant drank too much whisky, Lincoln replied, "Ah, yes. . . . By the way, can you tell me where he gets his whisky? He has given us . . . successes . . . and if his whisky does it, I should like to send a barrel of the same brand to every general in the field."*

On March 20, General Halleck said in a dispatch to Grant:

The eyes and hopes of the whole country are now directed to your army. In my opinion, the opening of the Mississippi River will be to us of more advantage than the capture of forty Richmonds.

By this time Grant, in cooperation with Admiral Porter, had devised a plan aimed at breaking the long and frustrating deadlock. It was a plan of great daring, one viewed with heavy misgivings by many of Grant's subordinates. Even the aggressive Sherman, who had become Grant's right-hand man, considered the operation a dangerous gamble.

Grant's army was to pick its way through the swamps on the western side of the river to a point well below the city (with Sherman's corps staying behind temporarily to demonstrate north of the city and confuse the enemy). Porter was to take the fleet directly past Vicksburg's batteries in the night. The fleet would include three river steamers manned by army volunteers and carrying supplies—the supplies being vital, for Grant would be cutting himself off for a

*time from all connection with his northern depots. Once the army
and the navy were reunited down the river, the army would be ferried across for a campaign around Vicksburg's rear.*

Grant explains:

Admiral Porter proceeded with the preparation of the steamers
for their hazardous passage of the enemy's batteries. The great essential was to protect the boilers from the enemy's shot, and to conceal
the fires under the boilers from view. This he accomplished by loading the steamers . . . with bales of hay and cotton . . . adding
sacks of grain. . . . Before this I had been collecting, from St. Louis
and Chicago, yawls and barges to be used as ferries when we got below. By the 16th of April Porter was ready to start on his perilous
trip.

*Confederate officer S. H. Lockett, chief engineer of Vicksburg's de-
fenses, was later to write: "Gunboats had frequently passed the batteries during the operations of the preceding ten months, but up to
that time no one had dreamed that the ordinary river steamboats
could do so."*

*The evening of the sixteenth saw a clear and beautiful sunset and
a bright emergence of the stars. Though a slight haze settled over the
Mississippi, visibility remained good. Spectators from the Federal
camps gathered in boats along the Louisiana side of the river, well
below the fleet's rendezvous area but safely out of range of the Vicksburg batteries. Says a correspondent for the New York* Times:

There were in all perhaps thirty boats . . . each of which was
black with spectators, of whom not a few were ladies. These, and the
stars, were the witnesses. . . . I am bound to say that the stars were
the more serious and quiet portion of the gathering. The balance
passed the hours of waiting in jokes, laughter, choruses, and love-
making—which, together with a running fusilade of champagne
corks, indicated anything but an appreciation of the fact that the
drama about to open was a tragedy instead of a roaring farce.

Lights twinkled busily from the Vicksburg hillsides until about
ten o'clock, when they disappeared. And about the same moment
song and laughter on our side were hushed, as a shapeless mass of
what looked like a great fragment of darkness was discerned floating
noiselessly down the river. It was the *Benton* [Admiral Porter's flag-
ship]. It passed and disappeared in the night, and was succeeded by
another bank of darkness—the *Lafayette* [a second gunboat, with a
small wooden naval steamer and a coal barge lashed, for their pro-

S. H. Lockett.

Confederate batteries engaging Porter's fleet.

tection, to its side—the one away from the enemy]. . . . Ten . . .
noiseless shapes [including the three river steamers serving as trans-
ports] revealed themselves and disappeared, and then we knew that
all the actors in the play had given us the first scene of the first act.

According to Vicksburg engineer S. H. Lockett:
   The movement of the boats was soon discovered by the Confederate pickets who nightly patrolled the river in small boats. They

immediately crossed the river and fired several houses in the village of DeSoto, so as to illuminate the river.

A Confederate signal rocket had already alerted the batteries of Vicksburg and also of Warrenton, a few miles below. The upper batteries roared into action.

Writes Federal newsman Albert Richardson:

. . . the Mississippi bank was ablaze. Our ironclads promptly replied with their heaviest guns, while the transports, hugging the Louisiana shore, ran by as fast as possible. The . . . burned houses [made] the night as light as day. Again and again the transports were struck . . . but the men stood gallantly at their posts. . . .

"The sight," says General Grant, "was magnificent but terrible. I witnessed it from the deck of a river transport run out into the middle of the river and as low down as it was prudent to go."

Grant's wife and children were with him on the transport. Writes an aide to the general, James Harrison Wilson: "One of the Grant children sat on my knees with its arms around my neck, and as each crash came, it nervously clasped me closer, and finally became so frightened that it was put to bed."

Frederick Dent Grant, twelve years old at the time, later recalled: "On board our boat, my father and I stood side by side on the hurricane deck. He was quietly smoking, but an intense light shone in his eyes."

The people of Vicksburg, both soldiers and civilians, had swarmed out into the streets. In the firelight, they could be seen running about, some of them shouting and gesticulating "as if they were mad." Among the civilians were ladies in their most fashionable evening attire, for a grand spring ball had been interrupted. Shrieks rang out when sections of masonry crumbled under the impact of Federal shells. Galloping horses pulled fieldpieces into position alongside the heavy guns already lining the river's bank, and bodies of infantry ran to the wharves to harry the fleet with small-arms fire.

In the words of an unnamed officer of the Federal gunboat Lafayette:

. . . a perfect tornado of shot and shell continued to shriek over our deck and among all the vessels of the fleet . . . but not more than one in ten struck or did any damage. . . . They mostly went over. On running out [our] guns, a good view could be had, through the ports, of the rebel batteries, which now flashed like a thunderstorm along the river as far as the eye could see.

But the incessant spatter of rifle balls, the spray from falling shot, the thunder of steel-pointed projectiles upon our sides, did not incline one to take a very protracted view of the scenery.

A few discharges of grape, shrapnel, and percussion shell was all we could afford at the time to bestow upon our rebel friends in exchange for their compliments. At each round the Confederate artillerymen gave a shout, which seemed surprisingly near. At one time we could not have been one hundred yards from the Vicksburg wharves.

Our vessel, with the steamer and barge lashed to our starboard side, became almost unmanageable, drifted in the eddy and turned her head square round, looking the batteries in the face. At this time we seemed to be receiving their concentrated fire at less than a hundred yards from the shore. The smoke from our own and the rebel guns, with the glare of the burning buildings from the opposite shore, rendered it difficult for the pilots to make out the direction we were going.

The enemy, supposing we were disabled, set up a fiendish yell of triumph. We soon, however, backed round and once more presented our broadside to them, and slowly drifted past, as if in contempt of their impotent efforts. Shells burst all around the pilot house, and at one time John Denning, our pilot, was literally baptized with fire. He thought himself killed, but he brushed the fire from his head and found he was unhurt.

Writes a third newspaper correspondent who was among the Federal spectators:

After an interval of maddest rage, the upper guns of the enemy almost cease their fire. It is evident our boats have passed the first-reached batteries. . . . That no large portion of them is missing is evident from the activity of the forts at Warrenton and the answering thunders of our own guns. . . .

Just as the . . . longer and longer intervals of silence gave intimation that the exciting scene was nearly over . . . a new glow of light . . . climbed gently toward the sky.

"They are lighting another beacon!" shouted many voices.

But . . . the speakers were mistaken. The light . . . with slow and equal pace, was moving onward, passing down the stream! There was no disguising the truth—one of our own boats was on fire!

. . . The boat that burned was the transport *Henry Clay*. Her crew got safely to shore. She was set on fire by a shell exploding among the cotton with which her engines were protected. She was loaded principally with commissary stores and forage, including a large amount of soldiers' rations and oats for the cavalry.

About two and a half hours after the action began, the last Federal vessel passed out of range down the river. All gunfire ceased, the excitement in Vicksburg diminished, darkness returned to the river as the beacon fires died to embers, and the frogs in the marshes resumed their spring trillings.

The Union gamble had paid off. Marvels newsman Albert Richardson:

On the gunboats not a man was killed, and only eight were wounded. On the steamers and barges nobody was even hit. Before daylight the entire fleet, save the ill-fated *Henry Clay,* was received at New Carthage by Grant's infantry with shouts of delight.

To the soldiers who had run the steamers on this daring race, the general promptly gave furloughs for forty days and transportation to and from home.

A second midnight expedition of six transports and twelve barges passed the batteries six days later, with the loss of one steamer and six barges sunk, one man killed and half a dozen wounded.

The Confederates, according to S. H. Lockett, now turned an anxious watch on New Carthage:

Here there was a fleet of formidable gunboats, and transports and barges enough to ferry a large force across the river. This gave a serious and threatening aspect to the movement.

Grant's command at this time numbered between 40,000 and 50,000 men. Confederate General John C. Pemberton, in charge of the defense of Vicksburg, had an army of similar size, but it wasn't concentrated. Some of the units were manning posts to the north; others were scattered along the river to the south; and still others were many miles to the east.

The Confederates could not be sure of Grant's intentions. Not only had Sherman tarried to demonstrate north of the city, but Union cavalry commander Benjamin H. Grierson had undertaken a raid from the Tennessee border down through Mississippi and into

Louisiana. Grierson was highly successful in alarming the Confederates and diverting attention from Grant.

The Federal army began crossing the Mississippi, about fifty miles downriver from Vicksburg, on April 30. Grant now launched a lightning campaign against Pemberton's scattered and confused forces. In two and a half weeks the Confederates were beaten five times—in the battles of Port Gibson, Raymond, Jackson, Champion's Hill, and Big Black River. The last battle was only ten miles east of Vicksburg, on the eastern bank of the Big Black. The Confederates were routed; they fled across the river, some by bridge and some by swimming.

Confederate officer S. H. Lockett was on the scene:

The affair of Big Black bridge was one which an ex-Confederate participant naturally dislikes to record. . . . After the stampede . . . orders were issued for the army to fall back to Vicksburg. . . . General Pemberton rode on himself. . . . I was the only staff officer with him. He was very much depressed . . . and for some time . . . rode in silence. He finally said:

"Just thirty years ago I began my military career by receiving my appointment to a cadetship at the U.S. Military Academy; and to-day—the same date—that career is ended in disaster and disgrace."

I strove to encourage him, urging that things were not so bad as they seemed to be; that we still had two excellent divisions . . . which had not been engaged and . . . could occupy our lines at Vicksburg . . . ; that Vicksburg was strong and could not be carried by assault; and that Mr. Davis had telegraphed to him "to hold Vicksburg at all hazard," adding that "if besieged he would be relieved." To all of which General Pemberton replied that my youth and hopes were the parents of my judgment. . . .

It was Sunday, May 17. That afternoon the defeated troops poured into Vicksburg. Among those watching was an unknown diarist, a "young lady of New Orleans":

I shall never forget that woeful sight . . . humanity in the last throes of endurance. Wan, hollow-eyed, ragged, footsore, bloody—the men limped along, unarmed but followed by siege guns, ambulances, gun-carriages, and wagons in aimless confusion. At twilight two or three bands on the courthouse hill and other points began playing "Dixie," "Bonnie Blue Flag," and so on; and drums began to beat all about; I suppose they were rallying the scattered army.

Adds another eyewitness—no admirer of General Pemberton:

Many of the troops declared their willingness to desert rather than serve under him again. The stillness of the Sabbath night was broken in upon, and an uproar in which the blasphemous oaths of the soldier and the cry of the child, mingled, formed a scene which the pen cannot depict. . . .

There were many gentlewomen and tender children torn from their homes by the advance of a ruthless foe, and compelled to fly to our lines for protection; and mixed up with them in one vast crowd were the gallant men who had left Vicksburg three short weeks before, in all the pride and confidence of a just cause, and returning to it a demoralized mob. . . .

General Grant, as Southerner S. H. Lockett explains, wasn't far behind:

Early on May 18th the Federal forces appeared. . . . The next day . . . they came forward rapidly . . . with shout and cheer, and soon after rushed upon the main line of defense. . . . But . . . they were compelled to fall back. A second time they came forward in greater numbers and with more boldness and determination, but with even more fatal results. They were repulsed with great loss. . . . These assaults . . . were met by troops which had not been in any of the recent disastrous engagements, and were not in the least demoralized. These men . . . helped to restore the morale of our army.

The 20th and 21st of May were occupied by the Federal forces in completing their line, at an average distance of about eight hundred yards from our works. . . . On the 22d of May the gunboats [on the Mississippi] moved up within range and opened fire upon the river front. At the same time several dense columns of troops assaulted our lines in the rear. . . . Once, twice, three times they came forward and recoiled from the deadly fire poured upon them by the Confederates, who were now thoroughly restored to their old-time confidence. . . . Every assault was repulsed with terrible loss to the attacking parties. . . .

On the 25th the Federal dead and some of their wounded . . . were still in our front and close to our lines. The dead had become offensive and the living were suffering fearful agonies. General Pemberton, therefore, under a flag of truce, sent a note to General Grant proposing a cessation of hostilities for two and a half hours, so that the dead and dying men might receive proper attention. This was acceded to by General Grant, and from six o'clock until nearly dark both parties were engaged in performing funeral rites and deeds of mercy to the dead and wounded Federal soldiers. . . .

The truce ended, the sharpshooters immediately began their work and kept it up until darkness prevented accuracy of aim. Then the pickets of the two armies were posted in front of their respective lines, so near to each other that they whiled away the long hours of the night-watch with social chat. . . .

The events of the 27th of May were varied by an attack on our river batteries by the fleet.

The battery that was attacked by the Union gunboat Cincinnati *responded with a vengeance. According to a writer for the fleet's small newspaper (published on board Admiral Porter's flagship):*

Said battery . . . sent some ugly customers after our gunboat, which vessel retired on finding the place too hot for her, having first received three or four shots in her bottom [and others elsewhere]. Not wishing to be [further] annoyed by the enemy, she wisely sunk in three fathoms of water . . . when the officers and crew coolly went in to bathe.

About fifteen men were drowned. Prior to this, about twenty-five had been killed or wounded.

By this time General Grant had given up the idea of trying to take Vicksburg by assault:

I . . . determined upon a regular siege. . . . [O]fficers and men . . . went to work on the defences and approaches with a will. With the navy holding the river, the investment of Vicksburg was complete. . . . [T]he enemy was limited in supplies of food, men, and munitions of war. . . . These could not last. . . .

My line was more than fifteen miles long, extending from Haines' Bluff [in the north] to Vicksburg, thence to Warrenton. The line of the enemy was about seven. In addition to this, having an enemy at Canton and Jackson, in our rear, who was being constantly reinforced, we required a second line of defence facing the other way. I had not troops enough. . . . General Halleck [in Washington] appreciated the situation and, without being asked, forwarded reinforcements with all possible dispatch. . . .

The enemy's line of defence followed the crest of a ridge from the river north of the city eastward, then southerly around to the Jackson road, full three miles back of the city, thence in a southwesterly direction to the river. Deep ravines . . . lay in front of these defences. . . . [T]he line was necessarily very irregular. . . .

The work to be done, to make our position as strong against the enemy as his was against us, was very great. . . . We had no siege guns except six thirty-two pounders. . . . Admiral Porter, however, supplied us with a battery of navy guns of large calibre, and with these, and the field-artillery used in the campaign, the siege began. . . .

The enemy did not harass us much while we were constructing our batteries. Probably their artillery ammunition was short; and their infantry was kept down by our sharpshooters, who were always on the alert and ready to fire at a head whenever it showed itself above the rebel works. . . .

The labor of building the batteries and intrenching was largely done by the pioneers, assisted by Negroes who came within our lines and who were paid for their work; but details from the troops had often to be made. The work was pushed forward as rapidly as possible, and when an advanced position was secured and covered from the fire of the enemy, the batteries were advanced.

The Federals shelled not only the Confederate lines but the city itself. Writes a resident named Edward S. Gregory:

Even the fire on the lines was not confined to them in its effects, for hardly any part of the city was outside the range of the enemy's artillery. . . . Just across the Mississippi . . . mortars were put in position and trained directly on the homes of the people. . . . Twenty-four hours of each day these preachers of the Union made their touching remarks to the town. All night long their deadly hail of iron dropped through roofs and tore up the deserted and denuded streets. . . .

. . . the women and children of Vicksburg took calmly and bravely the iron storm. . . . [T]he ordinary atmosphere of life, the course of conversation, the thread of every human existence took in . . . the momently contingency of these messengers of thunder and murder. . . . How many of them came and burst, nobody can have the least idea. . . . They became at last such an ordinary occurrence of daily life that I have seen ladies walk quietly along the streets while the shells burst above them, their heads protected meanwhile by a parasol held between them and the sun. . . .

Vicksburg hangs on the side of a hill whose name is poetical—the

Sky Parlor. . . . Its soil was light and friable, and yet sufficiently stiff to answer the purpose of excavation. Wherever the passage of a street left the face of the hill exposed, into it and under it the people burrowed, making long ranges and systems of chambers and arches within which the women and young took shelter. In them all the offices of life had to be discharged, except that generally the cooking stove stood near the entrance, opportunity to perform upon it being seized and improved during the shells' diversions in other quarters. Sometimes the caves were strengthened by pillars and wooden joists, and beds and furniture were crowded in them. . . . It was rather a point of honor among men not to hide in these places, which were reserved for the women and children.

New caves kept appearing. "Negroes who understood their business," *explains the wife of a Confederate officer, "hired themselves out to* *dig them, at from thirty to fifty dollars, according to the size."*

Though vulnerable to the heavier shells, the caves at least shielded *their occupants from the fragments of the lighter ones. It was diffi-* *cult, however, to keep the children inside. News of two misfortunes* *among the young reached the officer's wife in the course of one day:* *"A fragment had . . . struck and broken the arm of a little boy* *playing near the mouth of his mother's cave." And, more tragically:*

A young girl, becoming weary in the confinement of the cave, hastily ran to the house in the interval that elapsed between the slowly falling shells. On returning, an explosion sounded near her. One wild scream, and she ran into her mother's presence, sinking

Cave life at Vicksburg.

like a wounded dove, the life-blood flowing over the light summer dress in crimson ripples from a death-wound in her side. . . .

Some of Vicksburg's residents remained in their houses, taking to their cellars when the shells came close. In this group was the "young lady of New Orleans," who recorded in her diary:

We are utterly cut off from the world, surrounded by a circle of fire. . . . The fiery shower of shells goes on day and night. . . . People do nothing but eat what they can get, sleep when they can, and dodge the shells. . . . Clothing cannot be washed, or anything else done. . . .

I think all the dogs and cats must be killed or starved. We don't see any more pitiful animals prowling around. . . .

The cellar is so damp and musty the bedding has to be carried out and laid in the sun every day. . . . The confinement is dreadful. . . . I don't know what others do, but we read when I am not scribbling in this. H. [the narrator's husband] borrowed somewhere a lot of Dickens's novels, and we reread them by the dim light in the cellar.

When the shelling abates, H. goes to walk about a little or get the "Daily Citizen," which is still issuing a tiny sheet at twenty-five and fifty cents a copy. It is, of course, but a rehash of speculations which amuses a half hour.

Today [May 28] he heard while out that expert swimmers are crossing the Mississippi on logs at night to bring and carry news. . . .

I am so tired of corn-bread, which I never liked, that I eat it with tears in my eyes. We are lucky to get a quart of milk daily from a family near who have a cow they hourly expect to be killed. I send five dollars to market each morning, and it buys a small piece of mule meat. Rice and milk is my main food; I can't eat the mule meat. We boil the rice and eat it cold with milk for supper. Martha [a Negro servant] runs the gauntlet to buy the meat and milk once a day in perfect terror.

The shells seem to have many different names. I hear the soldiers say, "That's a mortar shell. There goes a Parrott. That's a rifle shell." They are all equally terrible.

A pair of chimney-swallows have built in the parlor chimney. The concussion of the house often sends down parts of their nest, which they patiently pick up and reascend with. . . .

It is our custom in the evening to sit in the front room a little while in the dark . . . and watch the shells, whose course at night is shown by the fuse. [On June 5] H. was at the window and suddenly sprang up, crying, "Run!" . . . I started through the back room, H. after me. I was just within the door when the crash came that threw me to the floor. It was the most appalling sensation I'd ever known. . . . Shaken and deafened, I picked myself up. H. had struck a light to find me. I lighted mine. . . . The candles were useless in the dense smoke, and it was many minutes before we could see. Then we found the entire side of the room torn out. . . .

There is one thing I feel especially grateful for, that amid these horrors we have been spared that of suffering for water. The weather has been dry a long time, and we hear of others dipping up the water from ditches and mud-holes. This place has two large underground cisterns of good cool water, and every night in my subterranean dressing-room a tub of cold water is the nerve-calmer that sends me to sleep in spite of the roar.

One cistern I had to give up to the soldiers, who swarm about like hungry animals seeking something to devour. Poor fellows! My heart bleeds for them. They have nothing but spoiled, greasy bacon, and bread made of musty pea-flour, and but little of that. The sick ones can't bolt it. They come into the kitchen when Martha puts the pan of corn-bread in the stove, and beg for the bowl she mixes it in. They shake up the scrapings with water, put in their bacon, and boil the mixture into a kind of soup, which is easier to swallow than pea-bread. When I happen in, they look so ashamed of their poor clothes. I know we saved the lives of two by giving a few meals. . . .

The churches are a great resort for those who own no caves. People fancy they are not shelled so much, and they are substantial, and the pews good to sleep in.

This period of the siege saw a night fire, the work of arsonists, in the city's business district. The perpetrators were persons angered by merchants engaged in profiteering. Citizen Edward Gregory says that the blaze swept out of control:
There was nothing to do except to remove the articles of value from the houses within its range. A great crowd collected, notwithstanding the concentration of the mortar fire; and yet there were no remembered casualties. The whole block was burned, of course; and the wonder is, only one.

"A state of siege," Gregory asserts elsewhere in his narrative,
fulfils . . . all that is involved in the suspension of civilization.

Its influences survive; its appliances vanish. . . . Home was a den shared with others, perhaps with strangers. . . . That people had to wait on themselves was a matter of course. . . .

In this state of suspended animation, it is really wonderful how people continued to drag out their endurance from one hopeless day to another. Perhaps the very vigilance they had to exercise against the shells . . . kept the besieged alive. Every day, too, somebody would start or speed a new story of deliverance [by an army] from without that stirred up, although for a fitful season only, the hearts bowed down by deep despair. Now it was E. Kirby Smith, and now Joe Johnston, who was at the gates.

The faith that something would and *must* be done to save the city was desperately clung to. . . . It probably never had deep roots in the reason of the generals, the men in the lines, or the people. But at such times men do not reason. . . . Powerless to resist the tide of events, their only refuge is in the indulgence of a desperate hope, whose alternative is despair and madness.

Actually, for a time Vicksburg's hope was not altogether a vain one. Joe Johnston, who had gathered a small army east of the Big Black River, considered several plans for rescuing the situation. About June 20 General Grant received information that led him to believe that Johnston was preparing to attack him from the rear:

I immediately ordered Sherman to the command of all the forces [stretching] from Haines' Bluff to the Big Black River. This amounted . . . to quite half the troops about Vicksburg. . . . We were now looking west, besieging Pemberton, while we were also looking east to defend ourselves against an expected siege by Johnston. But . . . we were strongly fortified. . . . Johnston evidently took in the situation, and wisely, I think, abstained from making an assault on us because it would simply have inflicted loss on both sides without accomplishing any result.

In the meantime, Grant adds, "the work of . . . pushing forward our position nearer to the enemy had been steadily progressing." At one spot the Federals succeeded in undermining the Confederate works in preparation to laying an explosive charge. Grant goes on:

The enemy had countermined, but did not succeed in reaching our mine. . . . Our sap [i.e., mining trench] ran close up to the outside of the enemy's parapet. . . . The soldiers of the two sides occasionally conversed pleasantly across this barrier. Sometimes they exchanged the hard bread of the Union soldiers for the tobacco of the Confederates. At other times the enemy threw over hand grenades, and often our men, catching them in their hands, returned them.

The story of the mine is taken up by a Union correspondent, James C. Fitzpatrick, writing on June 25:

This morning the work was completed, an immense quantity of gunpowder was stored in the cavity prepared to receive it, and the fuse train was laid. At noon the different regiments . . . selected to make the assault upon the breach when it should have been effected, were marshalled in long lines upon the near slopes of the hills immediately confronting the doomed rebel fortifications. . . . The rebels seemed to discover that some movement was on foot, for . . . their sharpshooters kept up an incessant fire from the whole line of their works.

At length all was in readiness; the fuse train was fired, and it went fizzing and popping through the zigzag line of trenches until . . . it vanished. Its disappearance was quickly succeeded by the explosion. . . . So terrible a spectacle is seldom witnessed. Dust, dirt, smoke, gabions, stockades, timber, gun-carriages, logs—in fact, everything connected with the fort—rose hundreds of feet into the air, as if vomited forth from a volcano. Some who were close spectators even say that they saw bodies of the poor wretches who a moment before had lined the ramparts of the work.

Grant interjects:

I remember one colored man . . . who was thrown to our side. He was not much hurt, but terribly frightened. Someone asked him how high he had gone up.

"Dunno, massa, but t'ink 'bout t'ree mile," was his reply.

According to Charles E. Hooker, a Confederate officer: "Six men of the Forty-third Mississippi, engaged in countermining at the time of the explosion, were buried alive."

Immediately after the explosion, Hooker goes on to explain,

. . . a terrible outburst of cannon and musketry opened from the Federal lines, and a charging column entered the crater. But they got no farther, for the Confederates were ready and opened such a withering fire that it was instant death for one of the enemy to show his head. Not only that, but shells were lighted [at their fuses] and thrown over the parapet to explode among the Federals, causing a terrible loss of life.

Grant's men were unable to get more than a temporary hold on the crater, and their plans to do further digging against the enemy in this area had to be abandoned. But the game of mining and counter-mining was to be continued elsewhere.

The Negro who had landed in the Federal lines was taken to the headquarters of Union General John A. Logan, where he became a paid servant. To those who questioned him about his experience, he said that "somethin' busted" and blew him out of the Confederacy "plumb into de Union."

During the flurry of action that followed the explosion of the mine, the bombardment of the city had continued. That evening the "young lady of New Orleans" penned in her diary:

A horrible day. . . . We were all in the cellar when a shell came tearing through the roof, burst upstairs, tore up that room; and, the pieces coming through both floors down into the cellar, one of them tore open the leg of H.'s pantaloons. . . . On the heels of this came Mr. J. to tell us that young Mrs. P. had had her thighbone crushed. When Martha went for the milk, she came back horror-stricken to tell us the black girl there had her arm taken off by a shell.

For the first time I quailed. . . . I said to H., "You must get me out of this horrible place. I cannot stay. I know I shall be crippled."

Now the regret comes that I lost control, because H. is worried and has lost his composure because my coolness has broken down.

Morale in Vicksburg's defenses was also failing, but for a different reason. Says Confederate officer Charles Hooker:

On the 28th Pemberton received a communication signed "Many soldiers," containing these words: "Our rations have been cut down to one biscuit and a small bit of bacon per day, not enough scarcely to keep soul and body together, much less to stand the hardships we are called upon to stand. If you can't feed us, you had better surrender us, horrible as the idea is. . . . This army is now ripe to mutiny unless it can be fed."

The Federal newsmen were now calling the capture of Vicksburg "a foregone conclusion." Wrote Charles H. Farrell to the New York Herald:

A few days ago a rebel mail was captured coming out from Vicksburg, in which were letters from prominent men in the rebel army who state that they cannot hold out much longer. . . . So far as the siege of this place goes, I presume the people at home, in their easy chairs, think it ought to have been finished long since. To such let me say, could they be present here . . . and see the configuration of the country, its broken topography, its high and abrupt hills, deep gullies, gorges, and dilapidated roads, they would then realize the difficulties of the work. Then there is a large army to feed, great *matériel* to be brought into position, all of which demands large transportation and the united efforts of thousands of men.

General Grant acts independently of opinions of the public. He fully realizes the responsibility of his position and . . . he is determined to accomplish his work with as great an economy of human life as possible. He feels now that the prize is within his grasp. . . .

The Vicksburg Daily Citizen, *now printed on wallpaper, reported on July 2:*

The great Ulysses—the Yankee generalissimo surnamed Grant—has expressed his intention of dining in Vicksburg on . . . the Fourth of July. . . . Ulysses must get into the city before he dines in it. The way to cook a rabbit is "first catch the rabbit."

Elsewhere, the newspaper vouched for the palatability of mule steak and stewed cat.

That night Confederate commander Pemberton called a council of war. As recorded by S. H. Lockett:

We had been from the beginning short of ammunition. . . . We were short of provisions. . . . We were so shorthanded that no man within the lines had ever been off duty more than a small part of each day. . . . Our lines were badly battered, many of our guns were dismounted, and the Federal forces were within less than a minute of our defenses, so that a single dash could have precipitated them upon us in overwhelming numbers.

All of these facts were brought out in the council of war. . . . General Pemberton said he had lost all hopes of being relieved by General Johnston. . . . He then asked each officer present to give his vote on the question, *surrender or not?* Beginning with the junior officer present, all voted to surrender but two. . . .

General Pemberton said, "Well, gentlemen, I have heard your votes and I agree with your almost unanimous decision, though my own preference would be to put myself at the head of my troops and make a desperate effort to cut our way through the enemy. . . . Far better would it be for me to die at the head of my army, even in a vain effort to force the enemy's lines, than to surrender it and live and meet the obloquy which I know will be heaped upon me. But my duty is to sacrifice myself to save the army which has so nobly done its duty to defend Vicksburg. I therefore concur with you and shall offer to surrender. . . ."

According to the "young lady of New Orleans," the next day (July 3) began dismally for the people in the city:

Today we are down in the cellar again, shells flying as thick as ever; provisions so nearly gone, except [a] hogshead of sugar, that a few more days will bring us to starvation indeed. Martha says rats are hanging dressed in the market for sale with mule meat. There is nothing else.

In the lines, the negotiations for Vicksburg's surrender had begun. The forty-day siege was ending—on the same day, coincidentally, that Lee sent Pickett against Cemetery Ridge and lost the Battle of Gettysburg.

The morning of July 4 found General Grant at his headquarters awaiting General Pemberton's final acknowledgment of the surrender terms. Wrote a newsman who paid Grant a visit:

I . . . found everybody about his headquarters in a state of the liveliest satisfaction. . . . The General I found in conversation more animated than I have ever known him. He is evidently contented with the manner in which he has acquitted himself of the responsible task which has for more than five months engrossed his mind and his army. The consummation is one of which he may well be proud.

The Confederates laid down their arms that afternoon. Grant's men watched the procedure without cheering.

Vicksburg's citizens, deeply relieved that the ordeal was over at last, swarmed out of their caves and cellars and walked the streets in the sunshine. The "young lady of New Orleans" paid a visit to the waterfront:

Truly it was a fine spectacle to see the fleet of [Union] transports sweep around the curve and anchor in the teeth of the batteries lately vomiting fire. Presently Mr. J. passed us: "Aren't you coming? There's provisions on those boats—coffee and flour."

Arrival of Union fleet after Vicksburg's surrender.

. . . The townfolk continued to dash through the streets with their arms full, canned goods predominating. Towards five, Mr. J. passed again. "Keep on the lookout," he said, "the army of occupation is coming." And in a few minutes the head of the column appeared.

What a contrast to the suffering creatures we had seen were these stalwart, well-fed men, so splendidly set up and accoutred! Sleek horses, polished arms, bright plumes—this was the pride and panoply of war. Civilization, discipline, and order seemed to enter with the measured tramp of those marching columns; and the heart turns with throbs of added pity to the worn men in gray who were being blindly dashed against this embodiment of modern power.

Says Confederate officer S. H. Lockett:
A few minutes after the Federal soldiers marched in, the soldiers of the two armies were fraternizing and swapping yarns over the incidents of the long siege. . . . [A] hearty cheer was given by one Federal division "for the gallant defenders of Vicksburg!"

"I myself," writes Grant, "saw our men taking bread from their haversacks and giving it to the enemy they had so recently been engaged in starving out."
A few of the more mischievous Yankees went to the office of the

Daily Citizen and arranged for the last issue printed on wallpaper to carry the announcement that Grant had "caught the rabbit."

Grant rode down to the river to exchange congratulations with Admiral Porter on their joint victory. The general then returned to his headquarters outside the city and sent an aide to the nearest telegraph office with a report for Washington.

Grant wrote later:

This news, with the victory at Gettysburg won the same day, lifted a great load of anxiety from the minds of the President, his Cabinet, and the loyal people all over the North.

Port Hudson, Louisiana, a smaller post about 150 miles farther down the river, was still in Confederate hands, but only for the moment; as a result of Vicksburg's fall, it capitulated to another Federal force on July 8. Except for mopping-up operations, this concluded the long campaign for the Mississippi.

"The Father of Waters," said Lincoln, "again goes unvexed to the sea."

As for Grant, he considered the fate of the Confederacy sealed.

19

CHICKAMAUGA
AND CHATTANOOGA

IT WAS NOT REALLY CERTAIN *in July, 1863, that the Southern cause was lost. The Confederates clung to the hope that if they prolonged their resistance the North might yet grow utterly sick of the war and free them to end it. Only two weeks after Gettysburg and Vicksburg the South's morale was raised by news from the North that a new draft law had resulted in a series of riots.*

But the eastern half of the Confederacy—its heartland—was now virtually surrounded by Union land and naval forces. Control of the Mississippi extended to its mouth on the Gulf Coast; there the blockade took up, running eastward through the Gulf and then northward along the Atlantic Coast to Virginia (the blockade being augmented by several beachheads on Confederate soil); Union armies were strung in a southwesterly direction through Virginia, Tennessee, and Mississippi to the river, completing the encirclement.

The half of the Confederacy west of the river—Texas, Arkansas, and the greater part of Louisiana—had, from the beginning, seen its own share of military activity, and the strife would continue; but the eastern arena was ever the more vital one.

It was time for Northern strategists to turn their attention to Alabama, Georgia, and the Carolinas. Chattanooga, Tennessee, lying just north of the Georgia border and called the "Gateway to the Deep

South," became the next prime objective. Here were located gaps in the Cumberland Mountains formed by the meandering Tennessee River. The town itself, though it showed a population of only 2,545 in the census of 1860, was a major railroad center.

After his victory at Murfreesboro, Tennessee, at the very beginning of 1863, Union General William Rosecrans held his Army of the Cumberland at that place for nearly six months. Confederate General Braxton Bragg's Army of Tennessee was deployed some miles to the south, its chief object being to cover Chattanooga.

In late June—even as the Vicksburg campaign was being concluded—Rosecrans began moving southward. Bragg, flanked out of his position, fell back toward Chattanooga. But Rosecrans failed to keep up his pressure, stopping just south of Tullahoma to make additional preparations for the campaign. For one thing, he wanted to wait for Tennessee's corn crop to ripen so that his rations would be ample.

He began to move again in mid-August. At the same time, the Union Army of the Ohio, under Ambrose Burnside, launched a campaign against Knoxville, in eastern Tennessee. This effort would aid Rosecrans by impeding Bragg's communications with the East and enhancing his own.

The showdown between Rosecrans and Bragg finally came in mid-September. They had been maneuvering energetically for some days, Bragg having been forced to abandon Chattanooga and Rosecrans having established a headquarters there. The two armies at last deployed along the line of the Chickamauga Creek, south of Chattanooga and the Georgia border. The Federals held the position nearer the coveted town. Skirmishing occurred on September 18 as the two sides completed their dispositions. Bragg had just received some welcome reinforcements from the East—elements of Longstreet's corps. Longstreet himself was nearing the field with additional units. On the eve of the battle, each side had in the neighborhood of 60,000 men.

Relates Union Private Arthur van Lisle:

That night we threw out a heavy skirmish line, then ate our hardtack, drank our black coffee, and lay down to rest. We were very much worn with the heavy marching for several days and the . . . [skirmishing] of that afternoon, so we slept quite soundly . . . every man with his rifle at his side, which, in a half-conscious mechanical way, he would transfer to the other side as he rolled over in his sleep.

There was no sounding of the reveille the next morning, that

Federal troops on the march against Bragg.

memorable Saturday, September 19th, but every man was astir at the first dawning, still weary, stiff in every joint, bones aching, muscles sore. A pint of strong black coffee, however, relaxes the system, and soon we feel somewhat refreshed. An occasional shot is heard here and there, on the right or the left. But no one regards that, although we are expecting every moment either to be attacked or to make the attack ourselves. We are formed into line and rest at ease, but ready.

The Confederates, too, are stirring. . . . They advance upon us. . . . We are eager, anxious witnesses of this grand, warlike spectacle . . . and cannot restrain our admiration . . . yet we know too well what their approach portends. Involuntarily we seize our rifles and examine them critically to see that all is in order; we place our hands upon the cartridge-boxes to assure ourselves that they are un-fastened and well filled; we thrust thumb and forefinger into our cap-pouches to ascertain their condition, for no less depends upon these items than upon our courage. But all the while our eyes are intently fixed upon the advancing foe. . . .

On they come, that long gray line, so long that the flanks extend beyond our vision. Steady is their step and perfect their alignment, save here and there as they meet an obstruction in the way of a farm-house or a fence. There is heard to the right and left some irregular firing and occasional cannon shot, and then for a moment a crash and rumbling like the thunders rolling from cloud to cloud. In our immediate front, however, all is quiet. It is that dread silence that precedes the approaching storm.

On it comes, and now a general shout breaks forth. It is the rebel yell, "Hey—Yeh—Yeh! Hey—Yeh—Yeh!" They have started on the double-quick toward us. . . . We have witnessed similar demonstrations before and have withstood them. We only clutch our rifles more firmly and brace ourselves to receive the shock. . . . Suddenly they halt. They are probably eighty rods distant . . . and before they have time to adjust themselves in position, or bring their guns from a right-shoulder-shift, we are given the command, "Ready! Aim! Fire!"

A sheet of flame issues from our ranks; a cloud of smoke fills the air and obscures our vision. We reload and await results as we watch the vapor rising from the ground. We see a flash, as of sheet-lightning; we hear the report; we see our comrades falling, some never to rise again, some mortally wounded, weltering in blood, others crippled and writhing in agony.

Now "forward" is the order, and we advance on the enemy, leaving our stricken comrades behind us where they have fallen. The battle is on in earnest. We do not see the enemy's lines, for they are hidden by the intervening cloud of smoke; but we know where they are, and we keep up an incessant fire as we steadily but cautiously move on. The enemy, too, maintains his fire, pouring into our ranks a regular shower of lead.

All is turmoil and confusion. Artillery in our rear is firing over our heads into the enemy beyond. A battery pushes up to our line shotted with grape and canister, which it pours into the enemy before us. But our ranks are growing thin; our losses are frightful. It is becoming evident that the "Johnnies" are too many for us. We are without doubt doing terrible execution among them; but we certainly cannot long endure their murderous fire, which is sweeping along our lines and mowing down our men like grass. Our condition is desperate, our position untenable. We are forced to retire—only temporarily, we hope, for surely reinforcements will come to our aid.

I fall. I try to rise, but cannot. . . . My thigh is torn, the bone is shattered, although I did not feel the shot that struck me. Here I lie among the dead and wounded. Our men have fallen back. Over our prostrate forms the bullets are hissing and shells shrieking. In the endeavor to ease my cramped position my wounded limb becomes twisted; and, oh, the agony of pain which I now feel for the first time! What horror surrounds me! Here I am, helpless and bleeding, my flesh lacerated, my thigh-bone broken; the dead so ghastly, the dying and the wounded all about me; my regiment falling back, the enemy advancing. What will become of me?

. . . The rattle of rifles and the roar of artillery are simply awful. No sounds . . . can bear comparison to this deafening, deadly, rattling, crashing, roaring, thundering noise, which fills the heavens and shakes the earth.

Now the enemy falls back. Our boys are coming. Thank God—I shall be rescued! But . . . I am growing weak, oh so weak; my tongue is dry, my lips are parched. I cannot move my body, but with an effort I turn my head to see if my comrades are really coming. Oh, how I long for their presence; for I am so thirsty, and they will give me drink and carry me to a place of safety in the rear.

But, better than all this, the battle is not lost, for the troops in gray are still falling back, and our own boys are still advancing. I see the flag. . . . My eyes are riveted to that glorious old banner. . . . Will it recover its lost ground and save the boys who fell where it first advanced? Will it ever reach me?

. . . The battle . . . rages furiously, and the horrors which environ me are being enacted all over that bloody field for miles around. . . . Now there ensues a temporary lull in this pandemonium. . . . The end is not yet. The enemy open fire with even greater fury than before, and again take the offensive. . . . Our boys cannot withstand their withering fire and desperate onslaught, and are compelled to fall back to escape complete annihilation.

Backward and forward surge the contending lines; and now—oh, my God!—the enemy comes with a wild rush and that ominous, terrifying rebel yell. They are passing over me, stumbling over our dead and wounded, falling among us, passing on. We are left behind, and the moans and groans of Union and Confederate wounded mingle in the smoke-stifling air, while many a poor fellow's agony is ended by stray shots which strike in our midst.

Can I survive this awful anguish? Must I die here, to be laid in an unknown grave by the hands of the enemy? How long must I endure this torture of mind and body?

. . . The day is waning. What a terrible day it has been! Night approaches. What horrors will it bring forth? Surely if my comrades cannot help me I must die; and I must die here, with no friend to soothe my last moments or tell the story of my death to the loved ones at home. I am growing weaker and weaker from the loss of blood, which is now drying upon my body and stiffening my clothing. Fever is in my veins, and I am perishing from thirst. Oh for a drink! *Water, water,* WATER!

Again the firing slackens. . . . Have my comrades, my regiment, my brigade, been driven from the field? And what of our army?

. . . there comes a sudden crash of artillery. The fight is renewed; and here comes back [in retreat] the line of gray with its thinned and thinning ranks, trampling upon the dead and the wounded as they retire, for they keep their faces to the front. They are falling thick and fast, some of them upon our dead, and some upon their own. . . .

It was during this repulse . . . that a Confederate soldier, standing over me, bravely fighting, seeing my bloody side and parched lips, stooped down and, throwing the strap of his canteen over his head, put the nozzle to my mouth, saying as he did so, "Drink, Yank. I reckon you're powerful dry."

I drank, and never did Ganymede serve the gods with nectar more delicious or refreshing.

Meanwhile the shower of shot and shell and hissing balls from our front was frightful, and the brave Confederates were forced still farther back, and my benefactor with them, while I still held his old cedar canteen to my lips, draining its contents. . . . I offered to return it, feebly raising the canteen above my head with outstretched arm.

"Jest you keep it," I heard him shout back as he retired, loading his gun.

I never saw that noble, tender-hearted Confederate soldier again; but . . . the water from that old cedar canteen refreshed and revived me so that I survived . . . and . . . was rescued by my comrades. . . .

This is the way one man saw Chickamauga's first day, and his account epitomizes that part of the battle. It was costly and prolonged, with the lines swaying back and forth, and with the issue unsettled at sundown.

A Union staff officer, J. S. Fullerton, takes up the narrative:

On the evening of the 19th every indication pointed to a renewal of the battle early the next day. The night was cold for that time of

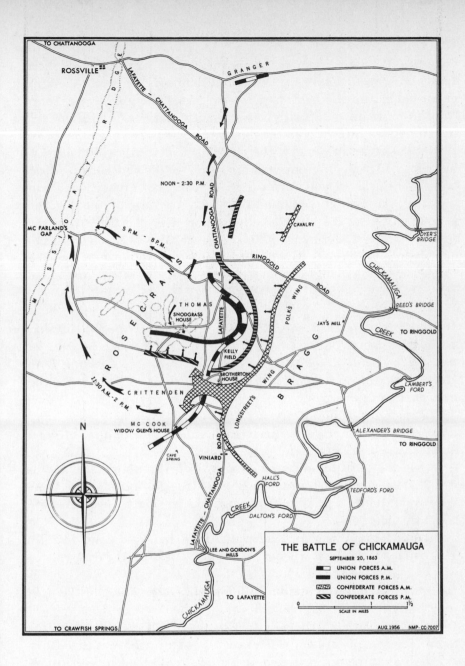

TO CHATTANOOGA

ROSSVILLE

GRANGER

LAFAYETTE - CHATTANOOGA ROAD

MISSIONARY RIDGE

NOON - 2:30 P.M.

MC FARLAND'S GAP

5 P.M. - 8 P.M.

CAVALRY

DYER'S BRIDGE

CHICKAMAUGA

RINGGOLD

ROSECRANS

THOMAS
SNODGRASS HOUSE

POLK'S WING ROAD

REED'S BRIDGE

CREEK TO RINGGOLD

JAY'S MILL

KELLY FIELD

LAMBERT'S FORD

BROTHERTON HOUSE

11:30 A.M. - 2 P.M.

CRITTENDEN

BRAGG

WING

LONGSTREET'S

LAFAYETTE - CHATTANOOGA ROAD

MC COOK
WIDOW GLEN'S HOUSE

ALEXANDER'S BRIDGE

TO RINGGOLD

CAVE SPRING

VINIARD

HALL'S FORD

TEDFORD'S FORD

N

CREEK

DALTON'S FORD

THE BATTLE OF CHICKAMAUGA

SEPTEMBER 20, 1863

UNION FORCES A.M.

UNION FORCES P.M.

CONFEDERATE FORCES A.M.

CONFEDERATE FORCES P.M.

0   1   1½

SCALE IN MILES

LAFAYETTE - CHATTANOOGA ROAD

LEE AND GORDON'S MILLS

TO LAFAYETTE

CHICKAMAUGA

AUG. 1956   NMP- CC-7007

TO CRAWFISH SPRINGS

the year. Tell-tale fires were prohibited. The men slept on their arms. All was quiet save in the field hospitals in the rear. A bright moon lighted up the fields and woods. Along the greater part of a front of eight miles [actually, according to maps, six miles or less] the ground was strewn with the intermingled dead of friend and foe.

The morning of Sunday, the 20th, opened with a cloudless sky, but a fog had come up from the warm water of the Chickamauga and hung over the battlefield until 9 o'clock. A silence of desertion was in the front. This quiet continued till nearly 10 o'clock. Then, as the peaceful tones of the church bells, rolling over the land from the east, reached the meridian of Chickamauga, they were made dissonant by the murderous roar of the artillery of Bishop Polk [on the Confederate right] who was opening the battle on [General George H.] Thomas's front [the Union left].

On the Confederate left, morale was high as the fight began. General Longstreet, Lee's "old war horse," fresh from the East, was on that part of the field. Among the officers with him was General John Hood, who wore a crippled arm in a sling, the result of the wound he took at Gettysburg.

Confederate Major William Miller Owen, who had been transferred west from Lee's army at an earlier date, said in a set of notes he made during the battle:

I had the pleasure of shaking hands with [Longstreet] as he was riding along the line this morning. . . . It is glorious to have these fellows out here. It recalls our old fights. I feel certain we will have a victory today.

10:45—Heavy firing on the right. Polk has . . . gone in. . . . He commands the right wing of the army; Longstreet the left.

Interposes Confederate Colonel William C. Oates, lately of the fight for Little Round Top at Gettysburg:

. . . the battle raged with varying success, Polk wholly failing to drive his enemy as had been expected. The reason was that Rosecrans, finding the attack aimed at his left, reinforced it with troops drawn from his right and center. Longstreet discovered this, and about 11 o'clock . . . ordered his entire wing forward. The first line . . . halted before the Union line. . . . The Union troops were behind the trunks of trees felled the night previous, and kept up a lively fire.

Again in Major Owen's words:

Our division, in advancing [to the front], passes the spot where Gen. Bragg is seated upon his horse. . . . He looks pale and careworn. . . .

The enemy seems to be fighting in detached bodies. Longstreet discovers, with his soldier's eye, a gap in their already confused lines. . . . The men rush over the hastily constructed breastworks . . . with the old-time familiar rebel yell; and, wheeling then to the right [toward Thomas's flank], the column sweeps the enemy before it, and pushes along the Chattanooga road towards Missionary Ridge in pursuit. It is glorious!

. . . Those troops of the enemy who were on Longstreet's left when he broke through the lines [the total making up a good part of the Union right] are falling back to positions of greater safety. . . .

Longstreet's work along the Chattanooga road is described by Confederate General D. H. Hill:

I have never seen the Federal dead lie so thickly on the ground, save in front of the sunken wall at Fredericksburg. But that indomitable Virginia soldier, George H. Thomas [who had remained loyal to the Union] was there . . . confronting . . . the forces of [Braxton Bragg,] his friend and captain in the Mexican War. Thomas . . . chose a strong position on a spur of Missionary Ridge. . . . Well and nobly did . . . his gallant troops hold their own. . . .

Some of the severest fighting had yet to be done after 3 P.M. . . . [T]he Federals were in the hands of the indomitable Thomas, and the Confederates were under their two heroic wing commanders, Longstreet and Polk.

In the lull of the strife I went . . . to examine the ground on our left. One of . . . [our] wounded men . . . was lying alone in the woods, his head partly supported by a tree. He was shockingly injured. He belonged to [Colonel Leon] von Zinken's regiment, of New Orleans, composed of French, Germans, and Irish.

I said to him, "My poor fellow, you are badly hurt. What regiment do you belong to?"

He replied, "The Fifth Confederit, and a dommed good regiment it is!"

The answer . . . touched me as illustrating the *esprit de corps* of the soldier—his pride in, and his affection for his command.

Colonel Von Zinken told me afterward that one of his desper-

Confederates at Chickamauga.

ately wounded Irishmen cried out to his comrades, "Charge them, boys! They have cha-ase (cheese) in their haversacks!"

On another part of the field, Confederate officer William Oates came upon "a boy . . . about fifteen years old . . . lagging in the rear and crying."

I spoke to him and told him not to cry; that he had not yet been hurt and he might live through the battle, and not to be so unmanly as to become frightened and go to crying. He replied, "Afraid, hell! That ain't it. I am so damned tired I can't keep up with my company."

On the Union side, a very young soldier made a name for himself that afternoon. He was Johnnie Clem, of Newark, Ohio. A Federal nurse who knew him, Mrs. Annie Wittenmyer, says that he was "a fair and beautiful child . . . about twelve years old, but very small of his age; he was . . . only about thirty inches high and weighed about sixty pounds." Johnnie was a veteran of several battles, and his hat had acquired three bullet holes. He seems to have carried a musket that had been sawed off to match his size. As Mrs. Wittenmyer tells it:

. . . [His] brigade . . . being partly surrounded by rebels, was retreating, when he, being unable to fall back as fast as the rest of the line, was singled out by a rebel colonel who rode up to him with the summons, "Scoundrel, halt! Surrender, you damned little Yankee!"

Johnnie halted and brought his gun into position as though he was about to surrender, thus throwing the colonel off his guard. In another moment the gun was cocked, fired, and the colonel fell dead from his horse.

His regiment was pursued, and a volley was fired at that moment, and Johnnie fell as though he had been killed, and lay there on the field until . . . [he was able] to slip away unnoticed.

And what of the Union army's top commander, General Rosecrans? At the time Longstreet broke through his lines to attack his left wing, he was with the right-wing troops. Federal staff officer Henry M. Cist says that Rosecrans, accompanied by James A. Garfield, his chief of staff (one day to be President of the United States), did everything he could to keep these men on the field:

But it was simply impossible to stem the tide. . . . He then concluded to go to Rossville [about four miles to the rear] and there determine whether to join Thomas on the battlefield or whether his duty called him [still farther rearward] to Chattanooga, to prepare for his broken army if his worst fears should be realized.

On reaching Rossville it was determined that Garfield should go to the front to Thomas . . . and that Rosecrans should go to Chattanooga and make the necessary dispositions for the troops as they came back in rout. . . .

While seated in the adjutant-general's office [in Chattanooga] . . . Rosecrans received a despatch from Garfield, who had reached the front. Hastily reading it over, he exclaimed, "Thank God!" and read the despatch aloud. In it Garfield announced . . . that he was then with Thomas, who had seven divisions intact with a number of detachments, that Thomas had just repulsed a heavy assault of the rebels, and felt confident that he could successfully resist all attacks against his position.

Waving this over his head, Rosecrans said, "This is good enough. The day isn't lost yet!"

. . . Thomas [had] . . . so to speak, placed himself with his back against a rock, and refused to be driven from the field. Here he stayed, despite the fierce and prolonged assaults of the enemy, repulsing every attack. And when the sun went down he was still there. Well was he called the "Rock of Chickamauga." . . .

At nightfall Thomas withdrew his troops to Rossville, and the two-day battle was over. Thomas's stand had saved the Union army, but the Confederates were left in full possession of the field. Casualties on both sides were staggering, the Federals losing about 16,000 and the Confederates about 18,000. General Hood, of the crippled arm, lost a leg; but after another period of recuperation his career as a field officer would continue. Among the Union dead was General William Haines Lytle, the poet, known best for his stanzas on the last moments of Mark Antony, beginning, "I am dying, Egypt, dying. . . ."

That night, says Southern staff officer J. Stoddard Johnston, "the Confederate army, worn down by long and arduous labors, with all commands mingled in promiscuous confusion, went to sleep on the battlefield, each where he found himself."

September 21 dawned, and the Confederates began to bury the dead and gather up the stores abandoned by the Federals. No pursuit was organized. According to Confederate General D. H. Hill, this was a great blunder: "A breathing-space was allowed [Rosecrans]; the panic among his troops subsided; and Chattanooga—the objective point of the campaign—was held."

But the Federals, all of whom were soon concentrated in and about the town, found their position one of hazard. Behind them was the Tennessee River, and before them was ground favorable to enemy occupation, including Lookout Mountain on their right and Missionary Ridge stretching diagonally (from southwest to northeast) across their front and past their left flank.

Writes Confederate Colonel Oates:

After Bragg had given Rosecrans two or three days to collect, reorganize, and reanimate his forces, strengthen and man his fortifications, he moved on Chattanooga, closed up about as close around as he could safely get, and went to digging and fortifying. . . . We were very scarce of rations, and for a day or two skirmished pretty lively with our Yankee neighbors over a cornfield to see who should have the most corn to parch. I believe we got the most.

Union General Phil Sheridan, still an infantry commander in the Army of the Cumberland, says further of the South's General Bragg:

He . . . began at once to erect permanent lines of earthworks on Missionary Ridge and to establish himself strongly on Lookout Mountain. He then sent Wheeler's cavalry north of the Tennessee, and, aided greatly by the configuration of the ground [about the town], held us in a state of partial siege. . . .

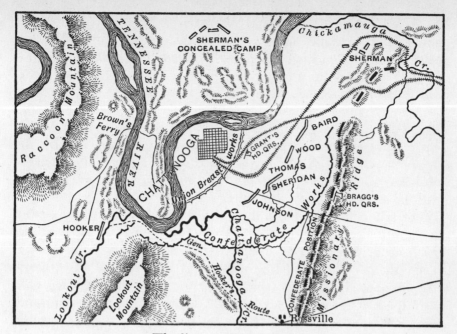

The lines at Chattanooga.

Relates W. F. G. Shanks, one of the Federal war correspondents in Chattanooga:

If there was little of beauty or elegance in the place when our troops retreated into it from Chickamauga, there was a great deal less a fortnight subsequently. . . . General Saint Clair Morton, the chief of Rosecrans's engineers, had no mercy. . . . Residences were turned into blockhouses; black bastions [i.e., projecting fortifications] sprang up in former vineyards; rifle pits were run through the graveyards; and soon a long line of works stretched from the river above to the river below the city, bending crescent-like around it. . . .

. . . the engineers alone did not despoil Chattanooga of its small modicum of beauty. The . . . quarters of the troops, composed of small dog-kennel-shaped huts, built of boards and roofed over with the shelter-tents with which the soldiers were provided, were scattered all over the town, in valley and on hillside. . . .

Life in Chattanooga . . . was dreary enough. . . . The enemy daily threw a few shells from the top of Lookout Mountain into our camps, but they were too wise to attack with infantry the works which . . . encircled the city.

Bragg preferred to rely for the final reduction of the garrison

upon his ally Famine—and a very formidable antagonist did our
men find him. . . . Bragg held the railroad line from Bridgeport
[a Union depot some twenty miles to the southwest] . . . thereby
. . . compelling [Rosecrans] to haul his provisions in wagon trains
. . . across the Cumberland Mountains.

*This roundabout route, more than sixty miles long, brought the
wagons to the bank of the Tennessee River opposite Chattanooga's
northwestern edge. They crossed over by pontoon bridge.*

    In the words of Union staff officer J. S. Fullerton:

The fall rains were beginning, and hauling was becoming each
day more difficult. Ten thousand dead mules walled the sides of the
road from Bridgeport to Chattanooga. In Chattanooga the men were
on less than half rations. Guards stood at the troughs of artillery
horses to keep the soldiers from taking the scant supply of corn allowed these starving animals. Many horses died of starvation, and
most of those that survived grew too weak for use in pulling the
lightest guns. Men followed the wagons as they came over the river,
picking up the grains of corn and bits of crackers that fell to the
ground.

Union correspondent Shanks explains that

The hundreds of citizens who were confined in the town . . .
suffered even more than the men. They were forced to huddle together in the centre of the town as best they could; and many of the
houses occupied by them during the siege surpassed in filth, point
of numbers of occupants, and general destitution, the worst tene-
ment-house in New York City.

*The Siege of Chattanooga had at least one very unusual aspect: Many
of the besiegers were as miserable as the besieged. Says Private Sam
Watkins, of the First Tennessee regiment:*

Our rations were cooked up by a special detail ten miles in the
rear and were sent to us every three days; and then those three days'
rations were generally eaten at one meal, and the soldiers had to
starve the other two days and a half. The soldiers were . . . almost
naked, and covered all over with vermin and camp-itch and filth and
dirt. The men looked sick, hollow-eyed, and heart-broken. . . .

    In the very acme of our privations and hunger, when the army
was most dissatisfied and unhappy, we were ordered into line . . .

to be reviewed by Honorable Jefferson Davis. When he passed us with his great retinue of staff-officers . . . at full gallop, cheers greeted him, with the words, "Send us something to eat, Massa Jeff. I'm hungry! I'm hungry!"

President Davis assured the men he had plans that would soon regain for them the bounty of the green fields of Tennessee. He also appealed to their patriotism, telling them they were fighting in the same kind of cause as their Revolutionary sires and that independence would be secured by "a vigorous, united, and persistent effort."

But in the present situation a major countereffort was being planned. Relates the Union's Phil Sheridan:

On October 16, 1863, General Grant . . . [was] assigned to the command of the "Military Division of the Mississippi," a geographical area which embraced the Departments of the Ohio, the Cumberland, and the Tennessee, thus effecting a consolidation of divided commands which might have been introduced most profitably at an earlier date. The same order that assigned General Grant relieved General Rosecrans, and placed General Thomas in command of the Army of the Cumberland.

At the time of the reception of the order, Rosecrans was busy with preparations for a movement to open the direct road to Bridgeport, having received . . . considerable reinforcements by the arrival in his department of the Eleventh and Twelfth corps, under General Hooker, from the Army of the Potomac. . . .

On the 19th of October, after turning the command over to Thomas, General Rosecrans quietly slipped away from the army. He submitted uncomplainingly to his removal, and modestly left us without fuss or demonstration—ever maintaining, though, that the Battle of Chickamauga was in effect a victory, as it had ensured us . . . the retention of Chattanooga. . . .

. . . the routine of fatigue duty and drills was continued as before, its monotony occasionally broken by the excitement of an expected attack, or by amusements of various kinds. . . . Mr. James E. Murdock, the actor . . . came down from the North to recover the body of his son, killed at Chickamauga, and . . . spent days, and even weeks, going about . . . giving recitations before the campfires and in improvised chapels which the men had constructed from refuse lumber and canvas. . . .

The pleasure he gave, and the confident feeling that was now arising from expected reinforcements, was darkened, however, by one sad incident. Three men of my division had deserted their colors at the beginning of the siege and made their way north. They were soon arrested and were brought back to stand trial for the worst offense that can be committed by a soldier, convicted of the crime, and ordered to be shot.

To make the example effective I paraded the whole division for the execution, and . . . in the presence of their former comrades the culprits were sent . . . to render their account to the Almighty. It was the saddest spectacle I ever witnessed; but there could be no evasion, no mitigation of the full letter of the law; its timely enforcement was but justice to the brave spirits who had yet to fight the rebellion to the end.

General Grant arrived at Chattanooga on October 23, and began at once to carry out the plans that had been formed for opening the shorter, or river road, to Bridgeport. This object was successfully accomplished by . . . Hooker's command . . . in concert with a force from the Army of the Cumberland. . . .

In Grant's words:

After we had secured the opening of a line over which to bring our supplies to the army, I made a personal inspection to see the situation of the pickets of the two armies. . . . I rode from our right around to our left. When I came to the camp of the picket guard of our side, I heard the call, "Turn out the guard for the commanding general."

I replied, "Never mind the guard," and they were dismissed and went back to their tents.

Just back of these . . . [across the Chattanooga Creek] were the guards of the Confederate pickets. The sentinel on their post called out in like manner, "Turn out the guard for the commanding general," and, I believe, added, "General Grant."

Their line in a moment front-faced to the north, facing me, and gave a salute, which I returned.

The most friendly relations seemed to exist between the pickets of the two armies. At one place there was a tree which had fallen across the stream, and which was used by the soldiers of both armies in drawing water for their camps. General Longstreet's corps was stationed there at the time, and wore blue of a little different shade from our uniform.

Seeing a soldier in blue on this log, I rode up to him, commenced conversing with him, and asked whose corps he belonged to. He was very polite, and, touching his hat to me, said he belonged to General Longstreet's corps. I asked him a few questions—but not with a view of gaining any particular information—all of which he answered, and I rode off.

It was now latter October, and the Union army was back on full rations. According to Phil Sheridan:

The four weeks which followed this cheering result were busy with the work of refitting and preparing for offensive operations as soon as General Sherman should reach us with his troops from West Tennessee. During this period . . . the enemy committed the serious fault of detaching Longstreet's corps—sending it to . . . Knoxville in East Tennessee [to confront the army under Ambrose Burnside]—an error which has no justification whatever, unless it be based on the presumption that it was absolutely necessary that Longstreet should ultimately rejoin Lee's army in Virginia by way of Knoxville and Lynchburg, with a chance of picking up Burnside enroute.

Thus depleted, Bragg still held Missionary Ridge in strong force [with two corps—one under William Hardee and the other under John Breckinridge], but that part of his line which extended across the intervening valley to the northerly point of Lookout Mountain was much attenuated.

By the 18th of November General Grant had issued instructions covering his intended operations. They contemplated that Sherman's column, which was arriving by the north bank of the Tennessee, should cross the river on a pontoon bridge [laid to reach a point to the left of the Union lines] . . . and carry the northern extremity of Missionary Ridge . . . ; that the Army of the Cumberland—the centre—should cooperate with Sherman; and that Hooker with a mixed command should continue to hold Lookout Valley and operate on our extreme right as circumstances might warrant.

On November 23, as the plan was about to be activated, it underwent a partial change. Phil Sheridan continues:

. . . Grant, becoming impressed with the idea that Bragg was endeavoring to get away, ordered Thomas [in the Union center] to make a strong demonstration in his front [i.e., toward Missionary

Ridge] to determine the truth or falsity of the information that had been received.

The information proved to be false. Thomas's advance, however, won the Federals possession of Bragg's outpost line at Orchard Knob, about a mile from the Missionary Ridge defenses.

On the following day, Sherman launched his part of the plan as originally conceived, crossing the river on the Union left and attacking at the north end of Missionary Ridge. At the same time, Hooker's forces on the Union right moved against Lookout Mountain. Sherman's advance soon came to a halt before a defense line under Pat Cleburne, though the first heights were occupied and held. Hooker, operating against inferior numbers, made steady progress.

Again in Phil Sheridan's words:

At first, with good glasses, we could plainly see Hooker's troops driving the Confederates up the face of the mountain. All were soon lost to view in the dense timber, but emerged again on the open ground, across which the Confederates retreated at a lively pace, followed by the pursuing line, which was led by a color-bearer, who, far in advance, was bravely waving on his comrades. The gallantry of this man elicited much enthusiasm among us all, but as he was a considerable distance ahead of his comrades I expected to see his rashness punished at any moment by death or capture. He finally got quite near the retreating Confederates, when suddenly they made a dash at him; but he was fully alive to such a move, and ran back, apparently uninjured, to his friends.

About this time . . . a cloud settled down on the mountain, and a heavy bank of fog obscured its whole face. After the view was lost, the sharp rattle of musketry continued some time, but practically the fight had been already won by Hooker's men, the enemy only holding on with a rear guard to assure his retreat across Chattanooga Valley to Missionary Ridge. . . .

This action on Lookout Mountain was to become known as "The Battle Above the Clouds."

Writes Union staff officer J. S. Fullerton:

As the sun went down, the clouds rolled up the mountain and the mist was blown out of the valley. Night came on clear, with the stars lighting up the heavens. . . . Away off to [the] right, and reaching skyward, Lookout Mountain was ablaze with the fires of Hooker's men, while off to [the] left, and reaching far above the val-

Hooker's attack on Lookout Mountain.

ley, the north end of Missionary Ridge was aflame with the lights of Sherman's army.

These sights on the army's flanks cheered the thousands in the center. The enemy's "great iron crescent," which had been holding them in dismal trenches for the past two months, was at last being made to recede.

Morale rose still higher at sunrise the next morning, November 25. A party of Hooker's men unfurled the Stars and Stripes on the very summit of Lookout Mountain. The sight inspired prolonged cheering.

That morning, says Phil Sheridan, "Bragg's entire army was holding only the line of Missionary Ridge, and our troops being now practically connected from Sherman to Hooker, confronted it with the Army of the Cumberland in the centre. . . ."

General Bragg was undismayed: "Though greatly outnumbered, such was the strength of our position that no doubt was entertained of our ability to hold it. . . ."

The troops on the ridge, explains Confederate officer J. P. Austin, had an excellent view of the approaches to their position:

The evolutions of the Federals, as they . . . formed on the plain below . . . presented the grandest military display the eye ever beheld! It had more the appearance of a great dress parade than an army forming for a desperate conflict. . . .

The invincible Cleburne, who occupied the right of the Confederate line, received the first shock [Sherman's troops renewing their attack of the previous day], and right nobly did he hurl it back, his artillery cutting broad swaths in their ranks.

Three times they rallied and renewed the assault, only to meet the same fate. Sometimes the lines were so close Cleburne's men were compelled to club their guns to beat them back. Cleburne held his lines. . . .

Six or seven hours had passed. Says Federal correspondent B. F. Taylor, writing for the Chicago Journal:

The brief November afternoon was half gone. It was yet thundering on the left . . . [though] Sherman was halted. . . . Hooker was . . . in Chattanooga Valley [on the right]. The Fourth Corps [under General Gordon Granger], that rounded out our centre [and had been picked to launch an attack], grew impatient of restraint. The day was waning. But little time remained to complete the commanding general's grand design.

Union staff officer Henry Cist describes the ground that lay before the army's center:

The enemy had originally four lines of breastworks. The first one on our front was captured by Thomas on the 23d, when Orchard Knob was taken. This left three lines of rifle pits remaining. The second one was about . . . a mile to the rear of the first, near the foot of the ridge. From here to the top was a steep ascent of some five hundred yards, covered with large rocks and fallen timber. About halfway up the ridge a small line of works had been thrown up. On the crest of the hill Bragg's men had constructed their heaviest breastworks, protected . . . by some fifty pieces of artillery. . . .

From his position in the Union center, correspondent B. F. Taylor watched the attack begin:

Let us take . . . just one glance at the surroundings. . . . Did ever battle have so vast a cloud of witnesses? The hive-shaped hills have swarmed [with both soldiers and civilians]. Clustered like bees, blackening the housetops, lining the fortifications—over yonder *across* the theatre . . . *everywhere,* are a hundred thousand behold- ers. Their souls are in their eyes. . . . I think of Bunker Hill as I stand here—of the thousands who witnessed the immortal struggle— and fancy there is a parallel. . . .

At half-past three a group of generals . . . stood upon Orchard Knob. . . . Generals Grant, Thomas, and Granger conferred. An order was given [that Granger send the Fourth Corps to take the line of rifle pits at the base of the ridge, then await further instructions], and in an instant the knob was cleared like a ship's deck for ac- tion. . . .

From divisions to brigades, from brigades to regiments, the order ran. A minute, and the skirmishers deploy; a minute, and the first great drops [of Confederate artillery fire] begin to patter along the line; a minute, and the musketry is in full play like the cracking whips of a hemlock fire.

Men go down here and there before your eyes. The wind lifts the smoke and drifts it away. . . . The divisions of [Thomas J.] Wood and Sheridan are wading breast-deep in the valley of death. . . . On moves the line of skirmishers . . . and after it, at quick- time, the splendid columns. . . . [B]ayonets glitter in the sun.` . . .

And so through the fringe of woods went the line. Now, out into the open ground they burst. . . . The tempest that now broke upon their heads was terrible. The enemy's fire burst out of the rifle pits from base to summit of Missionary Ridge; five rebel batteries . . . opened along the crest. Grape and canister and shot and shell sowed the ground with rugged iron and garnished it with the wounded and the dead. But steady and strong our columns moved on. . . .

Our artillery was doing splendid service. It laid its shot and shell wherever it pleased. . . . All along the mountain's side, in the rebel rifle pits, on the crest, [the hits] fairly dotted the ridge. . . . And all the while our lines were moving on . . . like a prairie fire.

The Confederate skirmishers were driven in. Writes Private Sam Watkins, of the First Tennessee:

. . . a column of Yankees . . . swept right over where I was standing. I was trying to stand aside to get out of their way, but the more I tried to get out of their way, the more in their way I got. I was carried [before them] I know not whither. We soon arrived at the foot of the ridge. . . .

The line of works there offered no safety for Watkins, nor for any other Confederate. Union staff officer Cist says that the Federals charged upon it,

. . . capturing it at the point of the bayonet and routing the rebels, sending them at full speed up the ridge, killing and capturing them in large numbers. These rifle pits were reached nearly simultaneously by the several commands, when the troops, in compliance with their instructions, laid down at the foot of the ridge awaiting further orders. Here they were under a hot, plunging, galling fire from the enemy in their works on the crest of the ridge.

Without further waiting, and under no orders from their officers, first one regiment, then another started with its colors up the ascent, until with loud hurrahs the entire line . . . advanced over and around rocks, under and through the fallen timber, [and] charged up the ridge. . . .

Federal newsman B. F. Taylor, not far behind, saw it all:

They dash . . . a little way, and then slacken; they creep up, hand over hand, loading and firing, and wavering and halting, from the first line of works to the second; they burst into a charge with a cheer, and go over it. Sheets of flame baptize them; plunging shot tear away comrades on left and right. . . .

Between the second and last lines of rebel works is the torrid zone of the battle . . . but our brave mountaineers are clambering steadily on. . . . They seem to be spurning the dull earth under their feet and going up to do Homeric battle with the greater gods. . . .

Among the Confederates who were retreating up the mountainside just ahead of the Federals was Private Sam Watkins:

They kept climbing and pulling and scratching until I was in touching distance of the . . . breastworks right on the very apex of Missionary Ridge. I made one jump, and I heard Captain [William B.] Turner, who had . . . four Napoleon guns . . . halloo out [the order to fire], and then a roar.

The next order was, "Limber to the rear!"

The Union charge up Missionary Ridge.

The Yankees were cutting and slashing, and the cannoneers were running in every direction. I saw [one] brigade throw down their guns and break like quarter horses. Bragg was trying to rally them. I heard him say, "Here is your commander," and the soldiers hallooed back, "Here is your mule."

The climactic moments on the summit are described by correspondent Taylor:

As the blue coats surged over . . . cheer on cheer rang like bells through the valley of the Chickamauga. Men flung themselves exhausted upon the ground. They laughed and wept, shook hands, embraced. . . . It was as wild as a carnival.

Granger [who had followed the corps after sending it forward from Orchard Knob] was received with a shout.

"Soldiers!" he said. "You ought to be court-martialed, every man of you. I ordered you to take the rifle pits, and you scaled the mountain!"

. . . his cheeks were wet with tears as honest as the blood that reddened all the route. . . .

But you must not think this was all there was of the scene on the crest, for fight and frolic were strangely mixed. . . . No sooner had the soldiers . . . straightened themselves, than up muskets—and away they blazed. One of them, fairly beside himself between laughing and crying, seemed puzzled at which end of his piece he should

load, and so abandoning the gun and the problem together, he . . .
fell to hurling stones after the enemy. . . .

Dead rebels lay . . . thick along the ridge. Scabbards, broken
arms, artillery horses, wrecks of gun carriages, and bloody garments
strewed the scene. And—tread lightly, oh loyal-hearted! . . . [B]oys
in blue are lying there. . . . A little waif of a drummer boy, [who
had] somehow drifted up the mountain in the surge, lies there, his
pale face upward, a blue spot on his breast. Muffle his drum for the
poor child and his mother!

Our troops met one loyal welcome on the height. How the old
Tennessean [a civilian with Union sympathies] . . . managed to get
there nobody knows, but there he was, grasping a colonel's hand and
saying, while the tears ran down his face, "God be thanked! I *knew*
the Yankees would fight!"

*The ridge, says Union staff officer Cist, was quickly carried in six
places:*

Regiments were captured almost entire; battery after battery
along the ridge was taken. In some cases the rebels were bayonetted
at their guns, and the cannon that but a moment before was firing on
our troops were by them captured, turned, and used against the rebels as they were driven in masses to the rear.

Confederate Private Watkins felt sorry for General Bragg:

The army was routed, and Bragg . . . looked so hacked and
whipped and mortified and chagrined at defeat; and all along the
line, when Bragg would pass, the soldiers would raise the yell, "Here
is your mule! Bully for Bragg. He's hell on retreat!"

Bragg wrote later:

No satisfactory excuse can possibly be given for the shameful
conduct of our troops . . . in allowing their line to be penetrated.
The position was one which ought to have been held by a line of
skirmishers against any assaulting column. . . . [B]ut one possible
reason presents itself to my mind in explanation of this bad conduct
in veteran troops who never before failed in any duty assigned them,
however difficult and hazardous. They had for two days confronted
the enemy, marshalling his immense forces in plain view and exhibiting to their sight . . . a superiority in numbers. . . . But our
veterans had so often encountered similar hosts when the strength

of position was against us, and with perfect success, that not a doubt crossed my mind.

Federal correspondent Taylor completes the day's story:

With the receding flight and swift pursuit, the battle died away in murmurs far down the valley of the Chickamauga. Sheridan was . . . in the saddle, and with his command spurring on after the enemy. Tall columns of smoke were rising. . . . The rebels were burning a train of stores a mile long. . . .

The sun . . . had hardly gone down, when up . . . rose the . . . full moon. The troubled day was done.

Next morning Grant launched an organized pursuit, but it soon ran up against the adamantine Pat Cleburne covering the retreat's rear. Bragg's columns gained the time they needed to escape, with Cleburne soon following. The Federals desisted.

Chattanooga's casualties were not excessive, the Federal total being about 5,800 and that of the Confederates about 6,700.

In a report to Secretary Stanton in Washington, Grant's quartermaster general, M. C. Meigs, rejoiced at the battle's outcome:

The strength of the rebellion in the [South's] center is broken. Burnside is relieved from danger in East Tennessee. . . . Georgia and the Southeast are threatened in the rear. And another victory is added to the chapter of "Unconditional Surrender Grant."

20

THE WILDERNESS CAMPAIGN

T HE WAR HAD FINALLY *produced the leader Lincoln had been looking for. In early March, 1864, Grant received orders to come to Washington to accept a congressionally created promotion to lieutenant general and to assume command of all Union armies, East and West—a total of more than half a million men. Already present in Washington when Grant received his summons was Horace Porter, an officer who had become acquainted with the general during the Chattanooga campaign and who was about to be appointed one of his aides-de-camp. Porter relates:*

On the evening of March 8 the President and Mrs. Lincoln gave a public reception at the White House, which I attended. The President stood in the usual reception room, known as the Blue Room, with several cabinet officers near him, and shook hands cordially with everybody as the vast procession of men and women passed in front of him. . . . Mrs. Lincoln occupied a position on his right. . . .

At about half-past nine o'clock a sudden commotion near the entrance to the room attracted general attention, and . . . I was surprised to see General Grant walking along modestly . . . toward Mr.

Lincoln. He had arrived from the West that evening and had come to the White House to pay his respects to the President. . . .

Although these two historical characters had never met before, Mr. Lincoln recognized the general at once from the pictures he had seen of him. With a face radiant with delight, he advanced rapidly two or three steps . . . and cried out, "Why, here is General Grant! Well, this is a great pleasure, I assure you," at the same time seizing him by the hand. . . .

The statesman and the soldier conversed for a few minutes, and then the President presented his distinguished guest to Mr. Seward. The Secretary of State was very demonstrative in his welcome, and after exchanging a few words, led the general to where Mrs. Lincoln was standing. . . . Mrs. Lincoln . . . and the general chatted together very pleasantly for some minutes.

The visitors had by this time become so curious to catch a sight of the general that . . . they became altogether unmanageable. . . . [Secretary Seward] succeeded in struggling through the crowd with the general until they reached the large East Room, where the people could circulate more freely. This, however, was only a temporary relief. . . . The vast throng surged and swayed and crowded until alarm was felt for the safety of the ladies.

Cries now arose of "Grant! Grant! Grant!" Then came cheer after cheer.

Seward, after some persuasion, induced the general to stand upon a sofa, thinking the visitors would be satisfied with a view of him, and retire; but . . . their shouts were renewed, and a rush was made to shake his hand. The President sent word that he and the Secretary of War would await the general's return in one of the small drawing rooms; but it was fully an hour before he was able to make his way there, and then only with the aid of several officers and ushers. . . .

The next day, March 9, the general went to the White House . . . for the purpose of receiving his commission from the hands of the President. . . . The next day, the 10th, he paid a visit by rail to the headquarters of the Army of the Potomac, near Brandy Station, in Virginia, about seventy miles from Washington. He returned the day after, and started the same night for Nashville, to meet Sherman and turn over to him the command of the Military Division of the Mississippi.

While in Washington, General Grant had been so much an object of curiosity, and had been so continually surrounded by admiring crowds when he appeared in the streets, and even in his hotel, that it had become very irksome to him. . . . The President had given him a cordial invitation to dine that evening at the White House, but he begged to be excused for the reason that he would lose a whole day, which he could not afford at that critical period.

"Besides," he added, "I have become very tired of this show business."

. . . General Grant returned to the capital on March 23. . . . He . . . had had Sheridan ordered East to take command of the cavalry of the Army of the Potomac. Sheridan . . . had been worn down almost to a shadow by hard work and exposure in the field. He weighed only a hundred and fifteen pounds, and as his height was but five feet six inches, he looked anything but formidable as a candidate for a cavalry leader. . . . [H]is appearance . . . gave rise to a remark made to General Grant . . . "The officer you brought on from the West is rather a little fellow to handle your cavalry." To which Grant replied, "You will find him big enough for the purpose before we get through with him."

The overall military situation at the time Grant took command is explained by the general himself:

The Union armies were now divided into nineteen departments, though four of them in the West had been concentrated into a single military division. . . . Before this time these various armies had acted separately and independently of each other. . . . I determined to stop this. . . . My general plan was now to concentrate all the force possible against the Confederate armies in the field.

There were but two . . . [major Confederate armies, both being] east of the Mississippi River and facing north. The Army of Northern Virginia, General Robert E. Lee commanding, was on the south bank of the Rapidan, confronting the Army of the Potomac; the second, under General Joseph E. Johnston [who had replaced the defeated Braxton Bragg], was at Dalton, Georgia, opposed to Sherman, who was still at Chattanooga.

Besides these main armies, the Confederates had to guard the Shenandoah Valley—a great storehouse to feed their armies from—and their line of communications from Richmond to Tennessee. [Nathan Bedford] Forrest, a brave and intrepid [Confederate] cavalry general, was in the West with a large force, making a larger command necessary to hold what we had gained in Middle and West Tennessee.

Entrusting Sherman with the details of the Western theater's most important campaign—that against Joe Johnston in Georgia—Grant concentrated on matters in the East. He goes on:

. . . the opposing forces stood in substantially the same relations towards each other as three years before, or when the war began; they were both between the Federal and Confederate capitals. It is true, footholds had been secured by us on the seacoast, in Virginia and North Carolina, but, beyond that, no substantial advantage had been gained by either side. . . .

That portion of the Army of the Potomac not engaged in guarding lines of communication was on the northern bank of the Rapidan. The Army of Northern Virginia confronting it on the opposite bank of the same river was strongly intrenched and commanded by the acknowledged ablest general in the Confederate army.

By about May 1, Grant was ready to attack. His plan was to press southeastward toward Richmond with Meade's army while supporting advances were being made by smaller forces in West Virginia, in Virginia's Shenandoah Valley, and, chiefly, up the James River from the Virginia coast.

Because of alert Confederates in their paths, the support forces would contribute little to the campaign except some raids on enemy property. For all practical purposes, the Army of the Potomac was on its own. It numbered about 120,000 men—the infantry corps of Hancock, Warren, Sedgwick, and Burnside; and a cavalry corps under Sheridan.

Lee had about 65,000 men—the infantry corps of Longstreet, Ewell, and A. P. Hill; and Jeb Stuart's cavalry corps.

According to Confederate General E. M. Law:

On the 2d of May, 1864, a group of officers stood at the Confederate signal station on Clark's Mountain, Virginia, south of the Rapidan, and examined closely through their field-glasses the position of the Federal army then lying north of the river in Culpeper County. The central figure of the group was the commander of the Army of Northern Virginia, who had requested his corps and division commanders to meet him there.

. . . General Lee expressed the opinion that the Federal army would cross the river at [the fords a few miles to the east]. Thirty-six hours later General Meade's army—General Grant, now commander-in-chief, being with it—commenced its march to the crossings indicated by General Lee.

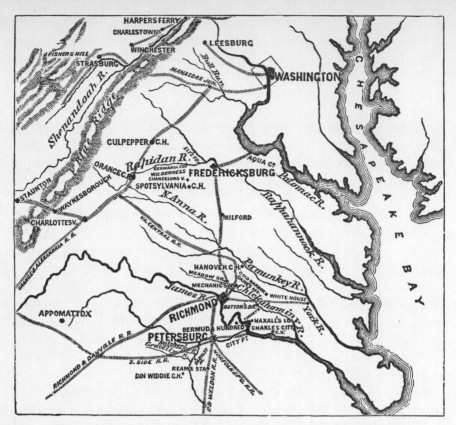

From the Rapidan to Petersburg: the Wilderness Campaign.

In the words of the regimental chaplain from Pennsylvania, the Reverend A. M. Stewart:

On the morning of May the 4th we, with the entire Grand Army of the Potomac, were in motion towards the Rapidan. The dawn was clear, warm, and beautiful. As the almost countless encampments were broken up—[with] bands in all directions playing lively airs, banners waving, regiments, brigades, and divisions falling into line . . . the scene, even to eyes long familiar with military displays, was one of unusual grandeur.

Adds Grant's aide-de-camp, Horace Porter:

The quick, elastic step and easy, swinging gait of the men, the cheery look upon their faces, and the lusty shouts with which they greeted their new commander as he passed, gave proof of the temper of their metal and the superb spirit which animated their hearts.

If the general's nature had been as emotional as that of Napoleon, he might have been moved to utter the words of the French emperor as his troops filed past him in moving to the field of Waterloo: "Magnificent, magnificent!" But as General Grant was neither demonstrative nor communicative, he gave no expression whatever to his feelings.

Explains Confederate General John B. Gordon (that indomitable fighter who had been temporarily blinded at Malvern Hill, had been wounded five times at Antietam but had returned to duty before Chancellorsville, had played a vigorous role at Gettysburg, and who was now one of Lee's most trusted lieutenants):

This advance by General Grant inaugurated the seventh act in the "On to Richmond" drama played by the armies of the Union. The first advance, led by General McDowell, had been repelled by Beauregard and Johnston at Rull Run; the next five, under the leadership respectively of McClellan, Pope, Burnside, Hooker, and Meade, had been repelled by Lee. . . .

Crossing the Rapidan with but little resistance . . . General Grant promptly faced his army in the direction from which Lee must necessarily approach. . . . Lee, in the meantime, was hurrying his columns along the narrow roads . . . in order to check Grant's advance. . . . General Grant . . . lost no time in pushing to the front. . . .

No substantial contact was made the first day. Writes Union soldier Warren Goss:

. . . we reached Chancellorsville and bivouacked near the blackened ruins of the old Chancellor House. Weather-stained remnants of clothing, rusty gun-barrels and bayonets, tarnished brasses and equipments, with bleaching bones and grinning skulls, marked this memorable field. In the cavity of one of these skulls was a nest with the three speckled eggs of a field bird. In yet another was a wasp nest. Life in embryo in the skull of death!

Union Private Frank Wilkeson takes up:

We walked to and fro over the old battlefield, looking at bullet-scarred and canister-riven trees. . . . It grew dark, and we built a fire at which to light our pipes close to where we thought Jackson's men had formed for the charge [on Hooker's right flank]. . . . The dead were all around us; their eyeless skulls seemed to stare steadily

Ruins of the Chancellor House.

at us. The smoke drifted to and fro among us. The trees swayed and sighed gently in the soft wind.

One veteran told the story of the burning of some of the Union soldiers who were wounded during Hooker's fight . . . as they lay helpless in the woods. It was a ghastly and awe-inspiring tale. . . . As we sat silently smoking and listening . . . an infantry soldier who had, unobserved by us, been prying into the shallow grave he sat on with his bayonet, suddenly rolled a skull on the ground before us and said in a deep, low voice: "That is what you are all coming to, and some of you will start toward it tomorrow."

As for Lee's soldiers on this eve of yet another campaign: Artillery adjutant Robert Stiles tells how their feelings were analyzed by an observant friend:

Billy . . . had just made his way back from furlough . . . and passed the night with an infantry regiment from his own county that contained many of his former schoolmates and friends and neighbors. . . .

He did not detect any depression or apprehension of disaster or weakness of pluck or purpose; but he says he did miss the bounding, buoyant spirit, the effervescent outbursts, the quips, the jests, the jokes, the jollities such as had usually characterized the first spring rousings of the army and the first meetings and minglings of the different commands as they shouted their tumultuous way to battle.

He says that there seems to have sifted through the ranks the conviction that the struggle ahead of us was of a different character from any we had experienced in the past—a sort of premonition of the definite mathematical calculation in whose hard, unyielding grip it was intended our future should be held and crushed. . . .

. . . if one army outnumbers another more than two to one, and the larger can be indefinitely reinforced and the smaller not at all, then if the stronger side will but make up its mind to stand all the killing the weaker can do, and will keep it so made up, there can be but one result.

Billy says the realization of this new order of things did not affect the resolution of the men, but that it did affect their spirits. I can only say I believe he is exactly correct.

The next day, May 5, dawned radiantly. Relates Union Private Theodore Gerrish:

. . . we were awake at an early hour. . . . The rising sun sent its rays of light down like golden needles through the tops of the pine trees. Little fires were kindled, our coffee was quickly boiled, and we sat down to our rude breakfasts with appetites such as are unknown in lives of luxury and ease. . . .

Some [of the men] were laughing and cracking their jokes about hunting for the Johnnies through the forest, of the grand times we should have marching down to Richmond and entering the rebel capital, how when the war was over "we would hang Jeff Davis to the sour apple tree" and then go marching home.

Another class, more thoughtful . . . were lying upon the ground, silent, alone . . . with compressed lips, seeming not to notice what was transpiring around them. They were thinking of wives and little ones far away, and wondering if they would ever see them again. Others were leaning against the trees, writing letters. . . .

Cavalry men soon came back with the thrilling intelligence that General Lee's army in great force was rapidly advancing. There was no time to lose. The field of battle which our commanding generals selected stretched its length for six miles through that great forest. . . .

The rebels evidently knew but little of our force, position, and intention, and it is safe to say we knew less of theirs; and thus the two great masses of men were hurled against each other. The rebels fought like demons, and under cover of the dense underbrush poured deadly volleys upon us. The air was filled with lead. Minie bullets went snapping and tearing through the pine limbs; splinters flew in

Fighting in the Wilderness. Federals in foreground.

every direction; trees were completely riddled with bullets in a moment's time; blood ran in torrents; death lost its terror; and men for a time seemed transformed to beings that had no fear. . . .

The rifle barrels touched, as from their muzzles they poured death into each other's faces; the ground shook with the roar of musketry; the forest trees were flaming with fire, and the air was loaded with death. . . . What a medley of sounds—the incessant roar of the rifle, the screaming of bullets, the forest on fire, men cheering, groaning, yelling, swearing, and praying!

Writes the Union's Chaplain Stewart:

What awful, what sickening scenes! No, we have ceased to get sick at such sights. Here a dear friend struck dead by a ball through the head or heart! Another fallen with leg or thigh broken, and looking, resignedly yet wistfully, to you for help away from the carnage. Another dropping his gun, quickly clapping his hand upon his breast, stomach or bowels, through which a Minnie has passed, and walking slowly to the rear to lie down and die. Still another— yea, many more—with bullet holes through various fleshy parts of the body, from which the blood is freely flowing, walking back and remarking, with a laugh somewhat distorted with pain, "See, the

rascals have hit me!" All this beneath a canopy of sulphur and a bedlam of sounds, like confusion confounded.

Night at length put an end to the carnage, and left the two armies
much in the same position as at the opening of the strife . . . both
unsubdued, and still fiercely confronting each other.

Early on Friday, the 6th, the work of death was resumed . . .
with various lulls, changes, and shiftings [occurring] in different
parts of the long, extended lines. . . .

During . . . a lull in the carnage, I was sitting on [my horse]
Jessie . . . in a place where the rebel line of battle had been the
previous day. Their wounded had been generally removed, while the
dead lay thickly scattered in all directions and positions. One of their
wounded, which had been either overlooked or they unable . . . to
remove him, lay near a tree where I stopped. Dismounting, I drew
near him with the familiar salutation:

"Well, friend, how are you getting along?"

Eyeing me with evident suspicion, mingled with some fierceness,
he slowly responded: "Wall, stranger, bad enough."

"Anything I can do for you?" was inquired.

Seeing I was not about to insult or kill him outright, his tone
and manner became greatly modified. . . . "Wall, if I could only
be turned over. Both my thighs seem broken, and lying just in this
one way since yesterday has made me awful tired."

Getting outside of him, and bending down, he was directed to
put his arms around me and help himself as well as he could. We
soon succeeded in getting him twisted over.

"Thar," said he. "That's better; thank ye."

"Got any water?"

"Nary a drop since yesterday."

A little was poured into his cup from my canteen.

"Could you eat a cracker?"

"Got nun."

Two were handed him. . . . By this time his fear and fierceness
were both gone, and his eyes filled with tears. . . .

"Got a wife?" I queried.

"Yes, yes; and a whole lot of children, away in North Carolina;
and oh, if I was only with Mammy now," meaning his wife.

Just then two of our young men came up with an empty stretcher.
I hailed them and asked if they would not carry this wounded enemy
back to our hospital.

"Certainly.'"

. . . This was too much, for all the wounded man's stoicism and animosity. Breaking down altogether, he commenced crying like a baby, and could only exclaim, as he was borne away, "Wall, now, this does beat all!"

That morning the Federals smashed a part of the Confederate line. General Lee, on horseback, dashed among the fugitives and implored them to rally. Longstreet's corps, coming up fresh, saved the situation. Lee, spurring his mount and waving his hat, joined the counterattack; but he was soon stayed by a chorus of anguished protests: "Go back, General Lee! Go back!" One of the men turned his horse by seizing its bridle.

Around midday, Longstreet's services were lost to Lee. As related by Southerner Robert Stiles:

It may not have been generally observed that Jackson and Longstreet were both struck down in the Wilderness, just one year apart . . . each by the fire of his own men [Longstreet, like Jackson, being with a mounted party that was mistaken for a group of the enemy].

I had been sent forward, perhaps to look for some place where we [artillerymen] might get into the fight, when I observed an excited gathering some distance back of the lines; and pressing toward it, I heard that General Longstreet had just been shot down and was being put into an ambulance. I could not learn anything definite as to the character of his wound, but only that it was serious—some said he was dead.

When the ambulance moved off, I followed it a little way, being anxious for trustworthy news of the general. The members of his staff surrounded the vehicle, some riding in front, some on one side and some on the other, and some behind. . . . They were literally bowed down with grief. . . . I rode up to the ambulance and looked in.

They had taken off Longstreet's hat and coat and boots. The blood had paled out of his face. . . . I noticed how white and dome-like his great forehead looked; and, with scarcely less reverent admiration, how spotless white his socks and his fine gauze undervest, save where the black-red gore from his breast and shoulder had stained it.

While I gazed at his massive frame, lying so still except when it rocked inertly with the lurch of the vehicle, his eyelids frayed apart till I could see a delicate line of blue between them; and then he very quietly moved his unwounded arm and, with his thumb and

Confederates assaulting the burning breastworks.

two fingers, carefully lifted the saturated undershirt from his chest, holding it up a moment, and heaved a deep sigh. He is not dead, I said to myself, and he is calm and entirely master of the situation. . . .

It would be nearly six months before Lee's "old war horse" returned to duty.

The general's wounding occasioned a lull in the fighting. The semiquiet lasted until about four o'clock. Then the Confederates launched an attack.

Northerner Warren Goss found himself literally on the hottest part of the field:

Flames sprang up in the woods in our front. . . . With crackling roar . . . it came down upon the Union line. The wind drove the blinding smoke and suffocating heat into our faces. . . . The line of fire, with resistless march, swept the thickets before its advance, then, reaching out its tongue of flame, ignited the breastworks composed of resinous logs, which soon roared and crackled along their entire length. The men fought the enemy and the flames at the same time. Their hair and beards were singed and their faces blistered.

At last, blinded by the smoke and suffocated by the hot breath of the flames, with the whole length of their intrenchments a crackling mass of fire, they gave way and fell back to the second line of log intrenchments. With a shout the rebel column approached . . . and attempted to seize the abandoned position. The impartial flames in turn drove them back. The fire soon consumed the logs, and the rebels planted their colors there.

The fire swept on and reached our second line of intrenchments. . . . The men formed at some places eight and ten ranks deep, the rear men loading the muskets for the front ranks, and thus undauntedly kept up the fight while the logs in front of them were in flames. Finally, blistered, blinded, and suffocating, they gave way.

The enemy yelled with exultation. They rushed forward and attempted to place their colors on this line of our defence. Their triumph was brief, for the last line of log defences was soon consumed like the first. Then, with a shout resembling the rebel yell, our men charged the enemy and swept them back from the field. . . .

The fire was the most terrible enemy our men met that day. . . . It is estimated that two hundred of our wounded were consumed. . . .

After sundown the Confederates made an attack on the right . . . creating considerable confusion. The night prevented them from following up their success.

Thus ended this terrible battle, the full details of which were hid in the tangled woods and darkling forests, where its mysteries will never be disclosed. It was a drawn battle. Both commanders, at its termination, arrived at the same conclusion—that further attack on those lines was hopeless. The losses on both sides were terrible.

But the Federals were far the greater sufferers, listing a figure of some 17,000, as compared with an unofficial Confederate figure of around 8,000.

The Union's Chaplain Stewart, who had been associated with much of the bloodshed, became involved in its aftermath also:

When the strife ceased . . . I went back about two miles to *one* of the large depots for the wounded—*hospital,* in this wilderness, there was none. Here about two thousand wounded had been collected. Such multiplied and accumulated suffering is not often seen. Not half the wounded from yesterday had yet been [taken care of]. All the surgeons present were exerting themselves to their utmost; the few nurses all busy. The Sanitary and Christian Commissions had perhaps a dozen delegates in all present. These were unceasing in the distribution of their various comforts to the sufferers; but what were . . . these among so many?

. . . When coming in from the field, my strength seemed almost wholly exhausted; but, on seeing such a mass of suffering and need, it revived; and I turned in to help during that seemingly long night. . . .

During the fore part of the night, an order came to have these wounded removed a number of miles towards Fredericksburg, and the work commenced, with all the ambulances which could be procured. . . . On Saturday morning, forty-seven who had died in this one locality . . . were laid in a row and buried in one ditch.

. . . our Union, our liberties, our hopes for the future must be very precious. This is their price.

That morning (May 7) was pridefully remembered by Confederate General John B. Gordon:

. . . I was invited by the commanding general to ride with him through that portion of the sombre woodland where the movement of my troops . . . had occurred on the previous evening. . . . It would be a matter of profound interest if all that General Lee said on this ride could be placed upon record. . . .

He discussed the dominant characteristics of his great antagonist: his indomitable will and untiring persistency; his direct method of waging war by delivering constant and heavy blows upon the enemy's front rather than by seeking advantage through strategic manoeuvre. General Lee also said that General Grant held so completely and firmly the confidence of the Government that he could command to any extent its limitless resources in men and materials, while the Confederacy was already practically exhausted in both.

He, however, hoped—perhaps I may say he was almost convinced—that if we could keep the Confederate army between General Grant and Richmond, checking him for a few months longer, as we had in the past two days, some crisis in public affairs or change in public opinion at the North might induce the authorities at Washington to let the Southern States go, rather than force their retention in the Union at so heavy a cost.

I endeavored to learn from General Lee what movements he had in contemplation, or what he next expected from General Grant. . . . Reports had reached me to the effect that General Grant's army was retreating or preparing to retreat, and I called General Lee's attention to these rumors. He had heard them, but they had not made the slightest impression upon his mind. . . . Indeed, he said in so many words: "General Grant is not going to retreat. He will move his army to Spotsylvania." [About ten miles to the southeast.]

I asked him . . . if there was special evidence of such purpose.

"Not at all," said Lee, "not at all; but that is the next point at which the armies will meet. Spotsylvania is now General Grant's best strategic point. . . . I have already made arrangements to march by the shortest practicable route, that we may meet him there."

During the moments when this high-level discussion was taking place, elsewhere on the field Confederate Private John Casler was being assigned to a burial detail:

As we started out to bury the dead, there was one of the Federals lying beside the road who had been killed about the first fire, and had lain there nearly three days. I had noticed him the first. I and another soldier started to bury him when the other fellow said, "Hold on until I search him."

I said that was no use, as he had been lying there so long and thousands of troops had passed him by, and that he had probably been searched before he got cold. But he kept on searching, and finally found forty dollars in greenbacks. I then wanted him to divide, but he refused to do so. After that I searched every one I helped to bury, but found nothing but a few pocket knives.

We got out of rations during this battle and could not get to our wagons, but the Yankees had four or five days' rations of hard-tack and bacon in their haversacks, and we would get them from the dead. I have been so hungry that I have cut the blood off from crackers and eaten them.

That evening, writes Union soldier Frank Wilkeson, the Northern army began to move:

Grant's military standing with the enlisted men this day hung on the direction we turned at the Chancellorsville House. If to the left [i.e., northward in retreat], he was to be rated with Meade and Hooker and Burnside and Pope—the generals who preceded him. At the Chancellorsville House we turned to the right [toward Spotsylvania]. . . . Our spirits rose. We . . . began to sing. The enlisted men understood the flanking movement. That night we were happy.

Federals emerging from the Wilderness on the march to Spotsylvania.

Returning to the Southern side and to John Casler:

On the 8th our corps moved on down the line, as General Grant was concentrating his force near Spotsylvania Court House. But General Lee had headed him off, and there was considerable fighting that day. Our whole line was formed in the evening, and that night we fortified again. . . .

There was considerable skirmishing and artillery firing on the 9th; and [Union] General Sedgwick, commanding the 6th United States Corps, was bantering some of his men—so it was reported by prisoners—about dodging their heads at the whistling of the Rebel bullets, and said that we could not hit an elephant at that distance. A moment afterwards he was killed, pierced through the brain by a Rebel bullet. He was one of their best corps commanders.

On the 10th they made a desperate attempt to carry our works . . . and succeeded in getting over the works at one point, but were repulsed and driven back to their lines.

Southerner Robert Stiles says that one Confederate unit that counter-attacked was led by "an old Captain Hunter" whose only weapon was a frying pan. It seems that Hunter had been frying a piece of meat as the Yankees arrived, and resented being cheated out of eating it. Stiles goes on:

When it became evident that the [Union] attack had failed, I suggested to the chaplain . . . that there might be some demand for his ministrations where the enemy had broken over; so we walked up there. . . . It was almost dark, but as we drew near we saw a wounded Federal soldier clutch the pantaloons of Captain Hunter, who at that moment was passing by, frying pan in hand, and heard him ask, with intense eagerness, "Can you pray, sir? Can you pray?"

The old captain looked down at him with a peculiar expression and pulled away, saying, "No, my friend. I don't wish you any harm now, but praying's not exactly my trade."

I said to the chaplain, "Let's go to that man."

As we came up, he caught my pants in the same way and uttered the same words, "Can you pray, sir? Can you pray?"

I bent over the poor fellow, turned back his blouse, and saw that a large canister shot had passed through his chest. . . . We both knelt down by him, and I took his hand in mine and said, "My friend, you haven't much time left for prayer, but if you will say after me just these simple words, with heart as well as lips, all will be well with you: 'God have mercy on me, a sinner, for Jesus Christ's sake.' "

I never saw such intensity in human gaze, nor ever heard such intensity in human voice, as in the gaze and voice of that dying man as he held my hand and looked into my face, repeating the simple, awful, yet reassuring words I had dictated. He uttered them again and again, with the death rattle in his throat and the death tremor in his frame, until someone shouted, "They are coming again!" and we broke away. . . . It proved to be a false alarm, and we returned immediately—but he was dead; yes, dead and half-stripped. . . .

As explained by Confederate Private Casler:

Each army would fortify at night—and through the day, when not fighting—in order to hold the ground they had gained and resist an attack.

On the night of the 10th, Sam Nunnelly came to me and said we would get over in front of our works that night and plunder the dead, as he knew there were plenty of them there that had never been searched. I told him I would not do it, as we would be in danger of being shot by our own men as well as the enemy. But he said he would go by himself and crawl around and play off wounded. So he went, and was gone all night, coming back at daylight. He got three watches, some money, knives, and other things. He would risk his life any time for plunder.

On the 11th there was some skirmishing and heavy artillery firing from both sides, and everyone who had to be near the front had a hole dug to get into.

That day a fierce cavalry battle took place at Yellow Tavern, a few miles north of Richmond, between dashing Jeb Stuart and tough little Phil Sheridan, whom Grant had sent on a raid around the Confederate army. The great Stuart was mortally wounded. Just five days earlier, a bullet had deprived Lee of his "old war horse." Now another bullet took his army's "eyes and ears." Stuart was as popular as he was courageous and capable, and the South was stunned by his death.

The heaviest fighting at Spotsylvania centered around a horse-shoe-shaped salient, or projection, in the center of Lee's lines. Grant launched an all-out attack on these defenses during the gusty, rainy, and misty dawn of May 12. Writes the general's aide-de-camp, Horace Porter:

The battle . . . was probably the most desperate engagement in the history of modern warfare. . . . It was chiefly a savage hand-to-hand fight across the breastworks. Rank after rank was riddled by shot and shell and bayonet thrusts, and finally sank, a mass of torn and mutilated corpses; then fresh troops rushed madly forward to replace the dead; and so the murderous work went on. Guns were run up close to the parapet, and double charges of canister played their part in the bloody work. The fence-rails and logs in the breastworks were shattered into splinters, and trees over a foot and a half in diameter were cut completely in two. . . .

The opposing flags were in places thrust against each other, and muskets were fired with muzzle against muzzle. Skulls were crushed with clubbed muskets and men stabbed to death with swords and bayonets thrust between the logs in the parapet which separated the combatants. Wild cheers, savage yells, and frantic shrieks rose above the sighing of the wind and the pattering of the rain, and formed a demoniacal accompaniment to the booming of the guns. . . . Even the darkness of night and the pitiless storm failed to stop the fierce contest. . . .

The action dwindled around midnight as the Confederates at last abandoned the salient's forward areas to occupy a new line at its base. Robert Stiles was present, and he tells this story:

After we got to our new position, I discovered that I had lost my pocket-knife, or some such trivial article of personal outfit, but difficult to replace; so . . . I went back on foot . . . to look, or feel for it. I had no difficulty in finding the spot where we had been lying, and began to grope and feel about for the knife, having at the time an unpleasant consciousness that I was running a very foolish and unjustifiable risk, for the minies were hissing and singing and spatting all about me.

There was a man near me, also on his hands and knees, looking or feeling for something. While glancing at the shape, dimly outlined, I heard the unmistakable thud of a bullet striking flesh. There was a muffled outcry, and the crouching or kneeling figure lay stretched upon the ground. I went to it and felt it. The man was dead. In a very brief time I was back in our new position and not thinking of pocket-knives.

Northern officer Horace Porter inspected the battleground the next day and found its sights "harrowing in the extreme."

Our own killed were scattered over a large space near the "angle," while in front of the captured breastworks the enemy's dead . . . were pilled upon each other in some places four layers deep, exhibiting every ghastly phase of mutilation. Below the mass of fast-decaying corpses, the convulsive twitching of limbs and the writhing of bodies showed that there were wounded men still alive and struggling to extricate themselves from their horrid entombment. Every relief possible was afforded, but in too many cases it came too late. The place was well named the "Bloody Angle."

Grant wasn't through at Spotsylvania. For some days he maneuvered his troops from flank to flank, seeking a way to shatter Lee's line. But each of his moves was skillfully countered.

Pennsylvania's Chaplain Stewart says in a letter from the field that the brigade he belonged to was withdrawn from the locality where it had fought on May 12, "leaving dead men and horses thickly strewn around and unburied."

On Wednesday the 18th at dawn, after a toilsome, sleepless night in changing position, we were brought to renew the bloody drama on this same spot. Within twelve rods of where we halted lay twelve

artillery horses, so close as to touch each other, now a mass of putre-
faction.

From where I stood, and in front of a rebel rifle pit, lay stretched
in all positions over fifty of our unburied soldiers, and within the
pit and lying across each other, perhaps as many rebel dead. It seems
almost incredible what a change of little less than a week had
wrought, by exposure to sun and hot air. The hair and skin had
fallen from the head, and the flesh from the bones—all alive with disgusting maggots.

Many of the soldiers stuffed their nostrils with green leaves. Such
a scene does seem too revolting to record. Yet, how else convey any
just conception of what is done and suffered here?

*The new Federal assault, in which three corps took part, was soon
repulsed. By the night of May 20, Grant's army was again in motion
southeastward. Lee set his troops on a parallel route, keeping between Grant and Richmond.*

*Said Chaplain Stewart in a letter from Hanover Court House
dated May 28:*

As to how we came here from Spotsylvania Court House, a volume would scarcely suffice to tell. What skirmishings and fight-
ings—what long, long, weary marches by day and night—what coun-
termarches, now far to the right, again away to the left—passing over
hot, dusty roads, corduroy bridges, and pontoons; through mud,
creeks, fields, woods, swamps, and sloughs; amid moonlight and
thick darkness, showers, thunderstorms, and sunshine.

Much of this may never, *can* never be written; and were it, could
not be understood by those not exercised therein.

No matter; we are here on the south bank of the Pamunkey
River, which we lately crossed on a pontoon bridge. Yes, here again
on the *Peninsula,* although from another point than formerly approached. Again on *this Peninsula,* where, two years ago, we endured so much, suffered so terribly, and from whence we retreated
so ingloriously. The future will tell whether this latter coming will
prove more successful than the first. . . .

Through the masterly tactics of Grant and the unparalleled
struggles of our soldiers, Lee has . . . fallen back . . . from post to
post [toward Richmond]; yet has each one of these recedings rendered our work of finally beating them more difficult; carrying us still
farther from our base of operations, supplies, and reinforcements.

Everyone with half a military idea will readily believe that our losses . . . were much greater than the rebels'. How could it be otherwise? Almost invariably we had to make the assaults upon Lee's veteran army, posted in rifle pits, behind breastworks, and in hiding places, where one soldier was equal to two making the attack.

These things are not written under any feeling of discouragement, much less to discourage others. We were never more hopeful. . . . They are especially written to preserve the reputation of our brave generals and still braver soldiers, should this war, of necessity, be continued far beyond the period when our ardent Northern expectation demands it to be finished.

Union soldier Warren Goss says of this part of the campaign:

Our army, operating in hostile territory, was like a swarm of locusts. . . . Where each man of an army takes a little, not much remains. I don't think we were very hard with these people, yet their fences fast melted away into campfires, and their chickens and turkeys and geese into goodly messes. . . .

The colored people whom we met . . . greedily gathered scraps of fat and beef thrown away around our camps, yet their faces were the most contented ones we saw in this country. Discontent and sullen anger, ill concealed, were written all over many of the white countenances. The few old darkies whom I talked with in most instances informed us that young "massa" was in the rebel army, and that the younger male servants were either beyond Richmond [presumably to keep them from falling into Union hands], or had been engaged in digging fortifications around it. . . .

The people at one of the home-like estates claimed to be Union people and requested a safety guard over their house. I was sergeant of the guard during a day around this place. . . . While seated near the house endeavoring to make a sketch of the picturesque homestead, with its background of foliage and Negro shanties, I was interrupted by a shadow falling across my small sketching-board, and upon turning was not unpleasantly confronted by a tall black-eyed miss who had been glancing over my shoulder.

"That's our place!" she exclaimed, evidently in surprise; and then, in apology for the rudeness, said, "You were so engaged you did not hear me speak, and I looked over your shoulder to see what you were doing. Where did you learn to draw?"

I told her; when she replied, "I was at boarding-school near there two years before the war."

. . . I got the impression that she had a tender attachment for a young gentleman in the North. Her questions were quite searching regarding people whom, as it chanced, I knew by reputation.

I finished the roughly executed sketch and presented it to her with such compliments as a susceptible young man of twenty-three years might make to a young lady, and thought to myself, "Here is one of those unwritten romances of war, the end of which I shall doubtless never know."

Most of the women the Federals met were, of course, loyal to the South. Chaplain Stewart had spoken with a number of these women since the army had crossed the Rapidan. "Former convictions," he states in another letter from the field,

have thus been greatly strengthened that the South stands today quite as much indebted for a successful prolongation of this struggle to her women as to her generals and soldiers in the field. Fully, fiercely, terribly, malignantly, have they entered into this conflict. In many localities I am fully persuaded that neither friend, relative, nor neighbor, capable of bearing arms, would be allowed to remain at home. The females in their zeal would find some means to drive him away into the military service. . . .

Not long since, during our numerous marchings and campings, I was called to visit, on . . . military duty, a family . . . from all appearances, previously to the war, the home of wealth, refinement, and luxury; but now, owing to the marching over and camping thereon of our immense army, everything was laid waste. Able-bodied slaves were all gone; a few, too old and too young for use, left as a burden; fences, cattle, crops, out-houses, all having disappeared; the old homestead, with a small yard enclosed by palings, alone remaining.

The family were a dignified old gentleman, several daughters, and some female relatives, the son being in the Southern army. . . . When speaking of the desolation of everything around, inquiry was made as to how they expected to get through the coming season.

"The Lord only knows, for I do not!" was the old gentleman's sad response.

A daughter of some twenty summers, full of life, energy, and bubbling over with Southern and Confederate sympathies, interposed, "Oh, never fear, we'll get through somehow. We are now living . . . on what, before the war, we carelessly threw away. Before this war commenced, the idea of doing what is called *work* never once entered my mind. Now I am laboring hard every day from morn to eve, and feel the better for it. We'll get along some way."

Thus it is that the Lord is strangely working a speedy and radical revolution in all the social feelings and habits of the South, lowering pride and vanity; levelling a self-constituted aristocracy to the ordinary grade of human sympathies and duties; developing also . . . the latent energies of what we have been wont to look upon as an almost effete race.

More than this also, God is unloosing those that were bound, elevating the lowly, removing stumbling blocks, and placing before a long-despised race new hopes, new desires, and new prospects, with the addition of a field hitherto unseen for rewarded energy and industry.

When this war has terminated with a restored Union and permanent peace, all the people of the South will be found in an entirely novel condition; full of energy, zeal, and self-reliance, henceforth to become vigorous yet loving competitors to the North in all the elements of national greatness. . . .

Skirmishing daily, the two armies continued moving southeastward on parallel lines, soon reaching Cold Harbor, a point only a few miles northeast of Richmond and very near Gaines's Mill, one of the McClellan–Lee battlefields of 1862. At Cold Harbor another major clash occurred. The South's Private Casler sums it up starkly:

On the 3d of June [Grant] was determined to fight the decisive battle of the war, and massed his troops and rushed them on our works amidst a storm of shot and shell that it seemed no men could stand; but they were repulsed with great slaughter. [Some 6,000 or 7,000 casualties were incurred.] The battle [at least the main part of it] did not last more than an hour. It was the most destructive that had been fought during the war, considering the length of time the engagement lasted.

According to the Union's Private Theodore Gerrish:

The situation was now a gloomy one; our losses through the campaign had been fearful; the army of General Lee was still between us and Richmond.

We now found ourselves, at a sickly season of the year, in the deadly swamps of the Chickahominy. . . . The sun glared down on

Federals in the trenches at Cold Harbor.

us. . . . The air was filled with malaria and death. The water was very poor and unhealthy. Sickness, as well as battle, was doing fearful work in our ranks.

We were now in the position from which General McClellan had been driven two years before. It was a fortunate thing for the destiny of this nation, in this dreary period, that we had at the head of our army a man who knew nothing of the word defeat—one who was equal to the emergency.

Undoubtedly General Grant was disappointed that the fruits of the campaign had not been more decisive, but he well understood that General Lee had lost heavily in the campaign and that it would be a difficult task for him to replenish his decimated ranks; and so he conceived the idea of throwing his army [southward] across the James River . . . [with intent to] capture Petersburg [some twenty miles below Richmond], cut the lines of railway connecting Richmond with the South, and thus compel the surrender of the rebel capital.

Southerner Robert Stiles says that on the night of June 12 Grant "folded his tents like the Arabs and silently stole away. . . ."
When we waked on the morning of the 13th and found no enemy

in our front we realized that a new element had entered into this move—the element of uncertainty. . . . [E]ven Marse Robert, who knew everything knowable, did not appear to know what his old enemy proposed to do or where he would be most likely to find him. . . .

. . . [Regarding] our search for Grant . . . there was nothing about it calculated to make an impression. . . . Of course, we crossed the Chickahominy, and then we worked down toward Malvern Hill. . . . We did not cross the James River . . . until the night of the 17th; but from that time everything seemed to have waked up, and though we saw no enemy, yet we knew where he was, and that Petersburg was his immediate objective. . . .

We made a rapid all-night march, which was a very trying one on account of the heat and the heavy dust which covered everything and everybody and rendered breathing all but impossible. We . . . arrived in Petersburg in the early morning, our division and our battalion being among the first of Lee's troops to arrive.

We were just in time. . . . General Beauregard [in charge of the city's defenses] had made admirable use of the scant force at his command and had successfully repulsed all . . . attacks [by the first Federal arrivals], but he did not have a garrison at all adequate to resist the countless thousands of Grant's main army. . . .

The whole population of the city appeared to be in the streets and thoroughly alive to the narrow escape they had made. . . . Ladies old and young met us at their front gates with hearty welcome, cool water, and delicious viands, and did not at all shrink from grasping our rough and dirty hands.

General Grant soon decided that Petersburg could not be taken by assault but would have to be invested.

Said the Union's Chaplain Stewart in a letter written on July 1:

Our flank movements have, in due time, brought us upon the south side of the James River and into a position from whence the spires of Petersburg are in full view. Soon, the old business over again, cannonading, long and loud. . . . Then rifle practice, sharp, continued, and bloody—hospitals with wounded to care for, and dead to bury.

Here is the Potomac army at a seemingly dead stand. No more flank movements practicable. Richmond not yet captured, nor soon likely to be. Notwithstanding the fearful amount of blood, toil, and treasure, with frequent change of base and locality during the past two months, yet has no apparent advantage been gained over Lee—

scarcely an insignificant rifle pit taken from the rebels and retained.

General Grant finds it a far different matter pushing aside Western armies and capturing Vicksburg to conquering Lee and entering Richmond. This, nevertheless, a dogged perseverance may yet accomplish—though before Petersburg, which is but an outpost of Richmond, we may be compelled to burrow for six months to come.

Grant's Wilderness campaign had cost him more than 50,000 casualties. During the campaign's progress, Washington sent him about 40,000 reinforcements. President Lincoln accepted the horrendous casualty reports without protest, but he must have agonized over them in private. They affected him not only as a man of conscience but as a politician. This was a presidential election year, and his conduct of the war was the leading issue.

Lee's army had been badly hurt (total casualties uncertain, but probably at least 20,000) and had received less than 15,000 fresh troops during the course of the campaign; but it was still relatively strong. An army on the defensive, fighting from behind stout breastworks, can do very well with modest numbers. Indeed, after Cold Harbor, Lee had even dispatched reinforcements under Jubal Early northwestward to the Shenandoah Valley, the resources of which were so important to the Confederacy. General Early succeeded in drawing a part of Grant's army away from Petersburg by pressing to the Valley's northern end and marching upon Washington. During the second week in July, the audacious Southerners actually demonstrated in the capital's suburbs, and Lincoln himself came briefly under their fire. Deficient in numbers, they soon returned to the Valley; but their act astonished the North.

All would have been well if the Siege of Petersburg could have been ended quickly. And this might have happened had success crowned an attempt to penetrate the Confederate works by means of a mine. A regiment composed chiefly of coal miners from Schuylkill County, Pennsylvania—the Forty-eighth Pennsylvania Volunteers— labored for a month tunneling under a key section of the defenses. The mine was exploded successfully on July 30, but the attack on the breach was badly managed, and the Confederates were able to rally and restore their line.

The people of the North made no secret of their dismay over the way things were going. A few months earlier they had seen Grant as the Union's savior. Now many of them were calling him "Butcher Grant." The general's position would have been better if Sherman had managed to achieve a quick and spectacular victory in the West. It is true that he had maneuvered and fought his way southward from Chattanooga to the outskirts of Atlanta, Georgia; but the city was still in Confederate hands.

All in all, the Union's morale was at a low ebb. The victories of Gettysburg, Vicksburg, and Chattanooga had lost their power to stimulate. It was already more than a year since Gettysburg and Vicksburg, and nine months since Chattanooga; and the end of the war seemed nowhere in sight.

21

FARRAGUT IN
MOBILE BAY

D AVID G. FARRAGUT'S CONQUEST *of New Orleans in 1862 had
earned him an historic honor: He became the nation's first
rear admiral. Now, in 1864, Farragut's chief concern as commander
of the Western Gulf Squadron was the maintaining of the coastal
blockade. The old sailor—his career spanned half a century, going
back to the War of 1812—was disgusted with the overall status of the
Union's work against the Confederates:*

What a disgrace that, with their slender means, they should,
after three years, contend with us from one end of the country to the
other. . . . I get right sick, every now and then, at the bad news.
. . . The only comfort I have is that the Confederates are more unhappy, if possible, than we are.

*As it turned out, it was Farragut himself who gave the Union its first
substantial lift that summer. His objective was Mobile Bay, in southwestern Alabama.*

Writes Southern editor and historian Edward Pollard:

The enemy had long contemplated the possession of Mobile Bay,
guarded at its entrance by two . . . fortifications. Here was a dif-

David G. Farragut.

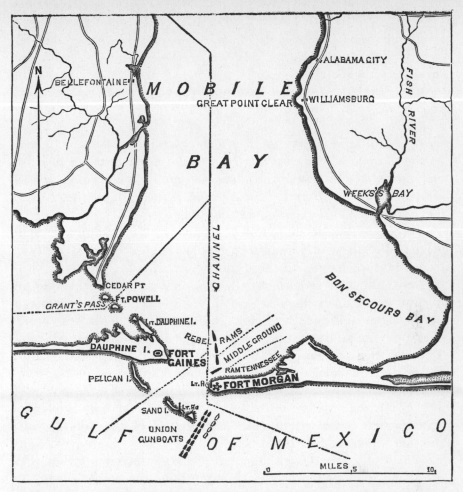

Federal fleet (bottom of map) is shown as it is about to pass Fort Morgan
and enter Mobile Bay. Confederate vessels await the entry.

ficult point to blockade; here was a nursery of the Confederate navy;
and here vessels were . . . being constructed for raising the
blockade.

*In charge of Mobile Bay's Confederate fleet (as yet a small one) was
Admiral Franklin Buchanan, who had commanded the* Merrimac *in
the famous fight at Hampton Roads—until he was shot in the leg by
a marksman on shore. Farragut and Buchanan had known each other
for many years, having fought the last of the West Indies pirates together as young men.*

Farragut had been unable to act against Mobile Bay as early as he wished because he lacked ironclad vessels and army support, the latter for land operations against the forts after he passed them with the fleet. In early August he was finally ready. His attack fleet was now an imposing one, containing fourteen wooden ships and four monitors.

On the afternoon of August 4, Farragut made a personal recon-noissance of the bay's entrance. He and his party were on board a small steamer, the Cowslip. *Among the admiral's assistants was an army signal officer, John C. Kinney, who was working with the navy for the first time. He describes what he saw:*

On the left, some three miles distant, was Fort Gaines, a small brick and earth work, mounting a few heavy guns, but too far away from the ship channel to cause much uneasiness to the fleet. [Still farther to the left was Fort Powell, also small, and of no threat at all to ships in the main channel.] Fort Morgan was on the right, one of the strongest of the old brick forts, and greatly strengthened by im-mense piles of sandbags, covering every portion of the exposed front. The fort was well equipped with three tiers of heavy guns—one of the guns, at least, of the best English make, imported by the Con-federates. In addition, there was in front a battery of seven powerful guns at the water's edge on the beach. All the guns, of both fort and water-battery, were within point-blank range of the only channel through which the fleet could pass.

The Confederates considered the works impregnable, but they did not depend solely upon them. Just around the point of land, be-hind Fort Morgan, we could see that afternoon three saucy-looking gunboats and the famous ram *Tennessee.* The latter [built along lines similar to those of the *Merrimac*] was . . . considered the strongest and most powerful iron-clad ever put afloat. She looked like a great turtle; her sloping sides were covered with iron plates six inches in thickness, thoroughly riveted together, and she had a formidable iron beak projecting under the water. Her armament consisted of six heavy Brooke rifles, each sending a solid shot weigh-ing from 95 to 110 pounds. . . .

In addition to these means of resistance, the narrow channel . . . had been lined with torpedoes [i.e., mines]. These were under the water, anchored to the bottom. Some of them were beer-kegs filled with powder, from the sides of which projected numerous little tubes containing fulminate, which it was expected would be exploded by contact with the passing vessels; but the greater part were tin cones fitted with caps.

Except for what Farragut had already accomplished on the Mississippi, it would have been considered a foolhardy experiment for wooden vessels to attempt to pass so close to one of the strongest forts on the coast; but when to the forts were added the knowledge of the strength of the ram and the supposed deadly character of the torpedoes, it may be imagined that the coming event impressed the person taking his first glimpse of naval warfare as decidedly hazardous and unpleasant. . . .

The scene on the *Cowslip* that afternoon of the 4th of August was a notable one as she steamed within range of the forts. The central figure was the grand old admiral, his plans all completed, affable with all, evidently not thinking of failure as among the possibilities of the morrow, and filling everyone with his enthusiasm. . . .

After the reconnoissance, the final council of war was held on board the *Hartford* [Farragut's flagship], when the positions of the various vessels were assigned and the order of the line was arranged. . . .

At sunset the last orders had been issued, every commander knew his duty, and unusual quiet prevailed in the fleet. The sea was smooth, a gentle breeze relieved the midsummer heat, and the night came on serenely and peacefully. . . . For the first hour after the candles were lighted below, the stillness was almost oppressive. The officers of the *Hartford* gathered around the wardroom table, writing letters to loved ones far away, or giving instructions in case of death. . . .

But this occupied little time; and then, business over, there followed an hour of unrestrained jollity. Many an old story was retold, and ancient conundrum repeated. Old officers forgot, for the moment, their customary dignity, and it was evident that all were exhilarated and stimulated by the knowledge of the coming struggle. There was no other "stimulation," for the strict naval rules prevented. Finally, after a half hour's smoke under the forecastle, all hands turned in.

The atmosphere on board the Confederate flagship, the ram Tennessee, was altogether different. For one thing, no prevailing spirit of optimism existed. The ram, though strongly built, had its defects.

Explains Fleet Surgeon D. B. Conrad (the same Conrad who served under Stonewall Jackson at First Bull Run):

Our engines had been taken from an old river boat. They were weak . . . and could only force us through the water about two miles an hour. . . . The rudder chains, by which the ship was steered, were found to be exposed to the enemy's shot, being in their whole length outside the iron deck; they were covered over by a slight coating of iron rail.

The capacity of the ram inboard to accommodate her crew was fearfully deficient. . . . We had been very uncomfortable for many weeks . . . in consequence of the prevailing heavy rains wetting the decks, and the terribly moist, hot atmosphere [within], which was like that oppressiveness which precedes a tornado. It was therefore impossible to sleep inside. Besides, from the want of properly cooked food and the continuous wetting of the decks [and bedding] at night, the officers and men were rendered desperate.

We knew that the impending action would soon be determined one way or the other, and everyone looked forward to it with a positive feeling of relief.

I had been sleeping on the deck of the admiral's cabin for two or three nights, when at daybreak on the 5th of August the old quartermaster came down the ladder, rousing us up with his gruff voice, saying, "Admiral, the officer of the deck bids me report that the enemy's fleet is under way!"

Jumping up, still half asleep, we came on deck, and sure enough, there was the enemy heading for the passage past the fort.

Farragut's monitors were in the lead and on the right flank, their object to pass nearest the fort's guns. The wooden vessels, all propelled by steam but some carrying sail also, followed in pairs (each pair a large vessel and a small) that were lashed together for mutual support during the first leg of the trip. They were to be separated when the fort was passed. The Brooklyn *was the large vessel of the first pair, and Farragut's flagship, the* Hartford, *was the large vessel of the second. The fleet's many colorful flags fluttered brightly in the first rays of the sun. On the gun decks the crews were at the ready.*

Writes the commander of the Confederate fort, General R. L. Page:

As they approached with a moderate wind and on the flood tide, I fired the first gun at long range, and soon the firing became general, our fire being briskly returned by the enemy. For a short time

Farragut's vessels going into action. Monitors are on side toward Fort Morgan.

the smoke was so dense that the vessels could not be distinguished, but still the firing was incessant.

Federal signal officer John Kinney says that the Confederate fleet
. . . took position across the entrance to the bay and raked the advance vessels fore and aft, doing great damage, to which it was for a time impossible to make effective reply. Gradually the fleet came into close quarters with Fort Morgan, and the firing on both sides became terrific.

In the words of Joseph Marthon, another Federal officer:
I was in charge of the howitzer placed in the maintop of the *Hartford* [i.e., on a platform built around the mainmast, high above the deck] . . . and used the gun while in range of Fort Morgan. . . .
The admiral climbed into the port main-rigging [the system of ropes leading to the maintop on the vessel's left side]. . . . Captain

[Percival] Drayton sent a quartermaster with a piece of lead-line to lash him to the shroud to prevent him falling in case of injury. After a short time the smoke grew more dense, when the admiral cast off the lashing, climbed up to the futtock-rigging [just below the platform], taking the lashing with him, where he lashed himself and remained during the action. . . .

My attention was called to the admiral's position by his hailing the top . . . asking "where this water was coming from." Upon looking about, I found that the water-breaker [a small cask of drinking water], placed in the hole of a coil of rigging I was sitting on, had been capsized by a piece of shell, knocking a hole in the top, and the water was running down on the admiral's head.

According to signal officer John Kinney:

The wooden vessels moved more rapidly than the monitors, and as the *Brooklyn* came opposite the fort and approached the torpedo line, she came nearly alongside the rear monitor. To have kept on would have been to take the lead, with the ram *Tennessee* approaching and with the unknown danger of the torpedoes underneath. At this critical moment the *Brooklyn* halted and began backing and signaling. . . .

The *Hartford* was immediately behind, and the following vessels were in close proximity; and the sudden stopping of the *Brooklyn* threatened to bring the whole fleet into collision, while the strong inflowing tide was likely to carry some of the vessels to the shore under the guns of the fort. . . .

[Word] was sent at once from the admiral, "Order the monitors ahead, and go on." But still the *Brooklyn* halted; while, to add to the horror of the situation, the monitor *Tecumseh,* a few hundred yards in the advance, suddenly careened to one side and almost instantly sank to the bottom [having fallen victim to a torpedo]. . . .

Says Southern observer D. B. Conrad:

Immediately immense bubbles of steam, as large as cauldrons, rose to the surface of the water, and only eight human beings could be seen in the turmoil. [Actually, twenty-one survived the disaster; ninety-three were trapped below decks.]

. . . Thus the monitor *Tecumseh,* at the commencement of the fight . . . went to her fate at the bottom of the Gulf. . . . Sunk with her was her chivalric commander, T. A. M. Craven. . . . The pilot, with whom I sometime afterwards conversed at Pensacola [while a prisoner of war] . . . told me that when the vessel careened so that water began to run into the mouth of the turret, he and Captain Craven were on the ladder together, the captain on the top step, with the way open for his easy and honorable escape.

The pilot said, "Go ahead, captain!"

"No, sir!" replied Captain Craven. "After you, pilot. I leave my ship last!"

Upon this the pilot sprung up, and the gallant Craven went down, sucked under in the vortex. . . .

Confederate General Page, in charge of Fort Morgan, says that as the Tecumseh *went down, "cheers from the garrison . . . rang out, which were checked at once; and the order was passed to sink the admiral's ship and then cheer."*

Oddly enough, the Federal fleet, too, rang with cheers as the Tecumseh *sank. The men somehow got the impression that the stricken vessel was the Confederate ram* Tennessee.

"Meantime," relates the Hartford's *John Kinney,*

the *Brooklyn* failed to go ahead, and the whole fleet became a stationary point-blank target for the guns of Fort Morgan and of the rebel vessels. It was during these few perilous moments that the most fatal work of the day was done to the fleet.

Owing to the *Hartford*'s position, only her few bow guns could be used, while a deadly rain of shot and shell was falling on her, and her men were being cut down by scores, unable to make reply. The sight on deck was sickening beyond the power of words to portray. Shot after shot came through the side, mowing down the men, deluging the decks with blood, and scattering mangled fragments of humanity so thickly that it was difficult to stand on the deck, so slippery was it. . . . The bodies of the dead were placed in a long row on the port side, while the wounded were sent below until the surgeons' quarters would hold no more.

A solid shot coming through the bow struck a gunner on the neck, completely severing head from body. One poor fellow . . . lost both legs by a cannon ball. As he fell he threw up both arms, just in time to have them also carried away by another shot. [This man survived, drawing much interest when he displayed himself at a postwar fair in New York.] At one gun, all the crew on one side were swept down by a shot which came crashing through the bul-

warks. A shell burst between the two forward guns in charge of Lieutenant [Herbert B.] Tyson, killing and wounding fifteen men. The
mast upon which the writer was perched was twice struck. . . .

Another signal message from the *Brooklyn* told of the sinking of
the *Tecumseh*—a fact known already—and another order to "go on"
was given and was not obeyed.

With the Brooklyn *and the three surviving monitors thus holding
all of Farragut's vessels in a position where they were "sitting-duck"
targets, the men of the small Confederate fleet saw a prospect of
victory.*

But at this supreme moment [says Southerner D. B. Conrad] . . .
Admiral Farragut's flagship, the *Hartford,* forged ahead; and Farragut, showing the nerve and determination of the officer and the
man, gave the order, "Damn the torpedoes! Go ahead!" And away
he went, crashing through their bed to victory and renown. Some of
the officers told me afterwards that they could hear the [torpedo
primers] snapping under the bottoms of their ships, and that they
expected every moment to be blown into high air. [Providentially,
the torpedoes had been rendered ineffective by their long exposure
to the water.]

The slightest delay at that time on the part of Farragut, subjected
as he was to the terrible fire of the fort and fleet, would have been disaster, defeat, and the probable loss of his entire squadron; but he
proved to be the man for the emergency.

We in the *Tennessee,* advancing very slowly, at the rate of about
two miles an hour, met the leading vessels of the enemy as they
passed, and fought them face to face; but their fire was . . . continuous and severe. . . .

A few of our men were slightly wounded, and when the last vessel had passed us and been fought in turn, we had been in action
more than an hour and a half. And then the enemy's fleet, somewhat
disabled, of course, kept on up the bay and anchored about four
miles away.

So [about 9:00 A.M.] ended the first part of the fight. Farragut
had already won half the battle. He had passed the fort and fleet and
had [his] wooden vessels and three monitors left in good fighting
trim.

The only Confederate vessel left to continue the fight was the Tennessee. *Of the three wooden gunboats (each of which had done its*

share against the Federal fleet), two had taken refuge under the guns of Fort Morgan, with one of the vessels having been badly damaged; and the third, the Selma, *commanded by P. U. Murphy, had been captured by the* Metacomet, *commanded by James E. Jouett—the two captains having known each other before the war.*

At its temporary anchorage, the Federal fleet was a scene of activity:

The crews of the various vessels [says John Kinney] had begun to efface the marks of the terrible contest by washing the decks and clearing up the splinters. The cooks were preparing breakfast [with Southerner P. U. Murphy, who was nursing a wrist wound, having accepted a cordial invitation to eat with his friendly enemy James Jouett on the *Metacomet*]; the surgeons were busily engaged in making amputations and binding arteries; and under canvas on the port side of each vessel lay the ghastly line of dead waiting the sailor's burial. As if by mutual understanding, officers who were relieved from immediate duty gathered in the wardrooms to ascertain who of their mates were missing. . . .

The Confederates on the Tennessee, *according to Fleet Surgeon Conrad, used these moments to seek both food and physical comfort:*

For us . . . to eat below was simply impossible, on account of the heat and humidity. . . . Soon hard-tack and coffee were furnished, the men all . . . creeping out of the ports of the shield to get a little fresh air, the officers going to the upper deck.

Admiral Buchanan . . . was stumping up and down the deck, lame from a wound received in his . . . engagement in the *Merrimac;* and in about fifteen minutes we observed that, instead of heading for the safe lee of the fort, our iron prow was pointed for the enemy's fleet. Suppressed exclamations were beginning to be heard from the officers and crew: "The old admiral has not had his fight out yet. He is heading for that big fleet. . . ."

. . . I, being on his staff and in close association with him, ventured to ask him, "Are you going into that fleet, admiral?"

"I am, sir!" was his reply.

Without intending to be heard by him, I said to an officer standing near me, "Well, we'll never come out of there whole!"

But Buchanan had heard my remark, and, turning round, said sharply, "That's my lookout, sir!"

. . . I may as well explain here why he did this much-criticized and desperate deed of daring. . . . He had only six hours' coal on

board, and he intended to expend that in fighting. . . . Then he
meant to go to the lee of the fort and assist General Page in the defense of the place. . . .

*The Federals, more than a little surprised by Buchanan's move, re-
occupied their battle stations and prepared to meet him.*

*John Kinney—who, incidentally, had been making signals for
Farragut from time to time—continued to observe with the fascina-
tion of an army man newly attached to the navy:*

Because of the slowness of the monitors, Admiral Farragut selected the fastest of the wooden vessels to begin the attack. While the
navy signals for a general attack of the enemy were being prepared,
the *Monongahela* . . . and the *Lackawanna* . . . were ordered by
the more rapid signal system of the army to "run down the ram," the
order being immediately repeated to the monitors.

The *Monongahela* . . . at once took the lead. . . . The ram
from the first headed for the *Hartford* and paid no attention to her
assailants, except with her guns. The *Monongahela*, going at full
speed, struck the *Tennessee* amidships—a blow that would have sunk
almost any vessel of the Union navy, but which inflicted not the
slightest damage on the solid iron hull of the ram. . . . Her own
iron prow and cutwater were carried away, and she was otherwise
badly damaged about the stern by the collision.

The *Lackawanna* was close behind and delivered a similar blow
with her wooden bow, simply causing the ram to lurch slightly to
one side. As the vessels separated, the *Lackawanna* swung alongside
the ram, which sent two shots through her and kept on her course
for the *Hartford,* which was now the next vessel in the attack.

The two flagships approached each other, bow to bow, iron
against oak. . . . The other vessels of the fleet were unable to do
anything for the defense of the admiral except to train their guns on
the ram, on which as yet they had not the slightest effect. It was a
thrilling moment for the fleet, for it was evident that if the ram
could strike the *Hartford* the latter must sink. But for the two vessels to strike fairly, bows on, would probably have involved the destruction of both, for the ram must have penetrated so far into the
wooden ship that as the *Hartford* filled and sank she would have carried the ram under water.

Whether for this reason or for some other, as the two vessels came
together the *Tennessee* slightly changed her course; the port bow of
the *Hartford* met the port bow of the ram, and the ships grated

against each other as they passed. The *Hartford* poured her whole port broadside against the ram, but the solid shot merely dented the side and bounded into the air. The ram tried to return the salute, but owing to defective primers only one gun was discharged. This sent a shell through the berth-deck, killing five men and wounding eight. The muzzle of the gun was so close to the *Hartford* that the powder blackened her side.

The admiral stood on the quarter-deck when the vessels came together, and as he saw the result he jumped on to the port-quarter-rail, holding to the mizzen-rigging, a position from which he might have jumped to the deck of the ram as she passed. Seeing him in this position and fearing for his safety, Flag-Lieutenant [J. Crittenden] Watson slipped a rope around him and secured it to the rigging, so that during the fight the admiral was twice "lashed to the rigging," each time by devoted officers. . . .

The *Tennessee* now became the target for the whole fleet, all the vessels of which were making toward her, pounding her with shot, and trying to run her down. As the *Hartford* turned to make for her again, we ran in front of the *Lackawanna*, which had already turned and was moving under full headway with the same object. She struck us on our starboard side, amidships, crushing halfway through, knocking two port-holes into one, upsetting one of the Dahlgren guns, and creating general consternation.

For a time it was thought that we must sink, and the cry rang out over the deck, "Save the admiral! Save the admiral!" The port boats were ordered lowered, and in their haste some of the sailors cut the falls, and two of the cutters dropped into the water wrong side up, and floated astern.

But the admiral sprang into the starboard mizzen-rigging, looked over the side of the ship, and, finding there were still a few inches to spare above the water's edge, instantly ordered the ship ahead again at full speed, after the ram.

The unfortunate *Lackawanna* . . . was making for [the ram] once more, and, singularly enough, again came up on our starboard side, and another collision seemed imminent. And now the admiral became a trifle excited. He had no idea of whipping the rebels to be himself sunk by a friend; nor did he realize at the moment that the *Hartford* was as much to blame as the *Lackawanna*.

Turning to the writer, he inquired, "Can you say 'For God's sake' by signal?"

"Yes, sir," was the reply.

"Then say to the *Lackawanna*, 'For God's sake get out of the way and anchor!' "

In my haste to send the message, I brought the end of my signal flag-staff down with considerable violence upon the head of the admiral, who was standing nearer than I thought, causing him to wince perceptibly.

It was a [rashly conceived] message, for the fault was equally divided, each ship being too eager to reach the enemy. . . . [I]t turned out all right. . . . The army signal officer on the *Lackawanna* . . . in the foretop . . . received the first five words, "For God's sake get out—" [and then] the wind flirted the large United States flag at the masthead around him, so that he was unable to read the conclusion of the message.

Meanwhile, the guns of Farragut's monitors were beginning to give the Tennessee *serious trouble. A 15-inch solid shot from the* Manhattan *struck her plating with such force that daylight was let through to her interior. But it was the* Chickasaw, *commanded by George H. Perkins, that fired the most destructive shots.*

According to Confederate officer James D. Johnston, second-in-command to Admiral Buchanan:

One of these missiles . . . struck the iron cover of the stern [gun] port and jammed it . . . so that it became impossible to run the gun out for firing, and Admiral Buchanan, who superintended the battery during the entire engagement, sent to the engine room for a machinist to back out the pin of the bolt upon which the port cover revolved. While this was being done, a shot . . . struck the edge of the port cover immediately over the spot where the machinist was sitting and [reduced him to bloody fragments]. . . . The same shot caused several iron splinters to fly inside of the shield, one of which killed a seaman, while another broke the admiral's leg below the knee.

Fleet Surgeon Conrad, summoned at once, tells what he found:

All of the gun's crew and the admiral were covered from head to foot with [the shattered machinist's] blood, flesh, and viscera. I thought at first the admiral was mortally wounded. . . .

I . . . asked, "Admiral, are you badly hurt?"

"Don't know," he replied, but I saw one of his legs crushed up under his body, and . . . I . . . raised him up with great caution;

and, clasping his arms around my neck, carried him on my back
down the ladder to the cockpit, his broken leg slapping against me
as we moved slowly along.

After applying a temporary bandage, he sat up on the deck and
received reports . . . regarding the progress of the fight. Captain
Johnston soon came down . . . and the admiral greeted him with:
"Well, Johnston, they have got me again. You'll have to look out for
her now; it is your fight."

"All right," answered the captain, "I'll do the best I know how."

*But by this time there really wasn't much that Johnston could do. He
relates:*

The steering apparatus had been completely destroyed . . . and
the smoke-stack had fallen, destroying the draught in such a degree
as to render it impossible to keep steam enough to stem the tide,
which was running out at the rate of over four miles an hour.

Realizing the impossibility of directing the firing of the guns
without the use of the rudder, and that the ship had been rendered
utterly helpless, I went to the lower deck and informed the admiral
of her condition, and that I had not been able to bring a gun to bear
upon any of our antagonists for nearly half an hour, to which he replied, "Well, Johnston, if you cannot do them any further damage
you had better surrender."

With this sanction of my own views I returned to the gun-deck,
and after another glance about the bay to see if there was any chance
of getting another shot, and seeing none of the enemy's ships within
range of our broadside guns, I went to the top of the shield [i.e., to
the topmost deck, which was out in the open] and took down the
boat-hook to which the flag had been lashed after having been shot
away several times during the fight.

While I was thus engaged, repeated shots came from the enemy's
vessels; but as soon as I [went down] to the gun-deck and had a flag
of truce attached to the boat-hook [and sent up] the firing ceased.
Having returned to the top of the shield, I saw one of the heaviest
ships of the fleet approaching rapidly, apparently for the purpose of
making another attempt to sink the ram.

Seeing the flag of truce, the commander [William E. Le Roy]
stopped his ship, but her momentum was too great to be overcome
in the short intervening space, and she struck the ram on the starboard quarter, but without injuring it. As she did so, her commander

James D. Johnston.

Tennessee (left foreground) makes her surrender.

hailed, saying: "This is the United States steamer *Ossipee*. Hello, Johnston; how are you? Le Roy— Don't you know me? I'll send a boat alongside for you."

The boat came and conveyed me on board the *Ossipee,* at whose gangway I was met by her genial commander, between whom and myself a lifelong friendship had existed. When I reached the deck of his ship, he remarked, "I'm glad to see you, Johnston. Here is some ice-water for you; I know you're dry. But I've something better than that for you down below."

. . . Within an hour after I was taken on board the *Ossipee,* Admiral Farragut sent for me to be brought on board his flagship, and when I reached her deck he expressed regret at meeting me under such circumstances. . . . His flag captain, Percival Drayton, remarked, "You have one consolation, Johnston. No one can say that you have not nobly defended the honor of the Confederate flag today."

I thanked him, but gave all the honor due to its defense to Admiral Buchanan, who was the true hero of the battle. And when the disparity between the forces engaged is duly considered, I am constrained to believe that history will give him his just meed of praise.

The battle had cost the Federals 145 killed (the figure including the 93 who were drowned) and 170 wounded, while the Confederates suffered only 12 killed and 20 wounded. The remains of the Confederate machinist who was torn to pieces were shoveled into buckets and thrown overboard.

The Union ship Metacomet *was turned into a hospital for the wounded of both sides. Writes the ship's commander, James Jouett:*

They lay in cots on the quarter-deck . . . side by side, chatting familiarly, taking medicine, tea, coffee, or wine, as the doctor thought best. 'Twas amusing to hear those poor fellows, who but an hour ago were trying to kill each other, now spinning yarns of olden times.

It remained for Admiral Farragut and his army supports to reduce the forts at the bay's entrance. Fort Gaines and Fort Powell were taken during the next two days. And a combined navy and army operation brought about the fall of the stronger Fort Morgan on August 23. Though the city of Mobile was still in Confederate hands (and would not fall until the war was about over), Federal control of the bay was complete; the port was tightly sealed.

Farragut's victory was a significant one. The people of the North, almost desperate for encouraging news, hailed it as a great one. For President Lincoln, the victory had considerable political importance. Coming at a time when his reelection was gravely in doubt, it helped to improve his chances.

22

SHERMAN'S MARCH

Lincoln's reelection—*his win over Democratic candidate George B. McClellan, deposed commander of the Army of the Potomac—was practically guaranteed when Sherman's troops, after four months of maneuvering and fighting in Georgia (months during which fame came to such places as Dalton, Resaca, New Hope Church, and Kennesaw Mountain), entered Atlanta on September 2, 1864. Here was a victory of truly great moment. Atlanta was a manufacturing center of vital importance to the Confederate war effort. Moreover, the city's fall opened Georgia to further conquest.*

One of the first things Sherman did was to order the evacuation of the inhabitants. "I was resolved to make Atlanta a pure military garrison or depot, with no civil population to influence military measures." In more than one occupied city, he says, he had seen large numbers of Federal troops taken from active duty "to guard and protect the interests of a hostile population." He admits that his decision had a punitive side, that it was intended in part to convince the South that he was in earnest.

The order, of course, was strongly protested. A written appeal to reconsider was sent to Sherman by the mayor and two councilmen. To this the general replied:

Gentlemen: I have your . . . petition to revoke my orders removing all the inhabitants from Atlanta. I . . . give full credit to your statements of the distress that will be occasioned, and yet shall not revoke my orders, because they were not designed to meet the humanities of the case but to prepare for the future struggles in which millions of good people outside of Atlanta have a deep interest. . . .

. . . I assert that our military plans make it necessary for the inhabitants to go away, and I can only renew my offer of services to make their exodus in any direction as easy and comfortable as possible.

You cannot qualify war in harsher terms than I will. War is cruelty, and you cannot refine it. And those who brought war into our country deserve all the curses and maledictions a people can pour out. I know I had no hand in making this war, and I know I will make more sacrifices today than any of you to secure peace. But you cannot have peace and a division of our country. . . .

You might as well appeal against the thunderstorm as against these terrible hardships of war. They are inevitable, and the only way the people of Atlanta can hope once more to live in peace and quiet at home is to stop the war. . . . We don't want your Negroes or your horses or your houses or your lands, or anything you have. But we do want, and will have, a just obedience to the laws of the United States . . . and if it involves the destruction of your improvements, we cannot help it. . . .

. . . the South began the war by seizing forts, arsenals, mints, custom-houses, etc., etc. . . . I myself have seen . . . hundreds and thousands of women and children fleeing from your armies and desperadoes, hungry and with bleeding feet. . . . Now that war comes home to you, you feel very different. You deprecate its horrors; but did not feel them when you sent carloads of soldiers and ammunition, and moulded shells and shot, to carry war into [Unionist areas of] Kentucky and Tennessee, to desolate the homes of hundreds and thousands of good people who only asked to live in peace at their old homes and under the government of their inheritance.

But these comparisons are idle. I want peace, and believe it can only be reached through union and war; and I will ever conduct war purely with a view to perfect an early success. But, my dear sirs, when peace does come, you may call on me for anything. Then will I share with you the last cracker, and watch with you to shield your homes and families against danger from every quarter.

Now you must go, and take with you the old and feeble, feed and nurse them, and build for them in more quiet places proper habitations to shield them against the weather until the mad passions of men cool down and allow the Union and peace once more to settle over your old homes at Atlanta.

Sherman's position at this time was not one of complete security. Though defeated at Atlanta, and heavily outnumbered, the Confederates posed a serious threat to Federal railroad communications northward to Tennessee, the campaign's starting point. General John Hood, of the crippled arm and the missing leg, was now the top Confederate commander, Joe Johnston having been relieved by President Davis for failing to stop Sherman's invasion.

In October Sherman found it necessary to march from Atlanta with a large part of his army to protect his rails from Hood's attacks. Hood retreated westward into Alabama. Sherman followed across the border, then abandoned the chase. Hood was expected next to invade Tennessee in an attempt to draw Sherman northward, but Sherman had no intention of becoming a party to this game. Leaving George Thomas, the Rock of Chickamauga, to defend Tennessee against Hood, he abandoned his communications to launch a new venture—a march from Atlanta to the sea.

This was a time of heartening news from the Virginia theater. Though Grant was still stalled before Richmond and Petersburg, Phil Sheridan was gaining the upper hand in the Shenandoah Valley, where a good part of Lee's supplies originated. On September 19, Sheridan (with the usual superior numbers) defeated Jubal Early at Winchester. Soon driving the Confederates from nearly the whole length of the Valley, the Federals launched a campaign against the Valley itself. An unrestrained torch was applied to mills, granaries, barns, railway stations, bridges, and other property useful to Lee's operations. General Early, though outnumbered at least 2 to 1, returned to the attack on October 19, surprising the Federals at Cedar Creek. The Confederates made smashing gains at first, but then they themselves were shattered by a counterattack led by Sheridan in person. The Shenandoah Valley had seen its last great battle.

In order for Sherman to make his march to the sea, he had to abandon Atlanta. Not wanting to return the city's war facilities to the enemy, he ordered them destroyed. A considerable part of the city went with them.

On the night of November 15, Major George Ward Nichols, an aide-de-camp to Sherman, wrote in his diary:

A grand and awful spectacle is presented to the beholder in this

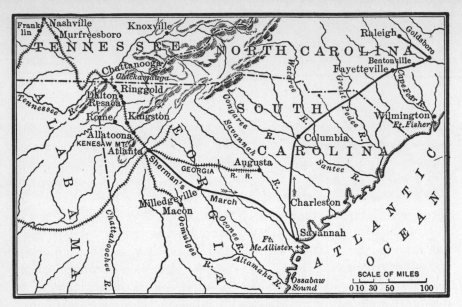

Route of Sherman's march through Georgia and the Carolinas.

beautiful city, now in flames. By order, the chief engineer has destroyed by powder and fire all the store-houses, depot buildings, and machine-shops. The heaven is one expanse of lurid fire; the air is filled with flying, burning cinders; buildings covering two hundred acres are in ruins or in flames; every instant there is the sharp detonation or the smothered booming sound of exploding shells and powder concealed in the buildings, and then the sparks and flame shoot away up into the black and red roof, scattering cinders far and wide.

These are the machine-shops where have been forged and cast the Rebel cannon, shot and shell that have carried death to many a brave defender of our nation's honor. These warehouses have been the receptacle of munitions of war, stored to be used for our destruction. The city which, next to Richmond, has furnished more material for prosecuting the war than any other in the South, exists no more as a means for injury to be used by the enemies of the Union.

Relates General Sherman:

About 7 A.M. of November 16th [my staff and I] rode out of Atlanta by the Decatur Road, filled by the marching troops and wagons of the Fourteenth Corps. . . . Behind us lay Atlanta, smouldering and in ruins, the black smoke rising high in the air and hanging like a pall over the ruined city. Away off in the distance, on the McDonough Road, was the rear of [General Oliver] Howard's column,

Atlanta in ruins.

One of Sherman's "bummers."

the gun-barrels glistening in the sun, the white-topped wagons stretching away to the south; and right before us the Fourteenth Corps, marching steadily and rapidly, with a cheery look and swinging pace that made light of the thousand miles that lay between us and Richmond.

Some band . . . struck up the anthem of "John Brown's soul goes marching on." The men caught up the strain, and never before or since have I heard the chorus of "Glory, glory, hallelujah!" done with more spirit or in better harmony of time and place.

Then we turned our horses' heads to the east. . . . The day was extremely beautiful, clear sunlight with bracing air, and an unusual feeling of exhilaration seemed to pervade all minds. . . . Even the common soldiers caught the inspiration, and many a group called out to me as I worked my way past them, "Uncle Billy, I guess Grant is waiting for us at Richmond!"

. . . There was a devil-may-care feeling pervading officers and men that made me feel the full load of responsibility; for success would be accepted as a matter of course, whereas, should we fail, this march would be adjudged the wild adventure of a crazy fool. I had no purpose to march direct for Richmond . . . but always designed to reach the seacoast first. . . .

The first night out we camped by the roadside near Lithonia. Stone Mountain, a mass of granite, was in plain view, cut out in clear outline against the blue sky. The whole horizon was lurid with the bonfires of rail ties, and groups of men all night were carrying the heated rails to the nearest trees and bending them around the trunks [forming what were called "Sherman's neckties"]. . . . I attached much importance to this destruction of the railroad, gave it my own personal attention, and made reiterated orders to others on the subject.

The next day we passed through the handsome town of Covington, the soldiers closing up their ranks, the color-bearers unfurling their flags, and the bands striking up patriotic airs. The white people came out of their houses to behold the sight, spite of their deep hatred of the invaders, and the Negroes were simply frantic with joy. Whenever they heard my name they clustered about my horse, shouted and prayed in their peculiar style, which had a natural eloquence that would have moved a stone.

One of the white citizens of the town was a young woman named Allie Travis:

Federals destroying a Georgia railroad.

The street in front of our house was a moving mass of bluecoats—
infantry, artillery, and cavalry—from 9 o'clock in the morning to a
late hour at night. All during the day squads would leave the ranks,
rush into the house, and demand something to eat, seize what they
could get, then go to the yard and garden to chase chickens and pull
up turnips. . . . When the first squad arrived, the chickens were
still in their house, so the task of catching them was easy. But when
they were turned out, the Yankees killed them with sticks and clubs.
Early in the morning, during a short calm in the storm, my mother
secured two fine turkeys from the yard, and, slipping them into our
house, put them separately in dark closets. The darkness and solitude
so awed them that they kept perfectly quiet, and so escaped Yankee
rapacity.

*Sherman's columns, moving on several roads, now headed toward
Milledgeville, then Georgia's capital. The general continues:*
We found abundance of corn, molasses, meal, bacon, and sweet
potatoes. We also took a good many cows and oxen, and a large number of mules. In all these, the country was quite rich, never before
having been visited by a hostile army. The recent crop had been ex-

cellent, had been just gathered and laid by for the winter. As a rule we destroyed none, but kept our wagons full and fed our teams bountifully.

The skill and success of the men in collecting forage was one of the features of this march. Each brigade commander had authority to detail a company of foragers, usually about fifty men, with one or two commissioned officers selected for their boldness and enterprise. This party would be dispatched before daylight with a knowledge of the intended day's march and camp; would proceed on foot five or six miles from the route traveled by their brigade, and then visit every plantation and farm within range. They would usually procure a wagon or family carriage, load it with bacon, corn-meal, turkeys, chickens, ducks, and everything that could be used as food or forage, and would then regain the main road, usually in advance of their train [i.e., their brigade's baggage train]. When this came up, they would deliver to the brigade commissary the supplies thus gathered by the way.

Often would I pass these foraging parties at the roadside, waiting for their wagons to come up, and was amused at their strange collections—mules, horses, even cattle, packed with old saddles and loaded with hams, bacon, bags of corn-meal, and poultry of every character and description.

Said an unnamed Federal newsman in a contemporary dispatch: "It is not unfrequently that an ancient hen is seen swinging from the pommel of a saddle, and a brood of young chickens following the horse."

Again in Sherman's words:

Although this foraging was attended with great danger and hard work [the danger in the form of roving detachments of Confederate cavalry and militia], there seemed to be a charm about it that attracted the soldiers, and it was a privilege to be detailed on such a party. Daily they returned mounted on all sorts of beasts, which were at once taken from them and appropriated to the general use; but the next day they would start out again on foot, only to repeat the experience of the day before.

No doubt, many acts of pillage, robbery, and violence were committed by these parties of foragers, usually called "bummers," for I have since heard of jewelry taken from women, and the plunder of articles that never reached the commissary; but . . . I never heard of any cases of murder or rape. And no army could have carried along sufficient food and forage for a march of three hundred miles [to the Georgia seacoast], so that foraging in some shape was necessary.

Adds aide-de-camp George Nichols:

As rumors of the approach of our army reached the frightened inhabitants, frantic efforts were made to conceal not only their valuable personal effects, plate, jewelry, and other rich goods, but also articles of food, such as hams, sugar, flour, etc. A large part of these supplies were carried to the neighboring swamps; but the favorite method of concealment was the burial of the treasures in the pathways and gardens adjoining the dwelling-houses. Sometimes, also, the graveyards were selected as the best place of security from the "vandal hands of the invaders."

. . . Wherever the army halted, almost every inch of ground in the vicinity of the dwellings was poked by ramrods, pierced with sabres, or upturned with spades. . . . Nothing escaped the observation of these sharp-witted soldiers. A woman standing upon the porch of a house . . . watching their proceedings, instantly became an object of suspicion, and she was watched until some movement betrayed a place of concealment. . . . It was all fair spoil of war, and the search made one of the excitements of the march.

On November 24, the same narrator told his diary:

We are in full possession of [Milledgeville,] the capital of the State of Georgia, and without firing a gun in its conquest. A few days ago, the Legislature, which had been in session, hearing of our approach, hastily decamped without any adjournment. The legislative panic spread among the citizens to such an extent as to depopulate the place, except a few old gentlemen and ladies and the Negroes, the latter welcoming our approach with ecstatic exclamations of joy . . . accompanying their words with rather embarrassing hugs, which those [marchers] nearest the sidewalks received quite liberally. . . .

But few of the troops were marched through the city. Two or three regiments were detailed . . . to destroy certain property designated by the General Commanding. The magazines, arsenals, depot buildings, factories of various kinds, with store-houses containing large amounts of government property, and about seventeen hundred bales of cotton, were burned. Private houses were respected. . . .

General Sherman is at the executive mansion, its former occupant having, with extremely bad grace, fled from his distinguished visitor, taking with him the entire furniture of the building. As General Sherman travels with a . . . roll of blankets and a haversack full of hard-tack . . . which is as complete for a life in the open air as in a palace, this discourtesy . . . was not a serious inconvenience. . . .

General Sherman's opening move in the present campaign has been successful in the highest degree. First marching his army in three columns [each by a different route], with a column of cavalry on his extreme right . . . he diverted the attention of the enemy, so that the Rebels concentrated their forces at extreme points, Macon and Augusta, leaving unimpeded the progress of the central columns. . . .

The roads each column was to follow were carefully designated, the number of miles each day to be traveled, and the points of rendezvous were given at a certain date. All of these conditions were fulfilled to the letter.

[General Henry] Slocum, with the 20th Corps, arrived at Milledgeville on the 22d instant, preceding [General Jefferson C.] Davis [no kin of the Confederate president], with the 14th Corps, one day. On the same day [cavalry commander Judson] Kilpatrick struck the Macon and Western road, destroying the bridge at Walnut Creek. The day following, Howard, with the 15th and 17th Corps, arrived at Gordon and began the destruction of the Georgia Central Railroad.

It was near here that the most serious fight of the campaign has occurred up to this date. . . . The enemy, about five thousand strong, advanced upon our troops, who had thrown up temporary breastworks, with a section of battery in position. . . . The Rebels were chiefly composed of militia, although a portion of Hardee's old corps was present, having been brought up from Savannah.

With the ignorance of danger common to new troops, the Rebels rushed upon our veterans with the greatest fury. They were received with grape-shot and musketry at point-blank range. . . . The Rebels . . . were soon in full flight. . . . A pretty severe lesson they have received.

Nichols goes on to say that Sherman's columns soon resumed their advance toward the sea.

As we journey from day to day [he wrote on November 30] it is curious to observe the attentions bestowed by our soldiers upon

camp pets. With a care which almost deserves the name of tenderness, the men gather helpless dumb animals around them; sometimes
an innocent kid whose mother has been served up as an extra ration;
and again a raccoon, a little donkey, a dog, or a cat. . . .

The favorite pet of the camp, however, is the hero of the barn-
yard. There is not a regiment nor a company, not a teamster nor a
Negro at headquarters, nor an orderly, but has a rooster of one kind
or another. When the column is moving, these haughty gamecocks
are seen mounted upon the breech of a cannon, tied to the pack-
saddle of a mule among pots and pans, or carried lovingly in the
arms of a mounted orderly; crowing with all his might from the interior of a wagon, or making the woods re-echo with his triumphant
notes as he rides perched upon the knapsack of a soldier.

These cocks represent every known breed, Polish and Spanish,
Dorkings, Shanghais and Bantams—high-blooded specimens travel-
ing with [others] of their species who may not boast of noble lineage.
They must all fight, however, or be killed and eaten.

Hardly has the army gone into camp before these feathery com-
bats begin. The cocks use only the spurs with which Nature furnishes them . . . and so but little harm is done. The gamecocks
which have come out of repeated conflicts victorious are honored
with such names as "Bill Sherman," "Johnny Logan" [one of Sher-
mans corps commanders], etc., while the defeated and bepecked victim is saluted with derisive appellations such as "Jeff Davis," "Beauregard," or "Bob Lee."

Cock-fighting is not, perhaps, one of the most refined or elevating
of pastimes, but it furnishes food for a certain kind of fun in camp;
and as it is not carried to the point of cruelty, the soldiers cannot be
blamed for liking it.

*The only opposition Sherman encountered during this part of his
march came from Joe Wheeler's cavalry. Relates one of Wheeler's
officers, J. P. Austin:*

The daily skirmishing with his advance guard had no more effect
than a fly would have on the back of a sea turtle. Sherman moved on
without any interruption, leaving a black and smoldering trail of
ruin behind him. Thousands of Negroes, with their plunder, flocked
to the Federal army as it passed through the country. When the
crowd became too burdensome, the Federals would take up their
bridges at the crossing of some river and leave their poor, deluded

followers on the opposite bank to ponder over the mutability of human plans and to cast a longing look at the receding forms of their supposed deliverers.

Another great throng of Negroes would soon fill the army's wake. Writes corps commander Henry Slocum:

It was natural that these poor creatures, seeking a place of safety, should flee to the army and endeavor to keep in sight of it. Every day as we marched on we could see, on each side of our line of march, crowds of these people coming to us through roads and across the fields, bringing with them all their earthly goods, and many goods which were not theirs. Horses, mules, cows, dogs, old family carriages, carts, and whatever they thought might be of use to them were seized upon and brought to us. . . . [A]t times they were almost equal in numbers to the army they were following. . . .

One day a large family of slaves came through the fields to join us. The head of the family, a venerable Negro, was mounted on a mule; and safely stowed away behind him, in pockets or bags attached to the blanket which covered the mule, were two little pickaninnies, one on each side. This gave rise to a most important invention . . . "the best way of transporting pickaninnies."

On the next day a mule appeared in column, covered by a blanket with two pockets on each side, each containing a little Negro. Very soon old tent-flies or strong canvas was used instead of the blanket, and often . . . nothing of the mule was visible except the head, tail, and feet—all else being covered by the black woolly heads and bright shining eyes of the little darkies. Occasionally a cow was made to take the place of the mule. This was a decided improvement, as the cow furnished rations as well as transportation for the babies.

Sherman had decided upon Savannah as his seaside objective, and he reached its environs on December 9. He placed the city under siege, at the same time moving against a waterfront fort (Fort McAllister), the capture of which enabled him to open up communications with a Federal fleet in nearby waters. One of the vessels was carrying a mountain of mail from home, which occasioned general rejoicing, since the men had been out of touch with their families for two months.

Savannah soon fell, its inadequate garrison (about 10,000 men) slipping away in the night. In a telegraphic message for President Lincoln dated December 22, Sherman said:

I beg to present you as a Christmas gift the city of Savannah, with one hundred and fifty heavy guns and plenty of ammunition; also about twenty-five thousand bales of cotton.

"This message," explains Sherman, "actually reached him on Christmas Eve, was extensively published in the newspapers, and made many a household unusually happy on that festive day." The delighted President sent Sherman a reply that began: "Many, many thanks for your Christmas present. . . ."

Sherman himself got a Christmas present in the form of good news from Tennessee. Earlier, the Confederates under John Hood had attacked a part of George Thomas's army at Franklin, some miles below Nashville. The Confederates suffered severely, with the stalwart Pat Cleburne among the dead. But Hood refused to accept this repulse as final; he gathered his battered forces for another try. Then, writes Sherman,

. . . on the 15th and 16th of December were fought, in front of Nashville, the great battles in which General Thomas so nobly fulfilled his promise to ruin Hood. . . . Rumors of these great victories [had] reached us . . . by piecemeal, but his official report came on the 24th of December. . . . I wrote at once through my chief of staff . . . to General Thomas, complimenting him in the highest terms. His brilliant victory at Nashville was necessary to mine at Savannah to make a complete whole. . . .

From the Virginia theater, no special news was forthcoming. "General Grant," says Sherman, "was still besieging Petersburg and Richmond, and . . . matters and things generally remained pretty much the same as when we had left Atlanta."

Savannah escaped harsh treatment. It was made a base of Federal operations. Again in Sherman's words:

As the division of Major General John W. Geary, of the Twentieth Corps, was the first to enter Savannah, that officer was appointed to command the place, or to act as a sort of governor. He very soon established a good police, maintained admirable order; and I doubt if Savannah, either before or since, has had a better government than during our stay.

The guard-mountings and parades, as well as the greater reviews, became the daily resorts of the ladies, to hear the music of our excellent bands. Schools were opened, and the churches every Sunday were well filled with most devout and respectful congregations. Stores were reopened, and markets for provisions, meat, wood, etc., were established, so that each family, regardless of race, color, or opinion, could procure all the necessaries and even luxuries of life, provided they had money. Of course, many families were actually destitute of this, and to these were issued stores from our own stock of supplies.

These stores—and here is another curious turn in this most unusual war—were augmented by food contributed by people in the North. It was sent down by ship.

Federal newsman Charles Coffin paid a visit to the occupied city on a mercy vessel from Boston. He discovered that the people "generally were ready to live once more in the Union."

The fire of Secession had died out. . . . At a meeting of the citizens, resolutions expressive of gratitude for the charity bestowed by Boston, New York, and Philadelphia were passed, also of a desire for future fellowship and amity.

A store at the corner of Bay and Barnard Streets was taken for a depot, the city canvassed, and a registry made of all who were in want. I passed a morning among the people who came for food. The air was keen. Ice had formed in the gutters, and some of the jolly young Negroes, who had provided themselves with old shoes and boots from the campgrounds of Sherman's soldiers, were enjoying the luxurious pastime of a slide on the ice. . . .

There was a motley crowd. Hundreds of both sexes, all ages, sizes, complexions, and costumes; gray-haired old men of Anglo-Saxon blood, with bags, bottles, and baskets; colored patriarchs who had been in bondage for many years, suddenly made freemen; well-dressed women wearing crape for their husbands and sons who had fallen while fighting against the old flag—[all] stood patiently waiting their turn to enter the building, where through the open doors they could see barrels of flour, pork, beans, and piles of bacon, hogsheads of sugar, molasses, and vinegar.

There were women with tattered dresses—old silks and satins, years before in fashion and laid aside as useless, but which now had become valuable through destitution. There were women in linsey-woolsey, in Negro and gunny cloth, in garments made from meal-bags; and men in Confederate gray and butternut brown; a boy with a crimson plush jacket made from the upholstering of a sofa; men in short jackets, and little boys in long ones; the cast-off clothes of soldiers; the rags which had been picked up in the streets and exhumed from garrets; boots and shoes down at the heel, open at the instep, and gaping at the toes.

[There were] old bonnets of every description, some with white and crimson feathers and ribbons once bright and flaunting; hats of every style worn by both sexes: palm-leaf, felt, straw, old and battered and well ventilated. One without a crown was worn by a man with red hair, suggestive of a chimney on fire and flaming out at the top. It was the ragman's jubilee for charity. . . .

Society in the South, and especially in Savannah, had undergone a great change. The extremes of social life were very wide apart before the war. They were no nearer the night before Sherman marched into the city. But the morning after, there was a convulsion, an upheaval, a shaking up and a settling down of all the discordant elements. The tread of that army of the West, as it moved in solid column through the streets, was like a moral earthquake, overturning aristocratic pride, privilege, and power.

Old houses, with foundations laid deep and strong in the centuries, fortified by wealth, name, and influence, went down beneath the shock. The general disruption of the former relations of master and slave, and forced submission to the Union arms, produced a common level. . . .

On the night before Sherman entered the place, there were citizens who could enumerate their wealth by millions; at sunrise the next morning they were worth scarcely a dime. Their property had been in cotton, Negroes, houses, land, Confederate bonds and currency, railroad and bank stocks. Government had seized their cotton; the Negroes had possession of their lands; their slaves had become freemen; their houses were occupied by troops; Confederate bonds were waste paper; their railroads were destroyed, their banks insolvent. They had not only lost wealth, but they had lost their cause. . . .

One could not ask for more courteous treatment than I received during my stay in Savannah. I am indebted to many ladies and gentlemen of that city for kind invitations to pass an evening with them. There was no concealment of opinion on either side, but with the utmost good feeling full expression was given to our differing sentiments.

"We went into the war in good faith; we thought we were right; we confidently expected to establish our independence; but we are whipped, and have got to make the best of it," was the frank acknowledgment of several gentlemen.

"I hate you of the North," said a young lady. It came squarely, and the tone indicated a little irritation.

"I am very sorry for that. I can hardly think that you really hate us. You don't hate me individually?"

"O, no. You came here as a gentleman. I should indeed be rude and unladylike to say that I hated you; but I mean the Yankees in general. We can never live together in peace again. For one, I hope to leave the country."

"If I were to reside here, you of course would treat me courteously so long as I was a gentleman in my deportment?"

"Certainly; but you are an individual."

"But if two individuals can live peacefully, why not ten—or a hundred—a thousand—all?"

She hesitated a moment; and then, with flashing eyes and flushed countenance, which added charms to her beauty, said, "Well, it is hard—and you will not think any worse of me for saying it—to have your friends killed, your servants all taken away, your lands confiscated; and then know that you have failed, that you have been whipped. . . .

"We have been able to have everything that money could buy, and now we haven't a dollar.

"I don't care anything about keeping the Negroes in slavery; but there is one feeling which we Southerners have that you cannot enter into. My old mamma who nursed me is just like a mother to me. But there is one thing that I never will submit to—that the Negro is our equal. . . ."

[I replied:] ". . . There never will be complete equality in society. Political and social equality are separate and distinct. Rowdies and ragamuffins have natural rights: they may have a right to vote; they may be citizens; but that does not necessarily entitle them to free entrance into our homes."

The idea was evidently new to the young lady—and not only to her, but to all in the room. To them the abolition of slavery was the breaking down of all social distinctions. . . . The thought was intolerable. . . .

The colored people who had taken up lands . . . under General Sherman's order met for consultation in the Slave Market, at the corner of St. Julian Street and Market Square. [Going there,] I passed up the two flights of stairs . . . and entered a large hall. At the farther end was an elevated platform about eight feet square—the auctioneer's block. The windows were grated with iron. . . .

A colored man was praying when I entered, giving thanks to God for the freedom of his race, and asking for a blessing on their under-taking. . . . Lieutenant Ketchum . . . who had been placed in charge of the confiscated lands, was present to answer their questions. . . . There was evidently a reluctance to becoming pioneers in such an enterprise—to leaving the city—unless the guaranty were sure. . . .

[Said one man:] "My bredren, I want to raise cotton, and I'm gwine." It was a short but effective speech. . . . He was going to improve the opportunity to raise cotton, even if he did not become a holder of the estate. . . .

"So will I!" And there was a general shaking of hands as if they were sealing a contract.

Having determined to go, they joined in singing the "Freedmen's Battle Hymn." . . . How gloriously it sounded . . . sung by five hundred freedmen in the Savannah slave-mart, where some of the singers had been sold in days gone by!

. . . The next morning, in the same room, I saw a school of one hundred colored children assembled, taught by colored teachers, who sat on the auctioneer's platform. . . . I listened to the recita-tions, and heard their songs of jubilee. The slave-mart transformed to a school house! Civilization and Christianity had indeed begun their beneficent work.

At the very end of Sherman's stay in the Savannah area, according to Coffin, the city experienced an unexpected conflagration:
The night of the 28th of January [1865] was a fearful one. . . . A fire broke out a little before midnight in a long row of wooden buildings at the west end of the city. The wind was fresh from the northwest, and the night exceedingly cold. My rooms were in the Pulaski House. I was awakened by a sudden explosion, which jarred the house. . . . There was another explosion. . . . It was the Rebel arsenal. . . .

Gradually I worked my way, under the shelter of buildings, to-wards the fire. . . . It was a gorgeous sight—the flames leaping high in the air, thrown up in columns by . . . thirteen-inch shells, filling the air with burning timbers, cinders, and myriads of sparks. The streets were filled with fugitives. The hospitals were being cleared of sick and wounded, the houses of furniture. It was grand but terri-ble.

General [Cuvier] Grover at once took measures to arrest the prog-ress of the flames by tearing down buildings and bringing up several regiments, which, with the citizens and Negroes, succeeded in mastering the destroying element. In the morning there was a wilderness of chimneys, and the streets were strewn with furniture.

It was amusing to see with what good humor and nonchalance the colored people . . . regarded the conflagration. Two Negro women passed me, carrying great bundles on their heads.

"I's clean burned out," said one.

"So is I!"

And they both laughed as if it was very funny.

With General Grant's approval, Sherman now began pressing northward through South Carolina. This would turn out to be a particularly vengeful march.

Somehow [writes Sherman] our men had got the idea that South Carolina was the cause of all our troubles. Her people were the first to fire on Fort Sumter, had been in a great hurry to precipitate the country into civil war; and therefore on them should fall the scourge of war in its worst form.

Even the people of Georgia, incidentally, wanted to see the South Carolinians suffer. Many Georgians had told Sherman they would forgive him what he had done to their state if he would be equally hard on South Carolina!

Sherman says that he spent one of the first nights of the new march at an abandoned mansion "with a majestic avenue of live-oaks whose limbs had been cut away by the troops for firewood." He goes on:

. . . desolation marked one of those splendid South Carolina estates where the proprietors formerly had dispensed a hospitality that distinguished the old regime of that proud state. I slept on the floor of the house, but the night was so bitter cold that I got up by the fire several times; and when it burned low I rekindled it with an old mantel-clock and the wreck of a bedstead which stood in a corner of the room—the only act of vandalism that I recall done by myself personally during the war.

This march was to be impeded by muddy roads, swollen streams, and brimming swamps for much of its length; yet an average of ten miles a day would be covered.

Confederate plans to oppose the march were meager. Cavalry

*officer J. P. Austin says that he and his comrades had spent the past
month "wallowing about in the swamps adjacent to [Savannah], sub-
sisting on what could be gleaned from the abandoned rice fields,
with now and then a turtle and a few small fish thrown in." Austin
continues:*

It was evident that [Sherman] contemplated forming a junction
with Grant somewhere in Virginia [in order to] wind up the ball in
short order. Now our old duties, skirmishing with Sherman's advance, commenced again. These skirmishes frequently resulted in
sharp and bloody engagements. . . .

The small force in Sherman's front offered but slight resistance
to his advance. He swept on with his army of sixty thousand men,
like a full developed cyclone, leaving behind him a track of desolation and ashes fifty miles wide. In front of them was terror and dismay. Bummers and foragers swarmed on his flanks, who plundered
and robbed everyone who was so unfortunate as to be within their
reach. . . .

Poor, bleeding, suffering South Carolina! Up to that time she
had felt but slightly—away from the coast [where the Federals had
been operating since 1861]—the devastating effects of the war; but
her time had come. The protestations of her old men and the plead-
ings of her noble women had no effect in staying the ravages of
sword, flame, and pillage.

Columbia's fate could readily be foretold from the destruction
along Sherman's line of march after he left Savannah. Beautiful
homes, with their tropical gardens, which had been the pride of their
owners for generations, were left in ruins. . . . Everything that
could not be carried off was destroyed. Thousands who had but recently lived in affluence were compelled to subsist on the scrapings
from the abandoned camps of the soldiers. . . . Livestock of every
description that they could not make use of was shot down. All farm
implements, with wagons and vehicles of every description, were
given to the flames.

The last stand made by our troops before reaching Columbia
was at the covered bridge over Broad River, where a desperate fight
took place; but it was all to no purpose. The bridge was burned, and
we fell back in the direction of Columbia. Hasty preparations were
being made to evacuate the place. General Beauregard, with a small
force, occupied the city. He succeeded in removing most of the government supplies.

Columbia in flames.

When the last of the stores had been sent out, the writer, with a detachment of cavalry, was ordered to remain and clear the city of [military] stragglers, and to remove all sick and wounded soldiers from the hospitals who were able to travel. . . . [T]hree soldiers . . . and myself were the last of the Confederates to leave Columbia [i.e., the last soldiers; many civilians remained in their homes]. . . . [W]hile Sherman's advance came in on one side of the city, we retired on the opposite.

We repaired to an elevation about a mile to the north of the city, and from that commanding spot witnessed the terrible conflagration which destroyed that proud and heroic city of the South. It was from this point that we saw the flames burst forth from public buildings, stores, and beautiful homesteads . . . which had long been the pride of a refined and cultured people.

Columbia was in flames. Then it was that the demons of fire [the Federal soldiers] commenced their exploits of rapine and pillage. Stores and dwellings were broken open and rifled of their contents. . . . Liquors were eagerly sought after. . . . Barrels of the stuff were rolled into the streets, the heads broken in. Then all could indulge without stint or restraint. Wines of a hundred years' vintage met with the same fate.

They were no respecters of persons. Ornaments were snatched from the persons of delicate females, and woe unto him who displayed a watch, fob, or gold chain; as he would be relieved of it in short order. Even houses of worship were not respected. The sacred vessels of the churches were appropriated by the drunken mob. . . .

As night approached, the destruction became more fierce and unrestrained. Valuable cabinets, elegant pianos, costly paintings—many of them imported from foreign lands, the work of some of the great masters—were ruthlessly smashed to pieces.

By 12 o'clock the city was one great sea of fire. From the position we occupied, the frightful conflagration seemed like the eruption of an hundred volcanoes, sending forth their lurid glare and lighting the horizon for miles around. Wreaths of flame shot upward and mingled with the clouds.

Columbia's fall made it necessary for the Confederates to evacuate their troops from Charleston, on the coast to the southeast. Sherman had bypassed the city, and he was about to cut it off as he swung northeastward toward North Carolina.

Southerner J. P. Austin goes on:

General Hardee, who was in command of the Confederate forces at Charleston, set fire to all the warehouses where cotton was stored when he left the place. The fire spread rapidly and ignited a large lot of powder which was in the depot of the N. E. Railroad, causing the loss of over two hundred lives.

An eyewitness to the appearance of Charleston after the troops withdrew says: "No pen, no pencil, no tongue can do justice to the scene. No imagination can conceive the complete wreck, the universal ruin, the utter desolation. . . ."

. . . This left South Carolina in the iron grasp of the Federal army. There she lay, prostrate at the feet of the conqueror. . . .

Sherman took the town of Cheraw, near the North Carolina border, on March 3. The next day his aide-de-camp, George Nichols, wrote in his diary:

We captured twenty-five cannon . . . Blakelys [and] twenty-pound Parrotts [foreign-made guns brought through the blockade], and two of Rebel manufacture. All but the Blakelys have been destroyed. These guns . . . will be carried . . . as trophies. General [Joseph A.] Mower fired them today in a salute in honor of the inauguration of Mr. Lincoln for his second term. Our honored President would have been as glad and proud as we, could he have heard the roaring of our cannon and our shouts of joy and victory. His first inauguration was not celebrated in South Carolina . . . but the glorification over the beginning of his second term goes to make up the deficiency.

Moving across the border into North Carolina, the Federals occupied Fayetteville on March 11. The city held a cluster of arsenal buildings that were assaulted both with battering rams and with fire. When the work was finished, not even the foundations remained.

By this time Confederate General Joe Johnston, relieved from command after failing to stop Sherman's advance toward Atlanta, had been called from semiretirement to face him anew. But the task of stopping Sherman was hopeless—particularly since fresh Federal troops in formidable numbers were moving to his support from newly captured Fort Fisher, on the North Carolina coast.

Johnston's once-magnificent hosts, laments Confederate officer J. P. Austin,

. . . had dwindled down to the veriest skeleton of an army. But he gathered its scattered fragments together and once more threw himself in front of Sherman's advancing columns. . . . A fierce engagement took place at Bentonville, North Carolina [on March 19]. It was maintained with the same old-time vigor for several hours [ending after nightfall].

[Two days later] Johnston was forced to give way to a vastly superior force and fall back in the direction of Raleigh. This was the last battle fought by General Johnston.

Sherman advanced to Goldsboro, there uniting with the troops from the coast. He expected now to help Grant with his effort in Virginia. But Sherman's work was finished. His extraordinary march, which had not only demoralized the South but had divested her of resources she could not afford to lose, had given Grant all the help he needed.

23

CONCLUSION
AT APPOMATTOX

BY MARCH, 1865, *Grant had been besieging Petersburg for nine months. His lines, which began southeast of Richmond, ran through Petersburg's eastern environs and then curved around the city in a southwesterly direction. Grant's current strength was about 125,000 men. Lee probably had less than half that number; moreover, faith in the cause had weakened, and desertions were rising.*

Lee's fortifications were strong, but this was a diminishing advantage. Grant had been extending the left of his lines farther and farther to the west, thus interfering with Lee's railway communications with the states to the south, and Lee had been forced to match each of Grant's moves with an extension of his right until his troops were spread thinly through about fifty miles of fortifications around Richmond and Petersburg.

In the words of Union General Andrew Humphreys:

During the whole period of our partial investment of Petersburg and Richmond, there were frequent affairs on the picket lines, especially in front of the Petersburg intrenchments, where the affair sometimes became of a serious character, drawing into it brigades, sometimes a division. . . . These attacks gave occasion for the exhibition of dexterity and daring on both sides, but did not result in any appreciable modification of the lines. The loss they entailed in killed and wounded was by no means trifling.

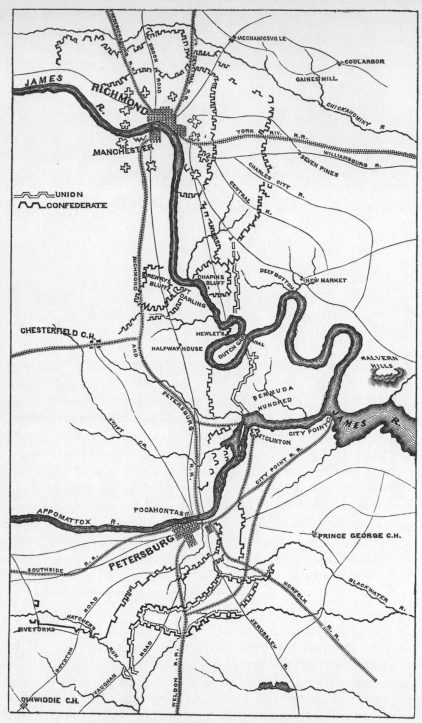

The defenses of Richmond and Petersburg.

Confederate General John B. Gordon says that many of Lee's wounded were carried into Petersburg:

There was scarcely a home within its corporate limits that was not open to the sick and wounded. . . . Its women, who were noted for culture and refinement, became nurses, as consecrated as Florence Nightingale. . . . Now and then . . . the subtle radiance of romance lighted up the gloom of the hospitals.

A beautiful Southern girl, on her daily mission of love and mercy, asked a badly wounded soldier boy what she could do for him. He replied:

"I'm greatly obliged to you, but it is too late for you to do anything for me. . . . I can't live long."

"Will you not let me pray for you? I hope that I am one of the Lord's daughters, and I would like to ask Him to help you."

Looking intently into her bewitching face, he replied: "Yes, pray at once and ask the Lord to let me be His son-in-law."

Union General Humphreys goes on to explain that

There had been indications for some time past that General Lee would abandon his Petersburg and Richmond intrenchments for the purpose of uniting with General Johnston, then in front of Sherman [about 150 miles to the southwest]. . . . Early in March, it was determined in a conference between Mr. Jefferson Davis and General Lee that as soon as the roads would admit of movement the Richmond and Petersburg lines should be abandoned. . . .

General Lee proposed in the meantime to make a sortie in order to gain some of the works . . . of . . . the Army of the Potomac [directly east of Petersburg] . . . and the ridge in their rear, with the expectation that this would oblige General Grant to concentrate there by drawing in his left . . . [which would ease the pressure he was exerting on Lee's escape corridor].

. . . General Gordon was selected for the service. . . . The point of attack was Fort Stedman, where the opposing lines were only one hundred and fifty yards apart; the pickets fifty yards apart. General Gordon was sanguine that this redoubt could be taken by a night assault, and that through the breach thus made a sufficient force could be thrown to disorganize and destroy Grant's left wing before he could recover and concentrate his forces from the right.

. . . General Lee placed at [Gordon's] disposal, in addition to his own corps, a portion of A. P. Hill's and a portion of Longstreet's, and a detachment of cavalry, in all about one-half of the army.

Gordon's plan was a bold one. Fifty axmen were to precede the attack, their job being to cut away the obstructions in front of the Federal lines. Three hundred men, divided into three teams, were to follow, their unusual duty being to pretend they were Federals and attempt to slip past Fort Stedman and seek out three additional forts believed to be behind it. In the meantime, the main attack would be hitting Fort Stedman and the lines that stretched away from its flanks. The attack's support troops were to arrive at the jumping-off point in due time by train.

Gordon writes that the attack was scheduled for the predawn hours of March 25:

All night my troops were moving and concentrating behind Colquitt's Salient. For hours Mrs. Gordon sat in her room in Petersburg, tearing strips of white cloth to tie across the breasts of the leading detachments, that they might recognize each other in the darkness. . . .

All things ready, at 4 A.M. I stood on the top of the breastworks, with no one at my side except a single private soldier with rifle in hand, who was to fire the signal shot for the headlong rush. This night charge on the fort was to be across the intervening space covered with ditches, in one of which stood the watchful Federal pickets.

There still remained near my works some of the debris of our obstructions . . . and I ordered it cleared away. The noise made by this removal, though slight, attracted the attention of a Union picket who stood on guard only a few rods from me, and he called out:

"What are you doing over there, Johnny? What is that noise? Answer quick, or I'll shoot."

. . . I expected him to fire and start the entire picket line to firing, thus giving the alarm to the fort. . . . The quick mother-wit of the private soldier at my side came to my relief. In an instant he replied:

"Never mind, Yank. Lie down and go to sleep. We are just gathering a little corn. You know rations are mighty short over here."

There was a narrow strip of corn which the bullets had not shot away still standing between the lines.

The Union picket promptly answered: "All right, Johnny. Go ahead and get your corn. I'll not shoot at you while you are drawing your rations."

. . . While this fraternal dialogue . . . was progressing . . . the last of the obstructions in my front were removed, and I ordered the private to fire the signal for the assault. He pointed his rifle upward, with his finger on the trigger, but hesitated. His conscience seemed to get hold of him. . . . His hesitation surprised me, and I again ordered: "Fire your gun, sir!"

He at once called to his kindhearted foe and said: "Hello, Yank! Wake up. . . . Look out; we are coming!"

And with this effort to satisfy his conscience and even up accounts . . . he fired the shot and rushed forward in the darkness.

As the solitary signal shot rang out in the stillness, my alert pickets, who had crept close to the Union sentinels, sprang like sinewy Ajaxes upon them and prevented the discharge of a single alarm shot. . . . Simultaneously . . . my stalwart axemen leaped over our breastworks, closely followed by the selected 300 and the packed column of infantry. . . .

. . . soon was heard the thud of the heavy axes as my brave fellows slashed down the Federal obstructions. The next moment the infantry sprang upon the Union breastworks and into the fort, overpowering the gunners before their destructive charges could be emptied into the mass of Confederates. They turned this captured artillery upon the flanking lines on each side of the fort, clearing the Union breastworks of their defenders for some distance in both directions.

Up to this point, the success had exceeded my most sanguine expectations. We had taken Fort Stedman and a long line of breastworks on either side. We had captured nine heavy cannon, eleven mortars, nearly 1000 prisoners, including General [N. B.] McLaughlen, with the loss of less than half a dozen men. . . .

I was in the fort myself, and relieved General McLaughlen by assuming command. . . . From the fort I sent word to General Lee, who was on a hill in the rear, that we were in the works and that the 300 were on their way to the lines in the rear.

Soon I received a message from one of these three officers . . . that he had passed the line of Federal infantry without trouble . . . but that he could not find his fort. . . . I soon received a similar message from the other two, and so notified General Lee. [Actually, no forts existed where the three teams were searching; the guns commanding the Stedman area were farther back, on the main defense line.]

Daylight was coming. . . . Our wretched railroad trains had broken down, and the troops who were coming to my aid did not reach me. The full light of the morning revealed the gathering forces of Grant and the great preponderance of his numbers. It was impossible for me to make further headway with my isolated corps, and General Lee directed me to withdraw.

This was not easily accomplished. . . . A consuming fire . . . caused a heavy loss to my command [many others being taken prisoner]. I myself was wounded, but not seriously, in recrossing the space over which we had charged in the darkness. . . .

This last supreme effort to break the hold of General Grant upon Petersburg and Richmond was the expiring struggle of the Confederate giant, whose strength was nearly exhausted and whose limbs were heavily shackled by the most onerous conditions.

President Lincoln was at City Point, a few miles behind the Federal lines, during Gordon's attack. Grant had invited him down from Washington for an extended visit with the army, and he was living on a steamer in the James River. Soon after the repulse, the President went to the front. Grant's aide-de-camp, Horace Porter, says that

. . . several hours were spent in visiting the troops, who cheered the President enthusiastically. He was greatly interested in looking at the prisoners who had been captured that morning. . . . The President carried a map with him, which he took out of his pocket and examined several times. He had the exact location of the troops marked on it, and he exhibited a singularly accurate knowledge of the various positions. Upon the return to headquarters at City Point, he sat for a while by the campfire and . . . entertained the general-in-chief and several members of the staff by talking in a most interesting manner about public affairs, and illustrating the subjects mentioned with his incomparable anecdotes.

On succeeding days, Lincoln spent much of his time visiting the various camps and hospitals. On one occasion, while walking through a camp, he came upon a squad cutting timber to build a cabin. He picked up an ax, and, while the men cheered his deft strokes, he cut a long log in two.

The President's main reason for coming down from Washington was that he wanted to share with Grant the moment of victory over the Confederate capital, a moment now close at hand.

Explains Southern General Fitzhugh Lee:

Lee, chained to his trenches by his necessities, and waiting for better roads on account of the weak condition of his artillery and transportation animals, gave General Grant the opportunity to get around his lines west of Petersburg, for which he had so long waited.

On March 28th, Grant sounded the *laissez aller,* as one writer puts it [meaning that he renounced restraint], and the next day great turning columns were put in motion to swing around the flank of Lee and get possession of his remaining lines of [railroad] transportation. . . . Five Forks, in front of the Southern right, became a strategic point.

The turning columns, which included Phil Sheridan's cavalry, functioned as a further extension of Grant's left. The original lines facing Petersburg and Richmond were maintained.

Confederate General Gordon relates:

. . . Lee . . . adopted the same bold, aggressive policy which had so repeatedly thwarted the flank movements of his great antagonist on every battlefield from the Wilderness to Petersburg. Withdrawing all the troops that could be spared from the trenches, Lee hurled [this] depleted but still resolute little army against Grant's heavy lines of infantry on the march to Five Forks, and [at first] drove back in confusion [a part] of the Federal army; but . . . the concentration upon Five Forks was accomplished. . . .

In the first encounter [at that place] General Sheridan's forces were repelled. . . . But soon the devoted little band of gray [led by Pickett of Gettysburg, who waved a bloodstained flag and sang, "Rally round the flag, boys; rally once again!"] was torn by artillery, harried by cavalry, and assaulted by infantry on every side; and the Confederate flags went down, while their brave defenders were surrounded by a cordon of fire. Five Forks fell, with the loss of large numbers of Confederates in killed, wounded, and prisoners [Pickett being among those who got away safely]. . . .

As General Lee rode back toward Petersburg from Five Forks . . . he said to one of his aides: "This is a sad business, colonel." In a few minutes he added: "It has happened as I told them in Richmond it would happen. The line has been stretched until it is broken."

This was the evening of Saturday, April 1. According to Federal newsman William Swinton (self-appointed historian of the Army of the Potomac):

Final assault on the Petersburg lines.

No sooner had the sound of musketry died away at the Five Forks than from the multitudinous throats of all the guns that studded Grant's lines before Petersburg there opened a prodigious clamor, and the darkness of night was illumined by the lurid light of hundreds of bursting shells and bombs. It was a paean to victory. . . .

Southerner Fitzhugh Lee says that the bombardment was continued all night:

At dawn on Sunday, April 2d . . . [the Federals] successfully assaulted the attenuated lines in their front. The task was easy, and [though] handfuls of brave men heroically resisted, like shooting stars their course was brilliant but brief. The . . . blue masses poured into the works. There were high parapets . . . and deep ditches; but . . . except here and there—notably at Fort Gregg—it was only a matter of physical agility to climb over them. Only small garrisons were in the forts, and very few men in the connecting lines. . . .

Lee's troops were forced back to an inner line . . . and there resisted all further attempts to break through them. Before 10 A.M. Lee knew he could only hope to cling to his trenches until night, and that [a] longer defense of Richmond and Petersburg was not possible. All his skill would be required to extricate his army . . . from the . . . lines. . . .

In the midst of the turmoil, excitement, and danger, Lee was as calm and collected as ever.

A. P. Hill was killed by Federal musket fire that morning. Fitz Lee eulogizes: "Hill . . . had rendered marked service throughout the whole war, and his light division had written many victories upon its proud standards."

Among the civilians in Richmond at this time was editor-historian Edward Pollard. His position with the Examiner *enabled him to keep well informed:*

It was eleven o'clock in the morning when General Lee wrote a hasty telegram to the War Department, advising that the authorities of Richmond should have everything in readiness to evacuate the capital at eight o'clock the coming night, unless before that time despatches should be received from him to a contrary effect.

A small slip of paper, sent up from the War Department to President Davis, as he was seated in his pew in St. Paul's Church, contained the news of the most momentous event of the war. . . .

The report of a great misfortune soon traverses a city without the aid of printed bulletins. But that of the evacuation of Richmond fell upon many incredulous ears. . . . There were but few people in the streets; no vehicles disturbed the quiet of the Sabbath; the sound of the church-going bells rose into the cloudless sky and floated on the blue tide of the beautiful day. How was it possible to imagine that in the next twenty-four hours . . . this peaceful city, a secure possession for four years, was at last to succumb . . . ?

As the day wore on, clatter and bustle in the streets denoted the progress of the evacuation and convinced those who had been incredulous of its reality. The disorder increased each hour. The streets were thronged with fugitives making their way to the railroad depots; pale women and little shoeless children struggled in the crowd; oaths and blasphemous shouts smote the ear. . . . In the afternoon a special train . . . [was prepared to carry] from Richmond President Davis and some of his Cabinet. . . .

When it was finally announced by the Mayor that those who had hoped for a despatch from General Lee contrary to what he had telegraphed in the morning had ceased to indulge such an expectation and that the evacuation of Richmond was a foregone conclusion, it was proposed to maintain order in the city by two regiments of militia; to destroy every drop of liquor in the warehouses and stores; and to establish a patrol through the night. But the militia ran through the fingers of their officers . . . and in a short while the whole city was plunged into mad confusion and indescribable horrors. . . .

It was an extraordinary night; [one of] disorder, pillage, shouts, mad revelry. . . . In the now dimly lighted city could be seen black masses of people, crowded around some object of excitement . . . swaying to and fro in whatever momentary passion possessed them. The gutters ran with a liquor freshet, and the fumes filled the air. Some of the straggling soldiers . . . easily managed to get hold of quantities of the liquor. Confusion became worse confounded; the sidewalks were encumbered with broken glass; stores were entered at pleasure and stripped from top to bottom; yells of drunken men, shouts of roving pillagers, wild cries of distress filled the air and made [the] night hideous.

But a new horror was to appear upon the scene and take possession of the community. To the rear-guard of the Confederate force . . . on the north side of James River . . . had been left the duty of blowing up the iron-clad vessels in the James and destroying the bridges across that river. . . . The work of destruction might well have ended here. But . . . the four principal tobacco warehouses of the city . . . were fired; the flames seized on the neighboring buildings and soon involved a wide and widening area; the conflagration passed rapidly beyond control. And in this mad fire, this wild, unnecessary destruction of their property, the citizens of Richmond had a fitting souvenir of the imprudence and recklessness of the departing Administration.

Morning broke on a scene never to be forgotten. . . . The smoke and glare of fire mingled with the golden beams of the rising sun. . . . The fire was reaching to whole blocks of buildings. . . . Its roar sounded in the ears; it leaped from street to street. Pillagers were busy at their vocation, and in the hot breath of the fire were figures as of demons contending for prey.

The sun was an hour or more above the horizon when suddenly there ran up the whole length of Main Street the cry of "Yankees! Yankees!" The upper part of this street was choked with crowds of pillagers—men provided with drays [i.e., wheeled carts], others rolling barrels up the street or bending under heavy burdens, and intermixed with them women and children with smaller lots of plunder in bags, baskets, tubs, buckets, and tin pans.

As the cry of "Yankees!" was raised, this motley crowd tore up the street, cursing, screaming, trampling upon each other, alarmed by an enemy not yet in sight, and madly seeking to extricate themselves from imaginary dangers.

Presently . . . following up the tangled mass of plunderers, but not pressing or interfering with them, was seen a small body of Federal cavalry, riding steadily along. Forty Massachusetts troopers, despatched by General [Godfrey] Weitzel to investigate the condition of affairs, had ridden . . . into Richmond. At the corner of Eleventh Street they broke into a trot for the public square, and in a few moments their guidons were planted on the Capitol and fluttered there, a strange spectacle in the early morning light.

A few hours thereafter, and Weitzel's troops were pouring through the streets of the city. A lady who witnessed the grand Federal entree . . . thus describes a portion of the scene:

"Stretching from the Exchange Hotel to the slopes of Church Hill . . . was the array, with its unbroken line of blue, fringed with bright bayonets. Strains of martial music, flushed countenances, waving swords betokened the victorious army. As the line turned at the Exchange Hotel into the upper street, the movement was the signal for a wild burst of cheers from each regiment.

"Shouts from a few Negroes were the only response. Through throngs of sullen spectators; along the line of . . . the . . . conflagration, [which had been] increased by the explosion of shells left by the retreating army; through curtains of smoke; through the . . . commotion of frightful sounds, moved the garish procession of the grand army. . . .

"A regiment of Negro cavalry swept by the hotel. As they turned the street corner they drew their sabres with savage shouts, and the blood mounted even in my woman's heart with quick throbs of defiance."

Meanwhile, the fire raged with unchecked fury. . . . The atmosphere was almost choking. Men, women, and children crowded into the square of the Capitol for a breath of pure air; but it was not to be obtained even there, and one traversed the green slopes [of the Capitol grounds] blinded by cinders and struggling for breath. Already piles of furniture had been collected there, dragged from the ruins of burning houses. And in uncouth arrangements—made with broken tables and bureaus—were huddled women and children with no other home, with no other resting place in Heaven's great hollowness.

Some tardy attempts were made to arrest the conflagration. In the afternoon the [Federal] military authorities organized the crowds of Negroes as a fire corps; but the few steam engines that played upon the flames were not sufficient to check their progress. It was late in the evening when the fire had burned itself out. . . .

As night came on, there was a painful reaction after the day's terrible excitement. A strange quiet fell upon the blackened city and its scenes of destruction. . . . Groups of women and children crawled under shelters of broken furniture in the Capitol square; hundreds of homeless persons laid down to sleep in the shadows of the ruins of Richmond. And, worn out by excitement, exhausted as by the spasm of a great battle, men watched for the morrow with the dull sense that the work of years had been ruined and that all they possessed on earth had been swept away.

While Richmond was filled with horror and destruction, and the smoke of its torment ascended to the skies, very different scenes were taking place far away in the cities of the North. [Here Pollard begins to speak of things he learned from Northern newspapers, which, all through the war, reached Richmond on a regular basis.] . . . With those fervors and shows characteristic of the Northern mind, Washington and New York were celebrating the downfall of the Confederate capital.

Bells were rung; wild and enthusiastic congratulations ran along the street; and vast crowds collected, whose fantastic exhibitions of joy, not content with huzzas, cheers and dancing in the streets, broke out into a blasphemous singing of hymns of the church. In New York, twenty thousand persons in the open air sung the doxology.

There was, of course, an unlimited display of flags; and as evidence of this characteristic exhibition it is said that half an hour after the news of the fall of Richmond was known, not a single large flag in the whole city of New York was left unpurchased. These symbols of loyalty not only floated over houses, but were fastened to carts, stages, and wagons.

The newspapers were mostly occupied with spread eagles and maps of Richmond. . . . The New York *Herald*—the organ par excellence of Yankee wind . . . declared that the taking of Richmond was "one of the grandest triumphs that had crowned human efforts for centuries."

. . . In his last despatch from Petersburg, General Lee had stated that sometime during the night of the 2d April he would fall back behind the Appomattox [River]. . . . When night [came], the air was luminous with the steady glare of the burning warehouses in Petersburg. For several hours, cannonading [of the Federal lines] was kept up; but about midnight the Confederates began their retreat. By three o'clock in the morning, Gordon's whole corps [Lee's rear guard], except a few pickets and stragglers, was safely across the river, and the bridge on fire. . . .

About the same time as the first Union troops entered Richmond on this Monday, April 3, General Grant rode into Petersburg. At his side was his aide-de-camp, Horace Porter:

Many of the citizens, panic-stricken, had escaped with the army. Most of the whites who remained stayed indoors. A few groups of Negroes gave cheers; but the scene generally was one of complete desertion.

Grant rode along quietly until he came to a comfortable-looking brick house with a yard in front . . . and here he and the staff dismounted and took seats on the piazza. . . . The general was anxious to move westward at once with the leading infantry columns, but he prolonged his stay until the President came up.

Mr. Lincoln soon after arrived, accompanied by Robert [his eldest son, who was on Grant's staff] . . . and by his little son, "Tad," and Admiral Porter [commander of the fleet on the James River with which Lincoln was staying].

He dismounted in the street and came in through the front gate with long and rapid strides, his face beaming with delight. He seized General Grant's hand as the general stepped forward to greet him, and stood shaking it for some time and pouring out his thanks and congratulations. . . . I doubt whether Mr. Lincoln ever experienced a happier moment in his life.

Grant soon afterward joined the troops pursuing Lee. As for the President, he was eager to visit Richmond, and he arranged to go there by boat the next day.

Federal newsman Charles Coffin was already in the city when Lincoln approached:

It was a little past noon when I walked down to the river bank to view the desolation. While there I saw a boat pulled by twelve rowers coming up stream, containing President Lincoln and his little son, Admiral Porter, and three officers.

Forty or fifty freedmen . . . on the bank . . . crowded round the President . . . in . . . wild joy at beholding the face of the author of the great Emancipation Proclamation.

As he approached, I said to a colored woman, "There is the man who made you free." . . .

"Dat President Linkum?"

"Yes."

She gazed at him a moment in amazement, joy, rapture, as if in supernal presence, then clapped her hands, jumped and shouted, "Glory! Glory! Glory!"

. . . Men, women, and children joined the constantly increasing throng. They came from all the streets, running in breathless haste, shouting and hallooing, and dancing with delight. . . .

No carriage was to be had, so the President, leading his son, walked to General Weitzel's headquarters—Jeff Davis's mansion. . . . The walk was long, and the President halted a moment to rest.

"May de good Lord bless you, President Linkum!" said an old Negro, removing his hat and bowing, with tears of joy rolling down his cheeks.

The President removed his own hat and bowed in silence. It was a bow which upset the forms, laws, customs, and ceremonies of centuries of slavery.

By this time thousands of people, both blacks and whites, had gathered in the vicinity. Says J. J. Hill, a black soldier who had entered Richmond with General Weitzel's occupation troops:

What a spectacle! I never witnessed such rejoicing in all my life. As the President passed along the street the colored people waved their handkerchiefs, hats and bonnets, and expressed their gratitude by shouting repeatedly, "Thank God for his goodness; we have seen his salvation." The white soldiers caught the sound and swelled the numbers. [Other soldiers had to be summoned to clear Lincoln's way.]

All could see the President, he was so tall. One woman standing in a doorway as he passed along shouted, "Thank you, dear Jesus, for this sight of the great conqueror." Another one standing by her side clasped her hands and shouted, "Bless the Lamb— Bless the Lamb." Another one threw her bonnet in the air, screaming with all her might, "Thank you, Master Lincoln." A white woman came to a window but turned away, as if it were a disgusting sight. A few

white women looking out of an elegant mansion waved their handkerchiefs.

*An aide to General Weitzel, Thomas T. Graves, was on the street
near the Davis mansion at this time:*

. . . I saw a crowd coming, headed by President Lincoln. . . .
Upon my saluting, he said, "Is it far to President Davis's house?"

I accompanied him. . . . At the Davis house he was shown into
the reception room, with the remark that the housekeeper had said
that that room was President Davis's office.

As he seated himself, he remarked, "This must have been President Davis's chair," and, crossing his legs, he looked far off with a
serious, dreamy expression.

At length he asked me if the housekeeper was in the house. Upon
learning that she had left, he jumped up and said with a boyish
manner, "Come, let's look at the house!" We went pretty much over
it . . . and he seemed interested in everything.

As we came down the staircase, General Weitzel came in . . .
and at once President Lincoln . . . realized that duty must be resumed. . . . [Later] I . . . heard General Weitzel ask President
Lincoln what he (General Weitzel) should do in regard to the conquered people. President Lincoln replied that he did not wish to
give any orders on that subject, but, as he expressed it, "If I were in
your place I'd let 'em up easy, let 'em up easy."

*Lincoln was well satisfied with that part of Grant's victory he had
shared. News of the final outcome was to reach him back in Washington.*

*The pursuit was well under way, with Lee continuing to head
westward. General Gordon, commanding Lee's rear guard, says that
he had an extra reason for feeling depressed over the abandonment
of Petersburg:*

I had left behind me in that city of gloom the wife who had followed me during the entire war. She was ill. But . . . I found
comfort in the hope that some chivalric soldier of the Union army
would learn of her presence and guard her home against all intru-
ders. My confidence in American manhood was not misplaced.

To bring up the rear and adequately protect the retreating army
was an impossible task. With characteristic vigor, General Grant
pressed the pursuit. Soon began the continuous and final battle.

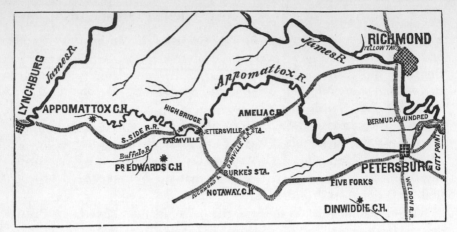

Petersburg to Appomattox.

Lincoln leaving the Davis mansion.

Fighting all day, marching all night, with exhaustion and hunger claiming their victims at every mile of the march, with charges of infantry in rear and of cavalry on the flanks, it seemed the war god had turned loose all his furies to revel in havoc.

On and on, hour after hour, from hilltop to hilltop, the lines were alternately forming, fighting, and retreating, making one almost continuous shifting battle. Here, in one direction, a battery of artillery became involved; there, in another, a blocked ammunition train required rescue. And thus came short but sharp little battles which made up the sideshows of the main performance, while the different divisions of Lee's lionhearted army were being broken and scattered or captured.

Out of one of these whirlwinds there came running at the top of his speed a boy soldier whose wit flashed out even in that dire extremity. When asked why he was running, he shouted back, ". . . I'm running 'cause I can't fly!"

. . . At Sayler's Creek, Anderson's corps was broken and destroyed; and General Ewell, with almost his entire command, was captured, as was General Kershaw, General Custis Lee—son of the general-in-chief—and other prominent officers. . . .

The roads and fields and woods swarmed with eager pursuers, and Lee now and then was forced to halt his whole army, reduced to less than 10,000 fighters [the thousands of others being unfit for duty as the result of wounds, sickness, hunger, exhaustion, discouragement], in order to meet these simultaneous attacks. Various divisions along the line of march turned upon the Federals, and in each case checked them long enough for some other Confederate commands to move on. . . .

General Lee was riding everywhere and watching everything, encouraging his brave men by his calm and cheerful bearing. He was often exposed to great danger from shells and bullets. . . .

On that doleful retreat . . . it was impossible for us to bury our dead or carry with us the disabled wounded. There was no longer any room in the crowded ambulances which had escaped capture. . . . We could do nothing for the unfortunate sufferers who were too severely wounded to march, except leave them on the roadside with canteens of water. . . .

On the evening of April 8th, [Lee's] little army, with its ammunition nearly exhausted, was confronted by the forces of Grant, which had been thrown across our line of retreat at Appomattox. Then came the last sad Confederate council of war. It was called by

Lee to meet at night. It met in the woods at his headquarters, and by a low-burning bivouac fire. There was no tent there, no table, no chairs, and no camp-stools. On blankets spread upon the ground or on saddles at the roots of trees, we sat around the great commander.

. . . no tongue or pen will ever be able to describe the unutterable anguish of Lee's commanders as they looked into the clouded face of their beloved leader and sought to draw from it some ray of hope.

There were present at this final council the general-in-chief; the commander of his artillery, General [William N.] Pendleton; General Fitzhugh Lee . . . [of] the cavalry; and General Longstreet and myself, commanding all that was left of his immortal infantry. . . .

If all that was said and felt at that meeting could be given, it would make a volume of measureless pathos. . . . It was finally determined that with Fitz Lee's cavalry, my infantry, and [Armistead] Long's artillery under Colonel Thomas H. Carter, we should attempt at daylight the next morning to cut through Grant's lines. Longstreet was to follow in support of the movement. The utmost that could be hoped for was that we might reach the mountains of Virginia and Tennessee with a remnant of the army, and ultimately join General Johnston. . . .

The Federals had constructed a line of breastworks across our front during the night. The audacious movement of our troops was begun at dawn. [It was now Sunday, April 9.] The dashing cavalry leader, Fitzhugh Lee, swept around the Union left flank, while the infantry and artillery attacked the front. I take especial pride in recording the fact that this last charge of the war was made by the footsore and starving men of my command with a spirit worthy of the best days of Lee's army.

The Union breastworks were carried. Two pieces of artillery were captured. The Federals were driven from all that portion of the field, and the brave boys in tattered gray cheered as their battle flags waved in triumph. . . .

The Confederate battle lines were still advancing when I discovered a heavy column of Union infantry coming from the right and upon my rear. I gathered around me my sharpshooters . . . and directed Colonel Thomas H. Carter of the artillery to turn all his guns upon the advancing column. It was held at bay by his shrapnel, grape, and canister. . . .

. . . Longstreet was assailed by other portions of the Federal army. He was so hardly pressed that he could not join, as contemplated, in the effort to break the cordon of men and metal around us. At this critical juncture a column of Union cavalry appeared on the hills to my left, headed for the broad space between Longstreet's command and mine. . . . I . . . detached a brigade to double-quick and intercept this Federal force.

Such was the situation . . . when I received a significant inquiry from General Lee . . . borne by Colonel Charles S. Venable of his staff. . . . The commander wished me to report . . . what progress I was making, and what encouragement I could give.

I said: "Tell General Lee that my command has been fought to a frazzle, and unless Longstreet can unite in the movement, or prevent these forces from coming upon my rear, I cannot long go forward."

. . . when General Lee received my message, he said: "There is nothing left me but to go and see General Grant, and I had rather die a thousand deaths."

My troops were still fighting . . . [though now on the defensive] when the final note from General Lee reached me. It notified me that there was a flag of truce between General Grant and himself, stopping hostilities, and that I could communicate that fact to the commander of the Union forces in my front. There was no unnecessary delay in sending that message.

A period of confusion and misunderstanding preceded the establishment of the truce, but then the guns fell silent everywhere. The cessation of hostilities came none too soon for the Confederates, for they were facing annihilation at the hands of overwhelming numbers.

According to Confederate officer William Miller Owen:

. . . General Lee . . . rode through our lines towards Appomattox Court-House. . . . By a singular coincidence, the meeting of the generals took place in the house of . . . [Wilmer] McLean, the same gentleman who in 1861, at the Battle of Bull Run, had tendered his house to General Beauregard for headquarters. He removed from Manassas after the battle, with the intention of seeking some quiet nook where the alarms of war could never find him; but it was his fortune to be in at the beginning and in at the death.

Lee, accompanied by only one staff officer, reached the McLean house first. In Grant's words:

I had known General Lee in the old army and had served with him in the Mexican War. . . .

When I left camp that morning I had not expected so soon the result that was then taking place, and consequently was in rough garb. I was without a sword, as I usually was when on horseback on the field, and wore a soldier's blouse for a coat, with the shoulder straps of my rank to indicate to the army who I was.

When I went into the house I found General Lee. We greeted each other, and after shaking hands took our seats. I had my staff with me, a good portion of whom were in the room during the whole of the interview.

What General Lee's feelings were I do not know. As he was a man of much dignity, with an impassible face . . . his feelings . . . were entirely concealed from my observation; but my own feelings . . . were sad and depressed. I felt like anything rather than rejoicing at the downfall of a foe who had fought so long and valiantly and had suffered so much. . . .

General Lee was dressed in a full uniform which was entirely new, and was wearing a sword of considerable value. . . . In my rough traveling suit . . . I must have contrasted very strangely with a man so handsomely dressed, six feet high and of faultless form. . . .

We soon fell into a conversation about old army times. . . . Our conversation grew so pleasant that I almost forgot the object of our meeting. After the conversation had run on in this style for some time, General Lee called my attention to the object of our meeting, and . . . asked for . . . the terms I proposed to give his army. I said that I meant merely that his army should lay down their arms. . . .

Then we gradually fell off again into conversation about matters foreign to the subject which had brought us together. . . . General Lee again interrupted the course of the conversation by suggesting that the terms I proposed to give his army ought to be written out. . . .

As I wrote . . . the thought occurred to me that the officers had their own private horses and effects, which were important to them but of no value to us; also that it would be an unnecessary humiliation to call upon them to deliver their side arms. . . .

When he read over that part of the terms about side arms, horses and private property of the officers, he remarked . . . that this would have a happy effect upon his army. Then, after a little further conversation, General Lee remarked to me . . . that in their

Grant and Lee discussing terms at the McLean house.

army the cavalrymen and artillerists owned their own horses; and he asked if he was to understand that the men who so owned their horses were to be permitted to retain them. . . .

I . . . said to him that I thought this would be about the last battle of the war . . . and I said further I took it that most of the men in the ranks were small farmers. The whole country had been so raided by the two armies that it was doubtful whether they would be able to put in a crop to carry themselves and their families through the next winter without the aid of the horses they were riding. The United States did not want them, and I would therefore [I told him] . . . let every man of the Confederate army who claimed to own a horse or mule take the animal to his home. Lee remarked again that this would have a happy effect. . . .

General Lee, after all was completed and before taking his leave, remarked that his army was in a very bad condition for want of food, and that they were without forage; that his men had been living for some days on parched corn exclusively, and that he would have to ask me for rations and forage. I told him, "Certainly." . . .

Lee and I . . . separated as cordially as we had met. . . .

When news of the surrender first reached our lines, our men commenced firing a salute of a hundred guns in honor of the victory. I at once sent word, however, to have it stopped. The Confederates were now our prisoners, and we did not want to exult over their downfall.

One of the officers of Lee's ravaged army who witnessed the general's return from the meeting with Grant was William Owen:

. . . whole lines of men rushed down to the roadside and crowded around him to shake his hand. All tried to show him the veneration and esteem in which they held him.

Filled with emotion, he essayed to speak, but could only say, "Men, we have fought through the war together. I have done the best I could for you. My heart is too full to say more."

We all knew the pathos of those simple words . . . and it was no shame on our manhood "that something upon the soldier's cheek washed off the stains of powder" . . . and that we could only grasp the hand of "Uncle Robert" and pray "God help you, General!"

Union General George A. Forsyth tells of an incident in the victor's journey from the surrender site:

General Grant, on his way to his field headquarters on this eventful Sunday evening, dismounted, sat quietly down by the roadside, and wrote a short and simple despatch ["General Lee surrendered the Army of Northern Virginia this afternoon on terms proposed by myself. . . ."], which a galloping aide bore full-speed to the nearest telegraph station, that on its reception in the nation's capital was flashed over the wires to every hamlet in the country, causing every steeple in the North to rock to its foundation, and sent one tall, gaunt, sad-eyed, weary-hearted man in Washington to his knees, thanking God that he had lived to see the beginning of the end, and that he had at last been vouchsafed the assurance that he had led his people aright.

Says Federal newsman and historian William Swinton of the situation at Appomattox:

As the armies were enemies no longer, there was no need of martial array that night, nor fear of surprise, nor call to arms; but hostile devisement gave place to mutual helpfulness, and the victors shared their rations with the famished vanquished. In that supreme moment these men knew and respected each other.

If one army drank the joy of victory, and the other the bitter draught of defeat, it was a joy moderated by the recollection of the cost at which it had been purchased, and a defeat mollified by the consciousness of many triumphs. If the victors could recall a Malvern Hill, an Antietam, a Gettysburg, a Five Forks, the vanquished could

The formal surrender. Confederates are shown stacking their muskets and furling their flags.

recall a Manassas, a Fredericksburg, a Chancellorsville, a Cold Harbor.

If at length the Army of Northern Virginia fell before the massive power of the North, yet what vitality had it shown! How terrible had been the struggle! How many hundreds of thousands of brave men had fallen before that result could be achieved!

Many Southerners found comfort in the knowledge that Lee's army had left upon the pages of history "a record of valor and devotion never excelled."

Swinton goes on:

And this is the glory of the Army of the Potomac, that it brought to the ground the adversary which had ever been the head and front of the revolt, and that in crushing it, it quelled the rebellion. For so decisive upon the issue of the war was the surrender of that army that the capitulation of all the other Confederate armies followed as a corollary therefrom, and the structure of the Confederacy, losing its keystone, fell with a resounding crash.

Three days after the surrender, the Confederates marched by divisions to a designated spot in the neighborhood of Appomattox Courthouse, and there the troops stacked their arms and deposited their accoutrements. Less than eight thousand presented themselves with muskets in their hands; but the capitulation included, in addition, about eighteen thousand unarmed. Paroles were then distributed to the men, and the Army of Northern Virginia passed out of existence.

The date was April 12, 1865. Two days later, the North's victory celebrations reached their climax. Down at Fort Sumter—now in ruins as a result of bombardments by the Federals—a special ceremony took place. Exactly four years after he lowered the American flag in surrender to the Confederacy, Robert Anderson, now a general, reclaimed the fort for the Union by raising the same flag above it.

In Washington that evening, President Lincoln, in the best of spirits, joined his wife and two young friends for a visit to Ford's Theater to see an English comedy entitled Our American Cousin.

Fort Sumter regained.

EPILOGUE

Lincoln's assassination was a blow not only to the people of the North but to those of the South as well. The new President, Andrew Johnson, tried to "let 'em up easy," but his leadership was inadequate and his wishes were negated by the radical Republicans in Congress. The years of Reconstruction, during which the South was exploited by Northern "carpetbaggers" and Southern "scalawags," were bitter ones for the defeated people. But, suffering and ill-feeling notwithstanding, all of the seceded states were back in the Union by 1870. The healing process could at least begin. It was dramatized at Chattanooga, Tennessee, on Memorial Day, 1877, when President Rutherford B. Hayes decorated the graves of the Confederate soldiers.

April, 1882. Theodore Gerrish, a Maine clergyman who was once a Union private, is at his desk penning the closing pages of his reminiscences. At this distance from the turbulent years, he can assess their meaning:

The results gathered from the Civil War are so many and of such importance that all must be convinced of the fact that the great sacrifice of human life was not made in vain. I will enumerate a few of them.

Slavery, that plague-spot upon the Republic, whose existence was a source of perpetual strife . . . perished. . . . States' Rights . . . was a legitimate offspring of slavery, and received its death-blow. . . . A few political "Rip Van Winkles" may now and then dolefully declaim about the sacred doctrine of States' Rights, but any political party that is simple enough to embody that doctrine within its platform of principles is doomed to defeat. . . . We rolled this heresy in its winding-sheet and laid it to rest upon the plains of Appomattox. . . .

. . . the Old South is passing from view. Mason and Dixon's line is no longer an impassable barrier, over which the nervous energy and skillful labor of the North is not allowed to pass. That line was blotted out in blood, and when the clouds of war passed, the South, with its genial climate, fertile soil, magnificent water-powers, and undeveloped mines . . . [asked] for honest labor, skillful enterprise, accumulated capital . . . and all were freely given. . . . A score of years only have passed, but already the South is thrilled with new life and is marching to the front. It . . . will pour a vast and magnificent stream of wealth into the treasury of our nation that will bring to it many elements of strength and add permanence to its institutions. . . .

"Our brothers in black" . . . fought heroically when marshaled under the stars and stripes, so that, when the war closed they had nobly earned the ballot that the Government placed in their hands. With deep interest . . . the old soldiers have watched their struggles and rapid development in all the elements of good citizenship since the close of the war. . . . Give the "brothers in black" an equal chance with other citizens. Let the General Government protect the rights of every citizen, without regard to color or race. That is all we ask, and that we have a right to demand. . . .

Our republic is at the front among the nations of the earth. . . . Europe had no faith in the permanence of our institutions. . . . But all that has changed. . . . Immigration is pouring like an infinite tide upon our shores; our population is over fifty millions of people; our resources are being developed; and our national outlook is most hopeful. . . .

Our dead are not forgotten. . . . The little mounds in the cemeteries . . . are becoming more numerous each year. . . . But a great portion of our dead are not in these cemeteries; their dust is . . . at Antietam, Fredericksburg, the Wilderness, and in the wild mountain gorges around Chattanooga. . . . They are safe. . . .

The survivors are [still] a numerous company. . . . Great changes [however] are taking place within our ranks. . . . Some of our comrades are now aged men . . . and we who then were mere lads are now sweeping on beyond the point of middle age. . . . We are now an army for which there are no recruits. . . . We shall all soon be "mustered out." . . . Many of us may not leave to our children much worldly wealth or high social position, but . . . I would rather have my boy stand by my grave and say, "My father was wounded in the Wilderness, and fought with Phil Sheridan at Five Forks, and saw Lee surrender at Appomattox," than to have him say that I was a millionaire or a member of the United States Senate. . . .

The country will always honor our memory. . . . Our graves will not be neglected when there are no Grand Army comrades to scatter their floral offerings upon them. This ceremony is to be handed from one generation to another. . . . Perhaps we may be permitted to view these ceremonies, looking down over the ramparts, a hundred years hence. . . .

Our country will be a great nation then; its resources will be well developed; it will probably contain two hundred millions of people, and . . . those people . . . will . . . thank God that, away back in the days of [civil] war and peril, there were men grand enough to sacrifice everything if, by so doing, they could save the nation from an untimely end. And as we survey it all, our reward will be sufficient, and we shall exclaim to each other, *"Satisfied, satisfied."*

APPENDIX

A Chronology of the War's Chief Events

1 8 6 1

APRIL 12	War begins with Confederate bombardment of Fort Sumter.
APRIL 14	Fort Sumter evacuated by its Union garrison.
APRIL 15	President Lincoln calls for 75,000 militia volunteers to serve for three months.
APRIL 17	Privateering against Union shipping initiated by Jefferson Davis.
APRIL 18	Federals abandon arsenal at Harpers Ferry, Virginia.
APRIL 19	Blockade of Confederate seacoast declared by Lincoln. Secessionist mob attacks Union troops marching through Baltimore, Maryland.
APRIL 20	Navy yard at Norfolk, Virginia, evacuated by Federals.
JUNE 10	Confederates beat back minor attack at Big Bethel, Virginia.
JUNE 11	Union success at Rich Mountain, in western Virginia, makes name for General McClellan.

JULY 21   First Battle of Bull Run (or Manassas), Virginia. Confederate victory.

JULY 27   McClellan placed in command of all Union troops in Washington area.

AUGUST 29   Fort Hatteras, North Carolina, captured by Federals.

OCTOBER 21   Confederates hurl back Federal advance at Ball's Bluff, Virginia.

NOVEMBER 7   Union forces capture Port Royal, South Carolina.

NOVEMBER 8   "Trent Affair" begins with Federal seizure of Southern commissioners on high seas.

1862

FEBRUARY 6   Fort Henry, Tennessee, falls to Union gunboats under Andrew Foote.

FEBRUARY 16   General Grant obtains unconditional surrender of Fort Donelson, Tennessee.

MARCH 9   Hampton Roads, Virginia, is scene of historic fight between *Monitor* and *Merrimac*.

APRIL 6–7   Battle of Shiloh (or Pittsburg Landing), Tennessee. Union victory.

APRIL 7   Federal troops, supported by gunboats, take Island Number Ten in Mississippi River.

APRIL 25   New Orleans, Louisiana, captured by Federal fleet under David Farragut.

MAY 3   Confederates evacuate Yorktown, on Virginia Peninsula, after siege by McClellan.

MAY 5   McClellan's advance clashes with Confederate rear guard at Williamsburg, Virginia.

MAY 8   Stonewall Jackson, busy confusing the Union troops in Virginia's Shenandoah Valley, scores a victory at McDowell.

MAY 15   Union naval force repulsed at Drewry's Bluff, on James River below Richmond.

MAY 25   Jackson defeats Federals at Winchester.

MAY 31–JUNE 1   McClellan withstands Confederate attack at Fair Oaks (or Seven Pines), east of Richmond.

JUNE 1   General Lee placed in command of Army of Northern Virginia.

JUNE 6   Federal forces capture Memphis, Tennessee.

JUNE 12–16   Jeb Stuart leads his cavalry on daring ride around McClellan's army.

JUNE 25   Beginning of Seven Days' Battles east and southeast of Richmond.

JUNE 26   Battle of Mechanicsville (or Beaver Dam Creek, or Ellerson's Mill).

JUNE 27   Battle of Gaines's Mill (or First Cold Harbor, or the Chickahominy).

JUNE 29   Battle of Savage's Station.

JUNE 30   Battle of Glendale (or Frayser's Farm, or White Oak Swamp).

JULY 1   Battle of Malvern Hill.

AUGUST 9   Pope's campaign against Lee begins with Battle of Cedar Mountain, Virginia.

AUGUST 29–30   Second Battle of Bull Run (or Manassas), Virginia. Confederate victory.

SEPTEMBER 4   Lee begins crossing Potomac into Maryland.

SEPTEMBER 14   Armies clash at passes through South Mountain, Maryland.

SEPTEMBER 17   Battle of Antietam (or Sharpsburg), Maryland. Union victory.

SEPTEMBER 19   Confederates bested at Iuka, Mississippi.

SEPTEMBER 22   Lincoln issues preliminary Emancipation Proclamation.

OCTOBER 3–4   Battle of Corinth, Mississippi. Confederates repulsed.

OCTOBER 8   Bragg's invasion of Kentucky ended by Battle of Perryville.

OCTOBER 9–12   Jeb Stuart raids Chambersburg, Pennsylvania, and rides around McClellan a second time.

NOVEMBER 7   McClellan removed as commander of Army of Potomac. Burnside instated.

DECEMBER 13   Battle of Fredericksburg, Virginia. Confederate victory.

DECEMBER 29   Sherman stopped at Chickasaw Bluffs, Mississippi.

DECEMBER 31–   Battle of Murfreesboro (or Stones River), Tennessee. Union
JANUARY 2   victory.

1 8 6 3

JANUARY 1   Emancipation Proclamation goes into effect.

JANUARY 19–23   Army of Potomac, under Burnside, makes "Mud March."

JANUARY 26   Burnside removed from command. Joe Hooker instated.

MARCH 3   Lincoln signs Federal Draft Act.

APRIL 16   Porter's fleet runs past batteries at Vicksburg, Mississippi.

APRIL 17   Cavalry raid through Mississippi begun by Grierson.

MAY 1   Port Gibson, Mississippi, taken by Grant.

MAY 1–4   Battle of Chancellorsville, Virginia. Confederate victory.

MAY 10   Stonewall Jackson dies.

MAY 12   Confederates defeated at Raymond, Mississippi.

MAY 14   Grant captures Jackson, Mississippi's capital.

MAY 16   Confederates retreat toward Vicksburg after Battle of Champion's Hill.

MAY 17   Confederate stand at Big Black River ends with rout.

MAY 18   Grant begins Siege of Vicksburg.

JUNE 3   Lee puts his army in motion for second invasion of the North.

JUNE 9   Union cavalry engages Stuart at Brandy Station, Virginia.

JUNE 14–15   Federal detachment at Winchester, Virginia, defeated by Lee's advance divisions.

JUNE 27   Hooker removed as commander of Army of Potomac. Meade instated.

JULY 1–3   Battle of Gettysburg, Pennsylvania. Union victory.

JULY 4   Vicksburg surrenders to Grant. Lee begins retreat to Virginia.

JULY 8   Port Hudson, Louisiana, capitulates.

JULY 13–16   Draft riots rock New York City. Other cities scene of lesser disturbances.

SEPTEMBER 2   Burnside occupies Knoxville, Tennessee.

SEPTEMBER 19–20   Battle of Chickamauga, Georgia. Confederate victory.

SEPTEMBER 23   Confederates begin Siege of Chattanooga, Tennessee.

OCTOBER 23   Grant takes command of Chattanooga's besieged forces.

NOVEMBER 23–25   Battle of Chattanooga (including Lookout Mountain and Missionary Ridge). Union victory.

1864

MARCH 10   Grant made general-in-chief of Armies of the United States.

MAY 4   Wilderness Campaign begins as Federals cross Virginia's Rapidan River.

MAY 5–6   Battle of the Wilderness.

MAY 7   Sherman begins drive toward Atlanta, Georgia.

MAY 8–19   Battles at Spotsylvania Court House, Virginia.

MAY 11   Jeb Stuart mortally wounded at Yellow Tavern, Virginia.

MAY 12   Sherman outflanks Johnston at Dalton, Georgia.

MAY 14–15   Battle of Resaca, Georgia.

MAY 25–JUNE 4   Sherman's advance stalled by Johnston in Campaign of New Hope Church.

JUNE 1–3	Battles at Cold Harbor, Virginia.
JUNE 12	Grant begins flanking movement across James River to Petersburg.
JUNE 18	Siege of Petersburg begins as Federal assaults fail.
JUNE 27	Sherman repulsed at Kennesaw Mountain, Georgia.
JULY 11–12	Confederates under Early demonstrate in Washington suburbs.
JULY 17	John Hood replaces Johnston as Federals reach environs of Atlanta.
JULY 17–SEPTEMBER 1	Series of maneuvers, skirmishes, and battles for possession of Atlanta.
JULY 30	Federals explode mine at Petersburg, but fail in their assault on breach.
AUGUST 5	Farragut damns the torpedoes and wins control of Mobile Bay, Alabama.
SEPTEMBER 2	Atlanta falls to Sherman's army.
SEPTEMBER 19	Sheridan defeats Early at Winchester, Virginia.
OCTOBER 19	Early repulsed in attack on Sheridan at Cedar Creek. Last major battle in Shenandoah Valley.
NOVEMBER 8	Lincoln elected to second term.
NOVEMBER 16	Sherman begins march to sea, leaving much of Atlanta in ruins.
NOVEMBER 22	Milledgeville, Georgia, occupied by troops under Sherman.
NOVEMBER 30	Hood makes costly assault at Franklin, Tennessee. Pat Cleburne killed.
DECEMBER 15–16	Thomas scores decisive win over Hood at Nashville. Last great battle in West.
DECEMBER 21	Sherman's army takes Savannah, Georgia.
DECEMBER 22	Sherman offers Savannah to Lincoln as a Christmas gift.

1 8 6 5

JANUARY 15   Federal landing force captures Fort Fisher, on North Carolina coast.

FEBRUARY 1   Sherman begins march through the Carolinas.

FEBRUARY 17   Columbia, South Carolina, ravaged by fire after falling to Sherman.
Confederates evacuate Charleston.

MARCH 11   Sherman takes Fayetteville, North Carolina.

MARCH 19–21   Confederates defeated at Battle of Bentonville, North Carolina.

MARCH 25   Gordon makes unsuccessful assault on Fort Stedman, in Union lines before Petersburg.

MARCH 29   Appomattox Campaign begins with flanking movement by Federals.

APRIL 1   Lee's troops defeated at Battle of Five Forks.

APRIL 2   Federals assault Petersburg defenses. Davis government flees Richmond. Night finds city in flames.
Lee begins retreat westward.

APRIL 4–5   Lincoln visits Richmond.

APRIL 6   Confederates defeated at Sayler's Creek.

APRIL 9   Lee surrenders at Appomattox Court House. Lee's army being keystone of Confederacy, stage is set for general surrender of Southern forces.

APRIL 14   Union victory celebrations climaxed by ceremony at Fort Sumter.
Lincoln shot at Ford's Theater. Dies the next morning.

MAY 23–24   Union armies parade in Washington prior to disbandment.

BIBLIOGRAPHY

ADAMS, F. COLBURN. *The Story of a Trooper.* New York: Dick & Fitzgerald, 1865.

ANGLE, PAUL M., AND MIERS, EARL SCHENCK. *Tragic Years, 1860–1865.* 2 vols. New York: Simon and Schuster, 1960.

Annals of the War. Philadelphia: The Times Publishing Company, 1879.

AUSTIN, J. P. *The Blue and the Gray.* Atlanta: The Franklin Printing and Publishing Co., 1899.

Battles and Leaders of the Civil War. 4 vols. Robert Underwood Johnson and Clarence Clough Buel (eds.). New York: The Century Co., 1884–1888.

BOTTS, JOHN MINOR. *The Great Rebellion.* New York: Harper & Brothers, 1866.

BROWNE, JUNIUS HENRI. *Four Years in Secessia.* Hartford: O. D. Case and Company, 1865.

CALDWELL, J. F. J. *The History of a Brigade of South Carolinians.* Philadelphia: King & Baird, 1866.

CARPENTER, F. B. *The Inner Life of Abraham Lincoln.* New York: Hurd and Houghton, 1868.

CASLER, JOHN O. *Four Years in the Stonewall Brigade.* James I. Robertson, Jr. (ed.). Dayton, Ohio: Morningside Bookshop, 1971. Facsimile of 1906 edition.

CATTON, BRUCE. *The Army of the Potomac: Mr. Lincoln's Army.* Garden City, N.Y.: Doubleday & Company, Inc., 1962.

———. *The Army of the Potomac: Glory Road.* Garden City, N.Y.: Doubleday & Company, Inc., 1962.

———. *The Army of the Potomac: A Stillness at Appomattox.* Garden City, N.Y.: Doubleday & Company, Inc., 1962.

———. *Gettysburg: The Final Fury.* Garden City, N.Y.: Doubleday & Company, Inc., 1974.

CHESNUT, MARY BOYKIN. *A Diary from Dixie*. New York: D. Appleton & Co., 1905.

CHITTENDEN, L. E. *Personal Reminiscences*. New York: Richmond, Croscup & Co., 1893.

CIST, HENRY M. *The Army of the Cumberland (Campaigns of the Civil War,* vol. 7). New York: Charles Scribner's Sons, 1882.

Civil War Naval Chronology. Compiled by Naval History Division, Navy Department. Washington, D.C.: Government Printing Office, 1971.

COFFIN, CHARLES CARLETON. *My Days and Nights on the Battle-Field*. Boston: Ticknor and Fields, 1863.

———. *Following the Flag*. Boston: Estes and Lauriat, 1865.

———. *The Boys of '61*. Boston: Estes and Lauriat, 1884.

———. *Drum-Beat of the Nation*. New York: Harper & Brothers, 1888.

———. *Marching to Victory*. New York: Harper & Brothers, 1889.

———. *Redeeming the Republic*. New York: Harper & Brothers, 1890.

COMMAGER, HENRY STEELE. *The Blue and the Gray*. Indianapolis and New York: The Bobbs-Merrill Company, Inc., 1950.

COX, JACOB D. *Atlanta (Campaigns of the Civil War,* vol. 9) . New York: Charles Scribner's Sons, 1882.

———. *The March to the Sea: Franklin and Nashville (Campaigns of the Civil War,* vol. 10). New York: Charles Scribner's Sons, 1882.

CRAFTS, WILLIAM A. *The Southern Rebellion*. Paperbound set; 50 parts. Boston: Samuel Walker, 1864–67.

CULLEN, JOSEPH P. *Richmond Battlefields;* Historical Handbook No. 33. Washington, D.C.: Government Printing Office, 1961.

———. *Where a Hundred Thousand Fell;* Historical Handbook No. 39. Washington, D.C.: Government Printing Office, 1966.

DERBY, W. P. *Bearing Arms*. Boston: Wright & Potter Printing Company, 1883.

DE TROBRIAND, P. REGIS. *Four Years With the Army of the Potomac*. Boston: Ticknor and Company, 1889.

DILLAHUNTY, ALBERT. *Shiloh;* Historical Handbook No. 10. Washington, D.C.: Government Printing Office, 1961.

DOOLADY, M. *Jefferson Davis and Stonewall Jackson*. Philadelphia: John E. Potter and Company, 1866.

DOUBLEDAY, ABNER. *Reminiscences of Forts Sumter and Moultrie, 1860–1861*. New York: Harper & Brothers, 1876.

———. *Chancellorsville and Gettysburg (Campaigns of the Civil War,* vol. 6) . New York: Charles Scribner's Sons, 1882.

DOUGLAS, HENRY KYD. *I Rode With Stonewall*. Chapel Hill, N.C.: University of North Carolina Press, 1940.

DRAPER, JOHN WILLIAM. *History of the American Civil War*. 3 vols. New York: Harper & Brothers, 1868–70.

DRAPER, WILLIAM F. *Recollections of a Varied Career*. Boston: Little, Brown, and Company, 1908.

DUYCKINCK, EVERT A. *National History of the War for the Union*. 3 vols. New York: Johnson, Fry and Company, 1868.

EDMONDS, S. EMMA E. *Nurse and Spy in the Union Army*. Hartford: W. S. Williams & Co., 1865.

ENGLISH, WILLIAM H. *Life and Military Career of Winfield Scott Hancock*. Philadelphia: J. C. McCurdy & Co., 1880.

EVANS, CLEMENT A. (ed.). *Confederate Military History*. 12 vols. New York, London, Toronto: Thomas Yoseloff, 1962. Facsimile publication of 1899 edition by the Confederate Publishing Company of Atlanta.

EVERHART, WILLIAM C. *Vicksburg; Historical Handbook No. 21*. Washington, D.C.: Government Printing Office, 1961.

FARRAGUT, LOYALL. *The Life of David Glasgow Farragut*. New York: D. Appleton and Company, 1879.

FISKE, JOHN. *The Mississippi Valley in the Civil War*. Boston and New York: Houghton, Mifflin and Company, 1900.

FORCE, M. F. *From Fort Henry to Corinth (Campaigns of the Civil War, vol. 2)*. New York: Charles Scribner's Sons, 1881.

GARLAND, HAMLIN. *Ulysses S. Grant, His Life and Character*. New York: Doubleday & McClure Co., 1898.

GERRISH, THEODORE. *Army Life: A Private's Reminiscences of the Civil War*. Portland, Me.: Hoyt, Fogg & Donham, 1882.

———, AND HUTCHINSON, JOHN S. *The Blue and the Gray*. Portland, Me.: Hoyt, Fogg & Donham, 1883.

GODDARD, SAMUEL A. *Letters on the American Rebellion*. Boston: Nichols and Noyes, 1870.

GOODE, JOHN. *Recollections of a Lifetime*. New York and Washington: The Neale Publishing Company, 1906.

GORDON, JOHN B. *Reminiscences of the Civil War*. New York: Charles Scribner's Sons, 1904.

GOSS, WARREN LEE. *Recollections of a Private*. New York: Thomas Y. Crowell & Co., 1890.

GRANT, U. S. *Personal Memoirs*. New York: Charles L. Webster & Company, 1894.

GREELEY, HORACE. *The American Conflict*. 2 vols. Hartford: O. D. Case & Company, 1864, 1867.

GREENE, FRANCIS VINTON. *The Mississippi (Campaigns of the Civil War, vol. 8)*. New York: Charles Scribner's Sons, 1882.

GUERNSEY, ALFRED H., AND ALDEN, HENRY M. *Harper's Pictorial History of the Great Rebellion*. 2 vols. Chicago: McDonnell Bros., 1866, 1868.

HANSEN, HARRY. *The Civil War*. New York: Bonanza Books, 1962.

Harper's Encyclopaedia of United States History. 10 vols. New York: Harper & Brothers, 1915.

HART, ALBERT BUSHNELL (ed.). *American History Told by Contemporaries, vol. 4*. New York: The Macmillan Company, 1910.

HEADLEY, J. T. *The Great Rebellion*. 2 vols. Hartford: Hurlbut, Williams & Company, 1863, 1866.

HILL, A. F. *Our Boys: The Personal Experiences of a Soldier in the Army of the Potomac*. Philadelphia: The Keystone Publishing Co., 1890.

HUMPHREYS, ANDREW A. *The Virginia Campaign of 1864 and 1865 (Campaigns of the Civil War, vol. 12)*. New York: Charles Scribner's Sons, 1883.

HUNTER, ALEXANDER. *Johnny Reb and Billy Yank*. New York: The Neale Publishing Co., 1904.

JOHNSON, ROSSITER. *Campfires and Battlefields*. New York: The Civil War Press, 1967.

JOHNSON, W. FLETCHER. *Life of Wm. Tecumseh Sherman*. Edgewood Publishing Company, 1891.

JONES, JOHN B. *A Rebel War Clerk's Diary*. Earl Schenck Miers (ed.). New York: Sagamore Press, Inc., 1958.

JONES, KATHARINE M. *When Sherman Came: Southern Women and the "Great March."* Indianapolis, Kansas City, and New York: The Bobbs-Merrill Company, Inc., 1964.

LARKE, JULIAN K. *General Grant and His Campaigns*. New York: J. C. Derby & N. C. Miller, 1864.

LEE, FITZHUGH. *General Lee of the Confederate Army*. London: Chapman and Hall, Ltd., 1895.

LEE, CAPTAIN ROBERT E. *Recollections and Letters of General Robert E. Lee*. New York: Doubleday, Page & Company, 1904.

LIVERMORE, MARY A. *My Story of the War*. Hartford: A. D. Worthington and Company, 1889.

LOGAN, JOHN A. *The Great Conspiracy*. New York: A. R. Hart & Co., 1886.

———. *The Volunteer Soldier of America*. Chicago and New York: R. S. Peale & Company, 1887.

LONG, E. B. (WITH BARBARA LONG). *The Civil War Day by Day*. Garden City, N.Y.: Doubleday & Company, Inc., 1971.

LOSSING, BENSON J. *Pictorial Field Book of the Civil War*. 3 vols. New York: T. Belknap & Company, 1868.

LUSK, WILLIAM THOMPSON. *War Letters*. Privately printed, 1911.

LYKES, RICHARD WAYNE. *Campaign for Petersburg*. Washington, D.C.: Government Printing Office, 1970.

MACLAY, EDGAR STANTON. *A History of the United States Navy,* vol. 2. New York: D. Appleton and Company, 1897.

McCLELLAN, GEORGE B. *McClellan's Own Story*. New York: Charles L. Webster & Company, 1887.

McCLELLAN, H. B. *The Life and Campaigns of Major-General J. E. B. Stuart*. Boston: Houghton, Mifflin & Company, 1885.

McPHERSON, JAMES M. *Marching Toward Freedom: the Negro in the Civil War*. New York: Alfred A. Knopf, 1965.

MELTZER, MILTON. *In Their Own Words: a History of the American Negro, 1619–1865*. New York: Thomas Y. Crowell Company, 1964.

MITCHELL, JOSEPH B. *Decisive Battles of the Civil War*. New York: G. P. Putnam's Sons, 1955.

MOORE, FRANK (ed.). *The Civil War in Song and Story*. New York: P. F. Collier, 1889.

———. *The Rebellion Record*. 12 vols. New York: G. P. Putnam, 1861–71.

MORTON, JOSEPH W., JR. (ed.). *Sparks from the Camp Fire*. Philadelphia: Keystone Publishing Co., 1892.

NICHOLS, G. W. *A Soldier's Story of His Regiment*. Kennesaw, Ga.: Continental Book Company, 1961. Facsimile of 1898 edition.

NICHOLS, GEORGE WARD. *The Story of the Great March*. New York: Harper & Brothers, 1865.

NICOLAY, JOHN G. *The Outbreak of Rebellion (Campaigns of the Civil War,* vol. 1). New York: Charles Scribner's Sons, 1881.

OATES, WILLIAM C. *The War Between the Union and the Confederacy.* New York: The Neale Publishing Co., 1905.

OWEN, WILLIAM MILLER. *In Camp and Battle with the Washington Artillery.* Boston: Ticknor and Company, 1885. Second edition by Pelican Publishing Company, New Orleans, 1964.

PALFREY, FRANCIS WINTHROP. *Antietam and Fredericksburg (Campaigns of the Civil War,* vol. 5). New York: Charles Scribner's Sons, 1882.

PENNYPACKER, ISAAC R. *General Meade.* New York: D. Appleton and Company, 1901.

PICKETT, GEORGE E. *The Heart of a Soldier.* New York: Seth Moyle, Inc., 1913.

PINKERTON, ALLAN. *The Spy of the Rebellion.* New York: G. W. Carleton & Co., 1883.

POLLARD, EDWARD A. *The Lost Cause.* New York: E. B. Treat & Co., 1866.

POND, GEORGE E. *The Shenandoah Valley in 1864 (Campaigns of the Civil War,* vol. 11). New York: Charles Scribner's Sons, 1883.

PORTER, HORACE. *Campaigning with Grant.* New York: The Century Company, 1897.

RICHARDSON, ALBERT D. *A Personal History of Ulysses S. Grant.* Hartford: American Publishing Company, 1868.

ROPES, JOHN CODMAN. *The Army Under Pope (Campaigns of the Civil War,* vol. 4). New York: Charles Scribner's Sons, 1881.

SHERIDAN, P. H. *Personal Memoirs.* 2 vols. New York: Charles L. Webster & Company, 1888.

SHERMAN, WILLIAM T. *Memoirs.* 2 vols. New York: D. Appleton and Company, 1875.

SPEARS, JOHN R. *The History of Our Navy,* vol. 4. New York: Charles Scribner's Sons, 1897.

STACKPOLE, EDWARD J. *They Met at Gettysburg.* New York: Bonanza Books, 1956.

STANLEY, DOROTHY (ed.). *The Autobiography of Sir Henry Morton Stanley.* Boston and New York: Houghton Mifflin Company, 1909.

STEPHENSON, NATHANIEL W. *The Day of the Confederacy.* New Haven: Yale University Press, 1920.

STEWART, A. M. *Camp, March and Battle-Field.* Philadelphia: Jas. B. Rodgers, 1865.

STILES, ROBERT. *Four Years Under Marse Robert.* New York and Washington: The Neale Publishing Company, 1903.

STILLWELL, LEANDER. *The Story of a Common Soldier; or Army Life in the Civil War.* Kansas City, Mo.: Franklin Hudson Publishing Co., 1920.

STOWE, HARRIET BEECHER. *Men of Our Times.* Hartford: Hartford Publishing Co., 1868.

SULLIVAN, JAMES R. *Chickamauga and Chattanooga Battlefields;* Historical Handbook No. 25. Washington, D.C.: Government Printing Office, 1961.

SWINTON, WILLIAM. *Campaigns of the Army of the Potomac.* New York: Charles Scribner's Sons, 1882.

TARBELL, IDA M. *The Life of Abraham Lincoln,* vol. 2. New York: McClure, Phillips & Co., 1902.

TAYLOR, WALTER H. *Four Years with General Lee.* New York: D. Appleton and Company, 1878.

TENNEY, W. J. *The Military and Naval History of the Rebellion.* New York: D. Appleton & Company, 1865.

TILBERG, FREDERICK. *Antietam;* Historical Handbook No. 31. Washington, D.C.: Government Printing Office, 1961.

———. *Gettysburg;* Historical Handbook No. 9. Washington, D.C.: Government Printing Office, 1962.

TOMES, ROBERT. *The Great Civil War.* 3 vols. New York: Virtue and Yorston, 1862.

Under Both Flags: A Panorama of the Great Civil War. Chicago: W. S. Reeve Publishing Co., 1896.

URBAN, JOHN W. *Battle Field and Prison Pen.* Edgewood Publishing Company, 1882.

VON BORCKE, HEROS. *Memoirs of the Confederate War for Independence.* 2 vols. New York: Peter Smith, 1938. Reprint of 1866 edition.

WEBB, ALEXANDER S. *The Peninsula (Campaigns of the Civil War,* vol. 3). New York: Charles Scribner's Sons, 1881.

WEBB, WILLARD (ed.). *Crucial Moments of the Civil War.* New York: Bonanza Books, 1961.

WILKESON, FRANK. *Recollections of a Private Soldier in the Army of the Potomac.* New York: G. P. Putnam's Sons, 1887.

WILLIAMS, T. HARRY. *Lincoln and His Generals.* New York: Alfred A. Knopf, Inc., 1952.

WILSHIN, FRANCIS F. *Manassas (Bull Run);* Historical Handbook No. 15. Washington, D.C.: Government Printing Office, 1961.

WILSON, JAMES HARRISON. *Under the Old Flag.* New York: D. Appleton & Co., 1912.

WITTENMYER, ANNIE. *Under the Guns: A Woman's Reminiscences of the Civil War.* Boston: E. B. Stillings & Co., 1895.

WOOD, WILLIAM. *Captains of the Civil War.* New Haven: Yale University Press, 1921.

WRIGHT, CHARLES. *A Corporal's Story.* Philadelphia: James Beale, 1887.

YOUNG, JESSE BOWMAN. *What a Boy Saw in the Army.* New York: Hunt & Eaton, 1894.

INDEX